S0-CFT-628

JOURNAL FOR THE STUDY OF THE NEW TESTAMENT SUPPLEMENT SERIES

19

Executive Editor, Supplement Series
David Hill

Publishing Editor
David E Orton

JSOT Press
Sheffield

Jesus and God
in
Paul's Eschatology

L. Joseph Kreitzer

Journal for the Study of the New Testament
Supplement Series 19

For Linda

Copyright © 1987 Sheffield Academic Press

Published by JSOT Press
JSOT Press is an imprint of
Sheffield Academic Press Ltd
The University of Sheffield
343 Fulwood Road
Sheffield S10 3BP
England

Typeset by Sheffield Academic Press
and
printed in Great Britain
by Billing & Sons Ltd
Worcester

British Library Cataloguing in Publication Data

Kreitzer, Larry Joseph
    Jesus and God in Paul's eschatology.—
    (Journal for the study of the New Testament
    supplement series, ISSN 0143-5108; no. 19).
    1. Bible. N.T. Epistles of Paul—Commentaries
    I. Title   II. Series
    227'.06   BS2650.3

    ISBN 1-85075-067-X
    ISBN 1-85075-066-1 Pbk

BS
2655
.E7
K7
1987

CONTENTS

Preface   9
Abbreviations   11

INTRODUCTION   15

Chapter 1
GOD, THE MESSIAH AND THE TEMPORARY KINGDOM
IN JEWISH PSEUDEPIGRAPHAL LITERATURE   29

  1. Pseudepigraphal Works of the Second
    to First Centuries BCE   32
    A. The Apocalypse of Weeks
      (*1 Enoch* 93.1-10 and 91.12-17)   32
    B. The Book of *Jubilees*   37
  2. Pseudepigraphal Works of the First Century CE   41
    A. *2 (Slavonic) Enoch*   41
    B. *4 Ezra* (2 Esdras)   52
    C. *2 (Syriac) Baruch*   69
    D. Summary of *4 Ezra* and *2 Baruch*   80
  3. Other Jewish Works Relevant to the Discussion   80
    A. Qumran Sectarian Literature   81
    B. Sibylline Oracles   84
    C. The Jewish Core underlying the Apocalypse of John   84
  4. Concluding Summary   85

Chapter 2
THE PAROUSIA AND THE FINAL JUDGMENT IN PAUL   93

  1. Views of Modern Scholarship on the
    Origin of the Doctrine of the Parousia   94
    A. Parousia as Church Addition:
      Glasson and Robinson   95
    B. Parousia and Church Abandonment:
      Schweitzer and Bultmann   97
  2. Final Judgment in Paul   99
    A. Throne of Judgment: The Jewish Pseudepigrapha   102
    B. Throne of Judgment: The Pauline Epistles   107

3. Day of the Lord in Paul 112
A. Referential Shift of 'Lord' from God to Christ 113
B. Referential Shift of Pronouns from God to Christ 124
C. Referential Shift of Description of the Day of the Lord
from God to Christ 125
4. Concluding Summary 128

Chapter 3
THE MESSIAH AND THE KINGDOM IN PAUL 131

1. Ἡ βασιλεία and βασιλεύω in Paul 132
A. 1 Corinthians 15.20-28 and the Kingdom of Christ 134
1. Scholarly Debate: Schweitzer and Davies 135
2. Scholarly Debate: Wilcke and Wallis 139
B. Psalm 110.1 and the Kingdom of Christ 146
C. The Christological Message of 1 Corinthians 15.20-28 149
2. Eschatological Theocentrism and Christocentrism:
A Summary Comparison of Jewish Pseudepigraphal
Literature and Paul 154
A. Diversity of Detail and Schematization 154
B. Functional Overlap between God and Christ 156
C. Presence of Textual Variants 156
D. Identification of Christ and God
within a Monotheistic Tradition 157
1. Ultimate Subordination—1 Corinthians 15.28c 158
2. Subordination in Worship—Philippians 2.11c 160
3. Nominal Clarification as Subordination 161
3. Concluding Summary 163

Chapter 4
CONCLUSIONS 165

Appendix
IMPLICATIONS FOR BIBLICAL STUDIES 171

1. The Question of the Relationship of the Pauline Corpus
to the Jewish Pseudepigrapha 171
2. Implications for the 'Son of Man' Debate 173
3. The Question of Development in Paul's
Eschatological Thought 177

4. The Question of the Nature of the Controversy
   at Corinth and Thessaloniki   180
5. The Integrity of 2 Thessalonians and its
   Relationship to 1 Thessalonians   181
6. The Question of Later Interpolations into the
   Pauline Epistles   182

Notes   185
Bibliography   253
Index of Textual References   277
Index of Modern Authors   289

PREFACE

This book is a slightly revised form of my PhD work completed at King's College, London, in 1985. I was fortunate to have been awarded a Tutorial Studentship within the Department of Biblical Studies at King's and count it a special privilege to have combined the roles of student and teacher of New Testament during the course of my study there. I have no doubts that this arrangement did much to make the time one of the most fulfilling and enriching of my life.

I wish to record my thanks to Professor Graham Stanton, who served as my supervisor at King's. He remains an inexhaustible source of inspiration and encouragement, not only as far as academic work is concerned, but also for his conviction of integrating his immense learning with an abiding commitment to the Body of Christ. One could not find a better representative for the motto of King's as an institution dedicated to both "Sancte et Sapienta". I gratefully acknowledge how fortunate I have been to have worked alongside and studied under him. Much of the inspiration for the book can be attributed to Graham; I claim the errors and short-comings for myself.

There are many others on the staff at King's who deserve special thanks as well. Michael Knibb played an especially important role in that he encouraged and nurtured my interest in Jewish pseudepigraphal literature. Leslie Houlden, Colin Hickling, Francis Watson, Richard Coggins, Ronald Clements, Grace Jantzen, Stewart Sutherland, Colin Gunton, Terry Tastard, and many others all helped to create an atmosphere which made study a pleasure and a joy. Their constant supportive interest in my work spurred me to produce that which I could not have otherwise achieved.

I also owe an immense debt to all the friends at the two Baptist churches with which I was in membership while in London, Northcote Road and Battersea Chapel. They will never know how much I relied upon them during those years. Theological study at the graduate level can be a lonely and isolating experience. I thank them that they helped to make it otherwise for me.

Many others have contributed to the production of this book and have been more important than they could ever possibly imagine. Prudence does not allow me the luxury of listing names, but they can rest assured that in my heart of hearts I know of their contribution and shall be ever grateful.

Most importantly, mention must be made of Linda, without whom I never could have finished, nor even begun, this project. A more loving and understanding companion could not be found; a more charitable and supportive partner could not be desired. I count it my supreme privilege in life to call her my wife. I dedicate the study to her.

Regent's Park College, Oxford
June 1987

ABBREVIATIONS

In connection with the nomenclature of the Dead Sea Scrolls material I have adopted the system of abbreviations suggested by Joseph A. Fitzmyer, *The Dead Sea Scrolls: Major Publications and Tools for Study* (1977), pp. 3-8.

AMWNE	*Apocalypticism in the Mediterranean World and the Near East: Proceedings of the International Colloquium on Apocalypticism, Uppsala, August 12-17, 1979*, edited by David Hellholm (J.C.B. Mohr: Tübingen, 1983).
ANRW	*Aufstieg und Niedergang der Römischen Welt*, edited by Wolfgang Haase (1979–).
AOT	*The Apocryphal Old Testament*, edited by H.F.D. Sparks (1984).
APOT	*Apocrypha and Pseudepigrapha of the Old Testament*, in 2 vols., edited by R.H. Charles (1913).
BASOR	*Bulletin of the American School of Oriental Research*
BCE	Before the Common Era
BibTr	*The Bible Translator*
BibZ	*Biblische Zeitschrift*
BIOSCS	*Bulletin of the International Organization of Septuagint and Cognate Studies*
BTB	*Biblical Theology Bulletin*
CBQ	*Catholic Biblical Quarterly*
CE	Common Era
CP	*Classical Philology*
CTR	*Calvin Theological Review*
EQ	*The Evangelical Quarterly*
EvT	*Evangelische Theologie*
ExpT	*The Expository Times*
FS	Festschrift
HJ	*Heythrop Journal*
HTR	*Harvard Theological Review*
IDB	*The Interpreter's Dictionary of the Bible*
IEJ	*Israel Exploration Journal*
JAAR	*Journal of the American Academy of Religion*

JAOS	*Journal of the American Oriental Society*
JBL	*Journal of Biblical Literature*
JETS	*Journal of the Evangelical Theological Society*
JJS	*Journal of Jewish Studies*
JourRel	*The Journal of Religion*
JQR	*The Jewish Quarterly Review*
JSJ	*The Journal for the Study of Judaism*
JSNT	*The Journal for the Study of the New Testament*
JSOT	*The Journal for the Study of the Old Testament*
JTC	*Journal for Theology and the Church*
JTS	*Journal of Theological Studies*
JWSTP	*Jewish Writings of the Second Temple Period*, (Compendia Rerum Iudaicarum ad Novum Testamentum, Section Two: The Literature of the Jewish People in the Period of the Second Temple and the Talmud), edited by Michael Stone (1984).
KTR	*King's Theological Review*
LXX	The Septuagint
MT	The Masoretic Text
NIDNTT	*The New International Dictionary of New Testament Theology*, edited by Colin Brown, 3 vols. (1975-78).
NovT	*Novum Testamentum*
NTS	*New Testament Studies*
OTS	*Oudtestamentische Studiën*
PMRS	*The Pseudepigrapha and Modern Research with a Supplement*, compiled by James H. Charlesworth (1981).
RB	*Revue Biblique*
RevExp	*The Review and Expositor*
RHPR	*Revue d'Historie et de Philosophie Religieuses*
RQ	*Revue de Qumran*
SBL	The Society of Biblical Literature
SJT	*The Scottish Journal of Theology*
SO	The Sibylline Oracles
SPCIC 61	*Studiorum Paulinorum Congressus Internationalis*
TB	*Tyndale Bulletin*
TDNT	*Theological Dictionary of the New Testament*, edited by G. Kittel and G. Friedrich, translated by G. Bromiley, 10 vols. (1964-74).

TOTP	*The Old Testament Pseudepigrapha*, edited by James H. Charlesworth, 2 vols. (1983-85).
TOTPNT	*The Old Testament Pseudepigrapha and the New Testament*, by James H. Charlesworth (1985).
TS	*Theological Studies*
TZ	*Theologische Literaturzeitung*
VT	*Vetus Testamentum*
ZAW	*Zeitschrift für die alttestamentliche Wissenschaft*
ZNW	*Zeitschrift für die neutestamentliche Wissenschaft*

INTRODUCTION

Do any of the New Testament writers call Jesus 'God' or identify Jesus with God ontologically? This question has often provoked scholars to reconsider their theological presuppositions, open their New Testaments afresh, and take up their pens.[1] The Pauline epistles[2] have an important part in the ensuing debate,[3] Rom. 9.5[4], Phil. 2.6-11[5] and Col. 1.15-20[6] being particular areas of controversy. It has not gone unnoticed that most of the Pauline passages examined in this regard are liturgical hymns of pre-Pauline origin.[7] Yet another category of Paul's teaching, just as much a part of the earliest Christian tradition, also needs to be examined in connection with this question. I speak of his eschatological teaching.[8]

To what extent does Paul's thought have God as its focal point and to what extent does it have Christ as that focal point? Is it possible for us to determine where the primary concentration of attention lies for Paul as he expounds his understanding of the Christian faith? In short, how does Paul relate theocentricity and christocentricity within his thinking? This study proposes to examine Paul's eschatological teaching in an effort to come to a better understanding of his christological thought, especially as it revolves around this central issue of the interrelationship between the respective roles of God and Christ. We shall have opportunity to compare and contrast Paul's ideas on this important subject with those embodied in selected Jewish pseudepigraphal documents of roughly the same period. Such a comparison will highlight the contribution a specifically Christian ingredient has to make within eschatological texts of the period 200 BCE to 100 CE and enable us to understand more fully how Paul conceived of Jesus' relationship to God.

Precisely how Paul, and other early Christians, conceived of Jesus' relationship to God is a matter at the heart of much christological discussion. The whole issue, more than anything else, displays the limitations of language as a means of expressing, with any degree of exactitude, the significance of Jesus and his relationship to God. Karl Rahner remarks:

> how hesitant and groping the religious language of the NT authors

is, when they try to speak of the unity and distinction of God as Father . . . (and) Son.[9]

In attempting to summarize Paul's formulation of this relationship, I would like to suggest that he stops short of actually asserting absolute equality between Jesus the Messiah and God. Yet at the same time, for Paul, Jesus' identification with God is such that he cannot be fully explained or comprehended via human categories alone. Nor can Jesus' significance be assessed as simply another expression of the phenomenon of intermediary figures populating Jewish apocalyptic literature of the time. Within Paul's thought, Jesus transcends the boundaries of such categories without, at the same time, entirely usurping the position of God himself.[10]

We do not think that such a paradoxical formulation is restricted to the Pauline material. Worth noting is the classic article by C.K. Barrett[11] in which the paradoxical claims of John's Gospel are explored and an important clarifying point interjected. Barrett's cautious summary should help to guide our exploration of the Pauline passages:

> It is further to be observed that those notable Johannine passages that seem at first sight to proclaim most unambiguously the unity and equality of the Son with the Father are often set in contexts which if they do not deny at least qualify this theme, and place alongside it the theme of dependence, and indeed of subordination.[12]

As we shall see, the Pauline materials demonstrate a striking parallel to this assessment of Johannine theology.

The early Christians' understanding of Jesus' unique identification with God, as it is expressed within the New Testament documents, has long been recognized as an essential feature of their faith. Such identification has been explored from a number of angles by scholars and the resultant christological picture which has emerged is multi-layered and extremely complex. Several approaches have been used with great effect in recent years. Let us broadly outline four of these approaches and thereby help to set the context for our own study.

Occasionally, a single theological theme or motif has been employed to analyze the christological material of the New Testament documents. For instance, 'Wisdom theology' has made a very significant contribution to our understanding of christology, especially as it involves the question of the relationship of theocentricity and christocentricity.

It is possible to demonstrate that 'Wisdom' ideas and categories, which are generally descriptions of the work and activity of God, become christologically re-applied and serve as descriptions of the work and activity of Christ. In the midst of such reapplication rises the question of precisely how the roles of God and Messiah interrelate. As an example, it is quite easy to demonstrate the associations that a 'Wisdom theology' has with the doctrine of the creation of the world (as in Prov. 8.22ff.). To what extent, however, does the description of Christ as the 'Wisdom of God' encroach upon the prerogative of God in this matter? In what way does the association of 'Wisdom theology' with a human agent, Jesus, alter it from being properly described as 'theocentric' in character? More specifically, to take but one text which emphasizes Christ's role in creation, to what extent can Col. 1.16-17 still be described as maintaining a balance of theocentricity and christocentricity when the focus of concentration is so obviously Jesus Christ himself? Wisdom which is described as the personification of an attribute or quality of God is easy enough to understand within the context of first-century Jewish thought; but Wisdom which is so firmly and absolutely equated with the life and ministry of a known, individual person is much more difficult to comprehend, and to a certain degree is without precedent. The addition of this 'personal' factor within discussions of 'Wisdom theology' has tremendous christological implications. As the late G.B. Caird once commented:

> Jewish antecedents adequately explain all the terminology used in the New Testament to describe the pre-existent Christ, but they cannot explain how Christians came to belief in his pre-existence as a person; for the Jews had believed only in the pre-existence of a personification. Wisdom was a personification, either of a divine attribute or of a divine purpose, but never a person.[13]

These are by no means easy concepts to understand, but their discussion is essential if we wish to gain a clearer picture of the christological expression among the first generations of Christians. In any case, the importance of 'Wisdom theology' as a crucial, even monumental, means of christological expression for those first Christian thinkers and writers is without doubt.

The same sort of phenomenon of expression occurs with respect to 'Logos theology', and, to a lesser degree, with respect to 'Adamic theology'.[14] The Pauline materials have an important role to play in many such theological discussions. We could note, for example, the place that 1 Cor. 8.6-7 and Col. 1.15-20 have within 'Wisdom' studies or the role that Rom. 5.12-21; 1 Cor. 15.20-22, 44-49; and Phil. 2.6-11 all have within 'Adamic' studies.[15]

Another approach to the larger christological issue has been one which focuses on the hermeneutical use of Old Testament scriptures within the Christian tradition. Paul's epistles have a primary place in this specialized area of study with about one third of all Old Testament quotations or allusions found within the New Testament occurring in his letters. The importance of christology as the hermeneutical key to understanding these quotations is emphasized by E.E. Ellis:[16]

> the significance of the OT for Paul's theology can hardly be overestimated. His experience on the Damascus road radically altered his understanding of the Book, but it in no way lessened its importance for the apostle to the Gentiles. Rather, his knowledge of Christ opened to him a New Way in which he found the true meaning of the Scriptures.

At the same time there is little doubt that such Old Testament quotations and allusions contained within the New Testament reveal a great deal about the way Jesus' relationship to God was conceived by Paul and other early Christians. Richard Longenecker,[17] while emphasizing the Christian's reliance upon the Jewish scriptures, hits upon a crucial point:

> the Jewish context in which the New Testament came to birth, significant though it was, is not what was distinctive or formative in the exegesis of the earliest believers. At the heart of their Biblical interpretation is a Christology and a Christocentric perspective.

Such an assessment is widely recognized and accepted by Biblical scholars. Indeed, it would be possible to describe the hermeneutical use of Old Testament scriptures within the New Testament documents as essentially 'christological' in character. Yet, one specialized feature of the Christian's use of Old Testament texts has not been as thoroughly explored as perhaps it ought to be. This involves the way in which an outright *substitution* of christocentrism for theocentrism occurs within many of the Old Testament quotations or allusions. Certainly the meaning of many of these Old Testament texts has been considerably expanded and enriched by the interjection of a new christological element, but in many cases the central theological message itself has undergone a decisive change of emphasis by such a substitutionary process. In such cases the focus of concentration shifts dramatically from God to Christ. A good example is 1 Cor. 2.6-16, where Paul's discussion of spiritual gifts and Wisdom culminates in his quotation of Isa. 40.13, focusing on 'the mind of the Lord'. He goes on to further amplify this reference, and christocentrically redirect it, by emphasizing that the Christian has 'the mind of Christ' (ἡμεῖς δε νοῦν Χριστοῦ ἔχομεν). Of course, such redirection involves a shifting of the focus of concentration from God to Christ and serves as an example of the way in which theocentrism and christocentrism are interwoven in a complex pattern within many of the Old Testament quotations and allusions occurring within the New Testament documents. Thus, the study of the hermeneutical use of the Old Testament within the New remains a very valuable means of examining the christological question.

A third way in which christology has been approached has been by the study of the liturgical and sacramental facets of the early Christian faith. In particular, the way in which Jesus becomes the object of worship among the early Christians has a very important contribution to make in filling out our understanding of Jesus' relationship to God as it was understood by those believers. As a brief indication of this phenomenon, we note that the epistolary form of many of the New Testament documents demonstrates the close relationship between Jesus and God. More specifically, within the Pauline letters the way in which the greetings and benedictions are written speaks obliquely of Paul's understanding of Jesus' unique role and priviliged postion with respect to mediating God's blessings to the churches concerned. It is not without significance that each of the ten epistles within the Pauline corpus contains some textual evidence for the letter as channeling grace and peace from God *and* Christ.[18]

A far more substantial area of investigation has been the New Testament christological hymns themselves. In pursuing this subject scholars have subjected the hymnic material to rigid form-critical and historical-critical analyses.[19] These investigations have produced important results both with respect to the determination of the origin of much of the hymnic material, as well as the specialized way in which it is christologically presented by the New Testament writers. This christological presentation has prompted J.T. Sanders to conclude his study of the subject with these words:[20]

> As the New Testament Christological hymns appear in the New
> Testament writings, the meaning once conveyed by them is
> yearning toward, and receiving, further articulation.

It would not be amiss to suggest that one further such articulation
was undoubtedly the expression of the relationship between Christ
and God. Thus we find that the liturgical material which is
embedded within the New Testament documents particularly the
hymns and hymnic fragments, has an invaluable contribution to
make in any discussion of christocentricity and its relationship to
theocentricity. Ralph P. Martin has summarized this point well:[21]

> as Christ's saving achievement in bringing the world back to God
> implies that he has done what God alone can do, it was a natural
> step for a 'functional' christology to take on a trinitarian formulation.
> And that implies too that the first Christians made *in worship* the
> decisive step of setting the exalted Christ on a par with God as the
> recipient of their praise. Hymnody and christology thus merged in
> the worship of the one Lord.

Thus, the crucial point at which the christological hymns
contribute to our understanding of how Jesus' relationship to God
was conceived by the early Christians is that implicit within such
hymnic praise is *the transference of worship from God to Christ*. In
other words, acts of praise, adoration and worship which had
hitherto been directed to God and had a theocentric focus of
attention, now are directed to Christ and have a christocentric focus
of attention.

Finally, Martin's point leads us to consider that recent discussion
about the doctrine of the atonement, as it is expressed within the
New Testament, has been seen by some scholars as directly reflecting
upon the christological question. This is accomplished via the close
connection between the doctrine of the incarnation and theories
about the meaning of the atonement. Forty years ago Vincent Taylor
remarked:[22]

> how closely the doctrine of the Incarnation is connected with that
> of the Atonement, both as regards the ministry of Christ for man
> and the work of God in Him.

Leon Morris[23] makes a similar comment:

> The point ... is that the New Testament insists that both the
> Godhead and the manhood of Christ are concerned in this process
> of atonement.

We might at first think that such discussions have little bearing on the faith of the New Testament writers themselves, or that any theological interpretation of the atonement which implies Jesus' identification with God is a later formulation of faith. However, Martin Hengel has recently argued powerfully for a soteriological interpretation of the death of Jesus as foundational to the Christian movement *at its earliest stages*. Hengel sides with a number of scholars, and speaks for many more, when he says:[24]

> we agree ... that the vicarious atoning effect of the death or even the suffering of a righteous man was not unknown in the Palestinian Judaism of the first century AD ... Objections against deriving the soteriological interpretation of the death of Jesus from the earliest Aramaic-speaking community are therefore ... unconvincing.

The critical point here is that a human being, Jesus of Nazareth, was believed by the early Christians to have died as an atonement for not only their sin, but the sin of all mankind. Occasionally, when the early Christians expressed this tremendous truth, the focus of concentration shifts away from God to Christ and Jesus thereby rivals God for the central role in the reconciliation which is accomplished by his death.

All of this is to say that the christological question of Jesus' relationship to God has important repercussions in recent investigations into the origins of this doctrine of atonement. Any light shed upon just how that relationship was conceived by the early Christians is bound to aid us in our understanding of their interpretation of the significance of Jesus' death.

Each of these four approaches makes an important contribution to the overall understanding of how Jesus' relationship to God was conceived by the early Christians. Each approach has thus helped to clarify our understanding of the relationship of theocentricity and christocentricity. No doubt there are many more with an equally valid contribution to make to such an understanding which we have neither time nor space to list. Moreover, there is yet much essential work to be done on various facets of the subject before a clear and concise picture of New Testament christology emerges.

For our part, we wish to build upon this work of a number of previous scholars who have explored the relationship between theocentricity and christocentricity, by concentrating upon the eschatological teaching of Paul as a means to shedding additional light upon this central christological question. The connection between eschatology and christology within Paul's letters is often alluded to by Pauline scholars; indeed, most times it is an operating assumption. Yet the precise connection between eschatology and christology within Paul's thought has not received the full treatment it deserves.

We propose to redress that imbalance, at least in part, by specifically exploring Paul's eschatological thought for its christological content. We shall take advantage of the importance of Paul's use of the Old Testament within such material and shall give special attention to those passages within Paul's letters which deal specifically with eschatological matters. As a means to discussing these passages we shall concentrate on his use of Old Testament eschatological texts and their placement within similar contexts in the Pauline epistles. At the same time, we shall take advantage of other eschatological texts within Jewish pseudepigraphal literature and use them to sharpen our sensitivity to the ways in which the respective roles of God and Messiah are expressed in such texts. In this way, we shall be better able to appreciate Paul's teaching on the subject. Such a study will provide us with an important body of information which will allow us to understand more fully how the apostle handled the question of theocentricity and christocentricity.

To approach our subject in this manner means that we are taking advantage of the timely coalescence of two significant movements within Biblical scholarship of recent years. The first of these is the revival of the study of apocalyptic as a means to unlocking the meaning of the New Testament. Ever since Ernst Käsemann's memorable lecture in 1960[25] it has been increasingly obvious that apocalyptic writings have an important role to play within serious New Testament studies.[26] In the last 20 years or so it has become popular to conduct Biblical studies with a sensitive consideration of the apocalyptic element resident within the New Testament documents. The 1970s saw several major journals dedicate an issue specifically to the apocalyptic theme.[27] Major advances were also made within the field of systematic theology as a result of the interjection of an apocalyptic ingredient.[28] Most recently we have also seen the literary genre of 'apocalyptic' itself subjected to considerable investigation and clarification.[29] A related issue is the complex discussion surrounding 'Merkabah Mysticism' and its relationship to the visionary experiences described within apocalyptic writings.[30]

This rediscovery of the value of apocalyptic has quite naturally spilled over into Pauline investigations as well. A recent important example is J. Christiaan Beker's *Paul the Apostle: The Triumph of God in Life and Thought*.[31] Beker argues that the apocalyptic world-view was the coherent center of Paul's thought and rejects any assessment of his thought which attempts to 'suppress, delimit or compromise its apocalyptic texture' (p. 135).[32] While we cannot but agree with Beker's main point, his contribution is somewhat weakened by his inadequate examination of what precisely that 'apocalyptic texture' includes or involves. In particular, Beker's explanation of the relationship that christology has to such a 'texture' leaves much to be desired.

What is offered here is an attempt to correct that weakness and to explore Paul's eschatological thought more fully. In the course of our study we shall have occasion to interact with those Pauline scholars who have discussed Paul's eschatology and/or christology, but within our study we shall want to emphasize the mutual interpenetration of the two categories of thought. Such an integrated approach has not yet been used in exploring the Pauline material; but it can yield some important results. Thus we shall emphasize that any thorough study of the eschatological thought of Paul the apostle necessarily takes place within the central arena of much modern christological research.

The second of these significant movements within Biblical scholarship is the growth of research into the Jewish pseudepigrapha. The late 1960s and 1970s saw tremendous advances being made in the study of the pseudepigrapha.[33] Important seminar groups and research projects dedicated to the investigation of this crucial category of literature were organized.[34] Perhaps the most significant recent contribution is the publication of two new English editions of the pseudepigraphal texts in 1983-85.[35] The first of these works, in two volumes, is the combined effort of a team of international scholars under the editorship of James Charlesworth. This work was long needed and repaced the well-worn, 70-year old edition of R.H. Charles. It saw the pseudepigrapha included swell from 15 or so in Charles's edition to 65 in Charlesworth's, partly as the result of the discovery of additional materials during the interval and partly as a result of a wider definition of the category of 'pseudepigraphal' writings. The other edition, edited by H.F.D. Sparks, contains fresh translations of 25 of many of the most important apocryphal and pseudepigraphal documents.

Such an increase of material available for study and comparison provides us with an ideal opportunity to re-examine the New Testament afresh. The time is now ripe for such an examination of the christological element within Paul's eschatological teaching to be undertaken in the light of the new pseudepigraphal research.[36]

We shall explore Paul's eschatological teaching along two separate but related fronts: 1. His doctrine of the Parousia and belief in the Final Judgment. 2. His use of ἡ βασιλεία/βασιλεύω and his understanding of the Kingdom. As an introduction to these specifically Pauline subject areas, we shall begin the study with a detailed examination of relevant Jewish pseudepigraphal documents in an attempt to provide a comparative basis for examining the Pauline material. This extended exploration into the pseudepigraphal documents will help to show how the doctrine of the Parousia of the Messiah is closely related to an understanding of the eschatological Kingdom of the Messiah. It also enables us to examine more closely the precise relationship of God and messianic agent within the eschatological passages of these texts. This investigation into the Jewish pseudepigraphal material will thus enable us to establish the parameters of these concepts within eschatological texts and ultimately allow us to penetrate deeper into the heart of Paul's ideas on these subjects.

In Chapter 1 we examine those Jewish pseudepigraphal documents which seem to reflect the tension surrounding the respective roles of God and messianic agent, inherent within much eschatological teaching, by the specialized recasting of Jewish eschatological schemes. That is to say, we examine those pseudepigraphal documents which maintain a distinction between the temporary, earthly Kingdom and the eternal Kingdom of God which follows. At heart here is the assumption that such a bifurcated eschatological scheme is reflective of a tension between God and Messiah with respect to their eschatological roles and is a partial attempt at its resolution. It will be necessary to consider carefully just which documents do embody this distinction, since this is a matter of considerable scholarly debate.

The relevant documents are categorized into three groups: (1) pseudepigraphal works of the second to first centuries BCE; (2) pseudepigraphal works of the first century CE; (3) other relevant Jewish works. A detailed study of these documents will be helpful in establishing the guidelines of interpretation offered by such specialized eschatological texts, especially as they shed light on how the respective roles of God and Messiah are presented. Such an examination will also enable us to understand better Paul's teaching about the Parousia and the Final Judgment as well as his beliefs involving the Messiah and the Kingdom, as both relate directly to the critical issue of the interrelationship between theocentricity and christocentricity.

Chapter 2 explores the Pauline conception of the Day of Christ and attempts to reveal some of its christological implications. We begin with a brief discussion of the various attempts by scholars to trace the origin of the doctrine of the Parousia. This discussion suggests the importance of Jewish pseudepigraphal literature for any such attempt. We then move to a discussion of the Final Judgment in Paul. We demonstrate how Jewish pseudepigraphal literature, especially *1 Enoch* 37-71, contains striking parallels to Paul with respect to this judgment theme. These parallels are such that they suggest Paul's eschatology might be explored profitably by further comparing it with other themes contained within the Jewish pseudepigraphal documents, especially as they relate to the larger question of the respective roles of God and Messiah within an eschatological context. The extent to which the eschatological sections of Paul's letters directly reflect this theocentric/christocentric debate is then discussed via an in-depth study of the doctrine of the Day of the Lord. In particular, we are concerned to look at the manner in which the Jewish notion of the Day of Yahweh (יום יהוה) becomes transposed into the Christian idea of the Day of Christ, with the titles, descriptions, functions, and attributes normally used in reference to God now being assigned to Christ. It is our contention that such a theocentric/christocentric transposition is a reflection of a conceptual overlap in Paul's mind between Jesus and God, in which Jesus could be said to be in some special way identified with God.[37] The Pauline eschatological passages under discussion are categorized in three groups, depending upon the basis of the conceptual overlap concerned.

Chapter 3 is largely given over to a discussion of Paul's teaching on the Messiah and the Kingdom, examining it within the guidelines gleaned from our study of the pseudepigraphal documents. We begin with a survey of the Pauline use of βασιλεία and βασιλεύω. Of particular value for our study are the rare references to the Kingdom of Christ (βασιλεία τοῦ Χριστοῦ) within the epistles. We find the references to βασιλεία and βασιλεύω contained in 1 Cor. 15.20-28 a particularly important focal point in this regard. An extended discussion is offered on 1 Cor. 15.20-28 and its teaching regarding the Kingdom of Christ. We consider whether the passage might legitimately be said to teach or imply a temporary, messianic reign on earth. In this regard, we suggest that 1 Cor. 15.20-28 be specifically examined with respect to its christological message and seek to discover in what ways this passage helps reveal the inner workings of Paul's christological beliefs as they revolve around the critical theocentric/christocentric issue.

We move on to demonstrate how Paul's eschatological teaching, as a whole, may be profitably compared with that contained in many of the Jewish pseudepigraphal documents. Such a comparison is particularly helpful in illustrating Paul's understanding of Jesus' relationship to and identification with God the Father as expressed within his eschatological teaching. Thus we expose the delicate balance between theocentrism and christocentrism, which seems to pervade Paul's eschatological thought, as essentially compatible with that found in other select Jewish documents of roughly the same period which happen to have survived. Included within this section is an extended comment on the subordination of Christ to God within the eschatological sections of the Pauline epistles. This emphasis upon subordination is also demonstrative of the delicate nature of the question of theocentricity and its relationship to christocentricity and helps distinguish the specifically Pauline perspective on this issue.

In Chapter 4 we offer our final conclusions about the issue of theocentricity and christocentricity within Paul's eschatological thought.

An Appendix follows in which we discuss some of the implications our study has upon the larger world of Biblical scholarship in general and Pauline scholarship in particular.

We may summarize our study as focusing on the crucial transposition from the Old Testament concept of the Day of the Lord Yahweh to the New Testament concept of the Day of the Lord Christ within Paul's epistles. Several facets of this transposition are explored, including the theme of the Final Judgment and the concept of the

Messianic Kingdom. It is suggested that this transposition is a central part of the issue of theocentricity and christocentricity within Paul's letters. Such transposition is traceable, at least in part, through the complex tangle of beliefs and ideas concerning the Messiah and the Messianic Kingdom as contained within the Jewish pseudepigraphal writings of the period 200 BCE to 100 CE. Our task is to untangle—as far as we are able—these beliefs and to use the knowledge gleaned from them to arrive at a better understanding of Paul's eschatological teaching as regards the question of theocentricity and christocentricity. In so doing we shall find ourselves regularly transgressing the delicate boundary between eschatology and christology. As we step across this boundary we enter what C.F.D. Moule has poetically termed the 'borderlands of ontology':

> the religious experiences reflected in the New Testament are not adequately described in terms simply of the noble example or lasting influence of a great, human leader. If and when it comes to attempting some definition of their implications, it is necessary to speak of Jesus as himself divinely creative, to put him 'on the side of the Creator'; and that means indeed reaching the borderlands of ontology.[38]

provide __ with an opportunity __

Chapter 1

GOD, THE MESSIAH AND THE TEMPORARY KINGDOM IN JEWISH PSEUDEPIGRAPHAL LITERATURE

How do God and Messiah interrelate in Jewish writing of the period BCE 200–100 CE? It is worth drawing attention to the fact that within selected Jewish pseudepigraphal writings there is a remarkable degree of conceptual overlap between God and messianic agent. This overlap focuses on the respective eschatological roles of both God and his Messiah and is most clearly visible in those documents which teach a temporary, earthly Kingdom; generally this earthly Kingdom is associated with a temporary rule of the Messiah. These selected writings also display imprecision with respect to how this temporary, earthly Kingdom and the eternal, heavenly Kingdom of God are related. In this chapter we will analyze those works which make a distinction between the temporary, earthly Kingdom and the eternal, heavenly Kingdom of God which follows it, as these documents provide us with an opportunity to observe how the messianic role is highlighted and contrasted with the more generalized Eternal Age. From a methodological point of view these documents, notably *4 Ezra* and *2 Baruch*, are important in that they afford us an opportunity to see just how these two different expectations are expressed in relation to each other. It is this 'two-edged' characteristic of these select Jewish pseudepigrapha which is most important for our consideration of how God and Messiah interrelate. That is not to suggest, however, that other documents are irrelevant.

There are many examples of Jewish apocalyptic texts which speak of *either* God or the Messiah alone as the focus of the eschatological drama. A good example of messianic focus in this regard is the *Psalms of Solomon*, where the Davidic Messiah executes judgment upon the enemies of Israel and establishes a righteous Kingdom on earth. However, such texts are generally unable to help demonstrate very clearly how the respective roles of God and Messiah *interrelate*. Nevertheless, it is to suggest that the question of their interrelationship is most patent within those documents which do maintain the 'two-edged' feature. For this reason we shall be dealing primarily with those documents espousing a temporary Kingdom on Earth which eventually gives way to an Eternal Age to Come.

One might well ask how it is that this category of documents came into being. It is generally recognized that they reflect a compromise between the traditional eschatological expectations of the people Israel which fastened upon an earthly revival of the nationalistic, Davidic Kingdom, and a more transcendent, heavenly realm which involved the creation of a whole new world.[1] As David Russell has said concerning this point:[2]

> we find evidence, then, of a tension between a this-wordly Kingdom and an other-wordly Kingdom. In the earlier period especially the former of these predominates and even when, in later years, the influence of the latter makes itself increasingly felt it does not oust from people's minds the earlier hope whose roots can be traced back to the ancient prophetic expectations. In their teaching concerning a millennial or a temporary Kingdom to be followed, through resurrection and judgement, by 'the age to come' they were expressing a compromise which witnesses to the strength of that traditional faith which looked forward to the establishment of the rule of God not only over his own people in their own land, but also over all people throughout the whole earth.

There have been several attempts within scholarly circles to explore the implications of belief in a temporary, earthly (Messianic) Kingdom as it is developed within the intertestamental period. As long ago as 1898 Emil Schürer[3] called attention to a Messianic Kingdom of limited duration. The distinction between the temporary, earthly Kingdom and the eternal, heavenly Age to Come is also a standard feature in several of the pseudepigraphal studies of R.H. Charles.[4] J.W. Bailey[5] made the topic the subject of a very thorough journal article in 1934, while Albert Schweitzer did much to bring the subject into widespread discussion with his work on Paul first published in English in 1931.[6]

One can also find the concept of a temporary, earthly Kingdom discussed in the monumental *He That Cometh* by Sigmund Mowinckel.[7] We should perhaps also mention, in spite of his antiquated prejudices about the nature of the pseudepigraphal documents, G.F. Moore's study on Judaism, which also traces the theme through rabbinic sources.[8] The most recent work which deals with the subject at some length is the volume by D.S. Russell entitled *The Method and Message of Jewish Apocalyptic*.[9] Russell's work is a convenient place for us to begin our discussion. He specifies five works within Jewish apocalyptic writing which make a distinction between a temporary, earthly (Messianic) Kingdom and the subsequent Eternal Age of God:[10] 1. The *Apocalypse of Weeks* (*1 Enoch* 93.1-10 and 91.12-17); 2. The book of *Jubilees*; 3. *2 (Slavonic) Enoch*; 4. *4 Ezra* (2 Esdras); 5. *2 (Syriac) Baruch*.

Although Russell's list of five Jewish works is a helpful starting point, we should not assume that he has made an infallible listing of such documents. As we shall see in due course, there are several other possibilities which must also be considered, including some of the sectarian writings from Qumran. At the same time it must be stated that Russell's list itself needs to be updated and clarified in the light of further scholarly work.

Let us begin by examining each of these five documents listed above in turn and offer important and necessary corrections to Russell's assessment as to which documents do indeed teach a temporary, earthly Kingdom. It is important to determine just which documents contain such teaching before moving on to examine how this belief is integrated within the eschatology of the various documents as a whole. Having accomplished this we shall be in a position to appreciate how the question of the relationship of the respective roles of God and the Messiah is handled within them.

These five main documents we shall be considering easily divide up into two distinct categories: Those from the first and second centuries BCE and those from the first century CE. We shall proceed by examining each of these works in chronological order before moving on to consider some additional possibilities, including the sectarian materials from Qumran. In addition, we shall occasionally have opportunity to examine some other Jewish pseudepigraphal texts, particularly when they shed light on the role of intermediary figures within eschatological passages. These additional texts may not contain teaching of a temporary, messianic Age, but they do contain valuable information which is relevant to our central theme.

1. PSEUDEPIGRAPHAL WORKS
OF THE SECOND TO FIRST CENTURIES BCE

A. *The Apocalypse of Weeks (1 Enoch 93.1-10 and 91.12-17)*

The so-called *Apocalypse of Weeks* provides an interesting starting point to begin to consider the relationship between the eternal, heavenly Kingdom of God and the temporal, earthly Kingdom (generally associated with the Messiah) which precedes it.[11] It is perhaps the oldest of the documents which embody this distinction and probably dates to the period just prior to the Maccabean revolt because of its lack of a clear reference to that tumultuous era.[12] The *Apocalypse of Weeks* is contained in the fifth section of *1 Enoch* (chs. 91–104) which is commonly designated the *Epistle of Enoch*. The larger book of *1 Enoch*[13] is extant in full only in Ethiopic but important fragments exist in Aramaic, Greek and Coptic.[14] In 1978 Michael A. Knibb published an updated text of the Ethiopic with a translation informed by the Aramaic fragments of Qumran Cave 4.[15]

In the available Ethiopic manuscripts the order of the *Apocalypse of Weeks* itself has become somewhat shuffled during the compilation of *1 Enoch* and we are left with the second half of the *Apocalypse* (91.12-17) placed before the first half (93.1-10). However, this displacement has long been recognized and most translations freely correct the text for the sake of continuity.[16] The Ethiopic text, in translation,[17] reads as follows:

> (93.1) And after this Enoch began to speak from the books. (93.2) And Enoch said: 'Concerning the sons of righteousness and concerning the chosen of the world and concerning the plant of righteousness and uprightness I will speak these things to you and make (them) known to you, my children, I Enoch, according to that which appeared to me in the heavenly vision, and (which) I know from the words of the holy angels and understand from the tablets of heaven'. (93.3) And Enoch then began to speak from the books and said: 'I was born the seventh in the first week, while justice and righteousness still lasted. (93.4) And after me in the second week great wickedness will arise, and deceit will have sprung up; and in it there will be the first end, and in it a man will be saved. And after it has ended, iniquity will grow, and he will make a law for the sinners. (93.5) And after this in the third week, at its end, a man will be chosen as the plant of righteous judgment: and after him will come the plant of righteousness forever. (93.6) And after this in the fourth week, at its end, visions of the holy and righteous will be

seen, and a law for all generations and an enclosure will be made for them. (93.7) And after this in the fifth week, at its end, a house of glory and of sovereignty will be built for ever. (93.8) And after this in the sixth week all those who live in it (will be) blinded, and the hearts of all, lacking wisdom, will sink into impiety. And in it a man will ascend; and at its end the house of sovereignty will be burnt with fire, and in it the whole race of the chosen root will be scattered. (93.9) And after this in the seventh week an apostate generation will arise, and many (will be) its deeds, but all its deeds (will be) apostasy. (93.10) And at its end the chosen righteous from the eternal plant of righteousness will be chosen, to whom will be given sevenfold teaching concerning his whole creation. (91.12) And after this there will be another week, the eighth, that of righteousness, and a sword will be given to it that the righteous judgment may be executed on those who do wrong, and the sinners will be handed over into the hands of the righteous. (91.13) And at its end they will acquire houses because of their righteousness, and a house will be built for the great king in glory for ever. (91.14) And after this in the ninth week the righteous judgment will be revealed to the whole world, and all the deeds of the impious will vanish from the whole earth; and the world will be written down for destruction, and all men will look to the path of uprightness. (91.15) And after this in the tenth week in the seventh part, there will be the eternal judgment which will be executed on the watchers, and the great eternal heaven which will spring from the midst of the angels. (91.16) And the first heaven will vanish and pass away, and a new heaven will appear, and all the powers of heaven will shine for ever (with) sevenfold (light). (91.17) And after this there will be many weeks without number for ever in goodness and in righteousness, and from then on sin will never again be mentioned.

Before we go on to discuss the significance of the *Apocalypse of Weeks* for our study, we should perhaps say a word about the relevant Qumran Aramaic fragments discovered in Cave 4 in 1952. On palaeographic grounds Milik dates this manuscript (denoted 4QENg) to the middle of the first century BCE.[18] Two passages from 4QENg shed light on the Ethiopic *Apocalypse of Weeks*: I iii 23-25 and iv 11-26. The Aramaic manuscript fragments confirm without a doubt the unity of the *Apocalypse of Weeks* by running continuously from 93.9-10 to 91.11-17.[19] Milik goes on to trace how the literary genre of a Weeks Apocalypse develops.[10] He points to a variety of Hebrew and Aramaic texts which suggest such a motif and hypothesizes that the author of the Enochian *Apocalypse of Weeks* was also the composer of the *Epistle of Enoch* (chs. 91–104) and that he relied upon an already established cycle of ten weeks.[21]

The *Apocalypse of Weeks* contains an account of the history of the world divided into ten Ages or Weeks.[22] It is clear from the introduction given to the *Apocalypse* that the contents have been revealed to Enoch in a vision (93.1-2).[23] It is quite easy to pinpoint key events within the life of the nation Israel within this telescopic view of history: Enoch's birth, for instance, takes place within the first week, Abraham's within the third, the Mosaic Law is given to the nation in the fourth week, etc. The first seven weeks thus give a short synopsis of Israel's history down to the post-exilic period. It is the contents of 93.9-10 and 91.12-17 which most concern us, however, for there we have a description of the rise of an apostate generation as well as the elected righteous in the seventh week, the judgment of the sinful and the erection of a new temple in the eighth week, the revelation of the righteous judgment to the world in the ninth week, and finally, the eternal judgment followed by the passing away of the first heaven and the appearance of a new heaven within eternity in the tenth week.

The important point we want to glean from the Apocalypse of Weeks is the distinction made between a temporal, earthly, (Messianic?)[24] Kingdom set up in the eighth week and the eternal, heavenly Kingdom of God which appears in the tenth and final week. R.H. Charles highlights this distinction by comparing the *Epistle of Enoch* with two earlier sections of the book (chs. 6–36 and the so-called *Book of Dreams* contained within chs. 83–90).[25] Charles argues that within these earlier sections the Messianic Kingdom is eternal and is preceded by the final judgment of God while in chs. 91–104 the Messianic Kingdom is temporary (via the influence of the Apocalypse of Weeks?) and is followed by the judgment. Likewise, resurrection, according to Charles, within the earlier sections of *1 Enoch* is to this Messianic Kingdom whereas in 91–104 it is into this eternal Kingdom.

The most comprehensive treatment of the *Apocalypse of Weeks* published to date is the monograph by Ferdinand Dexinger.[26] He attempts to analyze the *Apocalypse* in light of recent studies within the field and submits these sections from *1 Enoch* to an exhaustive textual and literary-critical investigation.[27] While Dexinger's thesis involves a complex reconstruction of the various redactional forces at work behind the *Apocalypse of Weeks* which are not directly relevant to our study,[28] he does make two very important observations which must be mentioned. First of all, he makes it clear that the description of the eighth and ninth weeks (91.12-14) is intimately linked to the imminent revolt of the Maccabees against their Syrian oppressors.[29] Secondly, he wishes to point out that specifically 'messianic' connections to this earthly Kingdom are very weak. We find the figure of the Messiah nowhere clearly mentioned. Even the reference to the 'Elect Righteous of the eternal plant of righteousness' (93.10)[30] is of little value and probably only designates a righteous remnant within the nation Israel.[31] Despite this lack of a messianic link, it is nevertheless clear that a deliberate and parallel structure exists between the account of the earthly, temporary Kingdom and the eternal Age to Come which follows in the tenth week.[32]

One final point needs to be made. In reference to Charles's contention that the final section of chs. 91-104, as a whole, teaches a temporary, Messianic Kingdom, it should be pointed out that *no* passage from that section of *1 Enoch*, apart from the *Apocalypse of Weeks* itself, clearly details such a doctrine. Every other passage which reflects eschatological teaching is perfectly compatible with the bulk of the work in maintaining an eternal Kingdom on earth as the abiding hope of the faithful.

This does not mean that a comparison of the eschatology of the *Apocalypse of Weeks* with that contained in other sections of *1 Enoch* is futile. On the contrary, such a comparison is highly revealing, especially if we focus our concentration on the role assigned to Enoch throughout the various sections of the book.

It has now been demonstrated that R.H. Charles misled scholarship by his rendering of 71.14.[33] It now seems clear that we should understand Enoch himself to be the heavenly Son of Man throughout the *Similitudes*. At least this is the case once ch. 71 becomes closely associated with 37-70. We cannot rule out the possibility that ch. 71 is a later Jewish addition to the rest of the *Similitudes*,[34] in which case the identification of Enoch with the Son of Man in chs. 37-70 is not explicit.

However, even if we were to go so far as to concede this identification of Enoch with the Son of Man in chs. 37-71 to be a *post-Christian phenomenon*, we are still left with the unusual role Enoch plays in other earlier sections of *1 Enoch*.[35] For instance, in *1 Enoch* 12-14, Enoch has an intermediary role between God and the fallen angels.[36] In fact, we have Enoch actually pronouncing

God's judgment upon those wicked angels. In addition, we have the *Animal Apocalypse* of *1 Enoch* 85-90 where Enoch serves as God's 'recording agent' and assists him thereby in executing final judgment.[37]

One is tempted to speculate whether the explicit messianism of the *Similitudes* is all that dissimilar to the veiled, implicit suggestions of Enoch's activity (with respect to final judgment) contained within earlier sections of *1 Enoch*. Our evaluation of the messianism within the *Similitudes* must not be prejudiced by our schemes of a developing New Testament christology.[38] It may be that the exalted Son of Man, Messiah-figure is nothing more that the logical outworking of Enoch speculations with the added (post-Christian?) ingredient of a titular use of 'son of man'. In short, we need not make the contribution of *1 Enoch* 37-71 to New Testament christological study dependent upon our successful resolution of the 'Son of Man' problem. We must also take note of Enoch's role within the whole of the book and recognize that he has a significant part to play within the eschatological judgment.

To return to the *Apocalypse of Weeks*, how does all of this help us to understand its eschatology? First of all, we need to be quite clear about the *non-messianic* nature of the temporary Kingdom within the Apocalypse. We simply have to admit that at this early stage it was possible to have a temporary, earthly Kingdom without a Messiah. At the same time, it appears that within sections of *1 Enoch*, God's action of final judgment is aided by intermediary figures, notably Enoch himself. These early Enochian speculations may have resulted in the submerging (or at least overshadowing) of the distinction between the earthly Kingdom and the Eternal Age to Come. At any rate we do not have the distinction outlined in the *Apocalypse of Weeks* developed anywhere else within the larger body of *1 Enoch*.

All in all, *1 Enoch* contains a wealth of diverse eschatological material, both with respect to intermediary figures and messianic formulas as well as to how the future historical timetable was envisioned. This has important implications for the use of these materials as background studies for the New Testament documents. The crucial point to be noticed here is the fact that *1 Enoch* embodies several different eschatological schemes and ideas in a manner which seems to cause no apparent difficulty to the final author(s) or redactor(s).[39] This diversity is especially noted with regard to the executor of final judgment. At times, God himself is that executor, while at times, he is aided by Enoch as a special intermediary figure. Such flexibility will prove highly illustrative as we turn to consider the eschatological teaching of Paul.

B. *The Book of Jubilees*

The book of *Jubilees*[40] has also been pointed to as making a distinction between the temporary, earthly (Messianic) Kingdom and the heavenly Age to Come which follows it.[41] The work of R.H. Charles is of particular importance in this regard.[42] He believed *Jubilees* to be the work of a Pharisee[43] written during the years 135–105 BCE in reaction to the hellenizing spirit which had beset Judaism. The author, in contrast to many of his contemporaries who associated the advent of the Levitical Messiah with the rise of the Maccabees, looked for the immediate advent of the Messianic Kingdom ruled over by a Judahic Messiah, that is to say a Messiah arising out of the lineage and tribe of Judah.[44]

According to Charles, this Messianic Kingdom, although already begun with the Maccabean ascension,[45] was to be gradually realized on earth and to be accompanied by a physical transformation of the world corresponding to the ethical transformation of man. Ultimately, all sorrows would pass and man would live to be 1,000 years old.[46] After death the righteous would enjoy spiritual blessedness for ever.

The two most important sections of *Jubilees* upon which Charles bases his interpretations of a gradually realized Messianic Kingdom are 1.27-29 and 23.26-31.[47]

> (1.27) And He said to the angel of the presence: 'Write for Moses from the beginning of creation till My sanctuary has been built among them for all eternity. (1.28) And the Lord will appear to the eyes of all, and all will know that I am the God of Israel and the Father of all the children of Jacob, and the King on Mount Zion for all eternity. (1.29) And the angel of the presence who went before the camp of Israel took the tables of the divisions of the years— from the time of the creation—of the law and of the testimony of the weeks, of the jubilees, according to the individual years, according to all the number of the jubilees (according to the individual years), from the day of the (new) creation when the heavens and the earth shall be renewed and all their creation according to the powers of the heaven, and according to all the

creation of the earth, until the sanctuary of the Lord shall be made
in Jerusalem on Mount Zion, and all the luminaries be renewed for
healing and for peace and for blessing for all the elect of Israel, and
that thus it may be from that day and unto all the days of the
earth.

(23.26) And in those days the children will begin to study the laws,
and to seek the commandments, and to return to the path of
righteousness. (23.27) And the days will begin to grow many and
increase amongst those children of men, till their days draw nigh to
one thousand years, and to a greater number of years than (before)
was the number of the days. (23.28) And there will be no old man
nor one who is not satisfied with his days, for all will be (as)
children and youths. (23.29) And all their days they will complete
and live in peace and in joy, and there will be no Satan nor any evil
destroyer; for all their days will be days of blessing and healing.
(23.30) And at that time the Lord will heal His servants, and they
will rise up and see great peace, and drive out their adversaries.
And the righteous will see and be thankful, and rejoice with joy for
ever and ever, and will see all their judgments and all their curses
on their enemies. (23.31) And their bones will rest in the earth, and
their spirits will have much joy, and they will know that it is the
Lord who executes judgment, and shows mercy to hundreds and
thousands and to all that love Him.

However, in his treatment of these two passages and their
immediate contexts Charles betrays some confusion in his understanding of the relationship between the final judgment and the
advent of this Messianic Kingdom.[48] In 23.11 we have what may be
taken as a veiled reference to the final judgment as preceding the
Messianic Kingdom. Yet, according to Charles, the very nature of a
gradually realized Messianic Kingdom (his understanding of the
Kingdom within *Jubilees*), precludes such a possible interpretation of
this cryptic verse.[49] Hence the meaning of 23.11 is sacrificed for the
sake of the teaching in 23.23-27 where the final judgment comes at
the close of the Messianic Kingdom. Moreover, when Charles argues
for *Jubilees* as teaching a temporary, Messianic Kingdom (on the
basis of 23.23-27), he runs into difficulty with his own interpretation
of 1.17-18, 29. That passage contains no such hint of the temporary
nature of the Messianic Kingdom but, instead, seems to speak in
terms of an everlasting rule of God on earth.

Gene Davenport sought to solve this dilemma in his monograph
on *Jubilees* published in 1971.[50] He criticized Charles, and most

other commentators, for false methodological assumptions of solitary authorship and for the incorrect diagnosis of the redactional nature of the book. Davenport sought to examine the eschatological sections of *Jubilees* and assigned them to two separate redactors (R1 and R2), who reworked the original edition of the book, the *Angelic Discourse*. This *Angelic Discourse*, containing the body of *Jubilees* and running from 2.1 to 50.4, had no material specifically designed to teach eschatological doctrine even though eschatological presuppositions do show through.[51] According to Davenport, it was written primarily to teach and authenticate Torah. Davenport dates this first edition to the late third or early second century BCE.[52]

During the Maccabean struggles of 166-160 BCE this *Angelic Discourse* was reworked by R1 who added 1.4b-26; a phrase in 1.29; 23.14-20, 21-31; 50.5; thus interjecting a word of eschatological judgment as well as hope. The Seleucid oppression was seen as a judgment of God upon rebellious Israel, but their exile was shortly to come to an end. The revolution of the Maccabees was seen as the day of future judgment, now active, of which the *Angelic Discourse* had spoken.

According to Davenport, the work of a second redactor can also be detected. He assigns to R2: 1.10b, 17a, 27-28, 29c; 4.26; 23.21; 31.14; and possibly 50.6-13. This second reworking was done during the Hasmonean period, probably during the rules of Simon and John Hyrcanus (140-104 BCE),[53] and he suggests this redaction was designed to emphasize the central role of the sanctuary in Israel's life. Faithfulness to the Torah is thus supplemented by faithfulness to the Temple. This second redaction has a strong note of cosmic eschatology contained within it. The rejuvenation of the New Age begins in Zion and spreads from there to engulf all of creation (1.29c).

Davenport is thus able to avoid the problem of inconsistent teaching within *Jubilees* concerning the relation of the day of judgment to the coming Kingdom by uncovering different strata of authorship. In 23.11 (part of the Angelic Discourse), the judgment precedes the Kingdom while in 23.30 (the work of R1) this judgment follows it. Incidentally, Davenport is careful to avoid calling the Kingdom 'Messianic' and is critical of attempts to ground a messianic doctrine on 31.18 by pointing out that the crucial phrase 'one of your sons' is clearly an interpolation.[54]

Given the complex redactional nature of this book of *Jubilees*, what conclusions can be drawn about its teachings concerning the future? Davenport quite simply argues that, according to the final redactional stage of *Jubilees* (the work of R2), the present evil age brought about by man's sinfulness and rejection of the Torah is soon to be met with judgment. All faithful Israelites will turn to God and rise as a mighty army to purge their nation of wickedness, establish the New Temple at Zion, and thus inaugurate the New Creation which will eventually extend over the entire earth. Men will live to be 1,000 years old and will die in peace. In short, we have a gradually established, earthly Kingdom which shall endure for ever. There is no clear 'messianic' figure involved and, according to Davenport, no provision of resurrection of the righteous dead to share within that Kingdom.[55] If such is the case, *Jubilees* can be dropped from our consideration since there is no eternal, heavenly Kingdom which is seen to follow the temporal, earthly one. May we so easily dispense with a potential source of valuable information, especially given the fact that we have so little evidence to begin with? One more important verse needs to be examined before coming to a conclusion about the relevance of *Jubilees* for our study.

It should perhaps be pointed out that Davenport fails to note the importance of the reference to the joy of the departed spirits in 23.31a-b. In a similar manner while commenting on this same verse, VanderKam argues that in neither *Jubilees* nor in the Qumran sectarian literature[56] is there any firm teaching of a doctrine of the resurrection of the righteous.[57] He interprets 23.30, 31 together and argues that whatever may be envisioned in v. 30b ('And they will rise up and see great peace'), the meaning of a physical resurrection is precluded by v. 31a-b ('And their bones will rest in the earth and their spirits will have much joy'). We should not think that such opinions are universal. H.C.C. Cavallin, for one, is unconvinced by such attempts to wriggle out of any belief in life after death in *Jubilees*.[58]

In any case, it seems that one cannot establish clear and definite links between the final, universal judgment and the resurrection of the righteous dead. Nevertheless 23.31 does seem to speak of some sort of post-mortem existence for the spirits of the faithful dead. Whether we are justified, on the basis of this single verse, in concluding that there was indeed some sort of role for these righteous within a temporary, earthly Messianic Kingdom is another matter. Unfortunately, the nature of the post-mortem existence, and the relationship the righteous who are granted that existence have to such a Messianic Kingdom, are matters left unexplained in the book of *Jubilees*.

With respect to Charles's attempts to explain away the diversity of traditions concerning the chronological relationship between the final judgment and the advent of the Messiah, we should simply point out that such diversifications need not be explained as due to different sources. Surely one of the most characteristic features of Jewish eschatological works such as *Jubilees* is their ability to absorb such 'contradictory' traditions comfortably. Rather than resorting to complex redactional analyses like Charles's to 'solve' the inconsistencies, we do better to accept them as inherent in such eschatological speculations. The same criticism may also be levelled against Davenport since his redactional analysis is motivated by a similar reason and does not allow the variety of schemes contained within *Jubilees* to exist side by side.

Thus we are left with a considerable degree of inherent ambiguity within *Jubilees* with respect to its eschatological teaching. Within this 'limitation', it is doubtful if we can confidently use the book of *Jubilees* as supportive evidence for a distinction between the temporary, earthly Kingdom and the Eternal Age to Come. This conclusion holds primarily because such a distinction is not very clearly spelled out and depends entirely upon the ambiguous phrases in 23.31. Even if we were to concede that 23.31 does imply such an earthly Kingdom, it can in no way be properly designated as 'messianic'.

Thus if we choose to turn to *Jubilees* and use it to help illuminate our topic, we should do so only in a qualified manner. Unfortunately, *Jubilees* is not sturdy enough to serve as a foundational stone and should be cautiously used only as a supportive buttress in our task.

2. PSEUDEPIGRAPHAL WORKS OF THE FIRST CENTURY CE

A. *2 (Slavonic) Enoch*

A third work which has been pointed to as making a distinction between the temporary, earthly (Messianic) Kingdom and the heavenly, Eternal Age to Come is *2 (Slavonic) Enoch*.[59] The book has come down to us chiefly in two Slavonic versions which have been translated and edited into English initially by W.R. Morfil and R.H. Charles.[60] Their edition relied upon the longer of two recensions (designated A1) for the basic text—a view which has come under severe criticism by modern scholarship.[61] It is generally thought that the original language of *2 Enoch* was Greek,[62] and that it was the work of a member of the Jewish Diaspora living in Egypt[63] during the first century CE.[64]

Within the book of *2 Enoch* itself we have an introductory two chapters which set the stage for the material which follows containing a description of a vision of Enoch on which he ascends through the seven heavens, accompanied by two angels, to the very throne of God (chs. 3–21). God here speaks to Enoch and reveals to him the secrets of creation and imparts to him knowledge of what is to come. Then Enoch is commissioned to return to the earth (chs. 22–58). On his return he teaches his sons of the mysteries he has had revealed to him so as to prepare them for the coming judgment (chs. 59–66). A final section, sometimes known as the Melchizedek Fragment, runs from 69–73.[65]

Within *2 Enoch* there are two chief passages upon which a doctrine of a temporary, Messianic Kingdom have been based: 32.1–33.2 and 65.6-10. The first of these has God saying to Adam:

> (32.1) And I said to him, 'You are earth, and into the earth once again you will go, out of which I took you. And I will not destroy you, but I will send you away to what I took you from. Then I can take you once again at my second coming'. And I blessed all my creatures, visible and invisible. And Adam was in paradise for five hours and a half. (32.2) And I blessed the seventh day which is the sabbath in which I rested from all my doings. (33.1) On the eighth day I likewise appointed, so that the eighth day might be the first, the first-created of my week, and that it should revolve in the revolution of 7000; (33.2) so that the 8000 might be in the beginning of a time not reckoned and unending, neither years, nor months, nor weeks, nor days, nor hours like the first day of the week, so also that the eighth day of the week might return continually.

Charles is heavily dependent upon this passage in his interpretation of the Messianic Kingdom as corresponding to the rest within the seventh day of creation. This Messianic Kingdom is to be followed, according to Charles, by the eighth day, the Eternal Age to Come.[66] It should be noted, however, that this section (32.1–33.2) is not contained in the shorter (B) version and Charles's conclusions are of debatable worth as a result.

The second relevant passage is of lesser critical importance.[67] It reads:

> (65.6) And when the whole of creation, visible and invisible, which the Lord has created, shall come to an end, then each person will go to the Lord's great judgment. (65.7) And then all time will perish, and afterwards there will be neither years nor months nor days nor hours. They will be dissipated, and after that they will not be reckoned. (65.8) But they will constitute a single age. And all the righteous, who escape from the Lord's great judgment, will be collected together into the great age. And the great age will come about for the righteous, and it will be eternal. (65.9) And after that there will be among them neither weariness nor sickness nor affliction nor worry nor want nor debilitation nor night nor darkness. (65.10) But they will have a great light, a great indestructible light, and paradise, great and incorruptible. For everything corruptible will pass away, and the incorruptible will come into being, and there will be the shelter of the eternal residences.

However, it is not at all clear from either of these passages that a marked distinction is being drawn between a temporary Age and an Eternal Age.[68] In particular, the second passage of 65.6-10 can only be said to contain such a teaching when it is read in conjunction with the first passage of 32.1–33.2. And we are only able to extract such an interpretation from 32.1–33.2 if we take there to be a special relationship between the eighth day of creation and the first day in such a way that a periodization of history into a week of 1,000 year aeons results. Even then the 1,000 year aeons have to be assigned interpretative value: the seventh period of 1,000 years becomes associated with the temporary, earthly (messianic?) Age while the eighth period of 1,000 years becomes associated with the eternal, heavenly Age. This is precisely the basis upon which Charles proceeds to interpret these passages, but it must be admitted that such an interpretation as he suggests is far from certain.

Let us for a moment assume, however, that Charles is correct in his general approach of assigning the days with the significance of 1,000 year periods. Are we justified in going on to draw a further distinction between a temporary, *messianic* Age and the eternal Age to Come? After all, such a further deduction is not specifically made within *2 Enoch* itself. Let us examine these questions more fully.

The answer to these questions throws us right into the center of the debate concerning the two versions of this peculiar document. In particular we need to reconsider the thorny question of the text of *2 Enoch* 32-33. These chapters are, after all, the sole basis for the idea of a temporary, earthly Age as over against an eternal, heavenly Age within the work. As mentioned above, this section is missing from Charles's shorter manuscript (B) and has therefore often been omitted from consideration in most discussions about the temporary, messianic Age. However, given the fact that *all* manuscripts of *2 Enoch* are very late[69] it seems rather arbitrary to assert that since 32-33 is missing from *some* of the manuscripts, and given that those chapters are crucial for extracting a belief in the temporary, (Messianic?) Kingdom from *2 Enoch*, we therefore can justify the elimination of *2 Enoch* from our consideration of the topic.

F.I. Andersen[70] has compiled for us the most recent scholarly investigation into the Slavonic materials. He cogently argues that it is too early to draw firm conclusions as to the textual relationships of the 20 or so manuscripts[71] which include portions of *2 Enoch* in them. We do know that no single manuscript is given over to a text of *2 Enoch* by itself; consequently it must be remembered in any future textual reconstruction that the Slavonic Enoch legends must bear some relationship to these other Slavonic materials. Attempts to divide the manuscripts rigidly into either a short recension or a long recension (as Charles did so long ago, thereby setting the boundaries for studies of *2 Enoch* for nearly a century), are simplistic and do not recognize the complexity of the problem. Given the present state of textual research into *2 Enoch* we are unable to explain adequately the differences between the longer and the shorter recensions as due simply to either condensation or expansion of an *Urtext* by later editors.[72]

In short, the relevance of chs. 32-33 to the question of a Jewish notion of a temporary, earthly Kingdom as distinct from the Eternal Age to Come is again an open issue. These chapters cannot be ruled out of bounds on purely textual grounds. A more fruitful way forward is a reconsideration of the *content* of these chapters in light of other early Jewish and Christian writings. In this regard the *Epistle of Barnabas* may help to shed some light. This parallel has not yet been sufficiently explored by scholars. It is an important parallel to consider and rightly deserves our attention, especially since several relevant points converge within the work.

We have already noted above how Charles argued that in *2 Enoch* 33.1-2 there is a special relationship emphasized between the eighth day of creation and the first day. This relationship is grounded in the underlying assumption that the days of creation correspond metaphorically to 1,000 year periods in the earth's history. The seventh day is the 1,000 year period of sabbath rest (32.2) easily adaptable to a belief in a messianic Age, while the eighth 1,000 year period takes on the transcendent character of the subsequent Age to Come. Is there any supportive evidence for such an interpretation within other relevant Jewish or Christian documents?

Fortunately, we do have the one helpful parallel in the *Epistle of Barnabas*. We find the same sort of ideas expressed there in 15.2-4. Within that passage we find first of all an interesting reference to the six-day creation motif of Gen. 2.2:[73]

> (3) And God made in six days the works of his hands and on the seventh day he made an end, he rested in it and sanctified it. (4) Notice, children, what is the meaning of 'He made an end in six days'? He means this: that the Lord will make an end (συντελέσαι κύριος) of everything in six thousand years, for a day of the Lord shall be as a thousand years.

Ps. 90.4 is called upon to support such an interpretaion by the author of the *Epistle*.

We have this idea amplified further on in the same chapter (15.8). In his explanation of Isa. 1.13, the author of the *Epistle of Barnabas* intones polemically:

> Furthermore, he says to them, 'Your new moons and the sabbaths I cannot away with'. Do you see what he means? The present sabbaths are not acceptable to me, but that which I have made, in which I will give rest to all things and make the beginning of an eighth day, that is the beginning of another world (ἀλλά ὁ πεποίηκα ἐν ᾧ, καταπαύσας τὰ πάντα ἀρχὴν ἡμέρας ὀγδοής ποιήσω, ὁ ἐστιν ἄλλου κόσμου ἀρχήν).

The writer goes on at this point to associate the eighth day with the resurrection day of Christ in a manner reminiscent of Rev. 1.10.[75]

Now the decidedly anti-Jewish tone of the *Epistle of Barnabas* is manifestly evident throughout the book by the way in which the interpretations of the Old and New Covenants are set in juxtaposition via the exegesis of scriptural passages.[76] We should not, however, deduce from this that the *Epistle* does not embody pre-Christian, Jewish concepts relevant to our concern.[77] It may be that we have here in the *Epistle of Barnabas* the polemical use of a Jewish belief in a pattern of an eighth-day periodization of history similar to that found in *2 Enoch*. This is made all the more feasible when we consider that within ch. 4 of the *Epistle* we have mention of the author's reliance upon *Enochian sources*:

> The final stumbling block is at hand of which it was written, as Enoch says (περὶ οὗ γέγραπται, ὡς Ενὼχ λέγει), 'For to this end the Lord has cut short the times and the days, that his beloved (ὁ ἠγαπημένος αὐτοῦ) should make haste and come to his inheritance.

Far from seeking to derive this passage from *1 Enoch*[78] we might do better to see it as arising from material we now know as *2 (Slavonic) Enoch*. It is not dissimilar in content and meaning to *2 Enoch* 33.2 and 65.6-11 (cp. *SO* 8.424-27).

In short, we should not be so hasty to pass over the teaching of *2 Enoch* 32-33 with regard to the temporary, earthly Kingdom as over against the Eternal Age to Come. But we can hardly deduce from 32.1-33.2 the *messianic* nature of that Kingdom. Indeed, there are *no* clear and unambiguous messianic passages in the entire book.

There is, however, a strong and persistent note of radical monotheism running throughout the work which is penetrated only in a few brief passages in which the intermediary world encroaches upon the divine territory. The Most High God (*gospodi*) is described in terms emphasizing his sole prerogative in creation (24.2-5; 33.4; 47.3-6; 65.1-2; 66.3-5). The Lord himself is said to execute final judgment upon the earth (18.6; 44.3-5; 50.4). The distinction between the extensive and elaborate angelic host and the Lord God is fairly rigidly maintained. Angels may have thrones in various levels of heaven (of which there are either seven or ten depending upon the text of 22.1), but the throne of God himself is found only in the seventh or highest heaven (19.4; 20.3; 21.2; 22.2; 25.4-5). In only one instance, (21.4), is an angel, in this case Gabriel, addressed by Enoch as *gospodi*, the term normally reserve for God himself.

It is interesting to note how Enoch relates to the angelic throng. Enoch is enrolled into the angelic ranks in 22.6-10 and to him are revealed things which none of the other angelic beings have had disclosed to them (24.3-5). Yet, perhaps in keeping with the monotheistic streak running through the whole of *2 Enoch*, we have Enoch exhorting his children not to take advantage of his exalted position and depend upon him for intercession on their behalf as they have to stand before God on the day of judgment (53.1-2).[79] We may detect here a hint of a polemic designed to protect the transcendent nature of God, especially with respect to his initiative in final judgment.

Is there any other evidence of such ideas involving the exaltation of Enoch which might be worth considering? We should mention the brief allusion to Enoch's exaltation contained in the *Ascension of Isaiah* 9.9.[80] But this is so brief that it is of little value and adds nothing of significance beyond that material contained in *2 Enoch* itself. In addition, it is most probably a Christian work, or at least the Christian editing is such that it renders any attempt to recover a Jewish original impossible.[81]

The closest other parallel within pseudepigraphal literature is *3 Enoch*.[82] This complex work, sometimes known as the *Hebrew Apocalypse of Enoch*, is basically an account of the ascension of R. Ishmael to heaven and a transcription of the revelations he receives there. Of special interest for our study is the archangel Metatron, the angelic guide and mediator to R. Ishmael. The oldest section of *3 Enoch* is probably chs. 3–15 and it is this section which describes Metatron in the most exalted language.[83] For instance, he is continually designated the Prince of the Divine Presence (שר הפנים occurs 12 times in these chapters); he is said to have 70 names built upon the name of the 'King of the kings of the kings' (3.2; cp. 4.1).[84] At one point he is even titled the 'lesser YHWH' (12.5; cp. 48D.90).[85] All of this must be taken along with the fact that in 4.2 it is revealed to R. Ishmael that Metatron is none other than Enoch himself!

Apparently this exaltation of Enoch to the highest order of angelic ranks was thought to cause quite a stir among the other angelic beings for they are made to protest most vehemently (4.7; 6.2). Indeed, the dissenting murmurings are only quashed by a pro-clamation of divine acceptance of Enoch/Metatron to this position of supreme importance (4.8-9; 6.3). However, the theological implications of such exaltation to the heavenly realms of a human being, even one as privileged and righteous as Enoch, still present a trouble-spot if ch. 16 is any idication. P. Alexander[86] suggests that ch. 16 is a secondary addition to 3-15 and is specifically invoked to halt or retard these exalted speculations revolving around Enoch/Metatron. Such speculations were thought to undermine the unity of God by promoting a heavenly dualism[87] and this supplementary chapter is an attempt to redress the problem by having Metatron punished for his insolence by the angel Anapiel with 60 lashes of fire.[88]

In addition to the fascinating speculations contained in chs. 3-16, there is also a further account of the elevation of Enoch within certain manuscripts (notably A and B). This further account comes at the end of the work and is designated 48C.[89] This extra chapter is, for the most part, an expansion of the ideas and speculations contained in 3-15. It does also contain the curious designation of Metatron as the 'lesser YHWH' (48C.90).

There is much within this mysterious book of *3 Enoch* which stretches the imagination. However, the book presents a maze of difficulties both with respect to its textual history as well as its traditio-historical background. The position *3 Enoch* has within developing rabbinic Merkabah traditions is especially difficult to ascertain. Additionally, the work is extremely difficult to date. Although the rabbinic legends concerning R. Ishmael mention his death as occurring just prior to the outbreak of the Second Jewish Revolt in 132 CE, there is little assurance that any of the material contained within *3 Enoch* can be confidently dated to the second century CE. In all likelihood the work is much later. Alexander, for instance, suggests a date between the fifth and sixth centuries CE for the final redaction.[90]

With confidence we can say little more than that *3 Enoch* 3-15 is *probably* the oldest section of the book and that it *may* reflect ideas and traditions ultimately not too far removed from first-century CE consideration. This is admittedly not much to go on. With respect to the Enoch speculations contained within the work, it appears that *3 Enoch* provides us with some limited insight into the direction such speculations were heading. At best it serves as a 'tracer' in helping to highlight the trajectory of such developing Enoch speculations which may or may not prove relevant to earlier speculations of the same order.[91] We can say that the position of Enoch/Metatron within *3 Enoch* 3-15 encroaches most definitely upon that of God himself. This penetration into God's territory is so severe that at some point within the development of the book it was thought that correction was called for and ch. 16 added as a balancing ingredient.

It is interesting to note the way in which the 'Two powers in Heaven' controversy has been analyzed within recent New Testament christological studies. J.D.G. Dunn, for instance, has sought to include the implications of these Enochian speculations within his survey of developing christology. He sees *3 Enoch* as contributing evidence for a situation in which:[92]

> in the period between the two Jewish Revolts (70–132) messianic hope, apocalyptic fervency and/or merkabah mysticism inter-mingled in a speculation stimulated by and in part at least centered upon Dan. 7.13, and that in one case at least the rabbis judged the speculation to have gotten out of hand.

It should be noted that Dunn's approach, typical of the way in which Enochian speculations are used by those tracing New Testament christological development, tends to analyze the contri-bution of *3 Enoch* to the issue solely on the basis of its ability to support pre-Christian ideas of a pre-existent Son of Man figure. The link with Dan. 7.13f. as the backdrop of such speculations is assumed and is undoubtedly correct.

However, it is a weakness in Dunn's approach that he has sought to explore the contribution of *3 Enoch* toward a developing christology only on this very limited basis of the titular 'Son of Man' question. Why should its contribution be channeled along this single avenue? We may miss some of the importance of *3 Enoch* by focusing our attention narrowly upon the 'Son of Man' issue. There is, after all, another angle which needs to be explored more fully, namely the larger traditions of heavenly visions themselves.

This is all the more evident when we consider that Dan. 7.9ff., with its description of *both* the 'son of man' and the 'Ancient of Days', was a critical text within the 'Two-Powers' controversy. It also was a frequently discussed text within rabbinic writings which sought to correct the heresy by giving a 'proper' exposition of the passage. This has prompted Alan F. Segal to comment (p. 36):

> All of this makes it likely that Dan. 7.9f. is as central to the heresy as it is to the defense against it. It could be interpreted to describe a kind of heresy which Ex. 15.3 is supposed to deny.

The major point to be gleaned here is that within the rabbinic materials (especially those associated with R. Akiba) the two thrones of Daniel 7 and the figures who are described as seated upon them (are they both occupied by YHWH or is one occupied by the

Messiah?) constitute a matter of considerable rabbinic controversy and exegetical debate. Indeed Segal argues that Dan. 7.9ff. is among the earliest and most important texts discussed within the context of this 'Two-Powers' debate.[93] It appears certain that originally this debate would have been binitarian, and *not* dualistic, in nature. It derives ultimately from Old Testament theophanic traditions like Exodus 15 and 24 and attempts to interpret them in a manner consistent with the governing theological principle of the unity of God.

We must not overlook the place of eschatology within *3 Enoch* nor its ability to reflect earlier traditions involving the heavenly vision of Daniel 7 upon which christological thought could have been based. Certainly the fact that it clearly reflects something of the 'Two-Powers' controversy, which ultimately, it might be argued, involves rabbinic discussion and exegesis of controversial traditions of visions of God in heaven from the Old Testament, makes the eschatology of *3 Enoch* a fruitful ground for investigation. Unfortunately, within the book as a whole, eschatology plays a very minimal role. We find, for instance, that the awaited Messianic Kingdom is only briefly hinted at in 44.7-8; 45.5; 48A.10. As far as can be deduced this earthly Messianic Kingdom is of everlasting duration. But there is some justification for seeing within the brief messianic sections of the book some fluctuation of the Messiah's role. It appears that the Messiah in 45.5[94] plays an 'active' role in the establishment of this Messianic Kingdom. This should be contrasted with the seemingly 'passive' role the Davidic Messiah has in 48A.10. Indeed, in 48C it is the hypostatized Right Hand of God which brings about the final defeat of the wicked nations and ushers in the conditions of the Messianic Kingdom (cp. 44.7-10). When we pursue this question of final judgment a bit further we discover that *3 Enoch* may provide valuable evidence of the importance of the shift from God as the focal point within the heavenly vision to the Messiah (or an angel or some other hypostasis) as the focal point. We note that in 48C.9 it is Enoch/Metatron who is said to take over the role of God with respect to final judgment. This is accomplished by a quotation of Dan. 2.21 in which the original referent of God is replaced by reference to Enoch/Metatron as the executor of judgment. In other words there is a liberal shift of both subject and object of this verse from the original Danielic text which has the prophet Daniel exalting God himself in the passage. A similar substitution of referent involving Isa. 55.11 is found immediately following in 48C.10-11. The only missing element to tie all of the ends together for our discussion is the equation of the Messiah with this Enoch/Metatron figure. Surely that would be to ask too much from a single document!

In short, such Enochian speculations as we see in *2 Enoch* and *3 Enoch* may have a greater relevance to this background question of heavenly visions than is at first appreciated. We should not presume to exhaust the christological relevance of such texts simply by examining them for their contribution to a pre-existent 'Son of Man' concept. They may yet contribute on another plane.[95]

To return to *2 Enoch* itself, we might wish to go on and associate these exalted Enochian descriptions alluded to in 22-24 with those speaking of one of Enoch's descendant—Melchizedek. Here once again we have exalted speculations involving an important figure in Israel's past. As noted above, a few of the extant *2 Enoch* manuscripts (A, V, B, J, R) include a further midrash on Enoch's descendants, Methuselah and Melchizedek.[96] The latter figure is particularly interesting given his appearance both within Qumran texts and the New Testament documents. In spite of the fact that the circumstances surrounding his birth, as recorded in *2 Enoch*, are extraordinary (he has no earthly father and is delivered from his expired mother!), it is hard to demonstrate any direct relationship to either the Qumran texts or the New Testament legends.[97]

The point to remember for our considerations is that *2 Enoch* gives us very little indeed to support the view that it teaches a temporary, Messianic Kingdom. Nor does it offer much in the way of what might be termed the 'functional deity' of the Messiah. The exaltation of Enoch to the highest level within above the angelic host is significant, but does not clearly demonstrate that any identification between God and an intermediary figure was to be understood. However, within the closely related Enochian speculations of *3 Enoch* such an identification does occur as Enoch/Metatron quite clearly crosses the barrier separating God and the intermediary world. Yet we should not press too firmly the connection between the Enochian speculations of *2 Enoch* and those we see in *3 Enoch*. The complex textual and traditio-historical background of *3 Enoch* does not allow for anything but suggestive comparison.

About all that *2 Enoch* does for our study is to give us corroborative evidence of a Jewish[98] apocalypse which perhaps maintains a distinction between a temporary, earthly Kingdom and the Eternal Age to Come. Its distinctive eight-day world week may echo harmoniously with material incorporated in the *Epistle of Barnabas*. Indeed, it may be that such motif comparisons between *2 Enoch* and other Jewish and Christian writings are the only valid approach for marshalling the evidence of *2 Enoch*. At least that is the only avenue open at present given the very limited understanding we have of the history of *2 Enoch*. We shall have to withhold definitive judgment and await further clarification of the circumstances which gave rise to the book.

2 Enoch is thus a limited, but useful piece of evidence for our considerations, but it must be used very cautiously. And if caution is the rule for using *2 Enoch*, trepidation must be the watchword for following through the Enoch speculations and appealing to *3 Enoch*!

B. *4 Ezra (2 Esdras)*

It has long been recognized that *4 Ezra* as it now stands is a mixture of Jewish and Christian sources. Chapters 1-2 and 15-16 are Christian additions to the older Jewish core of the book which is contained in chs. 3-14.[99] This Jewish core is known as the *Ezra Apocalypse* and will be the focus of our discussion.[100]

The *Apocalypse of Ezra* can be divided into seven sections containing material claimed to have been given to the scribe Ezra while in Babylon (3.1). However, it is quite obvious that the setting of the Babylonian captivity is merely a literary device used by the author, writing in the first century CE, to address his contemporaries following the devastating suppression of the First Jewish Revolt by Titus and his legions.[101] Thus the *Ezra Apocalypse* (along with the closely related *2 Baruch*) is associated with the period immediately following the subjugation of Judea and the destruction of the Temple in 70 CE.[102] The seven sections may be outlined thus:

1.	3.1– 5.19	Dialogues concerning the problem of
2.	5.20– 6.34	theodicy between Ezra and the Angel
3.	6.35– 9.25	of the Lord[102]
4.	9.26– 10.59	The Vision of the Mourning Woman
5.	10.60 –12.51	The Eagle Vision
6.	13.1-58	The Vision of a Man Rising From the Sea
7.	14.1-48	The Legend of Ezra

1. *Authorship and Provenance*

A clarifying word about the authorship and provenance of the book is in order here. Although I accept the scholarly consensus that the *Ezra Apocalypse* is essentially the work of a Jewish author(s), this question of unity of authorship and provenance of *4 Ezra* is important for our study and we would do well to consider it briefly before moving on to examine areas of its eschatological teaching.

This is a problem all the more heightened when we realize that one of our fundamental texts dealing with the temporary, Messianic Kingdom within the *Apocalypse* (7.26-30), is beset by obvious Christian interpolations.[104] We should note that the present state of 7.26-30 betrays some Christian tampering, with the reference to 'Jesus' in v. 28 serving as a prime example. Fortunately, given the textual evidence available (the Syriac reading is 'the Messiah' while the Armenian is 'my child the Messiah') it is quite easy to eliminate the Christian interpolations and recover the original reading.[105] A second obvious Christian interpolation within the same verse involves the reference to the length of the messianic Age as lasting thirty years.[106] Yet in spite of these obvious Christian interpolations, the essentially Jewish authorship of the book has ever been seriously doubted.

At times, of course, it is notoriously difficult to decide whether a particular work of the New Testament period is of Jewish or Christian provenance.[107] Often the definitive criterion employed to decide the question is whether a book contains material fundamentally incompatible with either Jewish or Christian belief and practice. This criterion of incompatibility is crucial for it enables us to decide in either one direction or another. At the same time however, this is a criterion beset with methodological difficulties for it operates on the assumption of the mutual incompatibility of Christian and Jewish belief. It is hampered by the fact that Jewish and Christians had a great deal of *shared* belief and practice.

Fortunately within *4 Ezra* the Jewish character of the *Ezra Apocalypse* is such that it is quite clear the book derives from Jewish circles. The possibility of the work being a product of a *sectarian* Judaism[108] has received some recent attention.

E.P. Sanders[109] has put forward the case that within *4 Ezra* the 'covenantal nomism' characteristic of most of the literature of Palestinian Judaism has collapsed and one is left with only the shell of a legalistic perfectionism. According to Sanders, the *Ezra Apocalypse* is therefore at odds with the rest of the Jewish literature of the period in that its pessimistic view of the sinful human condition overpowers the salvific power of the covenant and propels one down the path of a 'works-righteousness' resulting in the salvation of a select, obedient few. Sanders's analysis is dependent, at least in part, upon his theory of multiple authorship of *4 Ezra*. He takes chs. 13–14 to be 'a saving appendix to make IV Ezra more palatable in Jewish circles'.[110] This viewpoint is to be contrasted with that of the main author of the book whose own ideas are expressed by those of an angel of the dialogues (3.1–9.25). It is within this angelic stance that we have 'the closest approach to legalistic works-righteousness which can be found in the Jewish literature of the period'.[111]

Sanders's work has not gone uncriticized,[112] but it does help us to focus the discussion on the salvific nature of the Law and in a roundabout way strengthens the case for the non-Christian authorship of the *Apocalypse*. Let us briefly examine the role of the Law within *4 Ezra*.

Although the teaching on the sinfulness of humanity as channeled through Adam within *4 Ezra* is very reminiscent of Paul (cp. *4 Ezra* 7.118 with Rom. 5.12-21!), it is this conception of the Law within the *Apocalypse* which is difficult to reconcile with the view of any Christian, be he or she a Jewish-Christian or a Hellenistic-Christian. Note, for instance, 7.20:

> Let many perish who are now living, rather than that the law of God which is set before them be disregarded.

Or again in 7.61 where God declares in connection with his judgment day:

> I will not grieve over the multitude of those who perish; for it is they who are now like a mist, and are similar to a flame and smoke—they are set on fire and burn hotly, and are all extinguished.

In the fourth section of 9.26–10.59 the permanence of the Law is declared in 9.29-37. Since within *4 Ezra* the delicate balance between Law and sin as a basic pattern of life has as its fulcrum the agency of the individual free-will, the force of this passage is to suggest that adherence to the Law is salvific. Verses 30-31 read:

> Hear me, O Israel, and give heed to my words, O descendants of Jacob. For behold, I sow my Law in you, and you shall be glorified through it forever.

In spite of the fact that the overwhelming trend of mankind was to follow the pattern of Adam and fall into sin and wickedness, nonetheless, there are individuals who are able genuinely to follow the Law and enjoy salvation thereby. Note 3.35-36 for instance:

> When have the inhabitants of the earth not sinned in your sight? Or what nation has kept your commandments so well? You may indeed find individual men who have kept your commandments, but nations you will not find.

It is difficult to imagine a Christian having such an exalted attitude toward the salvific potential of the Law. Within the New Testament even the Epistle of James does not eliminate the element of faith from its discussion. Yet within *4 Ezra* such a cooperation of faith and works is barely even hinted at.[113] In short, the exalted salvific nature of the Law is an expression of one strand of Judaism and the final author of *4 Ezra* is an adherent to such a belief. Sanders's analysis of *4 Ezra* is weakened by his assumption that the message of the final vision in ch. 13 is essentially incompatible with that contained within the earlier dialogues. In fact there is much to suggest that the final vision *itself* may contain the answer to the questions of theodicy raised by these early dialogues of 3.1-9.25. The Messiah figure within that vision is the means of bridging the gap between earthly and heavenly understanding, a matter to which we shall shortly return.

We should be wary of dialectical analyses, such as Sanders's, which are absolutely dependent upon particular source-critical analysis for their foundation. Such an approach should be resorted to only if theories of the essential unity of the work under consideration prove unproductive and unable to explain adequately its theological contents. Such is not the case with *4 Ezra*.

One final point on the question of authorship needs to be made here. We noted above that one of the most important messianic passages of the *Ezra Apocalypse* (7.26-30) exhibited signs of Christian interpolation. Yet even here we detect a distinctly non-Christian element in what seemingly is a clearly Christian idea. In vv. 29-30 we have a reference to the death of the Messiah:

> And after these years my son the Messiah shall die, and all who draw human breath. And the world shall be turned back to primeval silence for seven days, as it was at the first beginnings; so that no one shall be left.

On first inspection one is tempted to see the reference to the death of the Messiah as further evidence of the work of a Christian interpolator (perhaps from the same hand who inserted the variants in 7.28 discussed above?). This is especially true in light of the fact that no similar statement about the death of the Messiah is to be found elsewhere within Judaism. However, starkly absent from the passage is any reference to the resurrection or the inauguration of the Kingdom as achieved by means of the Messiah's death. These are features which we would normally expect to find in any Christian's writing! Such an interpretation of the significance of the event develops very quickly within the Church, and surely the lack of such an idea within a post-70 CE document stands as a glaring omission. It appears that here too the Jewish authorship of the document is demonstrated. The reference to the Messiah's death serves to emphasize the radical division which exists between the earthly Kingdom and the Eternal Age which follows. Here not even the Messiah himself is able to participate in the Eternal Age short of following the pattern of death determined for all men. It is difficult to imagine a Christian contemplating such an idea when the proleptic resurrection of Christ from the dead and the inauguration of the Future Age brought to pass via that resurrection were at the heart of the Christian faith.

We may therefore assume that the *Ezra Apocalypse* is the work of a Jewish author who made ample use of a variety of materials at his disposal so as to construct a word of hope to the distraught Jewish nation following the traumatic events of 70 CE.

2. The Messiah and the Messianic Kingdom in 4 Ezra

The Messiah figure in this *Ezra Apocalypse* is of great importance for New Testament studies as it may provide an invaluable piece of evidence to aid in solving the complex riddle of how the doctrine of a pre-existent, heavenly, Son of Man-figure arises. Because of the highly developed messianic ideas we find in *4 Ezra*, this theme becomes the subject of much discussion.[114] Within the *Ezra Apocalypse* we may take 7.28ff.; 11.37–12.1; 12.31-34; 13.3-52; 14.9 as definite references to the Messiah.[115] Each of these references is important in its own right, but we shall be especially concerned with those which emphasize the Messiah's role in relation to the Messianic Kingdom.

We want to concentrate on the idea of a temporary, Messianic Kingdom as taught within the Apocalypse so as to determine its implications for the larger eschatological issues. This means that we will be primarily concerned with the first and third of the references listed above since these two passages explicitly speak of the Messianic Kingdom. Our first major passage is found within the third vision of 6.35–9.25, where Ezra is in dialogue with the Angel of the Lord concerning the fate of the righteous and the wicked. Into this discussion is interjected a section which describes the appearance of the Messiah (7.26-30). We had occasion to quote part of the passage above; it is given in its entirety here:

> (26) For behold, the time will come, when the signs which I have foretold to you will come to pass; the city which is not now seen shall appear, and the land which now is hidden shall be disclosed. (27) And everyone who has been delivered from the evils that I have foretold shall see my wonders. (28) For my son the Messiah shall be revealed with those who are with him, and those who remain shall rejoice four hundred years. (29) And after these years my son the Messiah shall die, and all those who draw human breath. (30) And the world shall be turned back to primeval silence for seven days, as it was at the first beginnings; so that no one will be left.

A description of the resurrection of the dead and the last judgment of God follows in 7.31-44.[116]

The second major passage comes in the interpretation given to Ezra concerning the Eagle Vision of 10.60–12.51:

> (12.31) And as for the lion that you saw rousing up out of the forest and roaring and speaking to the eagle and reproving him for his unrighteousness, and as for all his words that you have heard, (32) this is the Messiah whom the Most High has kept until the end of days, who will arise from the posterity of David, and will come and speak to them, he will denounce them for their ungodliness and for their wickedness, and will cast up before them their contemptuous dealings. (33) For first he will set them living before his judgment seat, and when he has reproved them, then he will destroy them. (34) But he will deliver in mercy the remnant of my people, those who have been saved throughout my borders, and he will make them joyful until the end comes, the day of judgment, of which I spoke to you at the beginning.

Here we can see quite clearly that the Messiah serves as the instrument of God's judgment upon the wicked before setting up a time of freedom and joy which will last until the final day of judgment.[117] In other words, it is important to note the distinction made between the Messiah's reproval of the powers of evil in setting up the Messianic Kingdom and the day of judgment which includes that Kingdom. The Messianic Kingdom could even be described as the period between these two judgments.

3. *The Messianic Kingdom and the Larger Eschatological Context of 4 Ezra*

Far too often *4 Ezra* is catalogued with those Jewish works purported to teach a temporary, Messianic Kingdom by scholars who extract these two passages (7.26-30 and 12.31-34) from the larger eschatological teaching of the book. Methodologically it is incorrect to focus our attention on two specific occurrences within the *Apocalypse* and hope thereby to draw out all the significance of its eschatological teaching.

Indeed, it is only when the larger eschatological teaching of the *Ezra Apocalypse* as a whole is taken into account, and these two passages examined in light of the other eschatological sections, that a truer and more accurate (albeit a more complex!) picture emerges. It is this diversity of eschatological teaching within a single document which provides us with an important, and often overlooked, point to bear in mind. If we were to ignore this diversity of material in *4 Ezra* and proceed no further than the citation of the two passages quoted above as evidence for the teaching of a temporary, Messianic Kingdom within the *Apocalypse*, we would come away with an entirely inaccurate understanding of the eschatology of the book. We are not justified in summarizing the eschatology of *4 Ezra* as 'this book teaches the temporary, Messianic Kingdom of 400 years' duration'. The truth is that the *Ezra Apocalypse* is much more complicated and the question will not be satisfied by such reductionistic means. In particular we note two ways in which messianic diversity is demonstrated with respect to the Kingdom within *4 Ezra*.

a. *Messianic Diversity: The Appearance of the Heavenly City*
First of all, there is some confusion as to when the appearance of the Heavenly Jerusalem (a metaphor of the Kingdom) occurs in relation to the advent of the Messiah. In 13.32-36 the advent of the Messiah is *before* the coming of the Heavenly City described here as Zion:

(32) And when these things come to pass and the signs occur which I showed you before, then my son will be revealed, whom you saw as a man coming up from the sea. (33) And when all nations hear his voice, every man shall leave his own land and the warfare that they have against one another. (34) and an innumerable multitude shall be gathered together, as you saw desiring to come and conquer him. (35) But he will stand on the top of Mount Zion. (36) And Zion will come and be made manifest to all people, prepared and built, as you saw the mountain carved out without hands.

Compare this with the passage from the third vision quoted above (7.26-30) where the advent of the Messiah is *after* the appearance of the Heavenly City. Incidentally, there are two additional passages which describe the heavenly Jerusalem. We find it briefly mentioned in 8.52-54 and in the interpretation of the Vision of the Mourning Woman in 10.38-58. Both references clearly speak of God's rule on earth but as they do not contain specific mention of the Messiah they add nothing to help clarify the problem.

What are we to make of this before/after discrepancy as seen in 13.32-36 and 7.26-30? One way in which scholars have tried to explain the difficulty is by appealing to later redactions of an earlier Seer's work. For instance, G.H. Box proposed[118] that 7.26-27 were from a later redactor who interjected all the passages describing a Messianic Kingdom upon the earth into the Seer's composition, which originally did not allow for such an intermediate messianic Age. Thus 12.34 is also by the redactor's hand because it too is inconsistent with the preceding context. Box suggests the reason for such confusion is historically grounded in the destruction of Jerusalem and the debate as to whether or not it was to be restored before the appearance of the Heavenly City.

Several voices have been raised to criticize such a redactional assessment[119] and reassert the unity of the *Ezra Apocalypse* as a whole. Jacob Myers, although admitting that minor interpolations and insertions are evident, argues for the substantial unity of the *Apocalypse*.[120] He follows David Russell in this regard.[121] Similarly, the recent monograph of Egon Brandenburger[122] has also argued quite persuasively for the unitary authorship of the *Apocalypse*.

In addition, the structure of the book, with its seven-fold division and repetition of structural features, tends to support theories of the essential unity of the book.

In short, fanciful attempts to explain away the discrepancies of the book by the detection and labeling of sources and the assigning of authors run into great difficulty. They may be prompted by our desire to impose a logical consistency upon an author to whom inconsistency was not an issue. The essential unity of the book, under a single author, is beyond reasonable doubt. In any case, extreme redactional theories are ultimately irrelevant to our point because they fail to explain how it is that the final redactor was able to hold such divergent messianic and eschatological beliefs together without any apparent difficulty. It is better to proceed without resorting to such complex redactional analyses and accept the inconsistencies at face value as evidence of a flexible and creative mind. In short, the author included within this composition differing views as to the time of the appearing of the Heavenly City in relation to the advent of the Messiah.

b. *Messianic Diversity: The Final Judgment*

The diversity of messianic expectations contained in *4 Ezra* can also be seen by examining the relationship between the final judgment and the Messianic Kingdom. Michael Stone has pointed out that there is an ambiguity within *4 Ezra* as to whether the consummation occurs before or after the Messianic Kingdom. This ambiguity is tied up with the flexibility of the term 'the end' (*finis*). As Stone comments:[123]

> It appears that (for IV Ezra) which particular event is called the end in any given passage is determined by the immediate context. It is clear that 'end' was a technical term in eschatological contexts, for it is used alone and without any referent in such contexts. Yet it is equally clear that it does not always refer to the same event (cf. 7.113; 12.34; 11.39-46; 6.25). 'End' evidently signified for the author something like 'the decisive point in the eschatological sequence'.

Stone goes on to categorize 7.113 and 12.34 as stating the end to be the Day of Judgment while 11.36-39; 6.25; 6.7-10; 5.41; 14.9 all place the end immediately before the Messianic Kingdom and thus prior to that Judgment Day.

Perhaps it is worth adding here that such flexibility is only brought to our attention by the interjection of the idea of a temporary, Messianic Kingdom into the eschatological thought of the writer. It gives us a comparative reference point by which we are able to recognize the free-handed way in which he was able to organize his thoughts about the future—at one point setting the end prior to the

Messianic Kingdom and at another setting it subsequent to that Kingdom.

In this connection another point needs to be emphasized which is often overlooked. What precisely is the role the Messiah plays with respect to that Final Judgment? More specifically, how is the messianic role defined in relation to that of God? A most fascinating discovery arises when this is looked at more carefully. It has frequently been pointed out that at times the Messiah plays a very passive role in executing final judgment upon the world (as in 7.26-30), while at other times he plays a very active role in the execution of that judgment (as in 12.31-34 and 12.21-49). At the same time we also want to note the way in which God's judgment is generally described as following the Messianic Kingdom regardless of the Messiah's active/passive role in the judgment of the nations and the institution of that Kingdom. Thus the 'passive' Messiah of 7.28-30 gives way to God who later judges absolutely (7.33-34):

> And the Most High shall be revealed upon the seat of judgment, and compassion shall pass away, and patience shall be withdrawn; but judgment alone shall remain, truth shall stand, and faithfulness grow strong.

Even in 12.31-34 where the earth is already subjected to the activity of the 'active' Messiah in judgment, we find that this messianic judgment is followed by a further judgment by God himself (referred to at the end of v. 34):

> But he will deliver in mercy the remnant of my people, those who have been saved throughout my borders, and he will make them joyful until the end comes, the day of judgment, of which I spoke to you at the beginning.

Indeed, it appears that within both these sections of *4 Ezra* the final act of judgment lies within the sphere of God's activities alone. (We can safely assume that the other generalized references to the eschatological judgment which do not specify their executor refer to the future judgment by God.)

Thus we find here that however exalted a role is given to the Messiah (whether he is active or passive in the establishment of his Kingdom and the execution of judgment open earth), it is always within the context of God's ultimate judgment and authority. In both of these messianic passages (7.28-30 and 12.31-34) this judgment activity on the part of the Messiah has been substantiated and verified by a subsequent judgment activity by God.

However, when we turn to the Vision of the man Rising from the Sea in 13.1-58 we find this pattern broken. What is unique about this vision when compared to the other two messianic visions is that there is *no* subsequent judgment by God following that of the Messiah. The importance of this omission of a confirming judgment of God becomes recognizable when we consider that, when viewed alongside the two earlier messianic sections, it can lead quite easily to a 'blurring' of the boundaries between God and Messiah in ch. 13 and contributes to a conceptual overlap between the two with respect to their roles in executing judgment upon the world.

We may sharpen the question further by phrasing it thus: Just who is executing the judgment in the vision of ch. 13? God himself or his messianic representative? Or, paradoxically, both? That is to say, is it possible that God himself is exercising Final Judgment in and through his messianic agent? I would like to suggest that this third option is the most likely and that this arrangement easily leads to a conceptual overlap between God and the Messiah with respect to this final judgment in this unusual chapter of *4 Ezra* 13. This conceptual overlap also results in a referential confusion between the two, as we shall see in a moment.

I think it no accident that the vision of Daniel 7 is behind this extraordinary passage in *4 Ezra*.[124] We see evidence of this influence in 13.3:[125]

> And I looked, and behold, this wind made something like the figure of a man come up out of the heart of the sea. And I looked, and behold, that man flew with the clouds of heaven.

It is precisely this same passage from Daniel which has perplexed scholars for years. The question is whether or not pre-existent, Son of Man-Messianic beliefs are implied. Yet we have to admit that the debate over the influence of Dan. 7.13f. upon development of such pre-Christian beliefs has recently bogged down in the marshes of the undateable *Similitudes of Enoch*.[126] This, so it has been argued, effectively removes the subject from any discussion of relevant first-century CE issues and casts doubts as to whether or not such an exalted concept of the Son of Man as we find in *1 Enoch* 37-71 was extant early enough[127] to have been influential within the early Church. Hopefully the messianism of *4 Ezra* can help to illuminate this whole question further by establishing a non-Christian belief in a Messiah-figure with transcendent qualities and theophanic associations parallel to, yet independent of, our earliest indications of such a belief within Christian circles.[128] It is in this regard that the vision of *4 Ezra* 13 is most important and the issue of final judgment within the vision a valuable piece of evidence for demonstrating the ambiguous roles of God and Messiah within a Jewish document which also contains mention of a temporary, Messianic Kingdom.[129] This is so because the vision in *4 Ezra* 13 easily would support an understanding of final judgment in which God and messianic agent are fused in activity and the transposition of focus from God to Messiah thereby easily facilitated.

But how far are we justified in stressing the omission of God's confirming final judgment in *4 Ezra* 13? Might it not be simply an oversight? A mere lapse of memory? More than likely its omission is best explained as yet a further indication of the flexibility within the apocalyptic genre with regard to schematic detail. However, several factors deserve additional consideration as we explore this passage more fully. First of all we have the curious dialogue between Ezra and God with which the interpretation of the vision concludes:

> (51) I said, 'O sovereign Lord, explain this to me: Why did I see the man coming up from the heart of the sea?' (52) He said to me, 'Just as no one can explore or know what is in the depths of the sea, so no one on earth can see my Son or those who are with him, except in the time of his day'.

Ezra is told that the reason he enjoys such a privileged status and is revealed these things is because of his adherence to the Law (13.53-56). In point of fact there is a contrast between the knowledge of men and the knowledge of God running through the entire *Apocalypse*. We find this specifically mentioned, for instance, in 4.21b:

> those who dwell upon earth can understand only what is on earth, and he who is above the heavens can understand what is above the height of the heavens.

Time and time again, especially within the first three sections preoccupied with the question of theodicy, we find Ezra's inability to comprehend the meaning of Israel's destruction by the Babylonians (Romans) explained by the angel Uriel as related to his inability to understand the heavenly things of God. Ezra lays bare his anguished thoughts on the subject to God in 5.23-29 and is told by God that the answer he seeks will be forthcoming provided Ezra can breach this separation between heavenly and earthly knowledge. In despair Ezra cries out (5.38):

> 'O sovereign Lord', I said, 'who is able to know these things except he whose dwelling is not with men?'

One's first impression suggests that God is meant, but can we be so sure? One is tempted to ask: Where would the author of *4 Ezra* have taken the habitation of the Messiah to be? In the earthly realms or in the heavenly? Now the Davidic lineage of the Messiah is certainly emphasized in *4 Ezra*, as is the Judean provenance of the Messianic Kingdom;[130] but the thrust of 13.51-52 (quoted above) surely leaves no doubt as to the heavenly nature of the Messiah. It is quite clear there that the Messiah serves as God's agent of action and as such is promoted to the heavenly sphere. If we were to associate 5.38 with the revelatory declaration of 13.51-52, we must entertain at least the possibility that 5.38 is a cryptic reference to the Messiah functioning as God's agent. At the very least we must admit that the verse could be (deliberately?) ambiguous. If it does refer to the awaited Messiah whose habitation is not among men, then it is this same Messiah who will be revealed and bridge the gap between the earthly things and the heavenly things. As hinted at above, the revelation of this heavenly Messiah in *4 Ezra* 13 may have been intended to serve as a culmination point for the book as a whole and thus help to solve the problem of how the dialogues revolving around theodicy (3.1-9.25) relate to the remaining chapters. In other words, the answer to the problem of theodicy of which the author speaks is resolved by the revelation of God's messianic agent.

If this suggestion is sound, it may indicate something of the way in which the hope of the author was inextricably bound to expectations of a messianic deliverance from the Roman oppressors, even in the face of the events of 70 CE.

This leads us to go further and explore the additional question of the relationship between God and his Messiah. In particular, the question arises as to what the ontological implications are for the Messiah's serving as God's agent in final judgment. At what point does functionalism encroach upon ontology?

How long, and under what circumstances, can the Messiah be seen to be functioning as God's agent before deity in some sense becomes attributed to him? These, of course, are exceedingly complicated questions and the process of answering them is equally involved.

The value of *4 Ezra* in attempting to answer some of these questions is that it is decidedly Jewish and yet espouses both a devoted monotheism as well as what we might call a 'functional deity' of the Messiah. Let me try to demonstrate what I mean by the phrase.

In 5.56 we have Ezra asking categorically of God:[131]

> I said, 'O Lord, I beseech you, if I have found favor in your sight, show your servant through whom you are going to visit your creation'.

Reply is given in the form of a series of declarations magnifying God's creative activities which culminate in 6.6:[132]

> I planned these things, and they were made through me and not through another, just as the end shall come through me and not through another.

In his comments on this passage, Myers suggests that it could have arisen in response to either Christian messianism or an elaborate Jewish angelology.[133] Is such an explanation adequate? I think not. There are other passages which emphasize the sole prerogative of God in creation and/or redemption. Note for example 3.4-5; 8.7. What is notable is that within a book containing such radically monotheistic statements as these we find messianic declarations such as 13.25-26:[134]

> As for your seeing a man come up from the heart of the sea, this is he whom the Most High has been keeping for many ages, who will himself deliver his creation; and he will direct those who are left.

In other words, it appears that the writer is flexible enough to assert the Lord God as sole Creator/Redeemer while at the same time paradoxically asserting the Messiah as Redeemer. The point, quite simply, is that the author of *4 Ezra* is able to hold his monotheism and this messianism in creative tension with no obvious reservations. Such a paradoxical juxtaposition (at least it is paradoxical from our modern vantage point) seems indicated when one compares 6.6 with 13.25-26. The radical monotheistic strands of the earlier sections of *Ezra Apocalypse*, when viewed alongside such exalted messianic passages as we find in ch. 13, drive us inevitably toward this conclusion.

Nor should we think that such a phenomenon is an isolated occurrence found only in *4 Ezra*. We find precisely the same thing in *Testament of Moses* 10.1-10.[135] There we read:

(10.1) Then his Kingdom will appear throughout his whole creation. Then the devil will have an end. Yea, sorrow will be led away with him. (2) Then will be filled the hands of the messenger, who is in the highest place appointed. Yea, he will at once avenge them of their enemies. (3) For the Heavenly One will arise from his kingly throne. Yea, he will go forth from his holy habitation with indignation and wrath on behalf of his sons. (4) And the earth will tremble, even to its ends shall it be shaken. And the mountains will be made low. Yea, they will be shaken, as enclosed valleys will they fall. (5) The sun will not give light. And in darkness the horns of the moon will flee. Yea, they will be broken in pieces. It will be turned wholly into blood. Yea, even the circle of the stars will be thrown into disarray. (6) And the sea all the way to the abyss will retire, to the sources of waters which fail. Yea, the rivers will vanish away. (7) For God Most High will surge forth, the Eternal One alone. In full view will he come to work vengeance on the nations. Yea, all their idols will he destroy. (8) Then will you be happy, O Israel! And you will mount up above the necks and the wings of an eagle. Yea, all things will be fulfilled. (9) And God will raise you to the heights. Yea, he will fix you firmly in the heaven of the stars, in the place of their habitations. (10) And you will behold from on high. Yea, you will see your enemies on the earth. And recognizing them, you will rejoice. And you will give thanks. Yea, you will confess your creator.

Here in vv. 1-2 we have the messenger of God, generally thought to be the archangel Michael,[136] described as executing the judgment of God upon the enemies of Israel. At the same time, later in the eschatological hymn, God himself is specifically said to be the executor of this judgment. We should not overlook the radically monotheistic statement in v. 7:

For God Most High will surge forth, the Eternal One alone (*solus*).

This tension led R.H. Charles[137] to postulate that the author of vv. 1-2 was not the same as the author of vv. 3-10. However, this is arbitrary and we must concur with J. Priest that such conclusions are far from reliable given the nature of the textual history of the Testament itself.[138] Instead, we are perhaps nearer to the truth if we simply acknowledge that the *Testament of Moses* is but another example of flexibility within Jewish pseudepigraphal writings with respect to the relationship between God and his agent of eschatological judgment.[139]

In short, it seems that the author of *4 Ezra* exhibits a creative tension between monotheism and messianism which retains all of the integrity associated with Jewish monotheism, while at the same time allowing for tremendous claims to be made for the Messiah's role. These claims are such that the 'functional deity' of the Messiah is asserted.

Such creativity leads us to a second reason why any attempt to explain the lack of a subsequent judgment by God in *4 Ezra* 13 needs to be carefully examined. It is this: all through the chapter we have fluid movement between God and messianic agent with respect to the final act of judgment.[140] In this context God is specifically mentioned in v. 29 while the Messiah is mentioned in vv. 26 and 37-38. The fluidity is most clearly illustrated in v. 49. In the passage immediately preceding this verse, we have the acts of the Most High with regard to the restoration of the ten tribes described (vv. 44, 47); but a final act of judgment is once again attributed to the Messiah in vv. 49-50, where God says:

> Therefore when he destroys the multitude of the nations that are gathered together, he will defend the people who remain. And then he will show them very many wonders.

Does a study of the various texts themselves help clarify this referential fluidity? We should remember that *4 Ezra* was probably written originally in either Hebrew or Aramaic. Unfortunately nothing remains of this earliest text nor indeed of its Greek translation (although the existence of the Greek translation is deduced from translation evidence within the Latin copies we do possess).[141] Thus we are dependent upon a variety of secondary translations for our study of *4 Ezra*, none of which aids very much in the reconstruction of the original Hebrew (Aramaic?) text. However, this variety of secondary translations does afford us an opportunity to compare the messianic features.

For instance, when we turn to the Armenian text, we note that it is significantly different from the Latin on a number of points. For instance, the crucial section of 5.56–6.6 is altogether unlike the Latin section discussed above in connection with the 'monotheistic/

messianic' tension. Indeed, the critical verse 6.6 is missing altogether! In its place the Armenian translation reads:

> I ask of you lord, do not turn away (your) face from me, who am asking you many things, but command me further to learn from you concerning which I wish to ask.

This is followed by a dialogue between Ezra and God which culminates in 6.1f-g:

> And I (Ezra) said to him, 'How will the Most High come, or when will his coming be?'. And he said, 'First of all, he will come after a little time in the form of a son of man, and he will teach hidden things'.

This association between God and 'a son of man' is even more interesting when we look at the messianic visions themselves. Basically the first two visions (7.26-30 and 12.31-34) of the Armenian text are not dissimilar in form and content to the Latin version upon which our comments above were based. However, the third vision of 13.1-58 is highly revealing with the interpretation of the vision given in vv. 25-26 setting the scene. There we read:

> (25) But this is the interpretation of the dream: the man whom you saw who ascended from the sea, (26) that is he whom the Most High will send after many times and through him he will save his creation and he will bring back those who remain.

Compare this with the statement contained in v. 32:

> And it shall come to pass when these signs happen which I told you, the Most High shall appear with great power. He is that man whom you saw, that he ascended from the sea.

In short the Armenian text seems to indicate an outright *identification* of this 'son of man' with the Most High! Anything we might have lost in our argument by the fact of the absence of 5.56–6.6 within the Armenian text is more than compensated for by its statements in 6.1f-g and 13.32.[142] We need only point out that here also there is diversity within the Armenian text itself as to the relationship between the Messiah and God, as the comparison between 13.25-26 and 13.32 shows.

Nor should we assume this to be a phenomenon restricted to the Armenian text. Apparently this fluctuation between God and messianic agent was confusing to the author of the Arabic text for he substitutes 'I' for 'he' in v. 49 and makes God the executor of judgment.[143]

In this concluding vision of *4 Ezra* 13 the fact that the author can freely alternate between God and Messiah as final Judge is a highly revealing indication of the author's conceptual overlap of the two. We find this fluctuation especially preserved and creatively expanded in a number of the secondary translations[144] of *4 Ezra*.

We now move on to consider the other major Jewish pseud-epigraphal document which teaches a temporary, Messianic Kingdom on earth: *2 (Syriac) Baruch*.

C. *2 (Syriac) Baruch*

The third book we need to examine in this section is *2 (Syriac) Baruch*.[145] Along with *4 Ezra*, we have here the most fully developed messianic, eschatological expectation.[146] *2 Baruch* is extant in its entirety in a single Syriac manuscript[147] which claims to be a translation from the Greek. However, scholars are divided as to its original language. Charles argued[148] for a Hebrew original which quickly becomes translated into Greek and from which the Syriac is later derived. Bogaert, on the other hand, feels a Greek original is more likely.[149] The question is unsolvable given our present state of evidence.

Charles[150] divided the body of *2 Baruch* (chs. 1–77) into seven sections, each of which is punctuated by a reference to Baruch's fasting in preparation for the next stage of revelation by God. Such a schema was thought to be the work of the final redactor of *2 Baruch*. The concluding chapters of 78–87 are an appendix and contain a letter from Baruch to the nine and one half Tribes of the Exile. However, we may outline the contents of the book thus:

1.	1.1–9.2	Description of the Destruction of Jerusalem
2.	10.1–20.6	Baruch Dialogues with the Lord
3.	21.1–30.5	The First Messianic Apocalypse
4.	31.1–34.1	Baruch Speaks to the People
5.	35.1–40.4	The Second Messianic Apocalypse
6.	41.1–43.33	Baruch Dialogues with the Lord
7.	44.1–47.2	Baruch Speaks to the People
8.	48.1–52.7	Baruch Dialogues with the Lord
9.	53.1–76.5	The Third Messianic Apocalypse
10.	77.1–26	Baruch Speaks to the People
11.	78.1–87.1	The Letter to the Nine and One Half Tribes

Here we can see the central place given to the Messianic Apocalypses within the structure of the book. Each of the Apocalypses is supported by a dialogue between Baruch and the Lord as well as a speech by Baruch to the people in which the contents of the messianic vision are delivered to them. In two out of three cases the dialogue with the Lord precedes the Messianic Apocalypse and the speech to the people follows it, but in connection with the second Messianic Apocalypse the order is varied slightly. The book is completed by an all-important introduction (1.1–9.2), which helps to set the tone and provides the historical setting for the work, and a conclusion (78.1–87.1), which attempts to bring the thrust of the book to bear within the life of the remaining Jewish community.

1. *Author and Provenance*

When reading *2 Baruch* one is immediately struck by its composite nature. Charles attempted to explain this by isolating no less than six different contributors to its final production. Each of these different contributing elements was determined by the slightly different emphases they bring to the role of the Messiah and the Messianic Kingdom.[151] However, Charles's isolation of documents behind the text of *2 Baruch* has not been well accepted.[152] Such elaborate fragmentation reads too much into subtle distinctions of the Messiah's function within the book and does not appreciate the latitude of thought present within individual works of the pseudepigrapha on the subject. We should accept the book as the work of a single author while recognizing his use of different background sources which are in part responsible for the variety of ideas contained within it. This is not to denigrate scholarly investigations into these various sources, for such investigations can yield important results.

A.F.J. Klijn, for instance, attempts to detect these different sources within *2 Baruch* and use them as a means to discovering the author's (by this he means the final redactor's) own theological ideas and opinions.[153] As an example, Klijn argues that it is possible to deduce the author's views on the destruction and restoration of the temple of Jerusalem by his redactional use of various temple traditions. In other words, Klijn wants to know whether we can determine whether, in the opinion of the author of *2 Baruch*, the destruction of the temple was to be met with faith in its earthly reconstruction or not. Klijn concludes that the author of *2 Baruch* was ultimately uninterested in a move to restore the earthly temple but believed instead in a decisive break between the present earthly Age and the glorious Age to Come. Thus he looks forward to the arrival of the heavenly temple within a heavenly Jerusalem and gives no support to any 'restoration' movement among the Jewish people who survived the tragic events of 70 CE. As will readily be apparent, such an interpretation carries with it important implications for the role of the Messiah within the eschatological expectations of the sources, as we shall see in due course. For now it is enough to say that any attempt to define rigidly the sources of *2 Baruch* are, at best, hypothetical and must always be examined in light of the teaching of the *whole* of the Apocalypse. Even Klijn's masterly analysis, however great its contribution, must be criticized along these lines. We must not allow severe source fragmentation theories to blind us to the way in which competing strands of tradition are woven together within a document yielding a single literary work containing many significant theological diversifications.

As in *4 Ezra* the setting of the book is the destruction of Jerusalem in 587 BCE and the ensuing period of the Babylonian captivity. Again a notable figure of the period is chosen as the medium of God's revelation. In *4 Ezra* this agent of revelation was the scribe Ezra; here it is Jeremiah's scribe Baruch. It is quite clear that the fictional setting is employed so as to allow the author to speak to the plight of the Jewish nation immediately following the events of 70 CE.[154] We see, for instance, in the Vision of the Forest and the Cedar (chs. 36–40), the use of the fourth empire of Daniel 7 in a manner similar to that pointed out in *4 Ezra* 12. Additionally, there is the prediction of the destruction of the second Temple in 32.2-4.[155]

2 Baruch contains a variety of intriguing theological discussions. In 6.1–8.5 the Chaldean army is pictured as surrounding Jerusalem with invasion imminent and yet it is revealed to Baruch that the destruction of the city and the Temple is to be attributed to God via his angelic instruments. It is an ironic twist, no doubt inspired by an unfailing belief in God's superiority over his enemies, which drives the author to have God destroy his prize possession rather than admit such an act was capable of being undertaken by the Chaldeans (Romans).

In 23.4-7 we have it declared that the End cannot come before the fixed number of men has been born. In 49.1–51.6 the nature of the resurrection body is discussed in such a way that it is clear a physical resemblance will exist between that resurrection body and the original, earthly form of the individual concerned. This is one of the rare places within Jewish pseudepigraphal literature where such a discussion occurs.

It is however within the three Messianic[156] Apocalypses that the most relevant sections for our discussion of the Messianic Kingdom arises. It is to these that we now turn. It is worth noting that the messianic features of *2 Baruch* are to be found *only* within these three Apocalypses. This phenomenon may ultimately be due to the author's use of special sources, but we cannot know for sure.

2. *The Messiah and the Messianic Kingdom in 2 Baruch*

In response to Baruch's question concerning the length of the tribulation preceding the judgment (26.1) we are given the first messianic section of chs. 27–30. The tribulation is described in the form of twelve woes that are to come upon the earth. Following these woes we have a picture of the Messianic Kingdom.

> (29.3) And it will happen that when all that which should come to pass in these parts has been accomplished, the Anointed One will begin to be revealed. (29.4) And Behemoth will reveal itself from its place, and Leviathan will come from the sea, the two great monsters which I created on the fifth day of creation and which I shall have kept until that time. And they will be nourishment for all who are left. (29.5) The earth will also yield fruits ten thousandfold. And on one vine will be a thousand branches, and one branch will produce a thousand clusters, and one cluster will produce a thousand grapes, and one grape will produce a cor of wine. (29.6) And those who are hungry will enjoy themselves and they will, moreover, see marvels every day. (29.7) For winds will go out in front of me every morning to bring the fragrance of aromatic fruits and clouds at the end of the day to distill the dew of health. (29.8) And it will happen at that time that the treasury of manna will come down again from on high, and they will eat of it in those years because these are they who have arrived at the consummation of time. (30.1) And it will happen after these things when the time of the appearance of the Anointed one has been fulfilled and he returns with glory, that then all who sleep in hope of him will rise.

Immediately following this description of the Messiah's return in glory (30.1), we are given a brief section dealing with the resurrection of the righteous dead.[157] The idealized picture of the messianic feast which awaits those living at the time is summed up by the reference to Behemoth and Leviathan in 29.4 (cp. *4 Ezra* 6.49-52). It should be noted that here the Messiah returns to heaven in glory at the conclusion of the Messianic Kingdom in contrast to *4 Ezra* 7.29-30, where he dies along with the rest of mankind.

The second Messianic Apocalypse is found in chs. 36–40, the Vision of the Forest and the Cedar. Baruch asks God for an interpretation to be given to this vision. Within the interpretation provided we see the influence of Daniel 7 and the re-interpretation of the fourth empire as symbolizing Rome (cp. *4 Ezra* 12.10-11, discussed above). The Messiah's conquest over this last world empire closes thus:

> (40.1) The last ruler who is left at that time will be bound, whereas the entire host will be destroyed. And they will carry him on Mount Zion, and my Anointed One will convict him of all his wicked deeds and will assemble and set before him all the works of his hosts. (40.2) And after these things he will kill him and protect the rest of my people who will be found in the place that I have chosen. (40.3) And his dominion will last forever until the world of corruption has ended and until the times which have been mentioned before have been fulfilled. (40.4) This is your vision, and this is its explanation.

The third Messianic Apocalypse is found within chs. 53–76. This longer and more developed section begins with the vision of the Cloud Rising from the Sea from which issues forth a series of twelve showers (alternating black and white waters), followed by a final deluge of black water and closing with a lightning storm which cleanses and heals the earth. Baruch prays that an interpretation be given and through the angel Ramiel learns that the twelve showers represent the successive ages of world history (periods of both good and evil; white and black) from the time of Adam up to the dawning of the messianic Age. The final deluge of black water is the last great rebellion of wickedness which precedes the Kingdom of the Messiah symbolized by the lightning storm in the vision. The Apocalypse concludes with a description of the Messianic Age:

> (72.2) After the signs have come of which I have spoken to you before, when the nations are moved and the time of my Anointed One comes, he will call all nations, and some of them he will spare, and others he will kill. (72.3) These things will befall the nations which will be spared by him. (72.4) Every nation which has not

known Israel and which has not trodden down the seed of Jacob will live. (72.5) And this is because some from all the nations have been subjected to your people. (72.6) All those, now, who have ruled over you or have known you, will be delivered up to the sword. (73.1) And it will happen that after he has brought down everything which is in the world, and has sat down in eternal peace on the throne of the Kingdom, then joy will be revealed and rest will appear. (73.2) And then health will descend in dew, and illness will vanish, and fear and tribulation and lamentation will pass away from among men, and joy will encompass the earth. (73.3) And nobody will again die untimely, nor will any adversity take place suddenly. (73.4) Judgment, condemnations, contentions, revenges, blood, passions, zeal, hate, and all such things will go into condemnation since they will be uprooted. (73.5) For these are the things that have filled this earth with evils, and because of them life of men came in yet greater confusion. (73.6) And the wild beasts will come out of their holes to subject themselves to a child. (73.7) And women will no longer have pain when they bear, nor will they be tormented when they yield the fruits of their womb. (74.1) And it will happen in those days that the reapers will not become tired, and the farmers will not wear themselves out, because the products of themselves will shoot out speedily, during the time that they work on them in full tranquility. (74.2) For that time is the end of that which is corruptible and the beginning of that which is incorruptible. (74.3) Therefore, the things which were said before will happen in it. Therefore, it is far away from the evil things and near to those which do not die.

3. *The Messianic Kingdom and the Larger Eschatological Context of 2 Baruch*

The comments made above in connection with *4 Ezra* are also applicable to *2 Baruch*. The eschatological teaching of this book is equally rich and diversified; indeed it is often thought (not without justification), that *2 Baruch* was dependent upon *4 Ezra* in this regard. The point to remember here is that the same approach we suggested as the proper means of examining the eschatological teaching of *4 Ezra* needs also to be employed in interpreting *2 Baruch*. It is equally dangerous to catalogue *2 Baruch* under the 'Temporary, Messianic Kingdom' file and thus fail to appreciate its full contribution to the issue of diversity in eschatology.

a. *Messianic Diversity: The Appearance of the Messianic Kingdom*

Within the first two Messianic Apocalypses we have a clear

indication as to the time of the appearance of the Messianic Kingdom in relation to the Eternal Age. This clarity is noted in 30.1 (where the Eternal Age is implied by the reference to the subsequent resurrection of the righteous dead); and in 40.3 (where the end of the Messianic Kingdom[158] is also the end of the earthly, corruptible world).

It should be pointed out that, in contrast to the two earlier Messianic Apocalypses (mentioned above) which make a clear distinction between the Messianic Age and the Age to Come, it is difficult to decide if in the third Messianic Apocalypse we have described the temporary, Messianic Kingdom on earth or the Eternal Age to Come which follows. Suffice it to say that the language of 74.2-3 speaks of the Messianic Age as if it were a transitional phase between the corruptible world and the incorruptible one. Are we, however, able to say anything more definite?

A.F.J. Klijn, in keeping with the logic of his arguments regarding the author's use of temple traditions mentioned above, also calls attention to redactional statements he feels are specifically designed to limit the time during which the Messiah is to reign on earth. He does this in order to try to arrive at some understanding of the author's beliefs concerning the nature of the Messianic Kingdom. According to Klijn, *2 Baruch* 30.1; 40.1-3; 74.2-3 are all especially important in this pursuit. As Klijn concludes:[159]

> In all these cases the author obviously tried to say that the times of the Anointed One belong to this world, the world of corruption. For this reason it has to come to an end to make place for the time of incorruption. This means that the author understood his sources and tried to add something to them. The author supposes a break between this world and the next one. The days of the Anointed One are a step in history in the direction of the incorruptible world. Then the final judgment takes place.

This may be all well and good and undoubtedly is a step in the right direction. However, Klijn carries his own arguments too far when he goes on to deduce the author's views of the Messianic Kingdom. Klijn comments:[160]

> The author's clear theological concepts were shaped by reinterpreting traditions passed down to him. He rejected the idea of a Messianic Kingdom on earth.

This is to take an unwarranted step beyond the evidence. Indeed one is prompted to ask why the author of *2 Baruch* has even bothered specifically to limit the length of the Messianic Age, as Klijn argues he does in 30.1; 40.1-3; 74.2-3, if he rejects the very idea of a Messianic Kingdom on earth. Would it not be much simpler to remove the offending passages altogether, especially if they remain undeveloped with respect to their specifically messianic content? Or alternatively, if the author maintains some degree of allegiance to the sources of these Messianic Apocalypses and cannot bring himself to delete them altogether, could not the specifically 'messianic' content of these passages easily be absorbed or transposed into beliefs surrounding the Eternal Age to Come? That is to say, that no distinction between the two be emphasized? After all, such an identification of the Messianic Kingdom with the Eternal Age is common enough in Jewish literature.

In short, is Klijn justified in claiming on the one hand, that the author of *2 Baruch* did not believe in a temporary, Messianic Age while on the other accusing him of redacting his sources in such a way as to teach precisely such a doctrine? In the end we have to admit that fanciful attempts to hypothesize what an author did and did not believe and why are very risky indeed; especially if they are ultimately dependent upon distinctions between competing eschato-logical schemes which probably caused the author no problems at all. Instead, I rather suspect that the diversity is inherent in the sources of the document themselves and that any interpretation must recognize and accept such diversity as evidence of flexibility of mind on the part of the final redactor of *2 Baruch*.

Additionally, Klijn does not recognize that there are indeed threads of a theology of 'the restoration of the temple' within the Apocalypse.[161] In addition to the brief, fleeting reference to the Second Temple in 32.2-3 mentioned above, we also have the restoration and resumption of temple worship mentioned in 68.5-6. Although it is indeed true that this restoration is only temporary and must be examined in light of the fuller expectation about the Coming Age, we must not overlook the secondary support such an idea might lend to belief in a temporary, Messianic Kingdom.

Such reasoning as Klijn's on this point fails to take into account the long tradition of Jewish belief in a temporary (Messianic?) Kingdom; a belief we see periodically cropping up in vestigial forms in the various documents discussed earlier like the *Apocalypse of Weeks* and *2 Enoch*. It is perhaps safer to assign the temporary nature of the Messianic Kingdom in *2 Baruch* to a competing eschatological tradition rather than to the redactional activity of an author dissatisfied with its implications. From this point it only needs to be pointed out that this differing tradition is faithfully preserved in spite of the author's alleged dissatisfaction with its theology.[162] All this speaks powerfully about the ability of the final author of *2 Baruch* to incorporate divergent messianic expectations within his work and yet to be relatively unconcerned about their essential 'incompatibility'.

However, with respect to the relationship between the Messianic Kingdom and the Eternal Age to Come, it does not appear that *2 Baruch* exhibits quite the unambiguous diversity we noted in *4 Ezra*. There we noted quite clearly that the appearance of the Heavenly City sometimes occurs after the advent of the Messiah and sometimes it occurs before his advent. It appears that in *2 Baruch* the issue is much more clearly defined with the Messianic Kingdom clearly preceding the arrival of the Heavenly City,[163] or any other metaphor of the incorruptible Age to Come. At least within the first two Messianic Apocalypses of 27–30 and 36–40 this is undoubtedly the case.

It is only within the third Messianic Apocalypse of 53–76 that any ambiguity might be said to exist at all. Particularly contentious is 74.2, where it is impossible to determine on which side of the divide the Messianic Kingdom stood (was it the end of the corruptible world or the beginning of the incorruptible one?). We may, of course, appeal to this passage as supportive evidence for a doctrine of the temporary, Messianic Kingdom within *2 Baruch* in light of the two earlier Messianic Apocalypses which leave no doubt on the matter. On the other hand, we are wisest if we simply allow the ambiguity to stand and do not try to force the passage in one direction or another.

In short, it appears that the teaching in *2 Baruch* concerning the appearance of the Messianic Kingdom is somewhat more internally consistent than that contained within *4 Ezra*. At the same time, the third Messianic Apocalypse (53.1–76.5) does demonstrate the difficulty one has in absolutely distinguishing between the earthly, Messianic Kingdom and the Eternal Age to Come in *2 Baruch*.

b. *Messianic Diversity: The Final Judgment*

The three Messianic Apocalypses of *2 Baruch* contain differing conceptions of the nature of the messianic role in the final judgment of the wicked as well. In the first Apocalypse of 27–30 we have a 'passive' Messiah while in the other two Apocalypses of 36–40 and

53–76 his 'active' character is revealed. This corresponds to the same fluctuation in role we saw exhibited in *4 Ezra*.

Following the approach we used above in examining the messianic role with respect to final judgment in *4 Ezra*, can we detect the same 'functional deity' of the Messiah within *2 Baruch*? One fact stands out when we consider the messianism of *2 Baruch*; it is restricted only to the Messianic Apocalypses themselves. It may well be that the lack of any further development of the messianic content of the work is due to an active polemic by the author deliberately to suppress these messianic sections from being used to undermine the sole prerogative of God as the Creator/Redeemer. After all, we should not overlook that *2 Baruch* does contain an important passage comparable to *4 Ezra* 5.56–6.6. Note *2 Baruch* 21.7-10:[164]

> (21.7) For you alone (all) this exists so that you may create at once all that you want. (8) You are the one who causes the rain to fall on earth with a specific number of raindrops. You know the end of time before it has arrived. Hear my prayer. (9) For only you can sustain those who exist, those who have gone and those who will come, those who sin and those who have proven themselves to be righteous, since you are the Living One, the Inscrutable One. (10) For you are the only Living One, the Immortal One and the Inscrutable One, and you know the number of men.

However, we must consider this polemic passage in the light of the larger issue of judgment as contained within the whole of the Apocalypse. When we do so we see the fluidity of role between God and messianic agent with respect to the final judgment. Thus *2 Baruch* parallels *4 Ezra* on this crucial point.

As mentioned above, God specifically declares that he is the Destroyer of Jerusalem and the temple (1.4). This destruction of Zion is only 'for a short time' and must be viewed in light of God's fuller purpose of presenting a new and heavenly Jerusalem to his people.[165] Not only does God destroy Jerusalem on account of the wickedness and disobedience of the inhabitants living there; he also stands firm as the final Judge of all. This is a persistent theme throughout the book. It is the avenging judgment of the persecuting nations by God which stands as the dominant and consoling message to a readership agonizing over the theological implications of the destruction of the temple. Baruch asks in 11.3:

> Who will judge over these things? Or to whom shall we complain about that which has befallen us?

The resounding answer comes that God himself is Judge. The future judgment of the nations by God helps to make sense of the otherwise senseless destruction of Zion. The judgment of the nations is therefore theologically linked to the devastation of Jerusalem and environs (cf. 13.3-12). In 19.3 God declares that he will judge everything that exists; in 48.32-41 the basis upon which such judgment is to be made is clarified: adherence to, or rejection of, the Mosaic Law. It is, however, within the concluding section of chs. 78–87 (the Letter to the Nine and One-half Tribes) that the note of God's judgment reaches a climax. Note especially 82.2 where Baruch tells the people of Israel:

> But you ought to know that our Creator will surely avenge us on all our brothers according to everything which they have done against us and among us; in particular that the end which the Most High prepared is near, and that his grace is coming, and that the fulfillment of his judgment is not far off.

Or again in 83.1-2, 6-7 where Baruch continues:

> (1) For the Most High will surely hasten his times, and he will certainly cause his periods to arrive. (2) And he will surely judge those who are in his world, and will truly inquire into everything with regard to all their works which were sins. (6) For the ends of the times and the periods will surely pass away and all which is in them together. (7) The end of the world will then show the greater power of our Ruler since everything will come to judgment.

Now the emphasis upon God as the Creator is a common feature throughout *2 Baruch* (cf. 14.17; 21.4-5; 54.13; 78.3; 82.2). We should note that the concluding reference within the book to this Creator also emphasizes that he is Judge. We said above that the Messiah has a fluctuating role when it comes to the final judgment on earth. The three Messianic Apocalypses are particularly revealing for their teaching about judgment, especially when we compare the larger issue of God's judgment over the nations.

We note the following results: 1. 27–30—the Messiah is revealed after the final judgment. There are no specific messianic connections with this judgment. 2. 36–40—the Messiah judges the nations and then rules for a short period of time. No subsequent judgment of those nations by God is indicated. We could be excused for taking the messianic judgment of the nations to be conclusive. That is to say, that the messianic judgment *was* the judgment by the Creator/Judge

God anticipated throughout the whole of *2 Baruch*. 3. 53–76—as in the second Messianic Apocalypse, the messianic judgment is conclusive. Indeed, 73.1 does much to render any subsequent judgment by God himself unnecessary and merely the introduction of a cause of confusion.[166] The description of the Messianic Age in 73.2–74.4 most probably reflects an earlier belief in which the identification of the Messianic Kingdom with the Eternal Age is assumed.

In short there is a great deal of latitude of thought within the teaching of *2 Baruch* with respect to its messianic content. All of this serves to illustrate the tremendous diversity which exists with respect to messianic expectation within *2 Baruch*.[167]

D. *Summary of 4 Ezra and 2 Baruch*

When the messianic eschatological passages of *4 Ezra* and *2 Baruch* are viewed as a whole they reveal a remarkable diversity. They range on the one hand from a passive messianic stand-in to an exalted figure very difficult in some respects to distinguish from God himself. I would like to suggest that this 'blurring' phenomenon is associated with a conceptual overlap between God and his messianic agent which, to a certain degree, is the inevitable by-product of loose eschatological speculations. It appears clear that the final authors of both *4 Ezra* and *2 Baruch* were able to integrate passages which taught a temporary, Messianic Kingdom alongside passages which emphasized God's Eternal Kingdom with no apparent difficulty. It is perhaps not unreasonable to suggest that a connection exists between the two. Thus, it appears that the seers were able to affirm belief in a temporary, earthly reign of the Messiah alongside belief in an eternal reign of God. We may take such a presentation to be an attempt to clarify the Messiah's role in relation to the eternal reign of God. In any case, such an integration of diverse eschatological beliefs does not entirely solve the question of the relationship between God and Messiah and we are left with an occasional glimpse of a residual referential confusion of the two.

3. OTHER JEWISH WORKS RELEVANT TO THE DISCUSSION

In addition to the five books mentioned above, which are generally said to make a distinction between the temporary, Messianic

Kingdom and the Eternal Age to Come, there are several other sources which are occasionally thought to support such a distinction. Included are: (A) specialized interpretations of 1QM, *Jubilees* and 1QH from Qumran; (B) sections of the *Sibylline Oracles*; (C) the Jewish apocalyptic core underlying the Apocalypse of John.[168] Each of these additional works presents difficulties, either in the form of a complex textual history or a particularly troublesome hermeneutical problem, which renders its contribution to our study of secondary importance. Yet each has received some scholarly attention in relation to our theme and therefore deserves brief consideration.

A. *Qumran Sectarian Literature*

When reading the War Scroll of Qumran (1QM) one is tempted to see within it a relevant parallel to the distinction between a temporary, Messianic Age and the eternal Kingdom of God. This is especially true within Column 1 of that scroll, where the final eschatological war is described. This war, which lasts 40 years, marks the end of the present Age of Wickedness and paves the way for the eternal Kingdom of God which follows. Strictly speaking, this document does not display quite the same type of descriptions of the Messianic Age as do, for instance, *4 Ezra* and *2 Baruch*. The War Scroll does, however, provide an interesting parallel to the temporary, Messianic Age of Bliss, even if the 40-year intervening period it describes is characterized by an unending battle between the Forces of Good and the Forces of Evil. Is there any other evidence from Qumran which might be relevant to our concern?

As mentioned above (pp. 32-33), the discovery of the *Apocalypse of Weeks* among the fragments of the Qumran Library of Cave 4 has furthered scholarly study of the eschatological expectations of the Essene community there.[169] In particular, Roger Beckwith has fastened upon the idea of the calendar of the Essene community and made that topic the subject of a detailed article probing the eschatological beliefs of the Qumran sect.[170] In this investigation, Beckwith's work is primarily dependent upon his interpretation of the book of *Jubilees*. He goes on to apply the results from his investigation into that document to the rest of the Qumran material in a way which is directly relevant to our study. His work is thus primarily a synthetical approach designed to uncover the Qumran community's eschatological belief, and as such warrants special attention. In other words, Beckwith is concerned to discover if the Essenes at Qumran believed in a temporary, Messianic Kingdom and whether we can deduce such a belief from the sectarian calendar of the community there.

Beckwith takes the book of *Jubilees* as foundational for his investigations since within it the history of the world is organized into a fifty-jubilee scheme with important events in Israel's life plotted to correspond to key seven-year intervals. Was such a *Jubilees* calendar influential at Qumran? And if so, are we able to ascertain the Qumran community's eschatological beliefs by its study? Beckwith answers both questions in the affirmative and points out the similarities between the calendar of the book of *Jubilees* and other sectarian Qumran materials (notably The Ages of the Creation 4Q180-181;[171] 11Q Melchizedek;[172] the Pseudo-Ezekiel Document of Cave 4; and the *Testament of Levi* 16-18).[173] The point uniting all of these works, and hence invaluable for determining the Essene eschatological calendar, is the periodization of history from Creation to Consummation into ten jubilee decades each lasting 490 years, or a total of 4900 years ($10 \times 10 \times 7 \times 7$).

Equally important was the fact that the Danielic reference to 70 weeks in 9.24-27 was also capable of being similarly schematized into one jubilee decade of 490 years' duration ($10 \times 7 \times 7$ or 70×7). It is this Danielic reference, coupled with the use of the Return from the Exile as a catalyst, which enables the Qumran community to interpret the events of the Maccabean Revolt as occurring within the eighth decade of these ten jubilee weeks and postulate thereby the advent of the Messiah at the end of that decade between 10 BCE and 2 CE. This, Beckwith argues, coincides remarkably well with the rampant messianic fervor we know to have existed at the time of the birth of Jesus.

Having established this, we can now move to consider the Essene expectations concerning the end of the world. Beckwith argues from *Jubilees* 47-50 that the date is between 974 and 978 CE according to Essene belief. The point to be noted is that we have the final two decades of jubilees (the ninth and the tenth) taken up with a Messianic Age of 980 years (490×2). Following these last two decades we have mention of the final judgment and the New Creation (largely drawn from the *Apocalypse of Weeks* 91.15-17).

What are we to make of all of this? Although Beckwith's analysis of eschatological expectations at Qumran makes for fascinating (albeit mathematically wearisome) reading, it stands at best as a hypothetical probability that the overarching calendar has been correctly deduced out of the mass of divergent schemes concerning the future resident in Qumran.[174] Perhaps it is better to recognize the tenuous nature of this deduction than to try to fit each eschatological chronology within such an interpretation. Instead we should allow each schema a bit more independent flexibility and freedom to express hope concerning the future. The propensity to harmonize must be checked. This is all the more needed when we consider that the Qumran community's eschatological beliefs cannot be viewed monolithically but must be examined as the product of several generations of reflection on what the future holds. We would expect these beliefs to adapt and change as the circumstances of the day do. In particular, the effect the Maccabean Revolt had within the eschatological expectations of the community (or its antecedents) must be more carefully examined.

Nevertheless, we are perhaps correct in agreeing with Beckwith that an eschatological calendar was operative, indeed influential, with respect to the Qumran community's eschatological beliefs. The influence of Dan. 9.24-27 upon such a calendar (whether it be conceived in 7-integer units or 10-integer units) was perhaps considerable.[175]

However, the crucial point at which Beckwith renders his reconstruction of Qumran eschatological belief improbable is when he tries to cast it into a rigid, two-stage 'Messianic Kingdom/Eternal Kingdom' mold. In other words, the ten week scheme of *Jubilees* is made to conform to that pattern which is introduced *only* through the *Apocalypse of Weeks* itself. Beckwith can point to no other Qumran document which speaks of eschatology in the same way that the *Apocalypse of Weeks* does. In short, he has interpreted *Jubilees* in light of the *Apocalypse of Weeks*, the result being that the true meaning of *Jubilees* is now possibly corrupted or lost entirely.

Indeed, there is much within the eschatological materials from Qumran which suggests such a systematic analysis as Beckwith's is far from certain. Quite simply, the eschatological belief of the Qumran community appears to be much more generalized and inexact than Beckwith suggests. We risk serious methodological error if we rely upon a generalized Qumran eschatological hope as corroborative evidence for pre-Christian, Jewish belief in the distinction between a temporary, Messianic Kingdom and the Eternal Age to Come in the manner suggested by Beckwith.

The only other document from Qumran which might be thought
to lend support to such a bifurcated eschatological hope is 1QH.[176]
This passage has often been pointed to[177] as expressing the hope of a
physical resurrection. Even if such an idea were accepted as being
intended by the writer of the hymn, there is no justification for
proceeding from this brief allusion to full-fledged belief in a
temporary, Messianic Kingdom as an integral part of eschatological
hope within the Qumran community.

B. *Sibylline Oracles*

The collection of diverse materials known as the *Sibylline Oracles*,
despite its 'oracular' genre, is generally thought to reflect Jewish
traditions and beliefs about the eschatological Age. Occasionally,
sections of the *Sibylline Oracles* are said to support a distinction
between a temporary, Messianic Kingdom and the Eternal Age to
Come. Book 3 is especially important in this regard. J.W. Bailey, for
instance, regards this section of the *Oracles* as implicitly supporting
such a distinction with 3.40-62, 741-761, and 767-784 all thought to
refer to the golden, Messianic Age while 3.796-808 is taken to refer to
the subsequent Eternal Age.[178] Such an interpretation is untenable,
however. When one examines the relevant sections closely it is
extremely difficult to imagine how such a distinction is maintained.
All the sections speak in a generalized way about the future and there
is no definite demarcation of this future hope into two distinct
stages.[179] It appears clear that the *Sibylline Oracles*, as a whole, are
united in generally presenting a consistent pattern of world history as
divided up into ten empires.[180] The tenth period is the climactic
Golden Age of the Future but is not further clarified in terms
relevant to our study. We should not therefore rely upon the *Sibylline
Oracles* in illuminating the bifurcated eschatological hope.

C. *The Jewish Core underlying the Apocalypse of John*

The final document we need to consider is the Apocalypse of John.
There is little doubt that within that book 20.4-6 does indeed teach a
temporary, Messianic Kingdom which gives way to the Eternal Age
to Come.[181] What *is* at issue is whether such a teaching is due to the
Christian authorship of the Apocalypse or whether it is due to the
adoption of such a teaching by the (Christian) author from his *Jewish*

apocalyptic sources. If we assume Christian authorship, how reliant is the author upon any Jewish sources; and how representative are any such sources in teaching a temporary, Messianic Kingdom? In other words, could the Apocalypse of John be further evidence for such a belief within *Jewish* eschatological texts?

Frankly, I am in two minds as to how that question should be answered. On the one hand, I would affirm that the Apocalypse seems to be very much in the tradition of Jewish eschatological writings both with respect to basic genre and its selection and use of motifs. On the other hand, I find it difficult to break the literary unity of the work and to label and identify those various Jewish sources. The work as it now stands is certainly a Christian composition and needs to be recognized as such.[182] I do not think that the Jewish core of the Apocalypse of John is recoverable simply by means of removing a few Christian textual emendations. In my opinion, the Christian character of the book is far too deeply embedded to allow such 'surgery' to be performed without 'losing the patient'. In short, we are unable to determine whether the belief of the temporary, Messianic Kingdom in 20.4-6 is ultimately due to such a teaching being resident within Jewish eschatological sources or, alternatively, whether it is due to the Christian redaction of those sources. What we can say with confidence, however, is that such a teaching, if it was indeed originally a part of any Jewish eschatological texts underlying the Apocalypse, was thought perfectly compatible with one branch of Christian theology involving the eschatological role of Jesus Christ. In short, we should not fail to recognize that the Apocalypse of John does contain teaching involving a temporary, Messianic Kingdom, nor that it also contains many striking statements which reveal how closely related are theocentricity and christocentricity within its author's thinking.[183] At the same time, we cannot establish for certain that such ideas are pre-Christian or that they were around early enough to have had an influence upon the development of christological thought. Thus, the contribution the Apocalypse of John can make to our understanding of Jewish eschatological texts and their significance for the development of Paul's christological thought is very minimal.

CONCLUDING SUMMARY

Let us now endeavour to draw some conclusions from our investigation into Jewish pseudepigraphal documents which apparently teach a temporary, earthly Kingdom. First of all, we should remind ourselves which writings may be legitimately held to contain such teaching and then move on to consider some of the implications of those documents. We may begin with the pseudepigraphal works of the second to first centuries BCE. Which documents dating to that period are relevant to the issue at hand?

We noted that D.S. Russell in his *Method and Message of Jewish Apocalyptic* lists three works in this category: *Apocalypse of Weeks* (*1 Enoch* 93.1-10 and 91.12-17), *Jubilees* and *2 (Slavonic) Enoch*.[184] Upon close examination of these three works we saw that in two of them (*Jubilees* and *2 Enoch*) the distinction between a temporary, earthly Kingdom and the Eternal Age to Come is rather speculative and dependent upon debatable exegesis of critical passages. For instance, whether we interpret *Jubilees* to maintain such a distinction is largely dependent upon how much weight we give to 23.31. In a similar vein, we can only make the distinction within *2 Enoch* by relying upon the textually troublesome 32.1-33.2 as linked to the rather vague passage in 65.6-10. It is only within the *Apocalypse of Weeks* that the distinction is clearly and unambiguously presented. In short, it would appear that Russell's idea that both *Jubilees* and *2 Enoch* belong to the category of documents which maintain a distinction between a temporary, earthly Kingdom and the Eternal Age to Come is a rather generous, and faulty, assessment. We are closer to the truth if we use both *Jubilees* and *2 Enoch* only as supportive and corroborative evidence for such a distinction. Both, quite simply, are too fragile to bear much weight in the matter. When we add to this the extreme textual and traditio-historical uncertainty which surrounds *2 Enoch* 32.1-33.2, we must realize the tenuous nature of any conclusions to the contrary.

Thus we are left with only the *Apocalypse of Weeks* as maintaining in any way the distinction between a temporary, earthly Kingdom and the eternal Age to Come. There is little doubt, however, about the fact that the *Apocalypse of Weeks* dates from the second century BCE; therefore it remains the earliest known document to exhibit such a distinction. We should perhaps also note again here that the *Apocalypse of Weeks* is firmly embedded within a larger document (*1 Enoch*) which nowhere else maintains such a distinction. Indeed, it appears that within most of the later extant textual evidence the continuity of the *Apocalypse of Weeks* is itself disrupted as it is broken into half and distributed between *1 Enoch* 93.1-10 and 91.12-17. Fortunately this situation is able to be corrected and verified by the discovery of fragments of the *Apocalypse* among the Dead Sea materials from Qumran. How or why the *Apocalypse of Weeks* becomes absorbed in the way it does within the larger body of *1 Enoch* remains a mystery. Yet it does embody a different conceptualization of the future from that contained within the rest of *1 Enoch*. We shall return to this point in a moment. For now we simply note that the *Apocalypse of Weeks* is the *sole* unambiguous evidence for belief in a temporary, earthly Kingdom in Jewish pseudepigraphal literature of the second to first centuries BCE.

This leads us quite naturally to make one further observation about the *Apocalypse of Weeks* before considering the first-century CE evidence. This involves the messianic nature of the temporary, earthly Kingdom. To put it quite plainly: the *Apocalypse of Weeks* has *no* specific material which suggests that the temporary, earthly Kingdom it teaches is in any way connected with a messianic figure. Attempts to get around this fact by appealing to a 'messianic' interpretation of the nation Israel are unlikely and highly suspect. In short, attempts to describe the *Apocalypse of Weeks* as teaching a temporary, *Messianic* Kingdom on earth are entirely wrong and misleading.

What about the Jewish pseudepigraphal writings of the first century ? When we turn to consider this first century evidence we find a much more elaborate and developed teaching within both *4 Ezra* and *2 Baruch*. Both of these documents quite clearly maintain a distinction between the temporary, earthly Kingdom and the eternal Age to Come. In addition, both documents quite clearly emphasize the messianic nature of this temporary, earthly Kingdom. The simple conclusion we must draw from this is that sometime between the writing of the *Apocalypse of Weeks* and the production of *4 Ezra* and *2 Baruch* a Messiah-figure becomes associated with the temporary, earthly Kingdom. In all likelihood this association results from a situation in which the national eschatological hope, centering upon the resurgence of a Davidic king who rules on earth in perpetuity, interacts with a more transcendent hope which focuses on God's heavenly, Eternal Kingdom. Within this interaction the Messiah becomes relegated to a temporary rule on earth which eventually gives way to the transcendent Eternal Age. We should not underestimate the shift which has occurred between the time of the writing of the *Apocalypse of Weeks* and that of *4 Ezra* and *2 Baruch* with regard to the Messiah. Some of the implications of such a reassessment of the messianic role are tremendously important, especially with regard to the parallel shift from God as the focus of concentration to the Messiah as the focus of concentration of eschatological activity. More will be said on this point directly.

At the same time we must hasten to add that the eschatological material within both *4 Ezra* and *2 Baruch* is extremely dynamic with respect to competing schematizations. In other words, it is false and misleading to categorize either book as simply teaching 'a temporary, Messianic Kingdom of 400 years' duration'. In reality such a doctrine is but one facet within both books which are rich with diversity on the matter. We should not oversimplify the issue; to do so is to impoverish ourselves and miss much of the contribution both *4 Ezra* and *2 Baruch* have to make towards understanding the eschatological thought contained within these pseudepigraphal documents.

In this respect *1 Enoch*, as a whole, shares an important heritage with both *4 Ezra* and *2 Baruch*. All three documents contain within themselves a variety of quite different conceptualizations about the future. Within *1 Enoch* the *Apocalypse of Weeks* is but one part of a very complicated patchwork; while within both *4 Ezra* and *2 Baruch* the various strands are woven together in such a masterful way that at times we miss, or fail to appreciate, the skill of the weaver. It takes an observant reader to detect this richness, but the diligent student is amply rewarded for the effort. This point cannot be overstated and speaks loudly and clearly for a very dynamic and fluid atmosphere which is often overlooked in modern scholarly investigations. The ability of the final redactor(s) of these works to incorporate such competing conceptualizations within their production must be given due consideration. This must be done even if it forces us to reassess our judgment about the alleged 'incompatibility' of much of this eschatological material. Nowhere is such a corrective ingredient needed more than within source-critical studies of these, and other pseudepigraphal documents.

To return to the critical issue of the shift from theocentric concentration to messianic concentration alluded to above: we emphasize once again that within both *4 Ezra* and *2 Baruch* the messianic role itself displays a great deal of diversity. This diversity exists not only with respect to his activity/passivity in the final judgment but extends, perhaps more significantly, to include the relationship he has with God. It is at this juncture that some of the most interesting implications of our investigation are to be found. In both *4 Ezra* and *2 Baruch* theocentric passages emphasizing God's activity in executing final judgment exist side-by-side with messianic passages which emphasize the Messiah's role in that same activity. At the same time this loose substitution of the messianic role for the theocentric one is also seen to thrive within the quite monotheistic and protective environment of both documents. In short, our ideas about the conceptual and theological restrictions of an 'orthodox monotheism' may have to be re-assessed in the light of these messianic passages and the respective roles accorded to Messiah and God within them.

Occasionally, we have cast our net a little wider and tried to fit this messianic diversity within the larger issue of intermediary figures as a whole. It becomes quite clear that within much of the pseudepigraphal literature the contents are filled with a plethora of intermediary figures who seem to be taking on an ever-increasing role and position. Much of the time these speculations center around a notable figure from Israel's past. We noted, for instance, that both Enoch and Melchizedek are subjects of such speculative midrashim. At the same time, the phenomenon was also manifesting itself with regard to angelic beings. Here the angel Michael is perhaps the most notable example. At times the two groups coalesce, as we noted in *3 Enoch*, where Enoch becomes transformed into the chief archangel Metatron.

Now we should not press our case too far in assuming that there is a *demonstrable* connection between the speculations of this increasingly exalted intermediary world and the specifically messianic expectations. At the same time we cannot help but notice the features that both categories share. In both categories God's activity, role and position in heaven are all more and more assumed by other entities (either an angelic figure, the Messiah himself, or some other hypostatization!). In this connection we cannot overlook the contribution that Enoch speculations, for example, have to make to our understanding of the shift from theocentrism to an emphasis on the messianic role. For this reason it has been most fruitful for us to turn to such books as the *Similitudes of Enoch*, *3 Enoch*, and the *Testament of Moses* in an effort to fill out our understanding more completely. Of course, none of these documents maintains the distinction between the Eternal Age to Come and a temporary, earthly Kingdom (messianic or otherwise!). Yet they are not without their importance for they contain much material that is illustrative to our theme.

In conclusion, it might be helpful to summarize some of the more important observations of our investigations into these specialized pseudepigraphal documents, notably *1 Enoch*, *4 Ezra* and *2 Baruch*. We noted the following points:

1. Diversity of detail and schematization is the general rule within all the eschatological texts examined. This diversity occurs without the slightest hint of concern for its being inconsistent with other competing materials internal to the document under consideration.

2. Within those documents which speak of a final eschatological judgment, there is a great deal of functional overlap between any intermediary agent and God himself as that activity is discharged.

3. The referential confusion between God and messianic agent with respect to this final judgment gives rise to a number of textual variants and readings among the various editions of the document now available to us for study.

4. Within those documents which speak explicitly of a Messiah, the functional overlap between messianic agent and God is so complete that it tends to slide into an identification between God and his agent in which the boundaries separating them are breached. This is accomplished in spite of the fact that both documents contain monotheistic sections exalting the transcendent nature of God alone. It is to be observed that this identification between God and the Messiah takes place within documents which contain a strong monotheistic tradition (such as embodied in *4 Ezra* 5.56–6.6 and *2 Baruch* 21.7-10). It appears that the two ideas of rigid monotheism and the identification of the Messiah with God are fused in paradox.

In closing, it is not unreasonable to assume that a connection exists between this referential confusion between God and Messiah and the fact that it is so readily seen in those documents which clearly espouse a distinction between the temporary, Messianic Kingdom and the Eternal Age to Come. That is to say, the latter distinction is an attempt to resolve the former referential confusion of God and Christ, which was apparently inherent within much eschatological teaching, by spelling out the Messiah's role more clearly and setting his activity within the bounds of an earthly, Messianic Kingdom of temporary duration. However, we must not presume that this subsequent distinction between a temporary, Messianic Kingdom and the Eternal Age to Come has entirely resolved the referential confusion which seems to be inherent in eschatological texts. We still can detect remaining lines of tension within our documents. What the distinction does seem to indicate is a growing sensitivity to the problem of the respective roles of God and Messiah within eschatological contexts. Thus, such a distinction represents a very creative approach to the handling of the controversy.

The focus upon a temporary, Messianic Kingdom prompts us now to consider more fully Paul's teaching on the subject. We now turn to consider how Paul's epistles also display a similar theocentric/ christocentric overlap with respect to certain eschatological motifs, including his teaching on the Parousia and Final Judgment as well as his discussion of the Messiah and the Kingdom.

Chapter 2

THE PAROUSIA AND THE FINAL JUDGMENT IN PAUL

In what ways does Paul's eschatological teaching reflect a theocentric/ christocentric overlap similar to that which we noted in selected Jewish pseudepigraphal writings? One way to answer this question is by considering an important aspect of Paul's eschatological teaching: his belief in the future Parousia[1] of Christ and its accompanying doctrine of the Final Judgment of the world. There can be little doubt that within the Pauline corpus the two concepts are welded together, for it is the End Judgment which helps to give the belief in the return of Christ its shape and form. The Lord Jesus returns at the future Parousia in order to execute judgment over all things and to begin to bring the salvific process to its consummation.

Thus in this chapter we shall be concerned primarily with the christological importance the Parousia doctrine has for Pauline theology. That is to say that Paul's belief in the Parousia of Christ, along with its accompanying doctrine of the Final Judgment, provides us with a dual motif in which fluctuation between God and his messianic agent occurs and a conceptual overlap between Christ and God can be clearly demonstrated. The importance of parallels within Jewish pseudepigraphal literature, which aid in our under-standing of how the respective roles of God and messianic agent are handled within eschatological passages, underlies the investigation into Paul's thought on the Parousia and Final Judgment.

Before proceeding to this central theocentric/christocentric issue in Paul, we first need to examine very briefly the debate about the rise of the Parousia doctrine. Within the context of this debate, the role which eschatological sections of Jewish pseudepigraphal texts have in helping to illuminate Paul's doctrine is particularly contentious. Any scholarly investigation in this area has to include a background of the Jewish pseudepigraphal literature relevant to the issue. Any scholarly investigation which does *not* take into account this body of pseudepigraphal literature remains impoverished and lacking in critical depth and understanding. It can also be very misleading. Such a methodological oversight also means that the christological importance of much of the eschatological material within the Pauline epistles is not fully appreciated.

Within this chapter we shall first examine: (1) scholarly attempts to determine the origins of Parousia belief. It will be demonstrated how various exegetical difficulties have arisen because Jewish pseudepigraphal materials, notably *1 Enoch*, have either been neglected, misunderstood or misapplied. This will prepare us to consider in more detail: (2) the Final Judgment in Paul. After a brief introduction to the judgment theme in Paul's epistles, we shall focus our attention on one particular motif, that of the throne of judgment, as a means of demonstrating the important contribution Jewish pseudepigraphal literature has to make to our topic. A second major area of eschatological teaching worth examining is: (3) the Day of the Lord in Paul. Here we shall be examining the way in which Old Testament theocentric texts are christocentrically reworked by Paul. This theocentric/christocentric transposition will also prepare the way for a further examination of Paul's thought when we move to consider his teaching on the Messiah and the Kingdom (Chapter 3). There we shall have an opportunity to examine more fully the parallels to Paul's eschatological teaching which exist within Jewish pseudepigraphal literature, especially with regard to the respective roles of God and Messiah. We now turn to the question of the origin of the Parousia belief before moving on to discuss Paul's handling of the Final Judgment and the Day of the Lord. These three areas form the three subsections of this chapter.

1. VIEWS OF MODERN SCHOLARSHIP ON THE ORIGIN OF THE DOCTRINE OF THE PAROUSIA

From where did Paul derive his belief in the Parousia of Christ?[2] At what point does it become an essential feature of the early Church's eschatological proclamation? There have been several attempts by scholars to unravel this mystery. We might broadly categorize their investigations in three groups: 1. Those which eliminate the doctrine from the beliefs of the earliest Church and explain it as a later intrusion into the faith of the believers (examples include T.F.

Glasson and J.A.T. Robinson). 2. Those which explain it as a culturally encapsulated motif of Jewish apocalyptic accepted by Jesus and/or the early Church which is modified, or even abandoned, as the gospel moves into the larger Hellenistic world (examples include Albert Schweitzer and Rudolf Bultmann). 3. Those which realize its essentially 'mythical' nature and attempt to explain its contemporary meaning through the use of modern philosophical systems (examples include Teilhard de Chardin and Paul Tillich).[3]

It would take us too far afield to examine each of these three categories at length. There have already appeared several good studies which have attempted to put them into proper perspective.[4]

We can readily see, however, that all three of these categories are united in that they agree (or imply) that a fundamental inconsistency was resident within the Church with respect to the doctrine of the Parousia of Christ. This is especially true within the first two categories. In the first, the Church changes from no belief in it to a later conviction of the doctrine of the Parousia; while in the second she changes from a firm belief in to a later de-eschatologization of that doctrine. Thus the first two categories are juxtaposed: one advocating the Church's later addition of this belief in the Parousia, the other advocating her abandonment of it. The fact that such diametrically opposed evaluations of the Parousia have been put forward and vigorously defended by competent scholars is indicative of the complexity which the doctrine of the Parousia poses. The third category remains largely unconcerned with the historical and ecclesiastical details of Parousia belief and tends to concentrate on the philosophical implications such a concept has for today. Although the philosophical task is critical for the doctrine to have contemporary meaning, we can safely lay aside this approach for our considerations within this study.

It may be useful if we briefly summarize the major ideas of some representatives of the first two categories, as both of these groups have an important bearing on our particular topic of the Pauline Parousia hope.

A. *Parousia as Church Addition: Glasson and Robinson*

In 1945 T.F. Glasson, building upon the foundational work of T. Colani, set as his task the discovery of the origin of the Parousia doctrine.[5] He challenged the presupposition that the belief in a messianic descent from the sky in glory was a pre-Christian, Jewish concept. Even the Son of Man figure in Dan. 7.13 was relegated to a symbolic role and provided no inspiration for a rise of a pre-Christian concept of the Parousia. Nor did Glasson feel such a concept was the product of the mind of Jesus, for he insists that Jesus did not teach that he would return from heaven in glory to judge the world. Instead, Glasson argues that we are probably correct in taking the Old Testament promises of the coming of the Lord God (such as Isa. 42.13 and Zech. 14.3-5) to be the foundation of the Parousia belief of the early Church as she identified Jesus as 'Lord' and transferred the apocalyptic imagery from God to him. This whole process of doctrinal development within the early Church was probably aided, so Glasson continues, by the prevailing myth and speculation concerning the Antichrist (as in 2 Thessalonians 2). Such speculations, Glasson concludes, served as a catalyst for the development of a Parousia belief within the early Church.[6]

In a similar fashion J.A.T. Robinson[7] has sought to explore the origins of the belief in the Parousia. By making a distinction between the traditional eschatological categories of 'visitation' and 'vindication' with respect to Jesus' teaching, and investing the former with meaning derived from Jesus' earthly ministry and the latter with meaning derived from the resurrection and exaltation, Robinson is able to argue that the earliest apostolic Christianity shows no evidence for an expectation of the Parousia. Thus, by integrating the present dimension of the rule of Christ begun at his resurrection and the Church's expectations of a future hope as based upon the continuing sovereignty of the Risen Lord, Robinson is able to bypass the need for a consummation in the form of a Second Advent.[8] Precisely what these 'Church expectations of a future hope' are is an open question and is certainly a weakness in Robinson's handling of the subject.[9] A good illustration of the way in which Robinson's approach is used in interpreting the eschatological texts within the New Testament is found in his handling of the perplexing passage in 1 Cor. 15.23ff.:[10]

> the difficulties derived from Paul's introduction of a second messianic movement into the primitive scheme, which viewed the End as a direct consummation of the sovereignty of Christ established at the Resurrection. The Parousia, so far from being required by this scheme, is by no means easy to fit into it.

B. *Parousia and Church Abandonment: Schweitzer and Bultmann*

As we shall see more clearly below when we move to consider the meaning of the βασιλεία τοῦ θεοῦ/Χριστοῦ within Paul, this same passage (1 Cor. 15.20-28) is used by Albert Schweitzer to support his interpretation of Pauline eschatological thought. Schweitzer sees Paul as adapting traditional Jewish teaching[11] on the subject in the light of Christ's resurrection and ascension. He feels Paul is driven by the impelling logic of Jewish eschatological thought, from belief in an imminent Parousia to a more mystical understanding of the believer's union with Christ.

At this point we simply note that, according to Schweitzer, this mystical element within Paul's thought does not represent an *elimination* of belief in the Parousia. Instead, it merely represents a *partial abandonment* in emphasis and re-interpretation in light of the delay of the Parousia. It is in this way that the Church is able to cope with a delay in the return of Christ itself.

That quality of Paul's theology which Schweitzer calls 'Christ-Mysticism' is thus the eventual product of a traditional Jewish understanding of eschatology which has been forced to accommodate the delay of the Parousia. As Schweitzer puts it (pp. 111-12):

> But now there happens something unexpected and hard to understand, namely, that since a time-interval has been interposed between the Resurrection and Return, the Resurrection of Jesus has become an independent event. But Paul refused to budge from the position that what belongs together, even though temporally separated, must still, as at first, be regarded as a unity. That which was to happen along with the Resurrection of Jesus is for him actually involved in it even though it is not visibly manifest. The Elect are the risen-along-with-Christ, even though they still have the external seeming of natural men.

For a very similar, but more radical, representation of this 'abandonment' category we turn to Rudolf Bultmann. According to Bultmann the eschatological Day of the Lord described within the Pauline corpus is a mythological construction used by Paul and adapted from the apocalyptic of first-century Judaism. The dominant note of Bultmann's discussion of the Day of Christ is closely linked to his understanding of the eschatological event as having already occurred in Christ's passion and, indeed, as still occurring wherever and whenever the Christian kerygma confronts mankind. Never-

theless, Bultmann interprets such passages as 1 Thess. 4.16ff. and
1 Cor. 15.20ff. as expressing the hope of the Christian faith in the
language of 'late Jewish' apocalyptic myth. We cannot today take
these myths at face value, argues Bultmann. Speaking of the
reference to Christ's coming as the Son of Man in eschatological
glory, Bultmann says:[12]

> This mythological method of representation is foreign to modern
> man, whose thinking is determined by science to whatever extent,
> if any, he himself actively participates in scientific research and
> understands its methods. We have learned the meaninglessness of
> speaking about 'above' and 'below' in the universe. We can no
> longer honestly accept the thought of Christ coming on the clouds
> of heaven.

Or again, even more succinctly:

> The kerygma is incredible to modern man, for he is convinced that
> the mythical view of the world is obsolete ... We can no longer
> look for the Son of Man on the clouds of heaven or hope that the
> faithful will meet him in the air (1 Thess. 4.15ff.).[13]

As far as Paul is concerned, Bultmann argues that the apostle
demonstrates some gradual development in his thought on the
subject and makes positive moves toward a de-mythologization of
the Parousia hope. Paul is, in effect, praised by Bultmann for his
attempts to de-mythologize the doctrine and thereby secures for
himself a prominent place within the history of the movement to re-
interpret the meaning of the Parousia for the living Church.

It is interesting to observe that the basis upon which scholars
evaluate the origin of Parousia belief often remains essentially
christological in character. Whether we take the Parousia doctrine to
be a later Church intrusion or an early Jewish notion in need of
demythologization is a question which has largely been determined
by our presuppositions as to the role and function of Jesus at the
beginning of the Christian movement. The intractable nature of the
opposing assessments of Jesus' role in the doctrinal development of
the Church has, unfortunately, blinded us to a large degree and
diverted our attention from the very Jewish pseudepigraphal
literature which may help us uncover the answers we seek.

In any case, there are two important observations to be made
about the Parousia and the Final Judgment as it is discussed within
the Pauline epistles which are above suspicion and which must help

to guide our present discussion. First of all we note the way in which Paul continues the Old Testament concept of the Day of the Lord, especially with reference to God's wrath or judgment as being made manifest in that Day. Secondly, we observe that this Day of the Lord has an obvious christological connection so that Paul can speak of the Old Testament idea and the coming Day of the Lord Jesus Christ interchangeably.[14] Let us consider the evidence supporting these observations in turn, trying, as always, to be sensitive to the christological ingredient concerned. These two observations form the major point of the remaining two subsections: (2) the Final Judgment in Paul; (3) the Day of the Lord in Paul. As the two categories are not entirely separable there will be some inevitable mixing in our discussion.

2. FINAL JUDGMENT IN PAUL

The Pauline epistles speak of the coming wrath (ὀργή) a total of 20 times.[15] Occasionally it is used with the article (Rom. 5.9; 9.22a; 12.19; 13.5; 1 Thess. 1.10; 2.16) while at times it is used anarthrously (Rom. 2.5a; 2.8; 3.5; 4.15; 9.22b; 13.4; 1 Thess. 5.9; Col. 3.8; cf. Eph. 2.3; 4.31).[16]

In a similar manner the phrase ἡ ὀργὴ τοῦ θεοῦ is found 3 times: (Rom. 1.18 [anarthrous] 5.6 Col. 3.6; cf. Eph. 5.6). The final instance of the word is Rom. 2.5b, where ἡμέρα ὀργῆς occurs.

Most of these references speak of the eschatological contents of this wrath and thus seem to speak of the retributive judgment of God on that Last Day. The wrath is primarily future; but it is not without present implications as well, as Rom. 1.18; 1 Thess. 2.16; Eph. 2.3; ? Rom. 4.15 (cf. Eph. 2.3) all demonstrate.[17]

Paul also uses the κρίνω word group frequently when speaking about God's judgment. The verb κρίνω occurs 39 times (Rom. 2.1 [3 times]; 2.3, 12, 16, 27; 3.4, 6, 7; 14.3, 4, 5 [2 times], 10, 13 [2 times], 22; 1 Cor. 2.2; 4.5; 5.3, 12 [2 times], 13; 6.1, 2 [2 times], 3, 6; 7.37; 10.15, 29; 11.13, 31, 32; 2 Cor. 2.1; 5.14; Col. 2.16; 2 Thess. 2.12. Three compound verbs built from the root verb κρίνω are also employed: συγκρίνω (3 times in 1 Cor. 2.13 and 2 Cor. 10.12 [2 times]); ἀνακρίνω (10 times in 1 Cor. 2.14, 15 [2 times]; 4.3 [2 times], 4; 9.3; 10.25, 27; 14.24); and κατακρίνω (5 times in Rom. 2.1; 8.3, 34; 14.23; 1 Cor. 11.32). The noun κρίσις is used in a similar manner to denote the judgment of God, although it occurs much less frequently. The noun itself occurs once in 2 Thess. 1.5 while its compound κατάκρισις appears twice, in 2 Cor. 3.9 and 7.3. We also note the *hapax legomenon* δικαιοκρισίας in Rom. 2.5. Paul uses κρίμα in connection with the judgment of God a total of 10 times (Rom. 2.2, 3; 3.8; 5.16; 11.33; 13.2; 1 Cor. 6.7; 11.29, 34; Gal. 5.10). The compound κατάκριμα appears three times, in Rom. 5.16, 18; 8.1.

As we noted in connection with ὀργή there is also a present/future tension within Paul's use of κρίνω and its cognates as they relate to the time of the execution of final judgment. If anything, the present dimension is even more strengthened in this regard. In both word groups much of the discussion about the Christian's position with respect to this judgment revolves around an ethical centre.[18] Paul exhorts his Christian readers to live lives worthy of Christ and warns them that a critical or condemning conduct within the community leads to judgment by God. Generally this divine judgment is described as indefinitely (but certainly!) hanging in the future; but at times the present force of its execution shines forth (as in 1 Cor. 11.29-32).

Finally it should be noted that at times παραδίδωμι is used within Paul to denote the delivering up of the wicked to justice or judgment. We find this especially in Rom. 1.24, 26, 28; 1 Cor. 5.5.[19]

We mentioned above that Paul continues the Old Testament idea of the Day of the Lord with respect to the Final Judgment but does so in a christological fashion. That is to say, he invests his understanding of the Day of the Lord with specific christological context. Let us examine this more closely.

It has long been recognized that this shift from God as the center of such eschatological hopes to Christ as the center is partly dependent upon the adaptation of certain eschatological texts from the Old Testament. T.F. Glasson sought to demonstrate this dependence and set up the following associations between the eschatological teaching contained within the Thessalonian epistles and the Old Testament:[20]

1.	Isa. 2.10, 19, 21	2 Thess. 1.9
2.	Zech. 14.5	1 Thess. 3.13
3.	Isa. 66.15-18	2 Thess. 1.8
4.	Isa. 66.5	2 Thess. 1.12
5.	Isa. 24.23 &	2 Thess. 1.10
	Ps. 68.35	
6.	Mic. 1.3;	
	Exod. 19.20; 34.5;	1 Thess. 4.16

	Num. 11.25;	
	Isa. 31.4	
7.	Isa. 26.21	1 Thess. 4 &
		2 Thess. 1
8.	Isa. 26.21	2 Thess. 1.9; 2.8
9.	Isa. 26.19	1 Thess. 4.16
10.	Isa. 27.13	1 Thess. 4.16
11.	Isa. 27.12	1 Thess. 4.17
12.	Isa. 13.6	1 Thess. 5.2-3

As will readily be appreciated, these associations contain varying degrees of dependence. Some are mere allusions, some suggestive parallel phrases, some actual quotations of the Old Testament passage concerned. Nonetheless, Glasson's point is well taken and undoubtedly correct. We would naturally assume that the Pauline conception of the Day of the Lord was reliant, at least in part, on the Old Testament teaching on the matter. It is beyond question that the Day of the Lord is ultimately a prophetic idea.[21]

I find it difficult, however, to follow Glasson's argument to its next step where he tries to apply this truth to his explanation of the origin of the Parousia doctrine in the New Testament. Quite simply, Glasson is too negative in his assessment of the contribution the Jewish pseudepigraphal literature makes to the issue. It is at this point that we can see how a faulty assessment of the Jewish pseudepigraphal literature yields misleading results for New Testament interpretation.

Glasson singles out *1 Enoch* (specifically the *Similitudes*) as the major pseudepigraphal representative in his discussion; but in his attempt to divorce Jesus' belief in his own return from the Parousia doctrine and attribute its rise to the later Church, he is driven to make unacceptable assumptions about the role of the Messiah in *1 Enoch* as compared to his role in the New Testament. He argues that Old Testament expectations of the Day of the Lord Yahweh are responsible for the eschatology of both *1 Enoch* and the New Testament; this is undeniably true. However, he goes on to maintain that there is a fundamental *difference* in the way those Old Testament expectations were developed within *1 Enoch* and the New Testament:

> The Old Testament said: 'The Lord will come'. The Enoch literature underlined this, and embellished the picture of the coming judgment, the Dream Visions (lxxxiii-xc) adding that God

would be assisted in the judgment by Michael, and the Similitudes (xxxvii–lxxi) that He would be assisted in the judgment by the Messiah. The New Testament repeated the OT message, 'The Lord will come', but interpreted it as 'the Lord Jesus'. In Enoch the Messiah comes with the Lord; in the NT the Messiah and the Lord are the same person.[22]

Glasson may be right in what he affirms, but he is wrong in what he implicitly denies. Certainly, the implication of his argument is misleading and tends to drive an unacceptable wedge between the New Testament documents and *1 Enoch*. It is incorrect to state baldly, that in the New Testament a union between Messiah and God exists which is *fundamentally and qualitatively different* from that found in *1 Enoch*.[23] In fact, the New Testament is in some respects remarkably similar to *1 Enoch* (and other Jewish works as well!) in its explanation of their relationship. It all depends on what points one is wishing to compare between the two bodies of literature. Glasson has here chosen to compare the specific notion of the Parousia itself. This narrow basis of comparison yields the exact results he intends. However, if we broaden the focus and examine the Parousia and the concept of Final Judgment together, quite a different result emerges.

Incidentally, there is no fundamental reason why the concept of the Day of the Lord within the Old Testament and the subsequent doctrinal development evidenced within the Jewish pseudepigraphal literature cannot work harmoniously in helping to illuminate the New Testament eschatological hope.[24] Indeed, reason would lead us to believe that such a synergistic approach is the most likely medium of such illumination. Any major differences which genuinely do exist between the conception of the Day of the Lord as recorded in Paul and the doctrine as found in the Jewish pseudepigrapha are to be explained by the two-stage Christ-event and not by a fundamentally different conception of the relationship between Messiah and God, as Glasson suggests. Let us examine the Jewish pseudepigraphal literature, including *1 Enoch*, more closely and see an example of one motif which renders Glasson's contention untenable, clearly displaying the weakness of his approach and rendering his conclusions about the origin of the Parousia all the more improbable as a result.

A. *Throne of Judgment: The Jewish Pseudepigrapha*

Several documents have an important contribution to make on this subject. The most important is *1 Enoch* 37-71. If we turn to the *Similitudes* and examine the judgment theme contained therein, some interesting observations come to light. Although the judgment motif is an underlying theme running throughout the whole of the *Similitudes* (especially within the latter two Parables), we shall focus our attention, for a moment, upon those passages which make reference to the Throne of Judgment.[25] There is little doubt that with respect to this motif the *Similitudes*, as a whole, are heavily dependent upon the vision of Daniel 7. This connection deserves some additional consideration as we seek to explore the meaning of the Throne within the *Similitudes*, and hence come to a better understanding of just how *1 Enoch* might be fairly and profitably used to illuminate the Pauline eschatological hope.

Within this attempt of additional consideration we need to examine carefully the relevant work of two scholars: Matthew Black and Seyoon Kim. The former has sought to consider the 'son of man' figure of Daniel 7, and the throne-theophany motif contained therein, from a traditio-historical viewpoint; the latter has sought to apply the results of such a consideration to Pauline christological studies. It will be beneficial if we briefly summarize both of these scholars' contributions before turning to a more direct consideration of the judgment-throne motif within the Danielic vision and its use in *1 Enoch* 37-71. The contributions of Black and Kim will go far in helping to set the backdrop against which Pauline christology, especially its relationship to the the judgment-throne idea, may be evaluated.

Matthew Black, following up a suggestion made by Zimmerli in his commentary on Ezekiel, has suggested that the Daniel 7 vision is based upon the throne-theophany in Ezek. 1.26-28.[26] Black suggests that within the Danielic vision the author of that work was contemplating an apotheosis of Israel at the end-time.[27] It is in this way that the 'son of man' was to be understood. Thus Black argues that a messianic interpretation of the Son of Man is not found in Daniel; but he does go on to argue further that it is the 'next logical development of the tradition of a corporate apotheosis of a righteous nucleus of the chosen people'.[28] It is precisely this next step in 'logical development' which Black suggests is at work in *1 Enoch* 37-71.

Within the critical chapter of *1 Enoch* 71, where Enoch is commissioned by God to be the Son of Man, Black transfers the 'Son of Man' vision of 46.1b to follow 71.10 in order to fill out the vision there more fully and support his general contention that the Son of

Man figure ultimately becomes an historic individual.[29] At least this is the case with the *Similitudes* as they now stand. Finally, Black suggests that the 'individualizing' interpretation of Daniel 7 might be a phenomenon widespread and early enough to influence other documents, including *1 Enoch*, and that such a possibility be entertained as a background to New Testament christology.

It is precisely such a suggestive possibility that Kim pursues in his monograph *The Origin of Paul's Gospel*. The basic contention of Kim's thesis is that the Damascus christophany serves as the critical, christological catalyst for Paul. It is within that christophanic experience that Paul came to understand Jesus to be the Image and Son of God, and it is from that understanding that the rest of Paul's christology was to stem.[30] Kim takes up the idea of throne-theophany visions and uses their traditio-historical consideration as supportive and corroborative evidence for his form-critical investigations into Paul's Damascus Road christophany. In other words, the throne-theophany vision, which characterizes many of the Old Testament prophetic calls, is brought into close associative relationship with Paul's Damascus Road vision and his apostolic commissioning by Christ. The way in which Daniel 7 adapts the vision of Ezekiel 1 makes it an important transitional point in such an association.[31] The critical point for our direct consideration is how this throne-theophany/Damascus christophany link might help explain the conceptual overlap between God and Christ within the eschatological sections of Paul's epistles. More specifically, does it help explain Paul's concept of the Day of the Lord?

The immediate answer, indirectly suggested by Kim,[32] is that such a conceptual overlap could easily arise given the presumption that Christ was understood as the Image of God and the fact that, according to Kim's form-critical analysis, such theophanic descriptions as we do have, often blur the distinction between God's image and any anthropomorphic agent of the theophany. Ultimately, Kim suggests that the Image christology, which he sees as inherently linked to the Damascus christophany, renders untenable an absolute distinction between functional and ontological categories of understanding, with respect to Christ as pre-existent Son.[33] As Kim summarizes:[34]

> (It) is a reasonable inference ... that the glorious, supernatural figure appearing in a vision can in himself be described either as being 'like a son of man' (= 'like a man') or 'like a son of God'

(= 'like God), and that what determines the seer's choice of one expression or the other depends on whether the figure is already known (or later turns out) to be a divine being or an exalted man.

The critical point in all of this is the way in which a heavenly being is described in human terms of appearance.[35] Kim cites Dan. 7.13,[36] *1 Enoch* 46, *4 Ezra* 13 and Revelation 1 as examples of this very process.[37] In other words, to put the matter in terms more directly relevant to our own pursuits, could it be that such a description of a heavenly being in terms of human appearance and within a theophanic context gives a partial answer to how it is that the Day of the Lord undergoes a change of referent from God to Christ? Could it be that this is how the Christian notion of a Day of the Lord Jesus arises?

The answer to such a question, at least as far as Kim's thesis is able to contribute, is absolutely dependent upon whether or not we presume that Christ was thought to be a 'heavenly being'. This is an operating presupposition of Kim's and his interpretation of Pauline christology is accordingly slanted.[38] In other words, the theophanic context as he describes it certainly *does* helps to explain how it is that such a critical referential change might occur. But what if we remove the critical component of Christ as being understood as a 'heavenly being' in the first place? Does the thesis of Kim's still stand? At the very least, we have to admit that his argument is seriously weakened if we exclude this critical factor.[39] His contribution, to a certain degree, is weakened by the fact that its conclusion derives directly from one of its premises. In any case, it may be that, as far as our interests are concerned, Kim's arguments are the long way around to our destination. It is much easier to demonstrate a conceptual overlap between God and messianic agent in their role as Final Judge within the *Similitudes* of Enoch.

Having looked at the throne-theophany motif and examined its relationship to Paul's Damascus Road christophany, we thus find that Kim's suggestions, although probably correct and certainly pursuing the right path, are not without their difficulties. Let us now cast our net in a slightly different direction and return to a more detailed consideration of the judgment-throne motif itself within *1 Enoch* and seek to determine what light it might shed on Paul's consideration of the theme. In so doing we will be considering the Danielic vision and its use within *1 Enoch* 37–71.

Within the Second Parable of 45–57 we have a clear use of the vision of Dan. 7.9-14 quoted in such a way so as to confirm the co-operation between God and Messiah with respect to who sits in judgment upon this throne of glory. The passage from Daniel 7 leaves no doubt as to the throne's occupant: the Lord God. Yet in *1 Enoch* 46.1 both God and Messiah are brought together at the judgment seat:

> At that place (the throne), I saw the One to whom belongs the time before time. And his head was white like wool, and there was with him another individual, whose face was like that of a human being.

This co-operation between God and Messiah with respect to the Day of Judgment is evident throughout the *Similitudes*.[40] The Ancient of Days is explicitly said to sit in judgment on his throne in 47.3 and 60.1-3. On the other hand, the Messiah (or as he is sometimes called, the Elect One), is said to sit in judgment on that throne in 45.3-6; 51.3; 55.4; 61.8; 62.2-5; 69.29.[41]

In short, we see that there is fluctuation within *1 Enoch* 37–71 with respect to the executor of Final Judgment. Sometimes God is specified as this executor while at other times the messianic agent is so designated. Do we have other examples of such fluctuation involving the throne motif within the pseudepigraphal literature?

We should briefly note that a similar phenomenon occurs within the *Testament of Abraham*.[42] There we find that in 13.1-2 the patriarchial figure Abel sits upon the throne of judgment in the first of three judgment cycles. The second and third cycles are performed by the Twelve Tribes and by God himself respectively.[43] We may take this to be further supportive evidence for a fluctuation with respect to the executor of final judgment within the Jewish pseudepigrapha. Attention should also be drawn to *T. Moses* 10.3-7, where God is said to rise up from his throne and go forth in judgment. This section is immediately preceded by a description of God's 'messenger' (*nuntius*) as executor of judgment. Although this messenger is not described as taking the throne, the context does supply a basis for confusion as to the identity of this executor of judgment.[44]

In short, there is some evidence of fluctuation between executors of final judgment within several of the Jewish pseudepigraphal documents. This fluctuation involves the ambiguous reference to the executor (whether God or agent) as seated on the Throne of Judgment.

How does this compare to Paul's teaching on the matter?

B. *Throne of Judgment: The Pauline Epistles*

We can also detect hints of precisely the same phenomenon within the Pauline epistles, again revolving around the idea of the Throne of Judgment. The clearest example of this fluctuation is in connection with the word βῆμα. It occurs in an eschatological context two times: once with reference to God (Rom. 14.10) and once with reference to Christ (2 Cor. 5.10).[45]

A more thorough investigation of these two Pauline verses is in order (and highly revealing!). First of all, let us consider the allusion to Eccl. 12.14 contained in 2 Cor. 5.10. The operative phrase in this verse is εἴτε ἀγαθὸν εἴτε φαῦλον which is perhaps derived from the concluding phrase of Ecclesiastes 12, ἐάν ἀγαθὸν καὶ ἐάν πονηρόν. The important point to note here is the fact that the thrust of the concluding verse of this Old Testament book is a clear reference to the Final Judgment by God:

> For God will bring every deed into judgment, including every hidden thing whether it be good or evil.

The action of God in judgment is clear and undoubtedly this judgment theme was part of the attraction of Eccl. 12.14 which led to Paul's decision to allude to it in 2 Corinthians 5.

The verse in Romans 14 incorporates material from two Old Testament passages from the prophet Isaiah. The first is the introductory declaration Ζῶ ἐγώ, λέγει κύριος derived from Isa. 49.18. This quotation has no direct connection with the judgment theme but the context of Isaiah 49 itself does lend itself to application to the idea of the Christian's resurrection via its discussion of the restoration of Israel. It is possibly this capacity which has served to link the quotation to the more specific issue of judgment itself. We see this judgment motif more clearly expressed in the second quotation of Rom. 14.11 taken from Isa. 45.23. The relevant section from the LXX reads: Ὅτι ἐμοὶ κάμψει πᾶν γόνυ, καὶ ὀμεῖται πᾶσα γλῶσσα τὸν θεόν.

We need to examine the larger context of both the Old Testament text and the New Testament quotation to extract their full significance for our study, always keeping in mind the difficulties inherent in such examinations with respect to their original context. Did Paul intend his reader to keep in mind the context of any given Old Testament quote or not? And if so, how wide do we need to cast our contextual net in order to retrieve the intended meaning? To a certain degree these problems can be overcome, at least with respect to Isa. 45.23, owing to the fuller treatment this verse receives in the Pauline epistles. That is to say that the meaning Paul assigns to the quote is to some degree clarified by the expanded treatment it receives elsewhere in his letters.[46]

Isaiah 45 is, of course, a messianic passage which brings together God and his anointed servant Cyrus (45.1, 13) in accomplishing the deliverance of the nation Israel. In the midst of an exalted messianic description of Cyrus, the Lord God is spoken of as Savior (45.15, 21). This description is done in very monotheistic terms which emphasize the Lord God as the 'only Righteous God and Savior'.[47] This theistic sense of Isa. 45.23 is to a certain degree maintained in the quotation of Rom. 14.10 itself; but as the larger context of 14.9-11 demonstrates, God and Messiah are more closely united than is sometimes recognized. We note, for instance, that v. 9 clearly associates Christ's death and resurrection with his Lordship (and his resultant role as Judge!). In v. 10 we have the specific mention of the judgment of God (τῷ βήματι τοῦ θεοῦ); while in v. 11 the Isaiah passages are quoted. We must not overlook the fact that 'Lord' most probably refers to God himself (via the force of τοῦ θεοῦ in v. 10), and that this, while quite natural, does represent a referential shift from the preceding christological use of the verb κυριεύσῃ in v. 9.[48]

We should at this point consider the thesis of George Howard regarding the replacement of the Hebrew tetragram יהוה by surrogates as the basis for confusion about the relationship between 'Lord God' and 'Lord Christ'.[49] Howard specifically discusses this passage from Romans 14 in some depth. He quite rightly points out that the textual evidence seems to indicate that in pre-Christian biblical texts the Hebrew tetragram was usually written regardless of the language of the text concerned. Most copies of the LXX, however, replace the tetragram with κύριος or an abbreviation of it, such as κς.[50] It is significant that virtually all surviving copies of the LXX are from Christian hands. Howard suggests that this process of replacing יהוה with surrogates such as κύριος and θεός (or their contracts κς and θς) dates to about 100 CE and is the work of Gentile Christian.

All of this has tremendous implications for our study. Could the referential confusion between Christ and God which we suggest exists within sections of Paul's writings be simply explained as our misreading of the whole problem based on a text altered by second-century Christian who no longer maintained the distinction which originally existed between יהוה and κύριος in their texts? Indeed, Howard suggests such is the case within several New Testament passages, the most important of which for our present consideration is Rom. 14.10-11. Following the implications of his thesis Howard argues that the κύριος of v. 11 originally stood within Paul's letter[51] as יהוה. He is able to argue for the originality of the textual variant of θεοῦ in verse 10 on the basis of consistency.[52]

Howard's important contribution warrants several comments. First of all, it should be noted that his program of correcting tetragram displacement succeeds best in those passages which clearly contain a recognizable quotation from or allusion to an Old Testament text. However, it is difficult to imagine how it helps to explain the ambiguous nature of such a phrase as 'Day of the Lord' nor does it give ample consideration to the way in which *descriptions* of the Day of the Lord Yahweh become descriptions of the Day of the Lord Christ. In short, it is difficult to imagine this theory of tetragram displacement provides the *whole* answer. Secondly, I find the assignation of 100 CE as the catalyst date for the whole process arbitrary. There is no compelling reason why this transition could not be dated much earlier, that is, in the Church's worship from the first point of contact with Greek-speaking Christians. Indeed, one is tempted to ask what was actually *said* when one came to pronounce יהוה within the public reading of Paul's letters to the churches concerned.[53] Surely κύριος was spoken within some Gentile Churches and no doubt some confusion would inevitably be left in the minds of some of the members of those congregations with respect to the relationship between Christ and God in certain key passages. Thirdly, we should not overlook the presence of competing traditions which seem to indicate a greater fluidity of thought than is often credited. For instance, even if Howard is correct in his interpretation of Rom. 14.10-11, we still have to contend with the complementary teaching of 2 Cor. 5.10 over the issue of Final Judgment; and there is no doubt as to the christocentric import of that verse.

Fourthly, Howard's thesis does not take into account the important contribution of Philo on this matter. Philo's writings can confidently be dated to much earlier than the arbitrary date of 100 CE to which Howard points as being decisive. Philo consistently uses κύριος rather than any form of the tetragrammaton within many of his Old Testament quotations. Indeed, the manner in which Philo explains his use of κύριος in these quotations is highly revealing.

Basically, Philo distinguishes between the 'beneficent power of God' (τὴν εὐεργετιδὴν δύναμιν) and the 'kingly power of God' (τὴν βασιλικὴν δύναμιν).[54] The former he associates with the name 'θεός' and the latter he associates with the name 'κύριος'. The beneficent power is primarily positive in its function and is responsible for creation, while the kingly power is primarily negative in function and is responsible for judgment. It may be that we detect here a slight reservation on Philo's part to associate God directly with judgment. Instead this function is relegated to the personification of one of God's names or titles. Could it be that a similar sort of dynamic was responsible, in part, for the relegating of judgment to be one of the Messiah's functions?

In conclusion, Howard's thesis may help to explain specific examples of textual variation within Old Testament quotations as they are contained in the New Testament, but its limitations must be recognized and the fuller answer pursued by investigating additional, supplementary possibilities. Such further investigation must include the contribution that Philo has to make to the issue.

To return to Romans 14, we note that in v. 12 the accountability of each individual Christian before God is reaffirmed in the midst of a discussion of his accountable ethical conduct before the Lord Jesus (13.14–14.8). In light of this interplay it is not surprising that we have the subsequent reference to the Kingdom of God in v. 17 which capitalizes on this ethical teaching (above, page 100). This statement is very similar to Paul's remarks in 1 Thess. 3.11-13.

There in 3.13 we find that Jesus and God are brought closely together with respect to the out-working of the Christian's life and salvation. In 3.11 both God the Father and the Lord Jesus (note the plural subject!) are spoken of as directing (κατευθύναι—singular verb!) Paul and his companions in helping to bring about the edification of the church at Thessaloniki. In 3.12-13 we see Paul's wish expressed that the Lord (ὁ κύριος) might engender true Christian love among the members of the congregation with a view to the instilling of an unblameable character capable of standing up to the Final Judgment. In 3.13 itself the Christians are said to stand before God the Father (ἔμπροσθεν τοῦ θεοῦ καὶ πατρὸς ἡμῶν) in the parousia of the Lord Jesus (ἐν τῇ παρουσίᾳ τοῦ κυρίου ἡμῶν Ἰησοῦ). Here we see, quite simply, how God and Christ are co-operative in Paul's description of the Parousia and Final Judgment. In 1 Thess. 3.13 we note how this co-operation is brought out by referring to both in an eschatological context.[55] On the other hand, we also not that Paul does often speak of one or the other, Christ or God, as the prime mover in this Judgment activity.

The point is that in 2 Cor. 5.10 the Christian is said to appear before (ἔμπροσθεν) the judgment seat of Christ, while here in 1 Thess. 3.13 he is said to appear before (ἔμπροσθεν) God the Father.[56] Perhaps too much should not be made of this as an absolute distinction since, as we have just noted, the Thessalonian reference is qualified by a further description of Christ's Parousia. Nevertheless, the passage of 1 Thess. 3.11-13 probably does exhibit something of a 'blurring' dynamic between Christ and God, especially when we consider the ambiguous use of ὁ κύριος in v. 12.

Finally, we mention in passing that this theme of the establishment of the Christian's blameless character is repeated throughout the Pauline epistles. It too underscores the conceptual overlap between God and messianic agent. For the most part it is generally God who is said to be the one responsible for the Christian's blameless character on the Day of the Lord (1 Cor. 1.8; Phil. 1.6, 10, 2.15; 1 Thess. 6.23). However, the specifically Christ-centred component may be indicated by Col. 1.22, where it appears that Christ presents the believers blameless before God. This seems indicated if we take the first αὐτοῦ in the phrase ἐν τῷ σώματι τῆς σαρκὸς αὐτοῦ to have Christ as its referent, and the second αὐτοῦ (later in the verse) to have God as its referent.[57]

Thus it is clear that within the Pauline epistles there is a great deal of interplay and conceptual overlap between God and Christ with respect to the execution of Final Judgment. This kind of interplay between Jesus and God with respect to Final Judgment is beautifully summarized in Polycarp's *Letter to the Philippians* (6.2):[58]

> If we pray to the Lord to forgive us, we ourselves must be forgiving, we are all under the eyes of our Lord and God, and every one of us must stand before the judgment-seat (βῆμα) of Christ, where each will have to give an account of himself.

As will be noted, Polycarp here combines elements of both Rom. 14.10 and 2 Cor. 5.10 into a single harmonized thought, not dissimilar, by implication at least, to that of Paul himself.

We shall have occasion to spell out in more detail this conceptual overlap between God and Messiah when we turn to our discussion of the Messianic Kingdom below. Here we simply note that *1 Enoch*

37–71 and Paul demonstrate remarkable similarity in how they conceive God and Messiah to co-operate in executing Final Judgment. This similarity suggests that the Jewish pseudepigraphal literature may be more significant for a study of Paul's eschatology than is often appreciated, particularly in allowing us to see how the respective roles of God and Messiah are expressed within such documents. Let us now turn to another important aspect of Paul's eschatological thought which directly involves us in the theocentric/christocentric issue.

3. DAY OF THE LORD IN PAUL

Without a doubt the idea of the Day of the Lord[59] is a standard feature within Paul's eschatological expectations. This eschatological Day of the Lord is of tremendous importance for the Christian believer.[60] It is the event which the Christian eagerly awaits,[61] for on that Day, the completion of our redemption, the resurrection of the body, is to be accomplished.[62] The Day of the Lord also has cosmic dimensions within the Pauline epistles, and the whole of the created order awaits it.[63]

However, we shall focus our attention more specifically upon the concept of the Parousia itself and seek to understand its contribution, not so much at an ecclesiastical level, but on a christological one. It is generally accepted that the Old Testament concept of the Day of the Lord Yahweh forms the basis of these Parousia expectations. Even so, there are a variety of specific terms used within the Pauline corpus to denote this eschatological event. They may be set out thus:[64]

1.	Day of the Lord Jesus Christ	1 Cor. 5.5
2.	Day of the Lord Jesus	1 Cor. 1.8;[65]
		2 Cor. 1.14
3.	Day of Christ Jesus	Phil. 1.6
4.	Day of Christ	Phil. 1.10, 2.16
5.	Day of the Lord	1 Thess. 5.2;
		2 Thess. 2.2
6.	The Coming of the Lord	
	A. Ἔρχομαι	1 Cor. 4.5; 11.26
		2 Thess. 1.10
	B. Πάρειμι	1 Cor. 15.23
		1 Thess. 2.19; 3.13; 4.15; 5.23

7. The Revelation of the Lord
   A. Ἀποκαλύπτω   1 Cor. 1.7;
                                   2 Thess. 1.7
   B. φανερόω   Col. 3.4
8. The End
   A. τὸ τέλος   1 Cor. 1.8; 15.24
                                   2 Cor. 1.13
   B. τὰ τέλη   1 Cor. 10.11[66]
9. The Day of Redemption   Eph. 4.30

Any detailed look at these alternative expressions will not fail to
note that a referential confusion and conceptual overlap between
God and messianic representative is frequently present in those
Pauline passages which speak of the Day of the Lord and are reliant
upon theocentric Old Testament texts which have been christologically reinterpreted. These and other relevant passages may be
usefully categorized as to the basis of the conceptual overlap
concerned. For our purposes we have attempted to group the
relevant texts into three different categories: (1) those which focus on
a referential shift of the word 'κύριος'; (2) those which focus on a
referential shift of third-person singular pronouns; (3) those which
focus on a referential shift of descriptive words or phrases revolving
around the Day of the Lord Yahweh.

We have already had occasion to demonstrate the way in which
Paul's letters contain a theocentric/christocentric overlap with
respect to the judgment-seat motif. There are many other examples
of such an overlap within Paul's eschatological writing. We have
isolated eleven such passages within the Pauline corpus and assigned
them to the appropriate categories outlined above.[67] Let us examine
each of these three categories in turn.

A. *Referential Shift of 'Lord' from God to Christ*

This referential shift occurs in a number of places within the Pauline
epistles and is not necessarily restricted to eschatological passages.
Note, for instance, how 2 Cor. 3.16 reinterprets Exod. 34.34 in a
christological fashion, yet within a context which can hardly be said
to refer clearly to the Parousia of the Lord.[68] It is impossible to
determine precisely at what point this type of transposition was
accomplished in the life of the Church, but if the exclamation of

1 Cor. 16.22 is any indication, it probably was a very early phenomenon indeed.[69] We have already noted above how Rom. 14.10 reinterprets Isa. 49.18 and 45.23 in a christological manner. We shall here focus our attention on other passages which accomplish this referential shift by a similar use of Old Testament theocentric texts.

1. *Joel 2.32 / Rom. 10.13*. The larger context of Joel 2.28-32 is clearly a prophecy proclaiming the eschatological Day of the Lord. We know that this larger context is amplified in Acts 2.16-21 in connection with the events of Pentecost.[70] Here, however, the meaning of the quotation is specifically linked to the Christian confession that 'Jesus is Lord' (Rom. 10.9).

The referential shift of κύριος is supported by several other conceptual ambiguities within Rom. 10.5-13. The allusion to Isa. 28.16 contained in v. 11 also embodies this point in that ἐπ᾽ αὐτῷ is made to refer to Christ.[71] Likewise, the extended allusion to Deut. 30.12-14 originally would have had God in mind. However, here in Rom. 10.5-13 the whole passage has as its prime referent the Lord Christ. The Parousia itself, of course, is behind the statement in Rom. 10.13 as it is that event which consummates the believer's salvation according to Paul.

2. *Isa. 45.23 / Phil. 2.10-11*. The hymn contained in Phil. 2.6-11 is a crucial christological passage, certainly among the most exalted texts within the Pauline corpus expounding Jesus' relationship to God. Fortunately, for our purposes, much of this christological debate can be safely by-passed as not directly relevant to our study.[72] Instead we wish to focus our attention upon the Isaianic allusion in 2.10-11 since it is here that our specific theme is contained. Nevertheless, a few clarifying comments on the hymn as a whole will help to set the tone for our investigation of 2.10-11 itself.

Several features of the Philippians hymn make it an extremely difficult passage to interpret, at least as far as Pauline theology is concerned. First and foremost is the question of its pre-Pauline form. How much of the hymn as it now stands is authentically Pauline and how much is Pauline interpolation into an earlier tradition? A corollary, which needs to be continually borne in mind, is the fact that if sections of the hymn are indeed pre-Pauline, the possibility exists that those sections might contain a slightly different christological emphasis (or at least stand as an earlier formulation of christological thought) than the authentically Pauline body of the epistle. In other words, the pre-Pauline nature and form of the hymn leaves us with an extra major consideration. We must admit the fact that the original author of the hymn may have had an entirely different meaning for it than Paul himself does. We should not necessarily presuppose that the christology of the hymn is identical to that of Paul. As will readily be appreciated, the basis upon which an evaluation of the Pauline christology of the hymn is made is to a large degree dependent upon what one takes to be Pauline inter-polations into the hymn.[73] This point has been a matter of considerable scholarly debate. I accept Jeremias's judgment that θανάτου δὲ σταυροῦ in v. 8,[74] ἐπουρανίων καὶ ἐπιγείων καὶ καταχθονίων in v. 10,[75] and εἰς δόξαν θεοῦ πατρός in v. 11 are all Pauline interpolations to the original hymn. In addition, his division of the hymn into three four-line stanzas seems to me to present the fewest difficulties.

A second major question is that of the setting of the hymn within the Pauline epistle. More precisely, this question involves the relationship v. 5 (τοῦτο φρονεῖτε ἐν ὑμῖν ὃ καὶ ἐν Χριστῷ Ἰησοῦ) bears to the hymn proper.[76] At first it might seem an irrelevant point, but it must be remembered that the answer is important given the fact that vv. 9-11 do not easily fit within the larger ethical-exhortative context of Phil. 1.27–2.18. Indeed, it might even be queried whether the third stanza of the hymn (vv. 9-11) properly belongs with the first two (vv. 6-7a and 7b-8).[77] However, there is no overriding reason why the third stanza must be amputated from the rest of the hymn in an arbitrary fashion. In fact, the exaltation discussed in the third stanza is closely linked with the first two[78] and serves as the logical result of Christ's obedience as discussed in them. In short, the three-stanza hymn has as its uniting point the presentation of Christ as the Obedient and (therefore) Exalted One.[79]

With these two preliminary considerations out of the way let us now move to examine the extended allusion to Isa. 45.23 contained in vv. 10-11. The critical phrase in these verses, which demonstrates a transference of description from God to Christ, is ἐν τῷ ὀνόματι Ἰησοῦ πᾶν γόνυ κάμψῃ καὶ πᾶσα γλῶσσα ἐξομολογήσεται. This is a loose reworking of the LXX of Isa. 45.23, which reads ὅτι ἐμοὶ κάμψει πᾶν γόνυ, καὶ ὀμεῖται γλῶσσα τὸν θεόν.[80] The focal point, of course, is the reference to ἐν τῷ ὀνόματι Ἰησοῦ, for it is here that the subject transference itself occurs. This prompts us to look at v. 9, where we read that God granted to Jesus τὸ ὄνομα τὸ ὑπὲρ πᾶν ὄνομα. Just what is meant by this enigmatic phrase? There have been two basic proposals: the name 'Jesus' (Ἰησοῦς) and the name 'Lord' (κύριος). There can be little doubt that the latter is intended,[81] especially in light of the fact that in v. 10 Ἰησοῦς is spoken of in preparatory fashion for the climactic phrase in v. 11 with which the hymn concludes: εἰς δόξαν θεοῦ πατρός. Thus, the contrast within the hymn is not between Ἰησοῦς and Ἰησοῦς Χρίστος, but between Ἰησοῦς and κύριος. Additionally, it should not be overlooked that κύριος occupies a prominent position within the structure of the hymn's last line. All this serves to confirm the probability that κύριος, and not Ἰησοῦς, is meant as τὸ ὄνομα τὸ ὑπὲρ πᾶν ὄνομα.[82]

Having established this probability we need to go on to try and glean what it means christologically for Jesus to be given the name of YHWH himself, for surely that tetragrammatic term is what lies behind the ambiguous κύριος. In all likelihood, what is intended here, at least initially, is the investiture of God's power, authority and office (as personified by his Divine Name)[84] upon Jesus Christ.[85]

The critical question at this junction is whether or not such an investiture can be said to affirm the ontological identification of Christ with God. And if so, at what point does this identification occur in relation to the Pauline epistles? We do, of course, know that in fourth-century Christianity such an affirmation is embodied in specific creedal formulation; but how do these relate to the Pauline letters?[86] Such questions are notoriously difficult to answer with precision, but at the very least we would have to admit that such an investiture as we see in Phil. 2.9-11 does seem to indicate a conceptual overlap between God and Christ in such a manner as to prepare the way for the later christological claims of the creeds. At the same time it is difficult to imagine any first-century Jew or Christian even remotely familiar with Isaiah 45 hearing this final stanza of Phil. 2.9-11 without recognizing that words of theistic import have now been applied to Jesus Christ.[87]

Thus, to a certain degree, the scholarly debate about whether το ὄνομα τὸ ὑπὲρ πᾶν ὄνομα in v. 9 is 'Ἰησοῦς' or 'κύριος' is solved in favor of the latter by the theistic allusion to Isa. 45.23 in v. 11

(provided that we maintain proper understanding of how vv. 9 and 11 interrelate). The two verses are mutually compatible in presenting Jesus as κύριος within a traditionally theistic, Old Testament context.

One final point needs to be considered in connection with our passage. It concerns the time of the application of this worship (the bowing of knees and the confessing of tongues) to Christ.[88] In pursuing this point we are drawn into a consideration of the context of Isa. 45.23 itself.[89] In 45.18-25 the Lord God is describing in quite dramatic fashion (emphasizing his sole prerogative in creation) the universal worship which one day will be accorded to him. Thus strictly speaking the passage is not a theophany, that is to say that nowhere is there specific mention of God's visitation upon the earth in final judgment. Nevertheless, the judgment theme itself is not lacking, as vv. 22 and 24 clearly indicate. The remarkable thing about the chapter as a whole is the way in which Cyrus functions as God's anointed agent of judgment. It is perhaps this feature which is partly responsible for the popularity of Isaiah 45 within Christian circles; as well as the easy adaption of κύρος to κύριος by the addition of a single iota.[90] In any event, while the setting of the prophetic passage itself is the time following the capture of Babylon by Cyrus, the important point for our purposes is the fact that the worship spoken of in 45.23 was still awaited and remained a future event. Given this contextual point it is perhaps not unreasonable to suggest that a future period of worship of Christ as κύριος is also indicated within the Philippians hymn. Thus we may adopt the textual variant ἐξομολογήσεται (future) in place of ἐξομολογήσηται (aorist) in v. 11.[91] The larger contextual appeal also gives occasion to mention in passing the suggestion made by J.A. Sanders[92] in calling attention to the divine adjectives in Phil. 2.1 which he argues should be associated with the κύριος Ἰησοῦς in 2.11. This gives additional support to the generalized atmosphere of conceptual overlap between God and Christ within the hymn itself.

3. *Zech. 14.5 / 1 Thess. 3.13.* We briefly discussed 1 Thess. 3.13 above in connection with the Final Judgment. Here we want to focus on the concluding phrase of that verse, as yet undiscussed, and draw out its implications as well. The final phrase is μετὰ πάντων τῶν ἁγίων αὐτοῦ and is part of the description of the Parousia of the Lord Jesus described in the passage. The phrase is taken from Zech.

14.5, the relevant phrase of which reads in the LXX: καὶ ἥξει κύριος ὁ θεός μου, καὶ πάντες οἱ ἅγιοι μετ' αὐτοῦ.[93] Now Zechariah 14 is part of an extended description, running from chs. 12-14, of the devastation to be laid upon the enemies of Israel with the arrival of the Day of the Lord.[94]

The quotation of this phrase from Zech. 14.5 in 1 Thess. 13.3 is significant in that it involves a clear referential shift of κύριος from God to Christ. The passage in 3.13 is made all the more important when we realize that it occurs with an additional reference to God the Father also present within the verse. Furthermore, the fact that the verse from Zechariah explicitly mentions κύριος ὁ θεός makes the Pauline double-object (of ἔμπροσθεν) clearly evident. It is extremely unlikely that the phrase in Paul is accidental and less than intentional. The introduction of the word παρουσία into 1 Thess. 3.13 should not overly concern us, but the future ἥξει of Zech. 14.5 easily accommodates such an introduction and is worth noting.

Several other passages from the Thessalonian correspondence also need to be considered briefly at this point, even though they do not have quite the same literal dependence upon Zech. 14.5 that 1 Thess. 3.13 exhibits.

4. *Zech. 14.5 / 1 Thess. 4.14.* It appears that 1 Thess. 4.14 also seems to rely upon the same Day of the Lord imagery from Zechariah. What is significant about this verse is that the subject of the visitation is God and not Christ: καὶ ὁ θεὸς τοὺς κοιμηθέντας διὰ τοῦ Ἰησοῦ ἄξει σὺν αὐτῷ[95] In other words, this allusion is much closer to the original theocentric intention of the oracle in Zechariah 14 insofar as the subject of the visitation is concerned.[96] And yet, at the same time, we cannot eradicate the christological component for the saints are described within the verse as τοὺς κοιμηθέντας διὰ τοῦ Ἰησοῦ.

5. *Zech. 14.5 / 2 Thess. 1.7-10.* We may also turn to two additional verses in 2 Thessalonians which are sometimes said to contain brief allusions to Zech. 14.5. They are 1.7 and 1.10, and are contained in an extended section of the epistle which is filled with various reflections of Old Testament Day of the Lord passages drawn from a host of prophetic sources. We shall discuss several of these reflections profitably, beginning with 1.7 and 1.10.

In 1.10 the operative phrase, at least as far as Zech. 14.5 is concerned, is ὅταν ἔλθῃ ἐνδοξασθῆναι ἐν τοῖς ἁγίοις αὐτοῦ. As will readily be appreciated, it is far from certain that the passage from Zech. 14.5 is in mind at all here. The only points of literal dependence are the words ἁγίοις and αὐτοῦ. However, the basic idea surrounding 1.10 is certainly within the realm of association with the concept of the Day of the Lord Yahweh.[97] We are on no less firm ground when considering 1.7. The operative phrase there is ἐν τῇ ἀποκαλύψει τοῦ κυρίου Ἰησοῦ ἀπ' οὐρανοῦ μετ' ἀγγέλων δυνάμεως αὐτοῦ. In order to assimilate this passage to an allusion to Zech. 14.5 we must equate the saints of the Lord (πάντες οἱ ἅγιοι μετ' αὐτοῦ) with the mighty angels (μετ' ἀγγέλων δυνάμεως αὐτοῦ). While this is not an impossible connection of thought, it is a somewhat weak basis for suggesting that Zech. 14.5 was explicitly in mind when 2 Thess. 1.7 was penned.[98] All this is to say that, at least as far as 2 Thess. is concerned, the description of the Day of the Lord in Zech. 12–14 is, at best, merely part of the image in the back of Paul's mind.[99]

We are on somewhat firmer ground when we examine the contribution other Old Testament passages which speak of the Day of the Lord have to make to 2 Thessalonians.

6. Isa. 66.4-6, 15 / 2 Thess. 1.6-12. Recently Roger Aus has discussed how the final vision of Isaiah 66 may have influenced messianic teachings in both Jewish and Christian circles.[100] In particular Isa. 66.7 has been shown to lend itself to messianic interpretations, as the Revelation 12 and the *Targum of Isaiah* 66.7 readily show.[101] In a similar manner, 2 Thess. 1.6-12 also exhibits a number of allusions to this vision of Isaiah 66 and reinterprets them christologically.[102] In all cases, Aus argues, these messianic interpretations of the Old Testament description of the Day of the Lord are carried along by the way in which the tribulations surrounding God's visitation on earth become readily associated with the messianic woes generally believed to precede immediately the appearance of the Messiah. This, of course, allows a strong point of contact to be made with regard to the persecution references in 2 Thessalonians and makes Aus's case for the christological use of Isaiah 66 in the Pauline letter all the more plausible as a result.[103]

In all Aus isolates four linguistic associations between the LXX and 2 Thessalonians 1 and three conceptual associations between the *Targum of Isaiah* and that chapter.[104] A close examination of these associations reveals that they are all individually quite weak in demonstrating literal dependence upon the Greek text of Isaiah; that is to say that never more than three consecutive words are directly quoted from the LXX of Isaiah 66 in the Pauline epistle.[105] Taken collectively, however, they speak strongly for the Day of the Lord vision from Isaiah as having a direct and demonstrable influence upon 2 Thess. 1.6-12. At the same time, Aus has argued for the suggestive possibility that this same passage of Isaiah 66 was interpreted messianically by select Jewish writings as well. If Aus's suggestion that the Targum of this passage also appears to have been influential upon the writer of 2 Thessalonians is correct, then the interesting question of the source of the messianic interpretation of Isa. 66.7 is raised.[106] In other words, is it not possible that the Targum reflects an earlier line of interpretation of the vision of Isaiah 66, a line of interpretation which emphasized the messianic fulfillment of that passage? We could even ask whether or not such a messianic interpretation was pre-Christian.

One final point needs to be added in our discussion of this important text from Isaiah 66 which is more directly relevant to our purpose. We note the way in which the critical phrase of 66.5 ἵνα τὸ ὄνομα κυρίου δοξασθῇ is adapted in 2 Thess. 1.12 to read ὅπως ἐνδοξασθῇ τὸ ὄνομα τοῦ κυρίου ἡμῶν Ἰησοῦ ἐν ὑμῖν. This adaptation, of course, depends upon a referential shift of 'κύριος' from God to Christ.

All in all, it appears that Isaiah 66 does seem to have had considerable impact upon 2 Thess. 1.6-12, even if that impact is not clearly a literal one. That is simply to say that the Day of the Lord ideas contained in Isaiah 66 are utilized in 2 Thessalonians even if the word-for-word quotation from the Old Testament vision does not occur. However, a more literal quotation from Isaiah does occur in 2 Thess. 1.9. It is to that passage that we now turn.

7. *Isa. 2.10 / 2 Thess. 1.9.* Here in Isaiah 2 we have another description of the calamitous events surrounding the Day of the Lord. In v. 10 men are exhorted to hide themselves 'from the face of fear of the Lord and from the glory of his power' (ἀπὸ προσώπου τοῦ φόβου κυρίου, καὶ ἀπὸ τῆς δόξης τῆς ἰσχύος αὐτοῦ).[107] This phrase is wholly adopted in 2 Thess. 1.9 with the only modification being the deletion of φόβου.[108] Here once again we see a clear case of the referential shift of 'κύριος' from God to Christ. Closer examination of Isaiah 2 also reveals more of its contribution to 2 Thess. 1.6-12. The phrase ἐν τῇ ἡμέρα ἐκείνῃ in 2 Thess. 1.10c probably derives

from its two-fold occurrence in Isa. 2.11, 17. It is difficult to say with confidence whether such a common phrase as ἐν τῇ ἡμέρα ἐκείνῃ was definitely taken over from Isaiah 2, but given the rather extended quotation in 2 Thess. 1.10c it is highly probable. If the phrase is indeed an allusion to Isaiah, it is interesting to note the *complete* phrase from Isaiah 2: καὶ ὑψωθήσεται κύριος μόνος ἐν τῇ ἡμέρα ἐκείνῃ.[109] This phrase serves as an exultant summary of the Day of the Lord vision itself. The strongly monotheistic tone of the phrase stands out as all the more interesting as it is applied to Christ in 2 Thessalonians.

A further possible allusion to an Old Testament passage occurs in 2 Thess. 1.10a, which reads ὅταν ἔλθῃ ἐνδοξασθῆναι ἐν τοῖς ἁγίοις αὐτοῦ. This might derive from Ps. 88.8 (ὁ θεός ἐνδοξαζόμενος ἐν βουλῇ ἁγίων), in which case the referential shift from God (θεός) to Christ is again decisive.[110]

One final instance of 'κύριος' in 2 Thessalonians is of related interest, although it does not strictly derive from an Old Testament text describing the Day of the Lord. Nevertheless, it is worth considering since it does demonstrate one additional feature about the use of Old Testament material to fill out the christological message of the book in a manner similar to our main concern. This occurs in 2 Thess. 2.8, where we find a fairly extended allusion to Isa. 11.4c-d which reads: καὶ πατάξει γῆν τῷ λόγῳ τοῦ στόματος αὐτοῦ, καὶ ἐν πνεύματι διὰ χειλέων ἀνελεῖ ἀσεβῆ. The relevant section from 2.8 reads: ὁ κύριος ἀνελεῖ τῷ πνεύματι στόματος αὐτοῦ.[111]

There are three points of literal correspondence: (1) the phrase τοῦ στόματος αὐτοῦ; (2) the dative noun πνεύματι; (3) the verb ἀνελεῖ.[112] This allusion in 2 Thess. 2.8 involves a fairly free-handed reconstruction, as can readily be seen.[113] In all probability the triggering idea is found in the reference to ἀσεβῆ in Isa. 11.5 which is linked to ὁ ἄνομος in 2 Thess. 2.8.

What is different about this Old Testament text when compared to the others from Isaiah we have been examining is the fact that 11.4-5 is decidely *messianic* in character. It is quite clear that the prophecy involves the coming of a new Davidic king, although the precise redactional forces behind its placing in the book of Isaiah are difficult to ascertain.[114] It is this Davidic Messiah who is to execute the judgment described in Isa. 11.3-5 which is subsequently alluded to in 2 Thess. 2.8.[115]

While there are other Old Testament descriptions of the Day of the Lord Yahweh which are similar to the description of the Messiah's judgment in Isa. 11.3-5 (such as Job 4.9 and Ps. 32.6) and may be responsible for the language and imagery of 2 Thess. 2.8, in my opinion the New Testament allusion derives solely from Isaiah 11. The important contribution of this passage in 2.8 is that it demonstrates how the writer of 2 Thessalonians is able to use *both* theocentric and messianic descriptions from Isaiah in his attempt to explain his understanding of Jesus' future role in judgment at the Parousia. The use of such dual descriptions is but another brief indication of how theocentricity and christocentricity are blurred within the Pauline corpus. Both categories of description are readily applied to Jesus without discrimination.

8. *1 Thess. 4.15-18.* In 1 Thess. 4.15-18 we have one of Paul's most developed discussions dealing with the Parousia of Christ. A great deal of scholarly controversy has raged over the phrase with which the passage begins: τοῦτο γὰρ ὑμῖν λέγομεν ἐν λόγῳ κυρίου. Does this mean that Paul is showing knowledge of an authentic word of Jesus which is unrecorded within the Gospel materials?[116] Fortunately, this puzzling question need not detain us. Whether or not the dominical saying which follows in vv. 15ff. ultimately derives from an authentic utterance by Jesus, it is quite clear that the κύριος of 15a refers to him. More directly relevant to our concern are the second and third instances of κύριος in the passage, namely, those found in vv. 16 and 17: αὐτὸς ὁ κύριος ἐν κελεύσματι ἐν φωνῇ ἀρχαγγέλου καὶ ἐν σάλπιγγι θεοῦ, καταβήσεται ἀπ' οὐρανοῦ, καὶ οἱ νεκροὶ ἐν Χριστῷ ἀναστήσονται πρῶτον, ἔπειτα ἡμεῖς οἱ ζῶντες οἱ περιλειπόμενοι ἅμα σὺν αὐτοῖς ἁρπαγησόμεθα ἐν νεφέλαις εἰς ἀπάντησιν τοῦ κυρίου εἰς ἀέρα.

Is this description ultimately dependent upon Old Testament ideas of the Day of the Lord, and does it therefore involve a referential shift of κύριος from God to Christ? Joseph Plevnik has offered an in-depth study of the passage,[117] concentrating on the four prepositional phrases in which the description of the Parousia is couched: (1) ἐν κελεύσματι; (2) ἐν φωνῇ ἀρχαγγέλου; (3) ἐν σάλπιγγι θεοῦ; (4) ἐν νεφέλαις. In each instance it is possible to find material within the Old Testament and/or pseudepigraphal literature related to the Day of the Lord which is similar to the descriptions found in the prepositional phrases. This is true even in the case of ἐν κελεύσματι, a *hapax legomenon* within the New Testament, although no clear and direct association with apocalyptic imagery itself can be established.

However, Plevnik has demonstrated a close connection with Day of the Lord imagery by exploiting the word גער and its meaning as a word of rebuke or command uttered by God, often in connection with a generalized theophanic description.[118] The phrase ἐν σάλπιγγι θεοῦ has a more demonstrable connection with Day of the Lord passages from the Old Testament.[119] A clear example is found in Zech. 9.14, where YHWH sounds the trumpet in connection with the final visitation in judgment.

More problematic is the phrase ἐν νεφέλαις. Primarily the difficulty lies in the associations this descriptive phrase has with Old Testament theophanies. Within the Gospels the Parousia of Christ is often spoken of as accompanied by clouds.[120] At the same time, many Old Testament passages contain the cloud-motif (Isa. 9.1 is a good example). However, the critical point to note here is that the cloud-motif in 1 Thess. 4.17 occurs in connection with the upward gathering (ἁρπαγησόμεθα) of the saints and *not* with the descent of the Lord from heaven (καταβήσεται ἀπ᾽ οὐρανοῦ). This distinction has prompted Glasson to insist that the Lord's Parousia as a descent from heaven is ultimately a misapplication of such description to the Lord Jesus, especially if it includes an appeal to Dan. 7.13. Nowhere, Glasson comments, in pre-Christian apocalyptic is the Messiah ever spoken of as 'descending' from the heavens. This is an important critical point for Glasson's contention that the doctrine of the Parousia cannot be derived from pseudepigraphal literature, such as *1 Enoch*, for he is able to interpret any messianic allusion to Dan. 7.13 within such documents as originally speaking of an ascension and not a descent. The descent-motif found in such passages as 1 Thess. 4.17 he attributes to direct transposition of such Day of the Lord texts as Mic. 1.3 (which contains the verb καταβήσεται).[121]

R.B.Y. Scott makes substantially the same point in his investigation of the phrase in Dan. 7.13a. Scott tries to separate the description of the 'clouds of heaven' from the vision of the coming of the son of man, associating the description instead with the throne scene in vv. 9-10.[122]

The crucial question is how and when this heavenly description becomes so firmly attached to the 'son of man' figure. Scott suggests that once the Messiah was thought of in supernatural terms his 'coming' becomes readily associated with the descent of the Lord. However, this argument becomes troublesome, at least in the present state of christological studies,[123] once it becomes questionable that the 'Son of Man' was understood to be a transcendent, messianic figure in the first century CE. However, such argumentation may be making too much of the alleged incompatibility of the theocentric/ descent motif and the christocentric/ascent motif and basing itself upon a fine distinction between the two which has already broken down by the New Testament period.[124]

B. *Referential Shift of Pronouns from God to Christ*

There is also one relevant passage within the Pauline corpus which deserves our attention since it contains a deliberate use of an added pronominal phrase within an Old Testament quotation. Thus this passage involves the application of theocentric ideas to a new christocentric subject and represents additional evidence for a referential shift and conceptual overlap in Paul's mind between God and Christ.

9. Isa. 28.16 / Rom. 9.33. We have already had occasion to note in connection with our discussion of Rom. 10.13 above (p. 114) that this verse from Isaiah 28 was christologically reinterpreted by Paul in Rom. 10.11. At this juncture we simply want to reiterate this point and call attention to the fact that the same verse is similarly reinterpreted in Rom. 9.33 as well.[125] We have also already noted the eschatological nature of this verse as used by Paul.[126] Two additional points are worth considering which heighten the christological force of the Isaiah quotation in Rom. 9.33. The first is the inclusion of the pronominal phrase ἐπ' αὐτῷ in the quotation[127] (this occurs in 10.11 as well). This additional phrase does not occur within all copies of the LXX of Isaiah[128] and there is little doubt that it is an attempt to smooth out the meaning of the cryptic phrase from Isaiah about the precious building stone (λίθον πολυτελῆ ἐκλεκτὸν, ἀκρογωνιαῖον, ἔντιμον) and associate it more clearly with Christ. Secondly, here in Rom. 9.33 Paul adds the additional allusion to Isa. 8.14, which brings out the scandalous character of the metaphorical stone concerned, by including the phrase λίθον προσκόμματος.[129] We should not overlook at this point that within the context of Isa. 8.14 this stumbling-block is said to be none other than the Lord himself.[130] In short, it appears that within Rom. 9.33 Paul has included the phrase επ' αὐτῷ within his quotations from Isaiah in such a way as to demonstrate his christological reinterpretation of theocentric passages from the prophet.

Let us now move on to consider a third way in which the transposition of theocentric Old Testament passages into expressions of christocentricity is achieved by Paul. This method is not as readily discernible as the previous two, but it is worthy of investigation in any case.

C. *Referential Shift of Description of the Day of the Lord from God to Christ*

In addition to those passages which clearly contain a shift in referent (κύριος) from God to Christ, and that one which involves the insertion of a pronominal phrase within a theocentric context, there are also similar passages which display the same sort of referential shift with respect to descriptions of the Day of the Lord Yahweh. These passages do not contain the ambiguous use of 'κύριος' or a relevant pronominal phrase, but nevertheless do clearly imply that the focus has shifted from theocentricism to christocentrism within the Pauline quotations.

10. *Isa. 59.20 / Rom. 11.26.* The first example involves the description of God as 'he who delivers' (ὁ ῥυόμενος). The description is a common Old Testament designation of God and gives opportunity for us to observe theocentric/christocentric fluctuation revolving around the concept in several Pauline texts. These texts either use the participial noun (ὁ ῥυόμενος), or forms of the verb (ῥύομαι), or related words and phrases.

Paul mixes three Old Testament texts together in Rom. 11.26-27 with varying degrees of literal reliance upon the LXX. We find Jer. 31.33 alluded to in 11.27a and Isa. 27.9 alluded to in 11.27b, while a fairly accurate quotation of the LXX of Isa. 59.20 occurs in 11.26.[131] The passage in Isaiah 59 is an extended section dealing with the future judgment and redemption of the people Israel by God himself. This theocentric emphasis is also carried into the surrounding context of Romans 11. The entire chapter focuses on God's deliverance of the Jews in accordance with his covenant.

We see additional indications of a similar designation of God as 'he who delivers' in other places within the Pauline epistles as well. We note, for instance, 2 Cor. 1.10, where the verb ῥύομαι is used three times in describing God's action on our behalf (θεός is specifically mentioned in v. 9). At the same time, three other passages speak of the deliverance of the Christian as the co-operative activity of God and Jesus Christ. In Col. 1.13 God the Father is spoken of as delivering us (ἐρρύσατο) from the domain of darkness and transferring us (μετέστησιν) into the kingdom of his son. We should also note Gal. 1.4 which speaks of Jesus Christ delivering us (ἐξέληται) in accordance with the will of our God and Father (κατὰ τὸ θέλημα τοῦ θεοῦ καὶ πατρός). The co-operative factor is also seen in Gal. 4.4-5, where God sends his son (ἐξεπέστειλεν ὁ θεός τὸν υἱὸν αὐτοῦ) so as to redeem us from the law (ἵνα τοὺς ὑπὸ νόμον ἐξαγοράσῃ). A pertinent question is whether Christ or God is the subject of ἐξαγοράσῃ. It is impossible to say for sure, although ὁ θεός has the advantage of consistency of case. If such a judgment is sound, we can say that in all four of these examples we see the theocentric ingredient quite clearly. However, in the final two relevant passages it is the christocentric ingredient which comes to the fore.

The first of these christocentric passages is 1 Thess. 1.10, which speaks of Jesus as the one who delivers us from the coming wrath (Ἰησοῦν τὸν ῥυόμενον ἡμᾶς ἐκ τῆς ὀργῆς τῆς ἐρχομένης). To be sure, the theocentric facet is not completely obliterated since it is clearly seen in v. 9. In terms of the description of the 'Deliverer', however, it is the christocentric facet which is operative in this case. Perhaps we should also at this point note the similar reference to Jesus as 'Savior' (σωτῆρα) in Phil. 3.20. Here there is no theocentric facet contextually near, but the use of κύριος in the verse may originally have borne such a connection in thought before it came to be christologically reinterpreted. It is worth mentioning that both of these final two references which emphasize Jesus as 'he who delivers' are thought by many to be pre-Pauline credal formulae and are thus reflective of a very early stage of christological expression.

In short, there is some evidence of a fluctuation between God and Jesus Christ when it comes to describing 'him who delivers'. Some of the passages emphasize the theocentric role in such a description, some emphasize the christocentric, and some demonstrate a co-operation between the two.

11. *Isa. 59.17 / 1 Thess. 5.8.* We have already discussed 1 Thess. 5.1-11 in another context above. However, there is an additional feature of a verse in this passage which deserves special comment in connection with our theme of Old Testament description of the Day of the Lord being referentially shifted from God to Christ. This

involves the allusion to Isa. 59.17 which occurs in 1 Thess. 5.8. This allusion focuses on the description of the donning of military equipment in preparation for the final judgment. In Isaiah 59 it is God himself who is spoken of as putting on this equipment. However, in 1 Thessalonians the allusion is freely adapted and the subject changed from God to the Christian believers. We also see free-handed substitution in that the δικαιοσύνην of Isaiah becomes changed into πίστεως καὶ ἀγάπης in Paul's letter. The main points of literal dependency in the allusion involve the verb ἐνδύω and the nouns θώρακα, περικεφαλαίον, and σωτήριον.

It is to be observed that the larger context of the passage in Isaiah quite clearly speaks of God's final judgment of the world. We have already noted above that Isaiah 59 was used by Paul to express himself christologically by the way in which v. 20 of the same Isaianic passage is adapted in Rom. 11.26. Here in 1 Thess. 5.8, however, the referential shift extends in a slightly different direction. In this verse the imagery of military equipment is reinterpreted and applied not directly to Jesus Christ himself, but to those who believe in him. In such an extension of application the description of the purpose of the armor (πανοπλία is also altered. In Isaiah 59 it is God himself who puts on the armor as a preparation for his active role in judgment. In 1 Thess. 5.8 the armor seems to have more of a protective role in that it preserves and safeguards the Christian in the Day of the Lord described. In short, there is indeed a demonstrable shift of Old Testament description of the Day of the Lord involved here. It should be noted that it is *not* one which directly involves Jesus Christ as the new subject.

However, given the fact that the Christians' position is directly dependent upon their Lord's (note the force of the ἀπαρχή analogy in 1 Cor. 15.20-22), is it possible to see 1 Thess. 5.8 as an example of a theocentric/christocentric shift *one step further removed*? It is interesting at this point to compare this description in 1 Thess. 5 with a similar one contained in Eph. 6.10-17.[132] Once again the imagery of Isaiah 59 is foundational, with an even greater literal dependence (focusing on ἐνδύω, θώρακα, δικαιοσύνης, περικεφαλαίον, and σωτηρία). Here, however, the armor is specifically said to protect the Christian from the attacks of the devil (ὁ διάβολος—v. 11) in the evil day (ἐν τῇ ἡμέρα τῇ πονηρᾷ—v. 13). The calamitous nature of the final Day of Judgment is still present, but the threat is perceived to come from another quarter.

The important point for us to note is the way in which the Old Testament description has become transposed into a description of extended christological importance. Is there any other indication as to how this sort of shift of theocentric description to the Christian believer might have been achieved? Fortunately, there is a passage from the book of Wisdom which has some relevance to this point. In Wis. 5.17-20 there is a description of how God arms himself with the full armor of his zeal (λήψεται πανοπλίαν τὸν ζῆλον αὐτοῦ) and brings about his righteous Final Judgment. All of this he does on behalf of his righteous followers (δίκαιοι—v. 15) and for their vindication. Once again the military imagery of Isaiah 59 underlies the rather expansive description (the same three common words ἐνδύω, θώρακα and δικαιοσύνη appear). It may be that this description of God's faithfulness in Wisdom 5 helps to explain in part how the theocentric description of Isa. 59.17 eventually becomes applied to the Christian believers in both 1 Thess. 5.8 and Eph. 6.10-17.[133]

In addition, the fact that the imagery of military equipment is so generalized and easily applied to any human subject makes it difficult to say for certain if 1 Thess. 5.8 is ultimately based upon a shift of theocentric description from God to Christ which is then further shifted from Christ to the believing Christians. What the passage does demonstrate, however, is that the imagery of military equipment is used for a variety of subjects, including God, Christ and the Christians.[134]

4. CONCLUDING SUMMARY

What can we conclude about Paul's teaching on the Parousia and Final Judgment? Are we better able to determine the position these eschatological topics have in a Pauline theology? We have made several important discoveries in the course of our exploration into Paul's eschatological thought. First of all, it needs to be emphasized once again that the Jewish pseudepigraphal literature stands as an important body of background material which enables us to understand more fully Paul's formulation of these doctrines. In particular, we have noted the way in which Paul's teaching on the judgment throne (βῆμα) is paralleled in several pseudepigraphal documents, including *1 Enoch* 37-71, the *Testament of Moses*, and the *Testament of Abraham*.

Secondly, we have also seen that there exists a conceptual ambiguity within sections of the eschatological teaching of the Pauline epistles with regard to these twin concepts of Parousia and Final Judgment. This conceptual ambiguity involves both God and his messianic agent and focuses on their respective eschatological roles. The ambiguity helps us understand the delicate balance between theocentricity and christocentricity in Paul's thought. In short, we have demonstrated how closely related christology and eschatology are within Paul's thinking. This relationship has hitherto not been sufficiently noted by New Testament scholars.

Finally, we have tried to demonstrate something of the way in which this conceptual overlap is enhanced by a reinterpretation of Old Testament theocentric passages into expressions of christo-centricity. We have outlined three specific ways in which such a transposition occurs in the Pauline epistles and grouped a number of passages from the Pauline corpus accordingly. It appears clear that for Paul, the fact that christology and eschatology are so closely linked is what determines his use of 'Day of the Lord' texts from the Old Testament as a means of expressing his understanding of the Christian faith. For Paul, the Day of the Lord Yahweh has become the Day of the Lord Jesus Christ.

Yet there remains another category of Paul's thought which exhibits a similar overlap of the Messiah's role and position with those of God's. In Chapter 3 we turn to discuss the Messiah and the Kingdom in Paul, where once again we can see how thin a divide separates the role of God from the role of Messiah in Paul's thought. As we consider this topic we shall have another opportunity to explore more fully the contribution Jewish pseudepigraphal documents have in demonstrating this phenomenon within eschatological passages.

Chapter 3

THE MESSIAH AND THE KINGDOM IN PAUL

As we come to discuss the Messiah and the Kingdom in Paul, it might be helpful if we briefly summarize our study this far. In Chapter 1 we examined a selected group of Jewish pseudepigraphal documents which taught a temporary, earthly Kingdom in order to see how the respective roles of God and messianic agent were presented. We noted that several of these documents exhibit a conceptual overlap between God and the Messiah, and we have suggested that the presence of a temporary, Messianic Kingdom on earth is a partial attempt at clarification of their respective roles. These selected documents are highly revealing in that they afford us an opportunity to see how God and Messiah interrelate within passages from Jewish texts.

In Chapter 2 we noted the way in which sections of Paul's eschatological teaching exhibited a similar conceptual overlap between God and messianic agent. This was especially true with regard to their respective roles in the execution of Final Judgment at the Parousia. Both of these two chapters prepare us for the present discussion. They help to place us in a position to examine Paul's teaching on the Messianic Kingdom more comprehensively. Specifically, we will want to consider how Paul's teaching on the Messiah and the Kingdom also reflects this central question of theocentricity and christocentricity. We shall try and relate our discussion here in Chapter 3 to what we have already highlighted with respect to the Pauline doctrines of the Parousia and the Final Judgment (Chapter 2), before moving to a summary comparison of Paul's eschatological teaching with the insights gleaned from our study of Jewish pseudepigraphal literature (Chapter 1).

We might well ask: what relationship does this doctrine of a Second Advent bear to this Messianic Kingdom? Let us begin to answer this question by noting that within Paul's eschatological teaching, as we now have it, there is a contrast implied between the Future Age and the Present Age.[1] This essential dualism undergirds all of Paul's teaching about the future. It also appears clear that for Paul the event which was thought to separate this Present Age from the Future Age was the Parousia of the Messiah. Thus it seems that for Paul, as indeed for the early Church at large, it was understood that the life, death, and resurrection of Christ somehow inaugurated this awaited Future Age upon earth. At the same time, it appears to have been consistently emphasized that this Messianic Age was merely inaugurated and awaited its consummation in the future. We see the Church thus pinning its hopes upon the future Parousia of Christ through which the Present Age will be brought to its consummation and the Eternal Age, with all its fulness, ushered in. How imminent this future Parousia was believed to be is a matter of considerable scholarly debate.

In any case, with this proleptic inauguration of the Messianic Age through the Christ-event, the sharp division between present and future is lost so that even now the Church is able to experience the effects of, and indeed participate in, the future Age. Paul tells us that the present age is passing away (1 Cor. 2.6; 7.29-31; 10.11), while the future is impinging upon it. The Christian is said to be in the process of being transformed (μεταμορφούμεθα) into the image of glory of the future Age (2 Cor. 3.18). He lives with a foot in each of the two realms: present and future.[2] The residing gift of the Holy Spirit within the believer stands as a guarantee (ἀρραβών) that this future salvation is secure (2 Cor. 1.22; 5.5; Eph. 1.14).[3] Note also the way in which the doctrine of the Spirit is combined with the future consummation in Rom. 8.22-23.

1. Ἡ βασιλεία AND βασιλεύω IN PAUL

When we move to consider the proclamation of βασιλεία τοῦ θεοῦ itself within the Pauline corpus we find it occupies a much less prominent role than in the Synoptic Gospels.[4] We find that the word βασιλεία itself occurs only twelve times: Rom. 14.17; 1 Cor. 4.20, 6.9, 10; 15.24, 50; Gal. 5.21; Eph. 5.5; Col. 1.13, 4.11; 1 Thess. 2.2; 2 Thess. 1.5. The corresponding verb βασιλεύω occurs nine times:[5] Rom. 5.14, 17 (2 times), 21 (2 times); 6.12; 1 Cor. 4.8 (2 times); 15.25. No doubt much of the meaning βασιλεία τοῦ θεοῦ carries in the

Synoptics has been adapted and expanded considerably from those categories and concepts we see within the Pauline corpus.[6] Let us examine more deeply Paul's use of βασιλεία/βασιλεύω.[7] How does Paul use the terms?

First of all we note that the phrase βασιλεία τοῦ θεοῦ and the corresponding verb βασιλεύω are used in an ethical context where Paul is speaking to a church concerning the behavior of some of its members. We find that this ethical exhortation is sometimes grounded in the believer's present experience of the force of the Kingdom: 1. Rom. 14.17 'The Kingdom of God is not eating and drinking, but justice, peace, and joy inspired by the Holy Spirit'. 2. 1 Cor. 4.20 'The Kingdom of God is not a matter of talk, but of power'. 3. 1 Thess. 2.12 'Live lives worthy of God who calls you into his Kingdom and glory'. 4. Rom. 6.12 'So sin must no longer reign (βασιλευέτω) in your mortal body exacting obedience to the bodily desires'. We should perhaps take the basic meaning of the Kingdom reference in Col. 4.11 to fit within this category as well.

Alternatively, at times the ethical exhortation has a very clear future dimension:[8] 1. 1 Cor. 6.9-10 'Surely you know that the unjust will never come into possession of the Kingdom of God. Make no mistake; no fornicator or idolator, none who are guilty either of adultery or of homosexual perversion, no thieves or grabbers or drunkards or slanderers or swindlers will possess the Kingdom of God'. 2. Gal. 5.21 'I warn you, as I warned you before, that those who behave in such ways will never inherit the Kingdom of God'. 3. 2 Thess. 1.5 '(Such sufferings) will prove you worthy of the Kingdom of God'.

A similar contrast of present and future using the verb is found within the Adam/Christ analogy of Rom. 5.14-21 with the sin of Adam resulting in the reign of death (ἐβασίλευσεν) and the obedience of Christ yielding the future reign (βασιλεύσῃ) of grace and righteousness.[9] The tension between the believer's present position in Christ and his future reigning with him in glory appears to be at the heart of Paul's sarcastic rebuke in 1 Cor. 4.8: 'You are already filled, you have already become rich, you have become kings (ἐβασιλεύσατε) without us, and I would indeed that you had become kings (ἐβασιλεύσατε) so that we might also reign with you (συμβασιλεύσωμεν).[10]

In addition to the strongly ethical context of these βασιλεία/βασιλεύω references, we note the more direct eschatological reference in 1 Cor. 15.50b: 'Flesh and blood can never possess the Kingdom of God'. Here Paul is concerned with the nature of the believer's resurrection existence as opposed to its ethical basis.[11]

The remaining three references to βασιλεία in the Pauline corpus are the most informative for our purposes, as they are all references to the Kingdom *of Christ*. We find, first of all in Col. 1.13, that the believer is said to have entered already into this Kingdom as a result of Christ's death and resurrection as instrumented by God: 'He (God) rescued (ἐρρύσατο) us from the domain of darkness and transferred us (μετέστησιν) into the Kingdom of his dear Son in whom our release is secured and our sins forgiven'. At the same time, within the Deutero-Pauline epistle to the Ephesians we have the curious reference in 5.5 to the future inheritance of the Kingdom of Christ and God[12] (ἐν τῇ βασιλείᾳ τοῦ Χριστοῦ καὶ θεοῦ). Once again we have here a strongly ethical context with the author listing patterns of life incompatible with such an inheritance.

Clearly within both of these passages (Col. 1.13 and Eph. 5.5), we have Christ and God brought within the closest possible connection with reference to the Kingdom.[13] Are we to understand the βασιλεία τοῦ θεοῦ and the βασιλεία τοῦ Χριστοῦ as synonymous?[14] What relationship do they have? Is it sufficient to explain the rise of a βασιλεία τοῦ Χριστοῦ in Paul simply on the basis of the centrality of the person of Jesus within traditional eschatological expectations of the βασιλεία τοῦ θεοῦ? Or do we need to look elsewhere for a more complete answer?

In 1 Cor. 15.20-28 (our final reference to the βασιλεία in Paul) we have a block of eschatological material particularly relevant to discussion of this topic of the Kingdom of Christ and its relationship to the Kingdom of God.[15] We find both the noun βασιλεία and the verb βασιλεύω together in vv. 24-25: 'Then comes the end, when he delivers up the Kingdom (βασιλείαν) to God the Father, when he has abolished all rule and authority and power. For he must reign (βασιλεύειν) until he has put all his enemies under his feet'.

The cryptic passage in 1 Cor. 15.20-28 has served as a focal point for discussion of the question of a future, Messianic Kingdom in Paul.[16] Let us examine this critical passage more closely.

A. *1 Cor. 15.20-28 and the Kingdom of Christ*

We have already noted in Chapter 1 some of the Jewish pseudepigraphal documents which teach an earthly, Messianic Kingdom of temporary duration. We should again note here briefly that the Apocalypse of John seems to be a *Christian* example of the same phenomenon. It is generally recognized[17] that the Apocalypse of John does indeed teach a future, earthly millennial Kingdom distinct from the Eternal Age which follows it. Rev. 20.1-6 quite clearly teaches that there will be two resurrections: the first, that of the righteous, who are raised to participate in the thousand-year rule of Christ on earth; and the second, of the rest of the dead (presumably the wicked and non-believers), who are raised to face eternal judgment at the end of the Messianic Age (cf. 20.11-16).

Is it possible to detect this belief in a millennial Kingdom, and its accompanying doctrine of two resurrections, within earlier Christian writers? There is some evidence which suggests that such a belief might underlie 1 Cor. 15.20-28. Certainly there have been many scholars who would so argue.[18]

Let us now turn to examine some of the scholarly debate about the nature of the Kingdom in 1 Cor. 15.20-28. A useful approach to this is to compare and contrast some of the interpretations of Pauline scholars.

1. *Scholarly Debate: Schweitzer and Davies*

One cannot approach the question of a temporary, Messianic Kingdom in Paul without giving due consideration to the work of Albert Schweitzer. His *Mysticism of Paul the Apostle* brought the question of Paul's eschatology to the centre of modern scholarly discussion.[19] Schweitzer emphasized the reliance of Paul upon traditional Jewish apocalyptic thought and felt Paul adopted the Jewish apocalyptic pattern with only one crucial modification.[20] The modification is that

> the first participators in the transient Messianic Kingdom clearly have the resurrection mode of existence, and the Elect of the last generation, even if they have died before the beginning of the Kingdom, will be able, through the resurrection, to become participants in it.

This significant alteration is, in essence, the introduction of the doctrine of two resurrections. Traditional Jewish eschatological thought emphasized only those alive at the time of the inauguration of the Messianic Kingdom as participants and the resurrection as the event which came at the end of the Messianic Age. According to Schweitzer the introduction of a dual resurrection motif is motivated by the fact of Christ's life, death and resurrection. In other words, the Jewish eschatological scheme did not originally allow for, nor even conceive of, the advent of the Messiah independent of the glory of the Messianic Kingdom as well. In Schweitzer's analysis the death of Christian believers threw the traditional Jewish scheme into disarray and drove Paul logically to postulate a special resurrection of deceased believers into the Messianic Age. Thus we have a doctrine of two resurrections taught by Paul.[21] In fact, Schweitzer goes on to explain the controversies within both the Corinthian and the Thessalonian churches which occasion Paul's letters as having arisen precisely because of this point.[22] The churches reflect the traditional Jewish eschatological belief which associated only the righteous who are alive at the beginning of the Messianic Age as its participants and taught that the resurrection of all men to judgment follows at the conclusion of that Age. In short, the delay of the Parousia and the death of believing Christians during that delay necessitated within Paul's thought a doctrine of two resurrections. For Schweitzer the Messianic Kingdom lies between these two resurrections. He appeals to 1 Cor. 15.20-28 for exegetical support of this doctrine but admits that Paul gave no detailed description of the Messianic Kingdom. Nevertheless, Schweitzer's work is critically important, for he is the first serious scholar to interpret 1 Cor. 15.20-28 as essentially a modified expression of traditional Jewish eschatological teaching. In this regard, Schweitzer is quick to point out its parallels with other eschatological writings of first-century Judaism (especially *4 Ezra!*).[23]

Schweitzer's work was severely criticized by W.D. Davies in his *Paul and Rabbinic Judaism*.[24] First of all, Davies disagreed that Paul must be made to conform too closely to current eschatological speculations. Paul must not be made a slave to first-century Jewish apocalyptic. Instead Davies tries to emphasize that for Paul the character of his eschatological teaching was more determined by the prime role accorded to Jesus. In response to Schweitzer's analysis of the controversies engulfing Corinth and Thessaloniki Davies argues that they arise out of Pauline teaching itself. Commenting on 1 Thess. 4.13-18 he says:

> The Thessalonian Christians had quite clearly been taught that the transformation of those 'in Christ' into the resurrection mode of existence would soon take place and that without the experience of death. Not only so but, as passages such as Rom. 6.1-14 show, the solidarity of Christians with their Lord was such that they had died

but also risen with Christ to life; a second death was unthinkable; they had already passed from death to life.[25]

Thus, we should note that both Schweitzer and Davies, while differing in their evaluation of how the doctrine of a Parousia of Christ arises within early Christianity, are agreed as to the disruption the two-stage appearance of the Messiah Jesus causes to the traditional, Jewish eschatological scheme.[26] Nowhere is this disruption made more clear than in 1 Cor. 15.20-28. At the same time, nowhere are the scholarly presuppositions of both Schweitzer and Davies made more visible than in their respective attempts at exegesis of this troublesome passage.

In particular, much discussion is given over in Davies's work to 1 Cor. 15.22ff., where he systematically attempts to render invalid a distinction between the future, Messianic Age and the Eternal Age to Come, as derived from these verses. This is accomplished in two major steps: 1. Any time-reference implied by the sequence ἀπαρχή-ἔπειτα-εἶτα in v. 24 is denied. 2. The meaning of τὸ τέλος is taken to be a technical one in which the phrase denotes the final consummation. By this Davies means the Kingdom of God independent of and sequential to the present Messianic Age. In effect, the Messianic Age is concluded with the Parousia of Christ which gives way to the Eternal Age to Come. Davies concludes:

> Paul's eschatology is far simpler than Schweitzer would have us believe. It contains no reference to a Messianic Kingdom such as is contemplated in Baruch, 4 Ezra, and Revelation and can be briefly summarized as the early expectation of the Parousia when there would be a final judgment, a general resurrection of the righteous dead (and possibly of all the dead), the transformation of the righteous living and ensuing upon all this the final consummation, the perfected Kingdom of God when God would be all in all.[27]

Two critical comments about Davies's work need to be made. One concerns a methodological point and the other an exegetical one. In interacting with Davies on these matters we are addressing our comments to a much larger field as well, for Davies's interpretation of 1 Cor. 15.20-28 is representative of a large number of Pauline scholars.

First of all, it is ironic that Davies criticizes Schweitzer quite heavily for overemphasizing the 'impelling logic' of Jewish eschatological thought, while at the same time he himself is guilty of the

same sort of error in that he imposes a logical consistency upon
Paul's eschatological thought which is perhaps just as unwarranted.
In the end, much of Davies's interpretation of 1 Cor. 15.20-28 is
governed, perhaps unconsciously, by a desire to present Paul's
eschatology coherently and systematically. Any departures from
what is perceived to be the 'norm' are sacrificed for the sake of this
consistency. To a certain degree, Davies's argument is thus a circular
one. Davies maintains that 1 Cor. 15.20-28 cannot be held to teach a
temporary, Messianic Kingdom because such a doctrine is inconsistent
with the rest of Paul's eschatological teaching. At the same time, the
reason Paul's eschatological teaching cannot include belief in a
temporary, Messianic Kingdom is because there is no clear example
of such a doctrine within Paul's writing on the subject. The tacit
assumption governing such argumentation is that the internal
consistency of Paul's belief-system must not be radically disturbed.

The flawed logic of Davies's position is also clearly seen in his
handling of the βασιλεία τοῦ Χριστοῦ. He quite rightly points out
that Paul very rarely speaks of the Kingdom of Christ. Indeed,
Davies goes on immediately to add the comment that: 'Whenever
Paul speaks of a Kingdom that is to come he thinks of a βασιλεία τοῦ
θεοῦ' (p. 295). He then lists six additional passages[28] from the body
of the Pauline corpus as support for this contention and concludes
that none of these other 'Kingdom' passages explicitly mentions a
temporary, Messianic Kingdom. In reality, all Davies has accomplished
here is to attempt to bury 1 Cor. 15.20-28 under the combined weight
of the rest of these Pauline texts which do speak of the Kingdom of
God. But we are still no closer to an understanding of the references
implying a Kingdom *of Christ* in 1 Cor. 15.20-28!

Such argumentation may produce a fine systematic theology, but
it does not help very much in highlighting the flexibility inherent
within a great deal of eschatological thought concerning the
Kingdom of God/Christ. To be fair, Davies does go on to pay
minimal attention to the only Pauline text which makes clear
reference to the βασιλεία τοῦ Χριστοῦ (Col. 1.13). However, he
dismisses it on the grounds that the Kingdom of Christ is there
regarded as a present fact (the implication being that it cannot
therefore be future as well). One is tempted to demand that the
sword be allowed to cut in the other direction and ask Davies
whether he takes the βασιλεία τοῦ Χριστοῦ to have any present
dimension in addition to its obviously future dimension. Or are we to

be forced into an either/or decision and allow ourselves to be robbed of much of the strength of eschatological teaching to assert paradoxically the Kingdom to be both present and future?

The second exegetical criticism of Davies involves his rather limited assessment of the term τὸ τέλος. He gives an admirable survey of the exegetical options involved but eventually settles on it being a 'technical phrase denoting the final consummation' (p. 25). However, the interpretation of this 'final consumption' is still a matter of considerable scholarly debate. We should remember that in *4 Ezra* a similar phrase[29] carried great flexibility and diversity in its use (pp. 60-61 above). If we learn anything from this pseudepigraphal book we see how the phrase can designate any number of points within the eschatological scheme.

We cannot assume, as Davies does, that τὸ τέλος must be equated only with the Parousia itself. In the end, it may be that a competing formulation to the ordinary eschatological scheme, or what we now recognize as the 'normal' scheme, is contained within 1 Cor. 15.20-28 and Schweitzer's interpretation is valid after all. Certainly we should not be too quick to dismiss the possibility that these troublesome verses simply reflect a slightly different conceptualization of what the future holds. There is no compelling reason why Paul's eschatological teaching cannot display the same sort of diversity in this regard that we noted in *4 Ezra* or *2 Baruch*. Let us now consider further scholarly debate over this passage of 1 Cor. 15.20-28.

2. Scholarly Debate: Wilcke and Wallis

Wilber Wallis's article of 1975 is the most recent effort given over to reasserting a millennial interpretation of Paul.[30] Wallis takes the monograph of Wilcke[31] to be his chief opposition in this attempt. Basically, the difference between the two scholars revolves around the same two key issues we saw surface in Schweitzer and Davies: (1) whether 1 Cor. 15.22 speaks of two resurrections;[32] (2) whether τὸ τέλος in 15.24 is synonymous with the Parousia. All the other differences in exegesis between the two scholars hinge upon their respective interpretations of these two points.

Let us first examine Wilcke's contribution to the subject. His book is a comprehensive one and strives to determine whether or not the idea of a temporary, Messianic Kingdom has any exegetical support within the Pauline epistles. At the same time, Wilcke does an admirable job of placing the doctrine of a temporary, Messianic

Kingdom within the history of Christian thought. Thus the monograph is laced with helpful quotations of and allusions to post-apostolic writers who expound on ideas associated with the doctrine of a temporary, Messianic Kingdom.[33] For our purposes we shall be considering only Wilcke's understanding of Paul's contribution to the issue.

Wilcke begins by noting that nowhere in any of the Pauline letters do we have the notion of a temporary, Messianic Kingdom explicitly detailed. However, he points out that some scholars have interpreted the ambiguous passage of 1 Cor. 15.20-28 as supporting such a doctrine and have occasionally extended that interpretation to cover the essential meaning of other Pauline eschatological passages as well, notably 1 Thess. 4.13-18. (Wilcke notes that occasionally 2 Thess. 1.5-12 and Phil. 3.10-14 are also interpreted in the light of the Corinthians pericope, but summarily dismisses them from any further consideration within his own monograph.) Thus Wilcke is primarily concerned with 1 Cor. 15.20-28 and 1 Thess. 4.13-18, and a major portion of his book is given over to a careful, verse-by-verse exegesis of these two passages.

At this point we should applaud Wilcke for one of his most important methodological observations in the study. He quite rightly makes it clear that 1 Thess. 4.13-18 cannot be seen as supporting either a doctrine of two ressurrections or explicit belief in a temporary, Messianic Kingdom. He correctly concludes that 1 Thess. 4.13-18 suffers exegetical violence if it is forced into the temporary, Messianic Kingdom pattern sometimes derived from the cryptic passage of in 1 Cor. 15.20-28. With this we cannot but agree.

However, I wonder if Wilcke does not commit exegetical violence himself with respect to the passage from 1 Corinthians 15 by trying to force it into a straight-jacket of interpretation and make it harmonize with 1 Thess. 4.13-18. His exegesis of 1 Cor. 15.20-28 deserves further consideration.

Wilcke is quite adamant that throughout 1 Corinthians 15 Paul has only one resurrection in mind, namely that of the believers. His argument is that this resurrection will occur at the Parousia; and it is at that time that the believers will enter into the Eternal Age. He thus denies that any exegetical support for a general resurrection (as distinct from a resurrection of those in Christ) is to be derived from either 15.20 or 15.22b.[34] Having thus rejected any basis for asserting

Paul's belief in a general resurrection, Wilcke is able to take the next step of associating the Parousia itself with the time of the granting of the Christian's resurrection body. In other words, if there is only one time of resurrection, how do we relate this event with the Parousia itself? For Wilcke there is a very close connection indeed. The Parousia is the event at which the Christian is granted his resurrection body.

Wilcke is equally adamant that τὸ τέλος in 15.24 is synonymous with this Parousia. After careful consideration he rejects any attempt to interpret τὸ τέλος as either an adjective (thus translating it as 'finally');[35] or of interpreting it as 'the Rest' (and thus setting up a third additional category of people to be resurrected).

In light of these two observations, Wilcke concludes that there is no room for an intermediate Messianic Kingdom after the Parousia; nor is there any mention in Paul of judgment subsequent to that event which would necessitate the second resurrection of the wicked.[36]

It should be noted how closely Wilcke's two observations are related in the forming of his conclusion about the temporary, Messianic Kingdom. Indeed, the second is dependent upon the first and flows directly from it. We shall have an opportunity to criticize Wilcke in a moment, but let us turn briefly to the work of Wallis and consider his interaction with some of Wilcke's results.

In direct contrast to Wilcke's two major observations, Wallis seeks to show that Paul does imply a doctrine of two resurrections and that he also makes an important distinction between the Parousia and τὸ τέλος in 1 Cor. 15.20-28. First with regard to the belief in two resurrections: Wallis also points out that the arguments for this belief hinges upon the meaning of πάντες in 15.22b. How comprehensive is the meaning of ἐν τῷ Χριστῷ πάντες? Does the πάντες in 22b have the same meaning as it does in 22a, ἐν τῷ Ἀδὰμ πάντες? Scholarly debate has raged over this battleground for many long campaigns and we have as yet no clear victor emerging.[37] Wallis has joined in the fray and has attempted to solve the meaning of the phrase in a way totally different to Wilcke's. Wallis has sought to affirm a univocal meaning to these phrases in v. 22 through an appeal to the same sense of comprehensiveness which prevails through the larger passage of vv. 20-28. In particular the quote of Ps. 8.6 in v. 27 is thought to substantiate this claim:

The comprehensiveness of the 'all' in Psalm 8.6 must decide the interpretation of 'all' in verse 22b, 'In Christ all will be made alive'. If 'all' in verse 22 does not have the same completeness as the 'all' in verse 27, a logical weakness enters Paul's argument.[38]

Wallis proceeds at this point to note that exegesis of this passage has tended to lead to two extremes. Either the verses were used to support a strict universalism in which 'all mankind' is redeemed, or, alternatively, they lead to a denial of the resurrection of the unbelievers.[39] Wallis himself opts for a middle way and answers the exegetical difficulties by postulating a doctrine of two resurrections. The second resurrection of the dead is connected with v. 26.[40]

Thus there is an essential difference between Wallis and Schweitzer as to the reason for their mutual belief in a Pauline doctrine of two resurrections. For Schweitzer the motivation for its development is the driving logic of Jewish apocalyptic which Paul adopts; while for Wallis the motivation is the comprehensiveness of Christ with respect to his authority and rule over the whole of the created order.

With respect to Wilcke's assertion that the Parousia is synonymous with τὸ τέλος, Wallis is equally dissatisfied. He asserts that εἶτα τὸ τέλος in v. 24 measures a time sequence between the Parousia and the final consummation. It is during this implied time interval that the future earthly reign of Christ is to take place. Wallis does not, however, leave his understanding of the 'millennial' reign dangling by such a thin and obscure exegetical thread. He goes on to appeal to the sequence of the two ὅταν clauses of v. 24 as supporting this idea of an earthly reign. He calls attention to the aorist καταργήσῃ and points out:

> The aorist subjunctive in the second hotan clause indicates that the destruction of Christ's enemies is prior to the event of the first hotan clause, the delivering over of the Kingdom at the telos; the delivering over follows the subjugation.[41]

A similar sequence is indicated by the parallel construction of vv. 27 (ὑπέταξεν) and 28 (ὅταν δὲ ὑποταγῇ).

Wallis is thus able to squeeze out of these verses room for a future Messianic Kingdom through appeal to the sequence implied by the tenses of the verbs used. We may outline the basic sequential scheme of vv. 23-28 which Wallis arrives at thus:

1. 23a—ἕκαστος δὲ ἐν τῷ ἰδίῳ τάγματι· ἀπαρχὴ Χριστός,
2. 23b—ἔπειτα οἱ τοῦ Χριστοῦ ἐν τῇ παρουσίᾳ αὐτοῦ,

3. 24b—ὅταν καταργήσῃ πᾶσαν ἀρχὴν καὶ πᾶσαν ἐξουσίαν καὶ δύναμιν,

4. 24a—εἶτα τὸ τέλος, ὅταν παραδιδῷ τὴν βασιλείαν τῷ θεῷ καὶ πατρί,

5. 28c—ἵνα ᾖ ὁ θεὸς τὰ πάντα ἐν πᾶσιν.

The meaning of step three is amplified in 28a—ὅταν δὲ ὑποταγῇ αὐτῷ τὰ πάντα, and expanded further in vv. 25-27—δεῖ γὰρ αὐτὸν βασιλεύειν ἄχρι οὗ θῇ πάντας τοὺς ἐχθροὺς ὑπὸ τοὺς πόδας αὐτοῦ. ἔσχατος ἐχθρὸς καταργεῖται ὁ θάνατος. πάντα γὰρ ὑπέταξεν ὑπὸ τοὺς πόδας αὐτοῦ. ὅταν δὲ εἴπῃ ὅτι πάντα ὑποτέτακται, δῆλον ὅτι ἐκτὸς τοῦ ὑποτάξαντος αὐτῷ τὰ πάντα. The meaning of step four is amplified in 28b—τότε καὶ αὐτὸς ὁ υἱός ὑποταγήσεται τῷ ὑποτάξαντι αὐτῷ τὰ πάντα.

The Messianic Age is thus implied by the reference to Christ reigning in v. 25. Wallis comments:

> A reign is essential to the destruction of Christ's enemies. Since the destruction of enemies must follow the Parousia, we must either conceive of the present reign of Christ as extending beyond the Parousia into the age to come, or think of a distinctive phase of His sovereign Lordship which will begin with the Parousia, and project into the age to come.[42]

As Wallis properly acknowledges, this is precisely the position of Oscar Cullmann.[43] A brief synopsis of Cullmann's thoughts will illustrate how close they are to the general drift of Wallis's argument.

As is well known, Cullmann has grounded his entire program of New Testament exegesis upon his understanding of the concept of linear time.[44] The way in which a distinction is made between the *Regnum Christi* and the Kingdom of God is a further and logical extension of this conception of linear time foundational to Cullmann's thought. He also notes the flexibility of the application of Ps. 110.1 in association with this Regnum Christi. Throughout most of the Ps. 110.1 references within New Testament it is clear that the ascension is reckoned as the event which inaugurates the reign of Christ.[45] However, in 1 Cor. 15.25, Cullmann argues that the use of the Psalm is in reference to a future event. He attributes such flexibility to the present/future tension characteristic of the entire New Testament[46] and is able thus to closely align Paul's message in 1 Corinthians 15 with that of the Apocalypse of John:

> The millennium and the apocalyptic events which precede it represent the part of the Regnum Christi which began with the ascension and which overlap into the future age.... The Regnum Christi is the more comprehensive concept, for this reign began almost two thousand years ago and will continue for an indefinite time in this age, whereas the millennium belongs to the final act of the Regnum Christi initiated by the Parousia, in which the Church will play a specially important part.[47]

The major distinction between the Apocalypse of John and Paul in the matter then is, according to Cullmann, the unspecific duration of the Messianic Kingdom in Paul.

To return to our discussion of Wilcke and Wallis, what shall we say about their respective attempts to plumb the depths of 1 Cor. 15.20-28? First, with regard to Wilcke's work: It should be noted that since its publication in 1967, Wilcke's monograph has remained the dominant authority for those who reject the idea of a messianic 'Zwischenreich' as derived from 1 Cor. 15.20-28. This is despite the fact that, to a certain degree, the monograph falls into the trap of circular argumentation in its rejection of the doctrine. Quite clearly, the reason why τὸ τέλος is equated with the Parousia is because such an interpretation is seen to be consistent with Wilcke's ideas about the meaning of the πάντες phrases in v. 22. At the same time, Wilcke is restrictive in his understanding of the meaning of τὸ τέλος itself. He is quite right to translate it as 'the End'; but he offers little explanation of just what is meant by this term τὸ τέλος. For instance, we are never convincingly told why τὸ τέλος cannot be a more comprehensive concept and include a general resurrection. In other words, the meaning Wilcke assigns to τὸ τέλος is supported by his interpretation of the πάντες phrases, while the meaning of the πάντες phrases is supported by his interpretation of τὸ τέλος. But what happens if we break out of such a circle by broadening the meaning of τὸ τέλος itself? After all, we did note above how diversely a similar term (*finis*) was used in *4 Ezra*. Surely we are justified in suggesting the possibility that a similar latitude of meaning might prove helpful in interpreting 1 Cor. 15.20-28.

Perhaps if Wilcke had given more consideration to the variety of eschatological thought within Jewish pseudepigraphal literature, and recognized how often in these documents competing eschatological schematizations occur within a single work, he might have been able to appreciate the possible variation 1 Cor. 15.20-28 gives to Paul's 'normal' eschatology. Surely it is a great weakness in Wilcke's work that so little attention is paid to relevant Jewish pseudepigraphal documents. A scant nine pages are given over to a discussion of the *Apocalypse of Weeks, SO* 3.652-731, *2 Baruch* and *4 Ezra*. No wonder that Wilcke's interpretation of 1 Cor. 15.20-28 ends up looking like a case of elaborate harmonization of Paul's eschatological teaching.

With respect to Wallis's article, which incidentally contains *no* supportive reference to any of the Jewish pseudepigraphal documents, two specific comments need to be made. First of all, it appears to me that Wallis is quite right in calling attention to the tangle of tenses contained within 1 Cor. 15.20ff. and in seeking to demonstrate thereby that the Parousia is not necessarily synonymous with τὸ τέλος. I would also affirm that the ἔπειτα/εἶτα clauses in vv. 23 and 24 *could* be causal in meaning but would also insist that the most natural reading of the text does support a temporal sequence easily consistent with the resultant teaching of a temporary, Messianic Kingdom.[48]

Secondly, we would wish to commend him on his ingenious interpretation of the meaning of the two ὅταν clauses in 1 Cor. 15.24. This surely is the most significant contribution he has to make to the study of the passage.[49] In addition, the interpretation based upon this observation serves as a complementary piece of evidence for his emphasis on the comprehensive sense of both πάντες clauses in v. 22. One of the great strengths of an interpretation such as Wallis's is that it provides a basis for an internally consistent meaning of these two controversial phrases.

However, whether or not we think Paul always intended there to be such an internal consistency when he used the Adam/Christ contrast is certainly another debateable issue. In the end, whether or not we agree with Wallis or Wilcke on this particular point is going to be determined largely by our own presuppositions about the mind of Paul. How consistent do we reckon him to have been when it came to expressing his eschatological thought?

Now the debate over the meaning of this passage in 1 Corinthians 15 also involves the idea of the time of the Messianic Kingdom as well. Let us examine the relationship between the Messianic Kingdom and the meaning of Ps. 110.1 in order to illustrate this point. A brief examination of this point will also reemphasize how elusive the meaning of these cryptic verses from the Corinthian letter can be.

B. *Ps. 110.1 and the Kingdom of Christ*

Above we mentioned Cullmann's comments on the quotation of Psalm 110.1 in our passage. That Ps. 110.1 was an extremely important text for the early Church's christological expression is evident and generally recognized.[50] It is the Old Testament text most frequently quoted or alluded to in the New Testament.[51] Not only does its frequency of quotation register its importance, but the manner in which it is used is also highly revealing. It generally occurs in passages filled with great christological wealth.

Of special significance to our study at this point is the relationship the use of the Psalm has with the rule of Christ in the Messianic Kingdom. More precisely, the question arises as to whether the quotation of the Psalm in 1 Cor. 15.20ff. is primarily with reference to a *future* exaltation or enthronement of the Messiah at the Parousia, or, alternatively, whether it is primarily speaking of the *past* resurrection/ascension/exaltation pattern characteristic of most of the New Testament witness concerning this text.

It is generally assumed[52] that in the earliest detectable strata of our Gospels (such as Mk 14.62?) such present/future formulations about the Kingdom were irrelevant given the prevailing understanding of the imminent Parousia. No expansive interval between the exaltation and Parousia was expected or anticipated. It was not until the delay of the Parousia prompted further thought and the Church had experienced the present power of the risen Lord in fellowship and worship did she begin to think in terms of a present/future dichotomy concerning the Messianic Kingdom.[53] Thus in one sense the Messiah was thought to be at present exercising his rule in the life of the Church, and to have been doing so since his resurrection and accompanying exaltation and enthronement. This exaltation of Christ to the right hand of God forms the basis of the Christian's relationship to God and instigates the according of worship to Christ.[54] On the other hand, this present rule of Christ was also thought to have its consummation in the future. So significant was this future consummation that at times the messianic rule was conceived as a wholly future event. This is especially true of 1 Cor. 15.20-28.[55] As Hay comments:

> 1 Corinthians 15.23 appears to refer to a period between the Parousia, when the limited number of 'those who belong to Christ' will be raised (cf. Rev. 20.4-5) and the 'end', when Christ shall have

conquered every foe (cf. Rev. 20.14-15)—an end which evidently means the rest of humanity.[56]

Thus we note that, according to Hay, the allusion to Ps. 110.1c in 1 Cor. 15.25 is primarily a reference to the future rule of the Messiah.[57] It must be admitted that such an interpretation is again highly contested by many notable Pauline scholars. Once again we also note that the basic objection to such an interpretation is that the eschatology of 1 Cor. 15.20-28 is rendered inconsistent with virtually all other major eschatological sections of Paul's epistles (1 Cor. 15.50ff. and 1 Thess. 4.13ff. in particular).[58]

Nevertheless, the thrust of the meaning of 1 Cor. 15.20-28, as a whole, is quite clearly futuristic. The evidence seems to me to reflect a diversity of eschatological belief in which Paul elaborates a slightly modified scheme in 1 Cor. 15.20-28 as compared to the rest of his discussions of the matter. I would go on to suggest that this modification quite possibly arises from traditional speculations about the future Messianic Kingdom and its relationship to the Eternal Age in a manner similar to those discussions we saw embodied in *4 Ezra* and *2 Baruch* in Chapter 1. In any case we should not be too overly concerned about such fluctuation and accept it as inherent in any protracted discussion about the future within Jewish apocalyptic.

Regardless of how we interpret the reign of the Kingdom in 1 Corinthians 15 (present or future or inaugurated), we are still struggling to explain the role of the Messianic Kingdom in relation to the future Age to Come. At the same time we are still trying to ground that role within a specific conception of temporality which may be totally inapplicable to, and incapable of expressing, the future.[59] Even if we were willing to accept that a linear concept of time (such as that suggested by Cullmann) was foundational to Paul and therefore relevant to his expression of the Regnum Christi, we still are left with the task of explaining the relationship between the *Eternal Age* and such a linear-time concept. It seems to me that the whole question of a temporary, Messianic Kingdom in Paul revolves around this conceptual problem.[60] Yet, ironically, it is in the very nature of discussion about the future that imprecision reigns. The lack of precedent itself makes this so. Indeed, it is naive to assume any firm degree of certainty of meaning can be attained when discussing these matters.

In the end, to formulate the debate entirely around whether or not Paul believed in a temporary, messianic reign after the Parousia is perhaps to misread the whole problem. We may be asking him (via his epistles) to pinpoint eschatological events with a certainty which should be expected of no one.[61] To a certain degree, we are ultimately handicapped by the genre of the eschatological literature itself in this matter. Such writing just does not easily lend itself to our sort of scholarly scrutiny.

What, then, are we able to confirm about Paul's eschatological thought? It seems likely that Paul remained absolutely convinced about the fact of the inauguration of the Messianic Age in the events of Jesus' life, death and ascension. Equally assured was the conviction that their future consummation and fulfilment lay in the events surrounding the awaited Parousia. When we try to press beyond this and demand a consistently precise and exact definition of events beyond the Parousia, we go too far.[62] These events are clothed in strained images and are lost in a blur of future wonder which does not allow for anything but rapturous awe. Investigation into the schema of Paul's eschatological thought is important and interesting, but may prove to be a large and well-disguised cul-de-sac if we do not recognize the inherent limitations and variations of the eschatological forms, language, and ideas in which it is couched.

Then how are we to try and solve this scholarly stalemate over the correct interpretation of 1 Cor. 15.20-28? One way is to approach the subject from a slightly different angle. We must learn to recognize the specifically christological import of these verses and use that as a basis upon which to proceed. Could we approach these verses from the standpoint of their ability to contribute to the larger theocentric/christocentric issue?

Such an approach is certainly not without its problems. Recently J. Christiaan Beker[63] has attempted to elucidate Paul's theology on the basis that it is rooted and grounded in an apocalyptic world-view. Beker notes the fact that the transformation of theology into christology within the history of the Church runs parallel to the de-eschatologizing of Paul's eschatology. This, Beker feels, results in a severe misinterpretation of Paul's thought.[64] He concludes (p. 363) that:

> Paul's apocalyptic theocentrism, then, is not to be contrasted with his Christocentric thinking, for the final hour of the glory of Christ and his Parousia will coincide with the glory of God, that is, with the actualization of the redemption of God's created order in his Kingdom.

Beker is quite right in insisting that we must not allow a false contrast to be set up between Paul's apocalyptic theocentrism[65] and his christology. At the same time Beker perhaps goes too far when he implicitly suggests that any developing christology is necessarily an abandonment of such an apocalyptic outlook. There is much within the apocalyptic texts themselves which provides the bais for an increasingly exalted christology.[66] Thus, we dare not allow ourselves to overlook the critical christological messages which are contained within many of the Pauline eschatological texts. Therefore, it may be much more fruitful to conduct our eschatological investigations with an eye toward their accompanying christological content. An investigation of the awaited Parousia and the eternal bliss it brings is most valuable, not for its ability to provide us with eschatological precision (which is by its very nature unobtainable), but for its ability to provide us with the setting in which christological proclamation can occur and be detected. On this basis, let us attempt an interpretation of 1 Cor. 15.20-28.

C. *The Christological Message of 1 Cor. 15.20-28*

The christological importance of 1 Cor. 15.20-28 is the subject of a recent article by J. Lambrecht.[67] As Lambrecht[68] clearly points out, the inter-relationship between theocentric and christocentric poles is at the heart of this passage. Just who is being spoken of in the various individual clauses of these few, brief verses? Which phrases have God as subject and which have Christ as subject? Are there any grounds for detecting a change of subject (from God to Christ or vice versa) within this passage and if so, at what point?

We are thrown into the midst of such questions when we note how Paul has adapted Ps. 110.1c in v. 25.[69] Several differences from the LXX occur, including (1) the interpretative reference to Christ's reign on earth (δεῖ γὰρ αὐτὸν βασιλεύειν) as a substitute for the LXX κάθου ἐκ δεξιῶν μου, (2) the replacement of ἕως ἄν by the more temporally explicit ἄχρι οὗ, (3) the addition of πάντας, (4) the replacement of ὑποπόδιον τῶν ποδῶν σου with ὑπὸ τοὺς πόδας αὐτοῦ (probably through the influence of Ps. 8.6, quoted in v. 27, (5) the change of grammatical subject from God (θῷ) in the Psalm to Christ (θῇ).[70]

It is the final point which is most important for our discussion. Nowhere else in the New Testament or in the early Christian quotation from or allusion to this Psalm does such a change occur. Seven out of the eight other known references to Ps. 110.1c retain the θῷ (cf. Mt. 22.44; Mk 12.36; Lk. 20.43; Acts 2.35; Heb. 1.13; *1 Clement* 36.5; *Barnabas* 12.10).[71] The only exception is Heb. 10.13, where οἱ ἐχθροι becomes the subject by force of the passive τεθῶσιν. Given that Christ is obviously the subject of 25a (δεῖ γὰρ αὐτὸν βασιλεύειν) it is quite natural that we should take there to be no change of subject for the remainder of the sentence (ἄχρι οὗ θῇ πάντας τοὺς ἐχθροὺς ὑπὸ τοὺς πόδας αὐτοῦ).[72] The rather loose quotation and reworking of the Psalm tends to support such a consistency of Christ as subject by allowing easy transfer of the contents of the Psalm from God to him. It thus appears that Paul has reworked the Psalm in order to serve his christological interest. We see quite clearly that an Old Testament function of God described in Ps. 110.1 (the subjugation of Israel's enemies)[73] becomes the activity of Christ in 1 Cor. 15.25.

If we are correct thus far we have a solution for another of the ambiguities within the passage the subject of καταργήσῃ in 24c. It has been argued that God is the subject of this verb and the whole passage decidedly theocentric.[74] However, since 24c and 25b are obviously parallels, both denoting the subjugation of enemies, the subject of καταργήσῃ is the same as 25b—Christ. Thus far we are on fairly sure ground and I would have little difficulty in agreeing with Lambrecht's analysis. It is, however, when he extends this christo-centric interpretation of the passage to include 27a that difficulties arise. More precisely, the issue revolves around the subject of ὑπέταξεν in 27a. Lambrecht takes Christ to be the subject. Such an interpretation ignores, however, the parallel in thought between the whole of vv. 27 and 28. In other words, 27a is the parallel of 28a and both speak of the subjugation of all things under the feet of Christ by God (note the passive ὑποταγῇ!). We should take God to be the subject and interpret the verse theocentrically instead. In so doing we are also able thereby to retain God as the consistent subject of ὑποτάξαντος in 27c and ὑποτάξαντι in 28b.[75] The clear force of 27b as a reference to the work of God is additionally brought into union with the thought of 27a.

This whole modification to Lambrecht's argument is made more sure by the clear quotation of Ps. 8.6 (LXX) in 27a which would naturally retain its original subject, God (in contrast to the less clear quotation of Ps. 110.1b in v. 25, which has undergone transposition and has Christ as subject).[76] In short, I would assert that 1 Cor. 15.23-28 contains a unique. blending of christocentricity and theocentricity. We see the christocentric facet first in vv. 23 to 26 and the theocentric facet next in vv. 27 to 28. It is perhaps not surprising that these same verse divisions (vv. 23-26 and 27-28) embody the references to Ps. 110.1 and Ps. 8.6 respectively.

One final piece of evidence helps to confirm this fluctuation between the christocentric and theocentric facets of this passage in 1 Corinthians. The connection between Ps. 110.1 and Dan. 7.13 is evident within the earliest strata of our Gospels (Mk 14.62); it is just possible that Dan. 7.27b (the LXX reads: καὶ πᾶσαι ἐξουσίαι αὐτῷ ὑποταγήσονται) provides the inspiration for, or at least contributed to, the idea of the subjugation of God's enemies in 1 Cor. 15.24ff.[77] If so, once again we have the referent of αὐτῷ changed from God in the LXX to Christ in the Pauline passage. In short, it appears that the phrase αὐτῷ in Dan. 7.27b is solved christologically by Paul in 1 Cor. 15.24ff. This is in spite of the fact that the Daniel passage in the LXX associates αὐτῷ with the people of God (λαῷ ἁγίῳ ὑψίστου).

We saw above that Ps. 110.1 was frequently employed by the early Church to fill out the christological message of the resurrection. Ps. 8.6 was often used to amplify this christological use of the enthronement Psalm and often occurs in conjunction with the more frequently occurring Ps. 110.1 (cf. Eph. 1.20-22; Heb. 1.13-2.8; Mk 12.36; Mt. 22.44; 1 Pet. 3.22). Perhaps the combination of the two texts, which was apparently an early Christian phenomenon,[78] paved the way for a functional and conceptual overlap between Christ and God in which the original messianic connections of Ps. 110.1[79] easily led to its christological use and to emphasis on Christ as the one who subjects all things unto himself in his rule as messianic King.[80] At the same time, the parallel note of the subjugation of the created order by God contained in Psalm 8 paradoxically retains its original subject (God) and does not undergo the same christological process.[81] The natural attraction between the two Psalms is partly a linguistic one (note the τῶν ποδῶν σου of Ps. 110.1 and the τῶν ποδῶν αὐτοῦ of Ps. 8.6), and partly a conceptual one centering on the idea of the subjugation of God's enemies.

It has been recently argued by J.D.G. Dunn[82] that the use of Ps. 8.6 by Paul is an extension of his Adamic christology and that the context of the preceding verses of the Psalm (vv. 4-6) are determinative in this regard:

> What is man that you are mindful of him, and the son of man that you care for him? You made him a little less than the angels, and crowned him with glory and honour, and set him over the work of your hands.

Several points need to be made in response. First, we have no way of determining whether or not the larger context of the Psalm has any necessary bearing on Paul's use of 6b. We simply do not know if Paul had the status of man in mind at all. To insist on the point is to run the risk of missing the crucial fluctuation between the christo-centric and theocentric sections of the passage. Furthermore, it can easily be demonstrated that early Christian authors often quoted from the Old Testament with little or no regard for the context of their quotation.[83] Secondly, even if such anthropological considerations were a constitutive element in Paul's mind here, we are still left with the clear theocentric thrust of 8.6b itself. There is no doubt that God is the one who subjects all things under the feet of man and that the focus is on the Lord's glory and majesty, as the even larger context of vv. 1-3 demonstrate. An appeal to the context of the Psalm is a double-edged sword and works for a theocentric interpretation as well.

In short, there is little to be said for the necessity of interpreting the quotation of Ps. 8.6 in 1 Cor. 15.27a christocentrically. There is at least an equal justification for interpreting the verse theocentrically. If so, we are left with the paradoxical juxtaposition of twin subjugation psalms, consecutively quoted, in which within the first section (vv. 23-26) Christ is the active subjugating agent and ruler of the Kingdom, while in the second (vv. 27-28) God is the active subjugating agent and any messianic rule is placed within the larger context of the ultimate rule and authority of God the Father. The independent spheres of meaning of the original context of these two Psalms within the early Church are probably responsible for such a phenomenon.[84]

Moreover, the close proximity into which these two Psalms are brought by their mutual subject matter of subjugation appears to have paved the way for a conceptual overlap and referential confusion between Christ and God, if the other Pauline quotation of Ps. 8.6 is any indication.

We catch a glimpse of this conceptual overlap when we turn to Phil. 3.21, the only allusion to Ps. 8.6 independent of Ps. 110.1 in the New Testament.[85] There we read that: ὅς (Christ) μετασχηματίσει τὸ σῶμα τῆς ταπεινώσεως ἡμῶν σόμμορφον τῷ σώματι τῆς δόξης αὐτοῦ κατὰ τὴν ἐνέργειαν τοῦ δύνασθαι αὐτὸν καὶ ὑποτάξαι αὐτῷ τὰ πάντα. Far from employing this passage as the capstone of an Adamic interpretation of Christology,[86] we should recognize the tremendous step it takes in bringing Christ and God into a conceptual overlap. For here in Phil. 3.21 we have Ps. 8.6, clearly associated with Christ as subject, and thereby serving a specifically christological interest. This stands in contradistinction to 1 Cor. 15.27-28, where the same Psalm is used to emphasize God as subject. If we are correct in our interpretation and analysis of 1 Cor. 15.20-28 we are left with no other conclusion than to recognize that a transference of referent has occurred between Christ and God with respect to the Psalm. Thus it appears that a conceptual overlap underlies the use of Ps. 8.6 in Phil. 3.21 and 1 Cor. 15.27a.

Not only does the christological shift from θῷ in Ps. 110.1 to θῇ in 1 Cor. 15.25 point to this overlap, but so too does the highly revealing use of Psalm 8 within the Pauline epistles. It is one thing to maintain a distinction of subject betweem the two halves of the eschatological passage of 1 Cor. 15.23-28 based upon traditional associations of the relevant Psalms; but the use of Ps. 8.6 in Phil. 3.21 is quite another matter. In the chronologically later Philippian passage theocentrism gives way to christocentrism and Christ assumes the prime role within the sense of the Psalm. Comparatively speaking, that is when we examine the use of Ps. 8.6 in both 1 Cor. 15.27a and Phil. 3.21, we can say that a definite transference of referent has occurred which serves as some indication of a conceptual overlap in Paul's mind.

Much of the time it is impossible to decide whether by the future Age Paul means the Messianic Age to Come or the Eternal Age to Come. Only occasionally, as in 1 Cor. 15.20-28, are the vestiges of a two-stage eschatology of Messianic Age and Eternal Age discernible. As we saw above, it appears that the conceptual overlap in Paul's mind between Christ and God is closely related to eschatological imprecision with regards to the relationship of the Messianic Kingdom to the Eternal Age to Come. This conceptual overlap is highlighted by the theocentric/christocentric fluctuation which surrounds Paul's discussions about the future.

We are now in a position to note again briefly the other two references to a Kingdom of Christ within the Pauline corpus. Above it was mentioned that Col. 1.13f. and Eph. 5.5 both contained references to this Kingdom. Both passages help to demonstrate the way in which the presence of a βασιλεία τοῦ Χριστοῦ tends to prepare the way for the conceptual confusion and overlap described above. This is evidenced first of all by the christological hymn which immediately follows the reference to βασιλεία in Col. 1.13. There can be little doubt that this christological hymn of Col. 1.15-20 refers to the cosmic Christ in language deliberately designed to induce reflections about God himself.[87]

Secondly, it is no wonder that in Eph. 5.5 we find the curious dual qualification τοῦ Χριστοῦ καὶ θεοῦ as descriptive of the singular βασιλείαν. We are perhaps not amiss, in the light of our discussion above, in translating the phrase as Bengel did so long ago, 'the Kingship of the Messiah, that is of God'.[88]

2. ESCHATOLOGICAL THEOCENTRISM AND CHRISTOCENTRISM: A SUMMARY COMPARISON OF JEWISH PSEUDEPIGRAPHAL LITERATURE AND PAUL

Finally, it is possible for us now to note that 1 Cor. 15.20-28 helps us to focus our attention on the crucial theocentric/christocentric fluctuation which occurs in Paul's teaching. The passage also enables us to consider how Paul's eschatological teaching compares with the observations noted within our survey of selected Jewish pseudepigraphal documents which display a similar fluctuation on this issue. In our study of those pseudepigraphal works we concluded by noting four such relevant observations. Let us now see how Paul's eschatological teaching compares with each of these observations in turn.

A. *Diversity of Detail and Schematization*

We noted in connection with our study of *1 Enoch*, *4 Ezra* and *2 Baruch* that all of these pseudepigraphal works, as they now stand, display competing eschatological schematizations. This speaks for a dynamic and fluid atmosphere of eschatological speculations which can be helpfully applied to our interpretation of the Pauline epistles. In other words, we should not be too hasty to construct a composite picture of Paul's eschatology and to conduct our exegesis of individual passages rigidly on that basis. If our investigations into the Jewish pseudepigraphal literature have yielded anything, they have shown the remarkable diversity of constituent eschatological texts with respect to order and detail.

The obvious Pauline evidence for the same phenomenon is readily seen when we consider that 1 Cor. 15.20-28, in all probability, reflects a slightly different eschatological schematization than most of the rest of his writings on the subject, such as 1 Thess. 4.13–5.11 or 2 Cor. 5.1-10. At the very least, we must admit that there are some grounds for interpreting 1 Cor. 15.20-28 as reflective of belief in a temporary, Messianic Kingdom on earth which lies in the future.

We might also explain the differing viewpoints of 1 Thessalonians and 2 Thessalonians with respect to the nearness of the Parousia of Christ as an additional manifestation of such diversity of eschatological detail. Here the essence of the argument has been the fact that 1 Thessalonians seems to expect the Parousia of Christ at any moment, while 2 Thessalonians seems to set down several preconditions for Christ's Second Advent. Finally, we have also had occasion to note brief indications of the diversity of eschatological detail in the course of our study, such as the plural τέλη in 1 Cor. 10.11. All of which means that 1 Cor. 15.20-28, in particular, must be allowed to stand independently and must be interpreted without being rigidly forced to conform to the pattern of other eschatological sections of Paul's epistles.

We also noted that within the pseudepigraphal materials there is little, if any, concern that such diversity registers as inconsistency on the part of the final author(s) or redactor(s). The same comment can be made with respect to 1 Cor. 15.20-28. There is no indication that Paul's teaching regarding a future Kingdom of Christ within that passage is in any way necessarily incompatible with the much more prevalent teaching of the present reality of that Kingdom. About all we can say on this point is that the impact of the resurrection of Christ upon Paul's eschatology is such that it renders the futuristic aspect of the Messianic Kingdom, such as is represented by 1 Cor. 15.20-28, secondary. It is probably for this reason that Paul only rarely speaks of the Kingdom of Christ as a strictly future event. Even so, it does seem that when occasion demands Paul can still assert, paradoxically, the future, Messianic Kingdom without fear of contradicting his teaching with regard to its present reality. We would do well to recognize that the brief, but much-debated section 1 Cor. 15.20-28 represents an example of diversity of detail within Paul's eschatological writings and brings him very near to other examples of such phenomenon we noted within the pseudepigraphal documents.

B. *Functional Overlap between God and Christ*

Within our discussion of Jewish pseudepigraphal documents which speak of a final eschatological judgment, we noted that when a messianic agent is involved there is a great deal of functional overlap between God and Messiah in discharging that judgment. In addition, we noted in Chapter 2 that Paul's eschatological teaching is also characterized by a similar functional overlap between God and Christ. We initially noted this functional overlap within the occurrences of βῆμα in Rom. 14.10 and 2 Cor. 5.10. We saw that the first passage was primarily theocentric in emphasis while the second was primarily christocentric in emphasis.

In addition, this functional overlap is seen most clearly by the way in which the theocentric Day of the Lord Yahweh has become christocentrically reinterpreted by Paul in terms of the Day of the Lord Christ. In this connection, we have noted how frequent it is that theocentric Old Testament passages have been redrafted so as to serve an abiding christocentric interest. We have also seen some evidence, here in this chapter, for a similar sort of theocentric/ christocentric overlap by the way in which Ps. 110.1 and 8.6 are used within the Pauline corpus, particularly in 1 Cor. 15.20-28 and Phil. 3.20-21. In short, it seems clear that Paul's eschatological writings are perfectly compatible with those select pseudepigraphal documents which we examined, notably *4 Ezra* and *2 Baruch*, in that they all clearly demonstrate an underlying functional overlap involving Messiah and God. This functional overlap is seen both in Paul's teaching on the Final Parousia and within his teaching on the Messianic Kingdom.

C. *Presence of Textual Variants*

We noted that within the Jewish pseudepigraphal literature we studied a number of significant textual variants are extant within passages which speak of God and messianic agent together in an eschatological context. The most important instance of this occurs in the Vision of the Man Rising from the Sea in *4 Ezra* 13. The variety of such emandations is a small index of the conceptual overlap which exists between God and messianic agent throughout the textual history of the document concerned.

In other words, passages which originally contained an ambiguity or inexactitude involving the subject (God or Messiah?) eventually find themselves burdened with a complex textual history which reflects attempts to resolve the question of referent. We also note that the same phenomenon occurs in eschatological sections of Paul's epistles, also apparently as an attempt to smooth out any referential difficulties. We noted, for instance, that the reference to the Kingdom of Christ (βασιλεία τοῦ Χριστοῦ) in Eph. 5.5 is beset with textual corrections. The same phenomenon also occurs with reference to βῆμα τοῦ θεοῦ in Rom. 14.10. In short, the subsequent textual emendations in certain key passages are indicative of a resident tension between theocentrism and christocentrism. The critical question is whether these textual emendations are catalysts for or merely reflections of the conceptual overlap involving theocentricity and christocentricity. We have tried to answer this difficult point, in part, by pointing out the close connection between such variants and the awkward task of conceptualizing the future in terms of either a Messianic Kingdom or the Eternal Age of God. In other words, the problem of describing the future, in terms of either a Messianic Kingdom or an Eternal Age of God, itself contributes to an atmosphere in which referential confusion might easily reign. Thus it seems reasonable to suggest that the complicated textual corrections and variations that occur on this point arise precisely because of an inherent ambiguity or conceptual overlap in the original texts themselves. I would suggest that the textual variations are reflections of a conceptual overlap involving God and Messiah and would insist that the subsequent alternative readings demonstrate the continuing problems some of these texts presented to later generations with regard to their subject matter, especially as they relate directly to the theocentric/christocentric question.

D. *Identification of Christ and God within a Monotheistic Tradition*

We noted that within select documents of the Jewish pseudepigrapha, namely *4 Ezra*, *2 Baruch* and *3 Enoch*, the functional overlap between God and Messiah is such that an identification between the two is set up. Theocentric boundaries are breached and the Messiah seems to have penetrated into divine territory. All of this takes place within writings which, at the same time, display a strong monotheistic tradition.

We have also suggested that one way in which this monotheistic tradition was preserved and protected was by the creative reworking of traditional eschatological schematizations in such a way that the Messiah is relegated to a temporary, earthly rule which is succeeded by the Eternal Age. In other words, the teaching of a temporary, Messianic Kingdom serves as a modicum of control and establishes the subordination of the Messiah to God within temporal terms. Our study of the Pauline teaching of the Messiah and the Kingdom indicates that, with only one possible exception (1 Corithians 15.20-28), this means of resolving the theocentric/christocentric problem was not pursued by the apostle, probably because of the impact of the Christ-event itself upon his theology.

However, is there any other evidence of how Paul sought to solve the theocentric/christocentric problem resident within much of the eschatological material within his epistles? Given the fact that for Paul the proleptic arrival of the Messianic Kingdom has necessitated a re-evaluation of his understanding of eschatology, in what ways does he appear to integrate his Jewish monotheism with his developing christology and handle the essential question of theocentricity and christocentricity? I believe there are one or two brief indications of attempts at such a resolution. They all involve in some way a subordination of Christ to God by means of a clarifying word or phrase within these very eschatological passages. Let us briefly examine three such indications of subordination.

1. *Ultimate Subordination—1 Cor. 15.28c*
The first, and most obvious, example of such subordination of Christ to God involves the phrase with which the section of 1 Cor. 15.20-28 concludes ἵνα ᾖ ὁ θεὸς τὰ πάντα ἐν πᾶσιν.[89] The meaning of this curious phrase is difficult to establish with precision. The ἵνα clause as a whole is dependent upon the verb ὑποταγήσεται in 28b and not upon the participle ὑποτάξαντι in the same clause.[90] Thus the note of Jesus' subordination is seen within the larger context of God's ultimate authority and rule. C.F.D. Moule states that the phrase may derive from 'a pantheistic cliché of Stoicism'.[91] There are other similar uses of πάντα and πᾶσιν in combination within the Pauline epistles, notably Col. 3.11 and Eph. 1.23. Whatever its ultimate source, this phrase of 1 Cor. 15.28c seems to speak of a proper relationship existing between God (ὁ θεός) and his creation (τὰ πάντα).[92]

The absolute use of ὁ υἱός in 1 Cor. 15.28b is another puzzling feature of the passage. This is especially noteworthy since it is the only time within the Pauline corpus that such an absolute use of ὁ υἱός occurs.[93] The old suggestion that it is a veiled reminder of ὁ υἱός τοῦ ἀνθρώπου remains unproven. It seems fair to suggest that the absolute form is a balance to the ὁ θεός which follows in 15.28c. Indeed, it may be that such a juxtaposition is in itself responsible for the absolute form of ὁ υἱός in 15.28b.

Oscar Cullmann calls this passage of 1 Cor. 15.28 'the key to all New Testament Christology'.[94] Such comment is prompted because the passage expresses so clearly the revelational unity of Jesus (ὁ υἱός) and God (ὁ θεός). Thus it is an ideal illustration of Cullmann's thesis that 'all Christology is Heilsgeschichte' and is functional rather than ontological in nature.[95] Such a functional/ ontological dichotomy as Cullmann suggests flows directly from his understanding of the nature of *Heilsgeschichte* itself and is exegetically somewhat forced. Certainly we can say that in 15.28c Paul closes the eschatological section of 15.20-28 on a theocentric note; but this final theocentric affirmation may arise precisely because the christocentric content of the previous verses impinged upon the ontological territory of God so much that the note of subordination of Christ to God was thought to be necessary as a concluding remark.

The nearest parallel in the Pauline corpus to the sense of 1 Cor. 15.28c is found in Eph. 1.10b, where it is said that 'all things will be summed up in Christ' (ἀνακεφαλαιώσασθαι τὰ πάντα ἐν τῷ Χριστῷ). The comprehensiveness of τὰ πάντα is further spelled out in 1.10c as 'the things in the heavens and upon the earth' (τὰ ἐπὶ τοῖς οὐρανοῖς καὶ ἐπὶ τῆς γῆς). The critical note of comparison with 1 Cor. 15.28c is the verb ἀνακεφαλαιώσασθαι.[96] Of related importance in the Pauline description of Christ as the 'head' (κεφαλή).[97] This occurs in 1 Cor. 11.3; Eph. 1.22; 4.15; 5.23; Col. 1.18; 2.10. 19. All these references establish an hierarchical order of authority with mankind being subordinated to Christ. In the Corinthians reference the hierarchical structure includes God as well and Christ is specifically said to be subordinated to God (κεφαλὴ δὲ τοῦ Χριστοῦ ὁ θεός). This statement is very reminiscent of 1 Cor. 3.23, where Paul constructs a relational hierarchy which concludes with the statement: 'you belong to Christ, but Christ belongs to God' (ὑμεῖς δὲ Χριστοῦ, Χριστὸς δὲ θεοῦ).

To return to the use of ἀνακεφαλαιώσασθαι in Eph. 1.10b, it is worth noting that no clear subordinating phrase comparable to 1 Cor. 15.28c is contained there. To be sure, the theocentric tone of the passage is not very far away (vv. 3-6 seem to have God as their operative subject); but a subordinating phrase along the lines of 1 Cor. 15.28c is absent. Exactly the same point can be made with reference to Col. 1.18c. There we find another christological statement in the phrase 'in order that he himself might be first in all things' (ἵνα γένηται ἐν πᾶσιν αὐτὸς πρωτεύων). If we take the verb πρωτεύω to have roughly the same meaning as ἀνακεφαλαιόω, we note that once again there is an absence of any direct theocentric qualifier like 1 Cor. 15.28c.[98]

In short, the christologically subordinating remark of Paul in 1 Cor. 15.28c is clear and unambiguous. This note of 'Ultimate Subordination' does not seem to have been universally sounded, as Eph. 1.10b and Col. 1.18c both indicate by their lack of a similar qualifying phrase. The concluding remark of 1.28c does seem to represent an attempt at resolving the theocentric/christocentric issue within one section of Paul's eschatological teaching.

2. Subordination in Worship—Phil. 2.11c

A second example of subordination of Christ to God within an eschatological context occurs in the much-discussed hymn, Phil. 2.6-11. Here, once again, the critical phrase is the concluding one of the passage: εἰς δόξαν θεοῦ πατρός.

The immediate question that arises when considering this phrase is whether or not it is a Pauline addition to the pre-Pauline hymn. It seems to me that such an explanation best suits the facts presently at our disposal.[99] Martin describes the phrase itself as the 'liturgical conclusion of the entire hymn'.[100] This is probably correct, but it is much more important for our considerations to examine *why* Paul has added, or included,[101] this line in 11c. Käsemann suggests that it was inserted by Paul specifically to express a subordinationist christology.[102] Käsemann's point is sound, even if one questions his attempt to relate it to an act of cosmic reconciliation through Christ's obedience to the Father.

The phrase εἰς (τὴν) δόξαν is a common one within Paul's writings, as Jeremias noted long ago.[103] It occurs in Rom. 3.7; 15.7; 1 Cor. 10.31; 2 Cor. 4.15; Phil. 1.11 and 1 Thess. 2.12. It is worth noting that in each of these six occurrences it is always the glory of God (δόξαν τοῦ θεοῦ) which is meant. At the same time, the christological message is not far away since in several of them, notably Rom. 15.7 and Phil. 1.11, the theocentric phrase is the culminating point of a christocentric statement.

In short it is not unreasonable to suggest that Phil. 2.11c was originally inserted into the christological hymn as a liturgical response. This response was specifically designed to preserve and protect the interests of Jewish monotheism and to interject a note of theocentrism within a highly exalted christocentric formulation of worship. Thus it is but one small indication of one way in which the christocentric/theocentric issue was handled within the early church. The very presence of such a qualifying phrase as εἰς δόξαν θεοῦ πατρός indicates something of the way in which Jewish monotheism expressed itself in light of the exaltation of Christ. Perhaps the integrity of such a monotheistic faith is preserved not by rigidly avoiding any instance in which God and Christ are functionally, or even ontologically identified,[104] but by the interjection of a clearly theistic element as the concluding remark in a given passage, such as we have here in 2.11c.[105]

3. *Nominal Clarification as Subordination*
One related observation needs to be made in connection with our discussion of the subordination of Christ to God as a theme. It involves the clarification of potentially ambiguous κύριος passages with the interjection of a nominal qualifier such as Ἰησοῦς or Χριστός or both. While this interjection does not strictly constitute subordination proper, it is, nevertheless, a parallel phenomenon designed to distinguish between the Lord (God) and the Lord (Jesus Christ).

In Chapter 2 we tried to demonstrate how Old Testament theocentric passages were transformed into christocentric ones. There we noted that one way in which this reinterpretation progressed was via the referential shift of κύριος from God to Christ. We also noted that many times this referential shift involved eschatological passages from Old Testament theophanies and took place in an environment conditioned by the conceptual overlap between God and messianic agent with respect to the execution of Final Judgment.

Here I would like to call attention to the fact that most of the references to the 'Day of the Lord' in the Pauline epistles are not left simply with the reference to κύριος unsupported or unclarified. This is true regardless of whether or not the reference includes a referential shift of κύριος from God to Christ in the manner involving Old Testament theophanies just described. For instance, we note that the nominal qualifier Ἰησοῦς is inserted in 1 Thess.

2.19; 3.13; 1 Cor. 1.8; 2 Cor. 1.14. With the exception of 1 Thess. 3.13, none of these references includes a direct allusion to an Old Testament theocentric text which has been christocentrically reinterpreted. In a similar manner, we also note that the dual nominal qualifier Ἰησοῦ occurs in 1 Thess. 5.23 and 1 Cor. 1.17. Again there is no direct Old Testament theocentric passage involved in either of these passages.

At times the immediate context of the passage concerned yields the clarification on this point. We see this, for instance, in 2 Thess. 2.2 (where κυρίου Ἰησοῦ Χριστοῦ is supplied by 2.1); 1 Cor. 11.26 (where κύριος Ἰησοῦς is supplied by 11.23); 2 Thess. 1.10 (where κυρίου Ἰησοῦ is supplied by 1.7); and 1 Thess. 4.15 (where Χριστῷ is supplied by 4.16).[106] Even in 1 Cor. 5.5 we see a number of textual variants within the tradition (mostly focusing on Ἰησοῦ and Ἰησοῦ Χριστοῦ), all designed to clarify the ambiguous κύριος which occurs there.

Only in 1 Thess. 5.2 and 1 Cor. 4.5 is ὁ κύριος not immediately qualified in some clear and decisive way. However, with regards to 1 Thess. 5.2, we might easily attach the reference to the larger context of 4.13–5.11 and clarify it in that manner. That leaves us with 1 Cor. 4.5 and its ambiguous reference to the 'coming of the Lord' (ἕως ἂν ἔλθῃ ὁ κύριος). Here the appeal to the immediate context is not very helpful since we have a mention of God in 4.1 and 4.5 and a mention of Christ in 4.1. We should not, however, overlook the fact that subordination of Christ to God is quite clearly spelled out in 3.23. Although this does not help us to solve absolutely who the κύριος of 4.4 is (God or Christ?), it does make any future judgment of Paul's conduct take place in the climate of Christ's subordination to God.

One final observation on this matter is worth noting. It appears that the ambiguous phrase 'Day of the Lord' was, almost without exception, qualified within the Pauline epistles. Can we detect any consistency in *how* it was qualified? Does Paul have a preference for which phrases he uses as qualifiers and can these be chronologically estimated? The evidence seems to me to suggest that some shift in the nominal qualifiers used has occurred during the course of Paul's epistolary ministry. It appears that, at least initially, the Parousia was known as the 'Day of the Lord *Jesus*', as the majority of reerences in the Thessalonian correspondence and in the Corinthian correspondence indicate. We also see the use of the 'Day of the Lord *Jesus*'

Christ' in 1 Cor. 1.7 and 5.5. In other words, it seems that the 'Jesus' component is crucial within any qualification in the earlier epistles. In the later Pauline epistles this 'Jesus' component is still occasionally used, as in Phil. 1.6, but its link with κύριος is not maintained. More frequently, we note that the phrase 'Day of Christ' serves as the norm, as in Phil. 1.10; 2.16; Col. 3.4. Perhaps this shift is indicative of a corresponding change of emphasis away from the human appellative 'Jesus' to an ever-increasing titular assessment of his life and ministry.

3. CONCLUDING SUMMARY

In this chapter we examined Paul's concept of the Messianic Kingdom and sought to explore that theme for what it could reveal to us about his christological thought. We focused particularly on the cryptic passage of 1 Cor. 15.20-28 in this regard and have used that passage as a forum to conduct our investigation. Within this critical text we noted that there is an important fluctuation between a theocentric facet (vv. 23-26) and a christocentric facet (vv. 27-28). This fluctuation is reminiscent of a similar phenomenon which occurs in several Jewish pseudepigraphal documents, notably *4 Ezra* and *2 Baruch* (discussed in Chapter 1).

Indeed, it is perhaps not surprising that 1 Cor. 15.23-28 has been interpreted by some as sharing the eschatological scheme which appears to underlie sections of those documents. That is to say, that 1 Cor. 15.23-28 may itself reflect the belief in an earthly, Messianic Kingdom of temperorary duration which eventually gives way to the Eternal Age to Come. To be sure, this bifurcated hope is modified within most of the rest of Paul's eschatological teaching in such a way that the future Parousia of Christ is generally viewed as the consummation of the Messianic Kingdom, instead of its inauguration. Nevertheless, this difficult passage of 1 Cor. 15.23-28 seems to slip into the same schematization we noted in both *4 Ezra* and *2 Baruch* and it is entirely possible to interpret the Corinthian passage in that light.

More importantly, we have sought to explore the question of theocentricity and its relationship to christocentricity within the eschatological sections of the Pauline letters by comparing them with the results of our investigations into the eschatological sections of selected Jewish pseudepigraphal documents. There are several ways in which Jewish pseudepigraphal documents provide important parallels to the Pauline eschatological passages and hep us in interpreting them. For instance, in our earlier study of the eschatological teaching of *4 Ezra* and *2 Baruch*, we noted the way in which both documents demonstrate a remarkable diversity with respect to eschatological detail. In addition, a complex history of alternative readings is present within the extant translation of some key eschatological passages in those two Jewish documents. We also noted that both documents contained passages which displayed a firmly monotheistic theocentrism (such as *4 Ezra* 5.56-6.6 and *2 Baruch* 21.7-10). This theocentric aspect is to be viewed alongside passages which spoke of the Messiah in very exalted terms, and we noted how there was a functional overlap between God and messianic agent which frequently manifests itself as a conceptual confusion between them. At times this conceptual confusion is so complete as to suggest an outright identification of messianic agent with God (as in some editions of *Ezra* 13).

Finally, we have suggested that it appears to be the case that one way in which this confusion involving God and messianic agent was partially resolved within some of the pseudepigraphal texts was by the relegation of the Messiah to an earthly rule of temporary duration. All of these summary points we found to harmonize, to a remarkable degree, with our observations about the Pauline eschatological passages and the way in which the respective roles of God and Christ are handled within such passages. Paul does not appear to pursue the teaching of a temporary, Messianic Kingdom beyond 1 Cor. 15.20-28, but he does attempt to clarify the respective roles of God and Messiah in other ways. We noted various ways in which Paul has directly addressed the theocentric/christocentric issue and interjected, or preserved, a note of subordination of Christ to God in several key places. In short, the concept of the Kingdom, whether earthly or not, and the role the Messiah has in that Kingdom, are important areas which display the close connection between the christological and eschatological dimensions of Paul's thought.

Chapter 4

CONCLUSIONS

Within our study we have been concerned with the question of theocentricity and christocentricity as it is expressed in Paul's eschatological thought. We have demonstrated that Paul's eschatological thought displays a remarkable degree of conceptual overlap between God and Christ in such a way that Christ is specifically identified with God. At the same time, we have noted briefly the manner and way in which Paul clarifies and qualifies the nature of this identification by means of the subordination of Christ to God in several key places. Thus, we have found the eschatological passages within the Pauline corpus an important forum for christological expression and an invaluable aid in understanding how Paul presents the respective eschatological roles of both God and Christ.

In examining Paul's eschatological teaching and its christological significance, we have pursued our study in the Pauline material along two separate but related paths: (1) Paul's doctrine of the Parousia and Final Judgment; (2) Paul's concept of the Messiah and the Kingdom. It appears reasonable to suggest that there is an important connection between these two categories of thought which allows us to concentrate on the critical question of how theocentricity and christocentricity interrelate. This connection focuses on Paul's conception of the Messianic Kingdom and its relationship to the Eternal Age to Come. It is in considering the relationship between these two categories that the messianic role is highlighted and brought to the center of discussion. Only then are we able to grasp how much the roles of God and Messiah interweave within the eschatological hopes of Paul. In conclusion, we would argue that both categories of Paul's thought, his belief in the Parousia and Final Judgment as well as his concept of the Messianic Kingdom, contain reflections of a conceptual tension between Christ and God and are thus extremely valuable for investigating the theocentric/christo-centric issue.

With respect to method, throughout our study we have seen the value of using relevant Jewish pseudepigraphal documents, as well as other supportive documents including the Qumran sectarian literature, as a means to illuminate the Pauline material. Indeed, Chapter 1 was specifically concerned with determining which of these various Jewish pseudepigraphal writings might legitimately be said to teach a 'bifurcated' eschatological hope and assessing the contribution such a belief had to make to our understanding of such texts. This 'bifurcated' eschatological hope is best described as a 'two-stage' process in which the Messiah enjoys an earthly rule of temporary duration which eventually gives way to the heavenly, Eternal Age of God. The importance of establishing which documents contain a doctrine of the temporary, Messianic Kingdom is to be seen in that the messianic role is therein more clearly defined in relation to the Eternal Age to Come. We are able to observe precisely how the messianic role overlaps with that of God by a careful comparison of both facets of the 'bifurcated' eschatological hope.

In particular, we saw that sections of *1 Enoch*, *4 Ezra* and *2 Baruch* are especially relevant in this regard, and we examined the eschatological teaching of each of these works in detail so as to understand better how the temporary, Messianic Kingdom functions within each book as a whole. Concurrently, our examination of the Jewish pseudepigraphal literature and the supportive documents enabled us to correct, or at least temper, some scholarly assumptions about other eschatological texts (such as *Jubilees*, *2 Enoch*, *Sibylline Oracles*) which are frequently asserted to express belief in a temporary, Messianic Kingdom. We discovered that some long-standing scholarly assumptions about these documents need to be jettisoned.

But why this extended investigation into Jewish pseudepigraphal literature? The short answer is that a study of how the 'bifurcated' eschatological hope was expressed within Jewish pseudepigraphal literature inevitably enables us to consider more carefully the question of theocentricity and christocentricity as it is handled within Paul's letters. The results gained from our study of the Jewish pseudepigraphal documents help set the parameters of discussion of eschatological texts in general and can be usefully applied to the Pauline material with regard to this crucial issue. This clarification of the methodological procedure is one of the most important contributions of our study.

With respect to the Pauline material itself, several important observations arise from our investigations. The first of these, as just noted, involves the place of Jewish pseudepigraphal documents in helping to understand the New Testament materials. This is particularly important with regard to the debate about the origin of the Parousia doctrine. Therefore, in our study of the Parousia and the Final Judgment in Paul (Chapter 2) we discussed the scholarly investigations into the origins of these two motifs and asserted the importance of Jewish pseudepigraphal material in illuminating those origins. In particular, we are critical of those attempts to undermine the relevance of *1 Enoch* 37-71 in this regard. Instead, we find, for instance, that the Pauline eschatological material contains significant parallels to several important features of *1 Enoch*. This is especially true with respect to the 'throne' motif and the fluctuation between God and messianic agent as occupants of that throne.

We suggest that the whole issue of the respective roles of God and Messiah within eschatological texts is ultimately related to the anthropomorphic language which occurs in theophanic or visionary texts. Without a doubt, Daniel 7 is of supreme importance in this regard, but other passages, such as Ezekiel 1, play a major part in the process. Such texts easily lend themselves to a creative reinterpretation, become readily coupled with a messianic expectation and frequently involve a Messiah (or intermediary) figure. In short, we would associate the rise of the doctrine of the Parousia of Christ with such texts as they become messianically reinterpreted. At the same time, there is no compelling reason why this reinterpretation could not have been a pre-Christian phenomenon, especially if we recall the prominent role intermediary figures, such as Enoch, play within eschatological texts which are clearly dated prior to the Christian movement. This means that the early development of a 'high' christology appears likely and that eschatological expectations involving the Day of the Lord play a major part in christological expression from the very beginning.

In this regard, we outlined the manner in which the Old Testament concept of the Day of the Lord Yahweh becomes transposed within the Pauline epistles into the Day of the Lord Christ. There are a variety of expressions which are used by Paul to denote this event and we sought to outline the specific bases upon which the christological transposition of the concept was accomplished. Three such bases can be distinguished: (1) there is a referential shift of 'Lord' from God to Christ; (2) there is a referential shift of pronouns from God to Christ; (3) there is a referential shift of descriptions of the Day of the Lord from God to Christ. We discussed eleven major instances within the Pauline epistles in which such a christological transposition occurs and grouped these occurrences into the three categories. Together these eleven passages offer considerable insight into how the question of theocentricity and christocentricity was handled within Paul's eschatological thought.

The Pauline teaching concerning the Messiah and the Kingdom (Chapter 3) also offers important material with regard to the central question of theocentricity and christocentricity. We examined the Pauline references to a βασιλεία and noted the rare discussions of a Messianic Kingdom. The most important of these references was the cryptic passage in 1 Cor. 15.20-28. We found this passage to be a 'bone of contention' among Pauline scholars, especially as to whether or not it taught, or implied, a temporary, Messianic Kingdom. Although there is a great deal of scholarly debate revolving around the interpretation of this passage, we concluded that 1 Cor. 15.20-28 probably does reflect belief in such a Kingdom even though this does mean that it is a modification to the rest of Paul's teaching on the matter. After all, a modification of this type is not uncommon within eschatological materials, such as *4 Ezra* and *2 Baruch*, and the diversity contained in those Jewish pseudepigraphal documents stands as a parallel to the diversity also evident within the Pauline corpus.

More importantly, we specifically analysed the christological content of 1 Cor. 15.20-28 and found it to contain a blend of theocentrism and christocentrism. This blend centers upon the use of Ps. 8.6 in v. 27a and the use of Ps. 110.1c in v. 25. In other words, the passage contains a blending of a christocentric facet (vv. 23-26) and a theocentric facet (vv. 27-28). Thus, 1 Cor. 15.20-28 makes its most important contribution at this christological level and helps to demonstrates how God and Messiah interpenetrate within Paul's thought. It is not unreasonable to suggest further that the conceptual overlap between God and Christ which we see in 1 Cor. 15.20-28 is, in part, explained by speculation over the precise relationship between the temporary, Messianic Kingdom and the Eternal Age to Come within eschatological thought in general. Here again we call attention to the fact that those Jewish pseudepigraphal documents which most clearly maintain the distinction between the temporary, Messianic Kingdom and the Eternal Age to Come, notably *4 Ezra* and *2 Baruch*, also support such a conceptual overlap between God and messianic agent.

In Chapter 3 we also included a summary of how Paul's handling of the question of the eschatological roles of both God and Messiah compares to that gleaned from our study of the relevant Jewish pseudepigraphal documents. We found there to be marked parallels within four major areas: (1) diversity of detail and schematization; (2) functional overlap between God and Christ; (3) textual variants involving the respective roles of God and Messiah within eschatological contexts; (4) identification of Christ and God within a monotheistic tradition. This final comparative point led us to consider the various ways in which Paul sought to interject a note of subordination within his teaching. In other words, it is important to observe how Paul partially resolves the theocentric/christocentric question within his eschatological thought by his inclusion of the idea of the subordination of Christ to God. The most important examples of such a note of subordination occur in 1 Cor. 15.28c and Phil. 2.11c. The manner in which Paul uses nominal clarification (the insertion of Ἰησοῦς or Χριστός to clarify an otherwise ambiguous use of κύριος) also has a bearing at this point.

In conclusion, the study has enabled us to appreciate how inmportant the eschatological sections of Paul's epistles are in relation to the question of theocentricity and christocentricity within his thought. At the same time, we have observed how closely Paul follows many of the conventions of other Jewish pseudepigraphal documents in his formulation of this theocentric/christocentric issue. This, of course, affirms the importance of such Jewish pseudepigraphal writings within our study and suggests that similar comparative studies might be profitably pursued. Most importantly, we have contributed to the understanding of New Testament christology as a whole and made progress in determining how it was that Jesus ultimately came to be regarded as the focus of Christian worship and adoration. We have shown that, at least with respect to Paul's eschatological teaching, the boundaries separating Christ and God are not always as fixed and rigidly determined as we sometimes assume. Instead Paul's thought contains a remarkable degree of flexibility in expression and demonstrates a clear overlap between

Christ and God with respect to their roles in the eschatological drama. At the same time, we have made some contribution to the larger question of christological expression itself, most importantly in its relationship to theistic expression, by demonstrating how thin the separation between 'functional' and 'ontological' statements involving Christ can be at times. Thus, by examining the christological element resident within Paul's eschatological thought, we have explored more fully one of the 'borderlands of ontology' which had hitherto not been accurately charted. We have found the expedition full and satisfying and to have been most rewarding in helping to reveal the richness and depth of Paul's christological thought.

Appendix

IMPLICATIONS FOR BIBLICAL STUDIES

Our study has several important implications for other scholarly investigations into the New Testament documents. We have here tried to catalogue six such implications and give a brief summary of how our work has a bearing on each of these additional areas of study. Space necessitates that our discussions of each be brief and succinct; therefore we have concentrated on the treatment each area has received within recent periodicals and books. Nevertheless, we hope that these brief comments will serve as some indication of the value a study of Paul's eschatological thought, such as is offered here, has for other dimensions of New Testament research.

1. The Question of the Relationship of the Pauline Corpus to the Jewish Pseudepigrapha

Hopefully the many advantages of using the pseudepigraphal parallels as a means to a better understanding of Paul's eschatological thought are readily visible. By means of such a comparison we can set Paul's eschatological teaching against the larger framework of other eschatological writings and are able to see his specific christological formulations more clearly. At the same time we are able to see just how closely Paul conforms to many of the conventions and patterns of the Jewish pseudepigraphal works we have examined. This is especially true with regard to some of the eschatological details (such as the 'throne' motif), as well as the overlap of the roles of God and Messiah within these documents.

However, this is not to say that such a use of Jewish parallel materials is without any inherent problems and difficulties. Samuel Sandmel, in a celebrated article,[1] cautioned against the extravagant use of Jewish literary parallels in interpreting the New Testament documents. He warned that, if not carefully applied, such parallels could be misleading, if not altogether counter-productive. For the most part, his comments are directed against the uncritical use of rabbinic sources in Gospel studies[2] and the unwarranted use of Philo in interpreting Paul. But might some of his caution be well directed in the use of the pseudepigraphal materials as well? Two comments need to be made in response.

First, it should be admitted that many of the pseudepigraphal materials are potentially troublesome in that they post-date the Pauline epistles. For instance, *4 Ezra* and *2 Baruch* were most likely completed at the end of the first century CE. That is to say, they are subsequent to the Pauline letters, at least as far as their final redaction is concerned, and it could be well argued that they be ruled out of bounds of any parallel consideration on grounds of date. Such a verdict would be a rash one in my opinion and runs the risk of eliminating an extremely valuable resource in New Testament interpretation. At the very least we must consider that these pseudepigraphal documents contain much material that must have been part of the oral traditions of the previous generation(s) and are therefore relevant for parallel studies.[3] A good example is the Vision of the Man Rising from the Sea in *4 Ezra* 13, which source-critical scholars date to around 66 CE.[4] In short, the dating criterion should not be the sole basis upon which these pseudepigraphal documents are judged as either relevant or irrelevant to New Testament studies. There are other compelling factors which must be taken into account.

Secondly, with respect to Sandmel's caution about the use of rabbinic materials for comparative work, it seems to me that at times there is a qualitive difference in how the rabbinic parallels and the pseudepigraphal parallels might be said to operate with respect to the New Testament writings. To a certain degree we see this difference reflected in that many of the pseudepigraphal documents are extant with a clear Christian redaction and obvious Christian textual emendations. Such is generally not the case with most of the rabbinic materials.

Happily, the majority of pseudepigraphal works manifestly exhibit that Christianity and Judaism had a great deal in common and suggest that any exploration into the literature of the one will reap benefits of interpretation and understanding within the literature of the other. Indeed, even to phrase the point in such a manner is perhaps to 'compartmentalize' the literature into 'Jewish' and 'Christian' camps in a way which is itself misleading. The division between the two is often very thin and there is much interpenetration of thought. At times it is absolutely impossible to decide whether a document is indeed 'Jewish' or 'Christian'.

Finally, it should be said that what we have attempted here is an examination of one very small aspect of thought within the Jewish pseudepigraphal writings and the epistles of Paul—the eschatological. Even there we were specifically concerned to see how this single category might help us to understand Paul's christology. Needless to say, the pseudepigraphal materials have much to offer in other areas of study as well. For instance, a thorough study of the sociological and anthropological forces which give rise to any given pseudepigraphal work might be helpful in illuminating the genesis of some of Paul's churches or the writings directed to those congregations. The larger question of the provenance of many of these works is a huge task which has, for the most part, yet to be undertaken but will surely yield huge benefits for serious New Testament work. In a similar vein, the manner in which these pseudepigraphal writings were preserved, and indeed revered, by Christians is surely a comment on their abiding impact and influence. A better understanding of this dynamic must prove to be invaluable in understanding the early Chruch.

In short, the time has now come for a much more wide-ranging investigation into the pseudeigraphal documents to be undertaken. This is not simply a necessity for the sake of Pauline or New Testament studies; these pseudepigraphal documents deserve the serious attention of scholars for their own sake. It is, however, to suggest that the minds of Paul and other early Christians might be made more accessible by investigating their thought in light of the Jewish pseudepigraphal materials which are now at our disposal.

2. *Implications for the 'Son of Man' Debate*

Within Biblical scholarship there have been recent advances in the understanding of the term 'Son of Man' within the New Testament documents. Within the past two decades we have witnessed a tremendous revolution within New Testament christological studies as the term 'Son of Man' has been subjected to extensive scholarly investigation. Geza Vermes, in many ways, has served to inaugurate this new stage of scholarship via his lecture 'The Use of "barnash/bar nasha" in Jewish Aramaic', delivered in Oxford in September 1965.[5]

Quite simply, this new approach to 'Son of Man' research involves an investigation into the meaning of the Aramaic expression 'bar nasha' which underlies the Greek ὁ υἱός τοῦ ἀνθρώπου. Vermes's point was to emphasize the essential *Aramaic* meaning of the phrase and to assert its use as a regular expression for 'man' as well as its use as a circumlocution for 'I' within given contexts. The effect of this was to undermine the long-held assumption that 'Son of Man' was a title in Aramaic and thus challenge a great deal of modern christological interpretation.[6]

Vermes's analysis sparked off an ensuing philological debate about the Aramaic phrase with Maurice Casey,[7] Joseph Fitzmyer,[8] John Bowker,[9] and Joachim Jeremias[10] all making important contributions.

At the same time, Vermes's work necessitated a re-evaluation of the 'titular' approach to the 'Son of Man' issue as it is deemed relevant to New Testament christological study. This re-evaluation has also helped to focus debate about the critical importance of both Daniel 7[11] and the *Similitudes of Enoch*[12] as background witnesses to the New Testament usage of the term. This process of re-assessment can also be traced via the vigorous debate among New Testament scholars, including Ragnar Leivestad[13] and Barnabas Lindars.[14] Both Leivestad and Lindars were concerned with interpreting the New Testament 'Son of Man' passages themselves in light of this latest Aramaic evidence. As any cursory comparison of the two attempts reveals, scholars are far from agreement as to the implications of the movement initiated by Vermes.

The latest round in the whole 'Son of Man' debate was sparked off by Barnabas Lindars's monograph *Jesus Son of Man* (1983).[15] Lindars, who here somewhat modifies his earlier stance, attempts to trace the development of the New Testament sayings which speak of the 'Son of Man' in light of all that has been gleaned in recent years about the nuance of the Aramaic 'bar nasha'. Thus, Lindars proceeds upon the possible assumption that the term 'Son of Man' was not a title within the New Testament period. At the same time, Lindars argues, we need to give some explanation as to how this Aramaic term does eventually attain titular status. He attempts to do precisely this via a careful analysis of the Gospels and concludes that the titular sense of the 'bar nasha' idiom is a result of the creativity of the Early Church as it re-interpreted the sayings of Jesus which included this idiom of circumlocution, 'bar nasha'.

The outcome of this whole philological movement is that it now allows for the possibility of making a distinction between the titular use of the phrase 'Son of Man' and other messianic expectations. It is precisely this sort of distinction which allows Lindars to erect his reconstruction of how messianic expectations developed within the New Testament, and his suggested 'solution' to the age-old 'Son of Man' question is the result. However, as Lindars would confirm, this is not to suggest that there is no correlation between the phrase 'Son of Man' and these messianic expectations, for the Gospel material testifies abundantly to their association *at some point*.[16] Lindars's major contention is that this association is primarily a phenomenon associated with the Early Church and not with Jesus.

Moreover, what an attempt such as that of Lindars does accomplish is that it provides a possible explanation to the 'Son of Man' problem. Such a comprehensive explanation as Lindars's is based upon its ability to clear away much of the 'Son of Man' overgrowth which is alleged to have long obstructed our view of the christological landscape. The result, according to Lindars, is that we are now able to examine the contour of the underlying christological bedrock more carefully and trace development more accurately. In effect, he claims that we no longer need run the risk of being misled as to the origin of christological thought by pursuing the illusive 'Son of Man' question since it is now deemed a titular 'dead-end'.

But do the facts not warrant any other possible solution? A word of caution should be heeded here. We should not assume, as Lindars seems to do, that since we can now seem to demonstrate that 'Son of Man' was not necessarily a title in Jesus' time, we can effectively remove him from its development or use as a title. Nor can we rule out Jesus' creative instigation of the phrase in a titular manner. Indeed, there have been some recent scholarly attempts to counter Lindars's thesis and to re-establish the possibility that there was a titular sense of the Aramaic phrase 'bar nasha' current in the first century CE.

Matthew Black[17] has argued for such an idea on the basis of a hypothetical reconstruction of how the present Ethiopic text[18] of *1 Enoch* expresses the underlying Greek, which he feels clearly betrays a titular sense. However, the further step of moving behind this Greek titular sense to an earlier Aramaic titular sense is much more difficult, as Black well appreciates. Nevertheless, he argues that there is justification for an emphatic statement in the Old Aramaic[19] which gives credibility to a titular sense of the phrase 'bar nasha'. This effectively rescues the phrase for re-consideration as part of the thought-world of Jesus. In any case, should Black's suggestion be untrue and it proved conclusively that 'bar nasha' was *not* an Aramaic title in the first century, we still cannot rule out a *a priori* Jesus' contribution toward the titular status of the term. Simply to assert the case that Jesus has no contribution to make in this regard, as Lindars does, is not to prove the case.

It should be noted that this whole debate as to whether the creativity of christological thought resided with Jesus or within the early Church is largely fought and won on the basis of the presuppositions of the debaters.[20] While such an observation is not condemning of either side of the debate, it is a point to be kept continually in mind when the arguments pro and contra are evaluated.

Our study in Paul's eschatological thought does not claim to have contributed directly to the 'Son of Man' issue so as to solve the problem in one direction or another. However, regardless of which way the issue is ultimately decided (if it is ever finally decided at all!), we can still fruitfully investigate the related area of Pauline eschatology. This is especially true if we examine the 'Son of Man' figure within the larger context of theophanic descriptions. It is at this juncture that we have hoped to make a small contribution. If Lindars is correct and the term 'Son of Man' no longer appears to be able to help provide the answer as to how a transcendent messianism arises, are we able to determine how such messianism *does* come about? Are we able, in any way, to help fill the christological vacuum left by the evacuation of 'Son of Man' as a relevant concept? I would like to suggest that the messianic sections of the pseudepigraphal literature, especially those which speak of a temporary Kingdom on earth, may provide a way forward by permitting us to associate the messianism contained therein with transcendent theophanic ideas and expectations. Lindars himself hints at the importance of theophany as a catalyst when commenting on *1 Enoch* 37–71 and *2 Esdras*, he says:[21]

> Both of these are post-Christian developments, but they are in no way dependent upon Christian thought, and they are independent

of each other. They take up long-standing court-room imagery of Jewish eschatology, and use the Danielic vision to identify the Messiah as God's agent in performing the judgment. This identification does not happen suddenly and without precedent in Jewish literature. The basic picture of Jewish eschatology is the coming of God himself to perform judgment.

If, on the other hand, Black is correct and it appears there is sufficient evidence to sustain a pre-Christian, Aramaic 'Son of Man' title, then we can certainly help to fill out the implications of that titular usage by a more comprehensive investigation of the theophanic motif within both the Jewish pseudepigraphal literature and the Pauline epistles. It is at this level that I have hoped to make a small contribution to the perplexing 'Son of Man' question and the attendant christological issues.

3. *The Question of Development in Paul's Eschatological Thought*

The question of whether or not Paul's eschatology develops is a long-standing one within Pauline scholarship.[22] For the most part, such development was seen by various scholars[23] as part of the gradual process of the 'Hellenization' of the gospel. These scholars have focused upon the later Pauline epistles (particularly Colossians and Ephesians) to substantiate this claim. The Corinthian correspondence also becomes an important focal point for this interpretative attempt, with the eschatological passages of 1 Corinthians 15 and 2 Cor. 5.1-10 special areas of controversy.[24] Recently the subject has been given a novel twist in direction by those who have sought to trace eschatological development within Paul's *earliest* writings, 1 and 2 Thessalonians. C.L. Mearns, for instance, has recently resurrected the argument and contends that a careful analysis of 1 and 2 Thessalonians reveals the probability that Paul's eschatological teaching has undergone a radical shift prior to the writing of those epistles.[25]

Basically, Mearns insists that prior to the writing of 1 Thessalonians, Paul's teaching was that of a thoroughly realized eschatology.[26] It was not until the death of some of the Christian believers occurred that a futuristic eschatology was deemed necessary. It is this fact which prompts the re-conceptualizing of the Parousia of Christ in terms of a 'Second Advent', so Mearns argues. In addition, this over-realized viewpoint quickly attaches itself to an over-inflated spiritual pride which demands Paul's correction.[27] Mearns supports his case by reconstructing the dialogue between Paul and the church at Thessaloniki and hypothesizing several layers of interaction.[28]

Mearns's thesis is complex and intertwined and does seem to answer, at least in part, many of the questions raised by a close examination of the eschatological sections of Paul's letters. It does, for instance, offer an explanation for many of the problems associated with the delay of the Parousia. Yet I remain skeptical on key points in Mearns's program. It seems to me that 1. he assumes that Paul's original eschatological teaching did not include belief in a future resurrection of the body without proving such to be the case. Why must it be that the Thessalonian conviction of this (if there is such a conviction), be laid at Paul's feet? 2. He assumes there to be two essentially incompatible truths which compel the development of eschatological thought forward: (a) eschatology is fully and entirely realized; (b) eschatology is imminent. We are led to believe that the incompatibility of these two perspectives is at the heart of the controversy at Thessaloniki and that an insistence upon their integration within Paul's thought is the very thing that has for so long blinded us to the real nature of the Thessalonian controversy. Yet, ironically, it is just such an integration of these two ideas that we are asked to believe was Paul's *final* conviction on the matter (as expressed in 2 Thessalonians). Why, I ask, is such an integration deemed possible only *after* Paul dialectically argues through these questions with the Thessalonians? Surely there is just as much to be said for arguing that, at least as far as Paul is concerned, the fusion of present and future elements of eschatological thought was long ago accomplished.[29]

One of the great weaknesses of theories such as Mearns's is their shallow handling of the question of the death of the believers. It is naively assumed that Paul had little or no contact with Christians who died prior to the writing of 1 Thessalonians.[30] I find it stretches my imagination to accept that such was the case, especially given the fact that Paul had already ministered for at least fifteen years or so within various Christian communities prior to penning that epistle. Are we seriously asked to believe that the subject of the death of the Christians had never arisen during that time? We shall have more to say about this point when we come to consider the nature of the Thessalonian controversy in great detail below.

Finally, we turn to a point more directly relevant to our own topic. It is axiomatic to Mearns's thesis that 'Second-Adventism' is a feature of early Christian apocalyptic and thus as secondary to this vexing question of eschatological development and the realized/ imminence issue.[31] Thus, the rise of the doctrine of the Parousia is explained entirely within the boundaries of eschatological schemes alone.[32] Nothing is said about how the theocentric/christocentric question contributes to the larger issue. Indeed, the relationship between christology and eschatology is one which remains essentially untouched within Mearns' argument. It is never questioned what impact the christological re-interpretation of the Old Testament Day of the Lord passages had upon the rise of a doctrine of the Parousia of Christ or upon the theory of eschatological development. Our own study has shown how interlocked are the two questions of eschatology and christology; any satisfactory explanation of development within Paul's eschatological thought which neglects the christological component does so at its own peril. The full and comprehensive answer must take into account this christological factor and adequately explain its contribution.

In short, the question of the development of Paul's eschatological thought cannot be examined in isolation from the larger question of the rise of the doctrine of the Parousia of Christ itself. We should not be too dismissive of the contribution that a careful examination of christocentricity and theocentricity has to make to this subject.

4. *The Question of the Nature of the Controversy at Corinth and Thessaloniki*

Above we briefly noted that one of the great weaknesses of theories of eschatological development in Paul's thought is the inadequate treatment given to the question of the death of believing Christians. This is especially evident when we consider that it is this very question which has been so often at the center of scholarly debate about the nature of the controversies at Corinth and Thessaloniki with which Paul is interacting in his epistles. Nowhere is such debate more clearly concentrated than in the eschatological passage of 1 Thess. 4.13-18.[33]

Recently, Joseph Plevnik has examined this passage while paying particular attention to the question of the resurrection of the dead.[34] He has offered an interesting interpretation which explains the basis of the Thessalonians' grief over the fate of the departed believers as the result of their understanding of the *method* of their participation (that is, translation), instead of taking the whole controversy to have arisen as a result of Paul's inadequate eschatological teaching with respect to the resurrection.[35] Plevnik supports this thesis via a study of 'translation-accounts' within apocalyptic literature.[36] In short, the result is that Plevnik has called into question the assumption that the Thessalonian controversy was ultimately based upon a fluctuation within Paul's teaching with respect to the resurrection body of the Christian believer at the Parousia. As Plevnik comments:

> The cause of grief in Thessaloniki was thus not connected with the absence of the Apostle's teaching of the resurrection of the dead, but rather with a misunderstanding of his unique depiction of the faithful's sharing in the glorious Parousia through their assumption.[37]

In other words, Paul's original eschatological teaching to the Thessalonians *did*, in all likelihood, include the idea of the resurrection of the dead. We should *not* assume such a teaching to have been an additional facet which is only later forged within Paul's mind via his interaction with the church at Corinth and his writing of 1 Corinthians 15. Such an evaluation has the added value that it also gives full weight to 1 Cor. 15.3ff. and the way in which the believer's resurrection is seen to flow directly from Christ's. At the same time Plevnik is quick to qualify the manner in which the teaching of 1 Corinthians 15 differs slightly from that contained in 1 Thess. 4.13-18 when he says:

> The difference in the two presentations is not due to Paul's having changed his mind, but rather to the actual problems to which he addresses himself. In 1 Thessalonians 4 he affirms that God can, in his power over death, restore the dead to life and so make them share not only in the Parousia of Christ but ultimately in life with the risen Lord in his (God's) presence forever. In 1 Corinthians 15 he affirms more directly that God will change our mortal bodies through the transformation which will affect both the dead and the living faithful.[38]

This explanation has the added attraction that it maintains the upward (earth to heavens) movement of the cloud motif (albeit with the resurrected bodies of believers in mind). This might be an important point for those who see a problem within the theophanic motif when it is associated with the downward (heavens to earth) Parousia of Christ.[39]

Thus it appears that investigations into the nature of the 'heresy' or disputed teaching at Corinth and/or Thessaloniki may have to be re-evaluated. This is especially true if it can be legitimately maintained that the dispute over the advantage of the believers living until the end of the age is ultimately derived from a latent belief in a temporary, Messianic Age on earth. As we have seen, there is some grounds for asserting that vestiges of just such a belief may underlie 1 Cor. 15.20-28. We should perhaps associate the nature of the controversy Paul has with the churches at Thessaloniki and Corinth with just such an expectation instead of assuming the problem to have arisen because of a shift in Paul's teaching with regard to the resurrection of the believers. The assessment of Albert Schweitzer with regard to this matter might be closer to the truth than we have been willing to admit.

This leads us quite naturally to consider a related aspect of Paul's eschatological teaching, especially as it relates to his earliest correspondence—the Thessalonian epistles.

5. The Integrity of 2 Thessalonians and its Relationship to 1 Thessalonians

The inauthenticity of 2 Thessalonians is in some quarters taken for granted. It is felt that a number of reasons are responsible for this judgment. Wolfgang Trilling[40] argues that the close literary dependence of 2 Thessalonians upon 1 Thessalonians leaves no other viable option. To be sure, the question of literary dependency is a difficult one, but it should not be separated in any way from a sensitivity to the occasional nature of the epistolary materials. At the same time, there are many scholars who would defend the apostolic integrity of 2 Thessalonians on other grounds. J.C. Hurd,[41] for instance, has recently argued that one of the reasons why the authenticity of 2 Thessalonians has been questioned involves an uncritical acceptance of the chronology of Acts. For our purposes we want to focus on the eschatological material within 2 Thessalonians, especially 2.1-10, which has been taken to be incompatible with that found in 1 Thessalonians. This incompatibility has served as the basis for asserting that 2 Thessalonians could not have come from the pen of Paul.

A good example of such argumentation is provided by John A. Bailey,[42] who bases his case for the pseudepigraphal nature of

2 Thessalonians upon a number of considerations, including the eschatological. Bailey insists that the dissimilarity of eschatology between 1 and 2 Thessalonians does militate against Pauline authorship. As he comments:[43]

> These two eschatologies are contradictory. Either the end will come suddenly and without warning like a thief in the night (I Thessalonians) or it will be preceded by a series of apocalyptic events which warn of its coming (II Thessalonians). Paul might have said both things—in differing situations to one church, or to different churches—but he can hardly have said both things to the same church at the same time, i.e. to the Thessalonians church when he founded it.

Quite simply, such an argument may be based upon an inadequate appreciation of the tremendous diversity of detail which is possible within eschatological texts. Indeed, as our study has shown, particularly with regard to *4 Ezra* and *2 Baruch*, such diversity of detail and schematization is typical of such texts. The same basic fluctuation in emphasis may be said to exist in Paul's Corinthian correspondence, if our interpretation of 1 Cor. 15.20-28 is correct and a comparison is made between that passage and others such as 1 Cor. 15.50-57 or 2 Cor. 5.1-10. In short, I would resist any attempt to base the inauthenticity of 2 Thessalonians on the alleged incompatibility of its eschatology with that of 1 Thessalonians. Such a foundation, it seems to me, is a very shaky one on which to build and violates one of the prime characteristics of eschatological material. The question of the inauthenticity of 2 Thessalonians is an open one, at least as far as the eschatology of the book is concerned.

6. The Question of Later Interpolations into the Pauline Epistles

Closely related to the question of the authenticity of 2 Thessalonians, in that it proceeds along the same lines of argumentation, is that of the question of later interpolations into the Pauline epistles. There have been one or two attempts to isolate sections of the letters on the basis that the eschatological viewpoint expressed is incompatible with the rest of the letter. The most important of these attempts centers on 1 Thess. 5.1-11.

For instance, Gerhard Friedrich has argued in a number of places[44] that 1 Thess. 5.1-11 is the work of an interpolator of the

Lucan school who has inserted these verses in order to counter Paul's belief in an imminent Parousia. At the heart of such arguments is the assumption that 5.1-11 is fundamentally incompatible with 4.13-18 which immediately precedes. Such an assumption cannot stand, and falls under the same sort of critiques we noted above in connection with the question of the authenticity of 2 Thessalonians. Indeed, the basis upon which theories of interpolations are argued is often very shaky and we should not admit any such theories when they employ eschatological texts in such a manner.[45]

NOTES

Notes to Introduction

1. Vincent Taylor, 'Does the New Testament Call Jesus God?', *ExpT* 72 (1961-62), pp. 116-18; R.E. Brown, 'Does the New Testament Call Jesus God?', *TS* 26 (1965), pp. 545-73; G.H. Boobyer, 'Jesus as "Theos" in the New Testament', *BJRL* 50 (1967-68), pp. 247-61; Victor Perry, 'Does the New Testament Call Jesus God?', *ExpT* 87 (1975-76), pp. 214-15; C.F.D. Moule, 'The New Testament and the Doctrine of the Trinity', *ExpT* 88 (1976-77), pp. 16-20; Richard L. Sturch, 'Can One Say "Jesus is God"?', in *Christ the Lord* (Guthrie FS), edited by Harold H. Rowden (1982), pp. 326-40.

2. Within this study I accept the Pauline authorship of nine out of the ten epistles commonly designated as the 'Pauline corpus'. Only in the case of Ephesians do I feel that the evidence is compelling enough to demand deutero-Pauline authorship. However, I admit that Colossians may have been reworked by a disciple of Paul's and demonstrates signs of editing to that effect. With respect to 2 Thessalonians, I do not share the prevailing scholarly scepticism directed against its authenticity, but would accept it as genuinely from the pen of Paul, especially since one of the main sources of such scepticism is an inaccurate interpretation of the eschatological material contained within the letter.

3. Walter Elwell, 'The Deity of Christ in the Writings of Paul', in *Current Issues in Biblical and Patristic Interpretation* (Tenney FS), edited by Gerald F. Hawthorne (1975), pp. 297-308.

4. W.L. Lorimer, 'Romans IX. 3-5', *NTS* 13 (1966-67), pp. 385-86; Bruce M. Metzger, 'The Punctuation of Rom. 9.5', in *Christ and Spirit in the New Testament* (C.F.D. Moule FS), edited by Barnabas Lindars and Stephen S. Smalley (1973), pp. 95-112.

5. See Ralph P. Martin, *Carmen Christi: Philippians II. 5-11 in Recent Interpretation and in the Setting of Early Christian Worship* (1967); Jean-François Collange, *The Epistle of St. Paul to the Phillippians* (1979), pp. 81-108.

6. See Eduard Lohse, *Colossians and Philemon* (1971), pp. 41-61; Ralph P. Martin, *Colossians: The Church's Lord and the Christian's Liberty* (1972), pp. 40-55, and his *Colossians and Philemon* (1974), pp. 55-66; Eduard Schweizer, *The Letter to the Colossians* (1982), pp. 55-88.

7. The pre-Pauline hypothesis with regard to these hymns is criticized by Seyoon Kim (*The Origin of Paul's Gospel* [1982], pp. 144ff.) as a part of the

author's general thesis of attributing the major concepts of Paul's thought to his Damascus Road experience.

8.   It would be naive to suggest that an examination of Paul's eschatological teaching (or anyone else's!) will enable us to solve this ontological question. Such an answer will ultimately only be found, if at all, in the philosophical debate over the nature and meaning of language itself. What an examination of eschatological texts will enable us to do, however, is to clarify their author's conceptual categories of Messiah and God as they relate to each other. What relationship these eschatological categories bear to reality itself is a matter we must leave to the linguistic philosophers.

9.   *Encyclopedia of Theology* (1975), p. 1756.

10.   An important recent contribution to this whole area is Christopher Rowland, *Christian Origins* (1985). Rowland argues powerfully that Christianity is best understood, at least from the standpoint of its origin, as a messianic sect within Judaism which drew much of its power from prevailing eschatological views of the day. Thus, Rowland acknowledges his debt to J. Weiss and Albert Schweitzer as interpreters of the New Testament and follows them in emphasizing the importance of eschatology for early Christianity. According to Rowland, the critical link between eschatology and christology within Christianity is to be found in the eschatological role that Jesus has as the one who brings the Kingdom of God. I would want to qualify some of the conclusions that Rowland draws in his investigations, particularly about the tension that the figure of Jesus caused between Jews and Christians, but his basic approach is very interesting and highly informative.

11.   '"The Father is Greater Than I: John 14.28 Subordinationist Christology in the New Testament"', reprinted in Barrett's *Essay on John* (1982), pp. 19-36.

12.   *Art. cit.*, p. 23.

13.   'The Development of the Doctrine of Christ in the New Testament', in *Christ For Us Today*, edited by Norman Pittenger (1968), p. 79.

14.   J.D.G. Dunn's *Christology in the Making* (1980), is an excellent survey of recent New Testament christological study and seeks to determine the origins upon which subsequent creedal formulations were built. Each of these three theological approaches, as well as others, is analyzed with a view to shedding light on the central christological question of Jesus' relationship to God.

15.   Regardless of how much we feel that 'Adamic theology' expresses only anthropological ideas, it seems to me that its contribution in some sense transcends the bounds of this anthropological category as well. No other human being is described in quite the same manner as Jesus is when he is designated 'Second Adam'; the typology at work goes beyond the bounds of the anthropological category. For a further discussion of this dynamic, see my unpublished MTh thesis 'Christ as Second Adam to Paul' (1982).

16. *Paul's Use of the Old Testament* (1957; reprinted 1981), p. 149.

17. *Biblical Exegesis in the Apostolic Period* (1975), p. 207.

18. See: Rom. 1.7; 1 Cor. 1.3; 2 Cor. 2.2; Gal. 1.3; Eph. 1.2; Phil. 1.2; Col. 1.2; 1 Thess. 1.1; 2 Thess. 1.2; Phlmn 3. Also note the benediction in Eph. 6.23. C.F.D. Moule, 'The New Testament and the Doctrine of the Trinity', *ExpT* 88 (1976-77), p. 17, describes this phenomenon as one of two 'implicit Christological "pointers"' which may be gleaned from Paul's epistles. The other is 'the fact that Paul seems to experience Christ as any theist reckons to understand God—that is, as personal, but as more than individual: as more than *a* person'. This point is made by Moule in a number of his writings, notable *The Origin in Christology* (1977), pp. 7ff., and is expanded by him under the heading of 'the corporate Christ'.

19. See Reinhard Deichgräber, *Gotteshymnus und Christushymnus in der frühen Christenheit* (1967); Klaus Wengst, *Christologische Formeln und Lieder des Urchristentums* (1973). Also note the excellent article by James H. Charlesworth, 'A Prolegomenon to a New Study of the Jewish Background to the Hymns and Prayers in the New Testament', *JJS* 33 (1982), pp. 265-85.

20. *The New Testament Christological Hymns* (1971), p. 144.

21. 'New Testament Hymns: Background and Development', *ExpT* 94 (1982-83), p. 136.

22. *The Atonement in New Testament Teaching* (2nd edn; 1945), p. 173.

23. *The Cross in the New Testament* (1965), p. 374.

24. *The Atonement* (1981), p. 64. Also, note the discussion in C.F.D. Moule's *The Origin of Christology* (1977), pp. 107-26. Sam K. Williams, *Jesus' Death as Saving Event: The Background and Origin of a Concept* (1975), stresses the importance of *4 Maccabees* in the development of this idea.

25. Published in Käsemann's *New Testament Questions for Today* (1969), pp. 82-107, and in *JTC* 6 (1969), pp. 17-46.

26. Whether we can go so far as to agree with Käsemann that 'Apocalyptic was the mother of all Christian theology' (*op. cit.*, p. 102), is another matter. Worth examining on this subject are Sophie Laws, 'Can Apocalyptic Be Relevant?', in *What About the New Testament?* (Christopher Evans FS), edited by Morna Hooker and Colin Hickling (1975), p. 93, for a humorous extension of this familial metaphor. This article contains an excellent critique of the whole issue.

27. In addition to the issue of *JTC* 6 cited above, note: *Interpretation* 25/4 (1971); *RevExp* 72/3 (1975); *CBQ* 39/3 (1977); *Apocalypse: Morphology of a Genre* (Semeia 14) (1979).

28. A good, introductory survey on this issue is Kurt Koch, *The Rediscovery of Apocalyptic* (1972). In addition, see Carl E. Braaten, 'The Significance of Apocalypticism for Systematic Theology', *Interpretation* 25 (1971), pp. 480-99; E. Frank Tupper, 'Revival of Apocalyptic in Biblical and

Theological Studies', *RevExp* 72 (1975), pp. 279-303.

29. In addition to the *Semeia* 14 volume mentioned above, special note must be made of the impressive work of Christopher Rowland, *The Open Heaven* (1982). Rowland tries to distinguish 'apocalyptic' as a literary genre from the larger category of 'eschatology'. Although his distinction is stretched a bit far at times (as in the way the *Sibylline Oracles* are ruled out of consideration, for instance), his contribution is immensely valuable and no doubt will remain the center of interaction for some time to come. T.F. Glasson, 'What is Apocalyptic?', *NTS* 27 (1980-81), pp. 98-105, handles the question in a similar fashion. Also note, I. Howard Marshall, 'Slippery Words: Eschatology', *ExpT* 89 (1977-78), pp. 264-69; Margaret Barker, 'Slippery Words: Apocalyptic', *ExpT* 89 (1977-78), pp. 324-29; and the three articles in *AMWNE* (1983), which deal with the subject; Lars Hartman, 'Survey of the Problem of Apocalyptic Genre', pp. 329-43; E.P. Sanders, 'The Genre of Palestinian Jewish Apocalypses', pp. 447-59; J.J. Collins, 'The Genre Apocalyptic in Hellenistic Judaism', pp. 531-48.

30. On this important area see Jacob Neusner, 'The Development of the Merkavah', *JSJ* 2 (1971), pp. 149-60; Christopher Rowland, 'The Visions of God in Apocalyptic Literature', *JSJ* 10 (1979), pp. 137-54; Alan F. Segal, 'Heavenly Ascent in Hellenistic Judaism, Early Christianity and their Environment', in *ANRW* II 23.2 (1980), pp. 1333-94; Ithamar Gruenwald, *Apocalyptic and Merkabah Mysticism* (1980); Chris Hauer, Jr, 'When History Stops: Apocalypticism and Mysticism in Judaism and Christianity', in *The Divine Helmsman* (Silberman FS) (1980), pp. 207-21; David J. Halperin, 'Merkabah Mysticism in the Septuagint', *JBL* 101 (1982), pp. 351-63; Ira Chernus, 'Visions of God in Merkabah Mysticism', *JSJ* 13 (1982), pp. 123-46; Mary Dean-Otting, *Heavenly Journeys: A Study of the Motif in Hellenistic Jewish Literature* (1984). David Winston Suter (*Tradition and Composition in the Parables of Enoch* [SBL Dissertation Series, 47: 1979], pp. 14-23), discusses the relationship between 'Merkabah Mysticism' and the Parables of Enoch. He concludes (p. 23) that the Parables of Enoch are 'proto-Merkabah' and belong to an early stage in the Merkabah tradition.

The relationship that such merkabah traditions and visionary description have to Paul's thought are discussed in J.W. Bowker, '"Merkabah" Visions and the Visions of Paul', *JSS* 16 (1971), pp. 157-73; Christopher Rowland, 'Apocalyptic Visions and the Exaltation of Christ in the Letter to the Colossians', *JSNT* 19 (1983), pp. 73-83.

31. Beker seeks to explore Pauline theology as motivated by Paul's apocalyptic ideas and conditioned by a vacillation between opposite poles labeled as 'contingency' and 'coherency'. This polarity is inherent in the nature of the epistolary evidence, according to Beker. Beker's thesis is flawed by his over-systematic attempts to present Paul's theology as well as his lack of consideration of literature later than the mid-70s. Nevertheless, it remains an important contribution. Also, see his more popular *Paul's Apocalyptic*

Gospel (1982). The conditional nature of Paul's eschatological teaching is also the subject of John Drane's 'Theological Diversity in the Letters of St. Paul', *TB* 27 (1976), pp. 3-26, where the author's earlier ideas presented in *Paul: Libertine or Legalist* with respect to law and grace are here applied further to include the eschatological realm. A similar point is made in John G. Gager, 'Functional Diversity in Paul's Use of End-Time Language', *JBL* 89 (1970), pp. 325-37.

32. Attempts to isolate this 'center of Paul's theology' have produced a flurry of monographs and articles, most of which are interacting with the traditional understanding of righteousness/justification as occupying that position. For a recent defense of the justification position, from a Lutheran standpoint, see John Reumann, *Righteousness in the New Testament* (1982). Beker's thesis is criticized on pp. 120-21. Also worth examining is C.J.A. Hickling, 'Centre and Periphery in the Thought of Paul', in *Studia Biblica 1978, III. Papers on Paul and Other New Testament Authors* (1980), pp. 199-214.

33. Charlesworth's *The Pseudepigrapha and Modern Research with a Supplement* (1981), is the best place to find bibliographical information detailing these advances. Also note: Gerhard Delling, *Bibliographie zur jüdisch-hellenistischen und intertestamentarischen Literatur 1900-1970* (1975); Daniel J. Harrington, 'Research on the Jewish Pseudepigrapha During the 1970s', *CBQ* 42 (1980), pp. 147-59. A comprehensive history of pseudepigraphal research is given in Charlesworth, *TOTPNT* (1985), pp. 6-17.

34. See James H. Charlesworth, 'The Renaissance of Pseudepigraphal Studies: The SBL Pseudepigrapha Project, *JSJ* 2 (1971), pp. 107-14; and his 'A History of Pseudepigraphal Research: The Re-emerging Importance of the Pseudepigrapha', *ANRW* II, 19.1 (1979), pp. 54-88. The SNTS has also established a Pseudepigraphal Study group which first met in 1976 and discussed the Testaments of the Twelve Patriarchs. The 1977 and 1978 sessions were dedicated to the books of Enoch. See James H. Charlesworth, 'Reflections on the SNTS Pseudepigrapha Seminar at Duke on the Testaments of the Twelve Patriarchs', *NTS* 23 (1976-77), pp. 296-304; and 'The SNTS Pseudepigrapha Seminars at Tübingen and Paris on the Books of Enoch', *NTS* 25 (1978-79), pp. 315-23. Charlesworth, *TOTPNT* (1985), pp. 94-141, gives a comprehensive survey of the SNTS Pseudepigrapha Seminars from 1976-1983.

35. *The Old Testament Pseudepigrapha* (hereafter cited as *TOTP*), 2 vols (1983-85); *The Apocryphal Old Testament* (1984).

36. Charlesworth (*TOTPNT* [1985], p. 4), writes to encourage New Testament scholars to 'join with the specialists who have demonstrated clearly the significance of the Pseudepigrapha for Christian origins and for the New Testament documents'. We have attempted to heed this call within this study.

37. If I may borrow an idea from Paul Tillich in illustration of the point I

am suggesting is operative in Paul's thought: Tillich (*Systematic Theology* 2 [1978], pp. 9ff.), makes a distinction between a 'sign' and a 'symbol' as they strive to express reality beyond themselves. Now, both point beyond themselves to that reality, but the 'symbol' distinguishes itself in that it *participates in the reality to which it points*; something of which the 'sign' is incapable. To apply this distinction to Paul, we might say that, for him, Christ is a 'symbol' pointing to God whereas all other intermediary figures are mere 'signs' pointing to Him. Of course, we may be dissatisfied with the arbitrary relegation of the intermediary world to the lesser 'sign' category; and perhaps we would wish to insist that *all* the intermediary figures 'participate in God's reality' and thus ought to be more correctly catalogued as 'symbols'. In this case we would at least have to say that, for Paul, Jesus occupies a position unique within the 'symbol' category and insist that Christ 'participates in the reality of God' to a degree that the other 'symbols' are not able. In short the suggestion is that, for Paul, there is a *qualitative* distinction between Jesus and other intermediary figures; a qualitative distinction which causes Jesus to merge with God in a way wholly consistent with Paul's monotheism when viewed from the standpoint of its being a creative tension within Paul's thought.

For a similar distinction between 'sign' and 'symbol' with reference to the meaning of 'the Kingdom of God', see Norman Perrin, 'Eschatology and Hermeneutics: Reflections on Method in the Interpretation of the New Testament', *JBL* 93 (1974), pp. 10ff.

In a similar vein, I am grateful to Chris Mearns for calling to my attention the distinction between *totus Deus* and *totum Dei* made a J.A.T. Robinson's *Truth is Two-Eyed* (1979), p. 107. However, to phrase the question in such clearly defined terms is perhaps to overstate the case.

38. C.F.D. Moule, 'The Borderlands of Ontology in the New Testament', *The Philosophical Frontiers of Christian Theology* (MacKinnon FS), edited by Brian Hebblethwaite and Stewart Sutherland (1982), pp. 1-11. The quotation is from p. 9.

Notes to Chapter 1

1. The sociological dynamics which gave rise to the apocalypticism we see characterizing segments of the ancient Jewish and Christian communities of the Near East are explored in S.R. Isenberg, 'Millenarism in Greco-Roman Palestine', *Religion 4* (1964), pp. 26-46. In addition, Paul D. Hanson has made a significant contribution in trying to answer this question regarding the rise of apocalyptic. In particular, note 'Jewish Apocalyptic Against its Near Eastern Environment', *RB* 78 (1971), pp. 31-58; *The Dawn of Apocalyptic* (1975); 'Prolegomena to the Study of Jewish Apocalyptic', in *Magnalia Dei: The Mighty Acts of God*, edited by F.M. Cross, W.E. Lemke &

P.D. Miller (1976); and the article of 'Apocalypticism' in *IDB Supplementary Volume* (1976), pp. 28-34. Also worth considering on this subject are: William R. Millar, *Isaiah 24-27 and the Origin in Apocalyptic* (1976); J.J. Collins, 'Jewish Apocalyptic against its Hellenistic Near Eastern Environment', *BASOR* 220 (1975), pp. 27-36; Michael Stone, *Scriptures, Sects, and Visions* (1980), pp. 37-47; J. Douglas Thomas, 'Jewish Apocalyptic and the Comparative Method', in *Scripture in Context* (1980), pp. 245-62; Howard C. Kee, *Miracle in the Early Christian World* (1983), pp. 146-73.

2. David Russell, *The Method and Message of Jewish Apocalyptic*, (1964), p. 297.

3. Emil Schürer, *A History of the Jewish People in the Time of Jesus Christ*, Division II, Volume II, pp. 175-77. This classic work is in the process of being revised and updated by Geza Vermes, Fergus Millar, and Matthew Black. Volume 1 appeared in 1973; Volume 2 in 1979 and Volume 3 in 1986. Included in Volume 2 is an excellent section on 'Messianism' (pp. 488-554) with a full and comprehensive bibliography.

4. We shall discuss some of the individual works below. For an overview of Charles's views on the matter, see his *A Critical History of the Doctrine of a Future Life in Israel, in Judaism, and in Christianity* (1899). Basically Charles names 100 BCE as the time when the distinction begins to be drawn.

5. 'The Temporary Messianic Reign in the Literature of Early Judaism', *JBL* 53 (1934), pp. 170-87. This article carries a comprehensive bibliography of the matter up to 1934.

6. *The Mysticism of Paul the Apostle*, pp. 84-90. See the critique of Schweitzer's interpretation of Paul on this matter in Hans Conzelmann's *1 Corinthians* (1975), p. 270 n. 63.

7. (1956), pp. 277-79.

8. *Judaism in the First Centuries of the Christian Era* (1927), II, pp. 323-95. For a criticism of Moore's work as well as an attempt to direct Jewish studies along the proper course, see Jacob Neusner, '"Judaism" after Moore: A Programmatic Statement', *JJS* 31 (1980), pp. 141-56.

9. See especially ch. 11 (pp. 285-303), which is given over to a discussion of the Messianic Kingdom.

10. Russell himself recognizes that the Messiah is not found in all five of these works (*op. cit.*, p. 309). Nevertheless, he persists in discussing all five within a chapter entitled 'The Messianic Kingdom'. I have designated those which do *not* contain mention of a Messiah-figure as books teaching a 'temporary, earthly (Messianic) Kingdom' thus retaining the term 'messianic' out of deference to Russell's grouping. However, as the discussion will show, this terminology is inadequate and potentially misleading. Ultimately I would call for a purification of the term with regards to the alleged 'messianic' nature of the temporary, earthly Kingdom within some of these Jewish documents. Russell does go on to outline other conceptualizations of

the future within the Jewish apocalyptic works. For instance, he says that the *Assumption of Moses* teaches the heavenly, Eternal Age of God as the awaited eschatological hope. He lists the following as teaching the earthly, Messianic Kingdom which lasts forever as that eschatological hope: Daniel; *1 Enoch* 6–36; *1 Enoch* 83–90; *Testament of the 12 Patriarchs*; *Sibylline Oracles* 3; *Psalms of Solomon* 17 & 18; and the *Similitudes of Enoch*.

11. See Russell, *op. cit.*, pp. 291-97; G.W.E. Nickelsburg, *Jewish Literature* (1981), pp. 145-46.

12. For a survey of *1 Enoch* within its historical setting consult Michael Stone, 'The Book of Enoch and Judaism in the Third Century B.C.E.', *CBQ* 40 (1978), pp. 479-92. James VanderKam, *Enoch and the Growth of an Apocalyptic Tradition*, 1984), pp. 144-49, suggests that the work was written between 175 and 167 BCE and argues that the author of the Weeks Apocalypse is the same as the author of the *Epistle of Enoch*. Matthew Black, *The Book of Enoch or 1 Enoch* (1985), pp. 287-95, suggests, on the basis of his interpretation of the 7th and 8th Weeks, that it was written after the Maccabean victories but before the reconsecration of the Temple, and thus dates the *Apocalypse of Weeks* to the time of Daniel, that is, prior to 165 BCE.

13. For a comprehensive bibliography of the literature dealing with *1 Enoch*, see: J.H. Charlesworth, *PMRS* (1981), pp. 98-103 and 278-83; *Semeia* 14: *Apocalypse*, edited by J.J. Collins (1979), pp. 31-32 and 51-52; *AOT* (1984), pp. 180-84.

14. The Greek fragments of *1 Enoch* unfortunately do not generally include material from the *Apocalypse of Weeks* itself. J.T. Milik, *The Books of Enoch* (1976), p. 264, does contain a discussion of a small fragment of the Chester-Beatty Michigan papyrus which may be relevant. The Coptic fragments are slightly more productive, preserving sections of 93.3-8. Matthew Black, *The Book of Enoch or 1 Enoch* (1985), pp. 1-8, contains a summary of the textual history of the book.

15. *The Ethiopic Book of Enoch*, 2 vols. Also note his contribution to *AOT* (1984), pp. 169-319.

16. See R.H. Charles, *The Book of Enoch* (1917), pp. 132-34. Michael Knibb feels that the displacement may be due to the judgment theme found in 91.1-10. Compare his *Ethiopic Book of Enoch*, II, p. 218. Also see the comments of Michael Stone, *JWSTP* (1984), p. 405.

17. The translation is taken from Knibb's *Ethiopic Book of Enoch*, II (1978), pp. 219-221 and 223-25.

18. Milik, *op. cit.*, p. 246. Knibb adopts Milik's views (*op. cit.*, p. 11).

19. The major difference between the Ethiopic and Aramaic texts is the linking of 91.11. In the Aramaic it is much shorter and altogether different in content from the Ethiopic. Knibb feels (*op. cit.*, p. 218) that the Ethiopic 91.11 is a redactional link designed to smooth over the violent change of

context from 91.1-10 to 91.11-17. Matthew Black argues, in 'The Apocalypse of Weeks in the Light of 4QENg', *VT* 28 (1978), pp. 464-69, that 91.11 was contained in the original Aramaic description of the seventh week and formed the basis of 91.5-10 which was composed later. He also attempts to complete the amputated ending of the Apocalypse in 91.17 by linking 92.3, 5 to it and thus finishing the Apocalypse on a note of resurrection of the righteous. Also note the discussion in Matthew Black, *The Book of Enoch or 1 Enoch* (1985), pp. 294-95.

20. Milik, *op, cit.*, pp. 245-59. On the possibility of Iranian ideas underlying such a periodization of history, see Geo. Widengren, 'Iran and Israel in Parthian Times with Special Regard to the Ethiopian Book of Enoch', in *Religious Syncretism in Antiquity* (1975), pp. 110-12.

21. Black, *art. cit.*, pp. 468-69, undermines Milik's thesis that the same author composed both the *Apocalypse of Weeks* and the *Epistle of Enoch* (91-104). Compare, Martin Hengel, *Judaism and Hellenism* (1974), pp. 180-96, where the origins of apocalyptic views of world history are discussed. This larger issue of apocalyptic historiography is discussed in the excellent article by L.L. Grabbe, 'Chronology in Hellenistic', *SBL 1979 Seminar Papers*, Volume II (1979), pp. 43-68. Also note: G.I. Davies, 'Apocalyptic and Historiography', *JSOT* 5 (1978), pp. 15-28, and Adela Yarbro Collins, 'Numerical Symbolism in Jewish and Early Christian Apocalyptic Literature', *ANRW* II 21.2 (1984), pp. 1221-87. The practical purpose of such apocalyptic schematizations about the future is emphasized in Lars Hartman, 'The Functions of Some So-Called Apocalyptic Timetables', *NTS* 22 (1975-76), pp. 1-14.

22. For an innovative, but highly speculative, attempt to interpret the *Apocalypse of Weeks* as a secret history of the Qumran sect, see Jeanie P. Thorndike, 'The Apocalypse of Weeks and the Qumran Sect', *RQ* 3 (1961), pp. 163-84. Thorndike co-ordinates the *Apocalypse of Weeks* with other Qumran sectarian scrolls to arrive at a history of the community prior to its installation at Qumran. Compare also G.W.E. Nickelsburg, 'The Epistle of Enoch and the Qumran Litrerature', *JJS* 33 (1982), pp. 333-48, where the *Apocalypse of Weeks* is seen as a scenario in which one is able to glean hints about the contemporary situation of the author of the epistle by his juxtaposition of the wicked and righteous in the seventh week of the *Apocalypse* (93.8-10, 91.11). This is to be compared with CD 1 and 1QS 8. Both the *Apocalypse* and the Qumran scrolls are thought to contain a common polemic against temple and cult.

23. We see here a link between this section of *1 Enoch* and the earlier *Book of Dreams* (chs. 83-90). For an assessment of the revelatory nature of apocalyptic, see Christopher Rowland, *The Open Heaven* (1982). The *Apocalypse of Weeks* is specifically discussed on pp. 163-65.

24. A persistent feature of R.H. Charles's works on the pseudepigrapha is his designation of this Kingdom as 'messianic', even where there is no

mention of a Messiah within the passage or book concerned. He does this knowingly. For a statement of his reasons, see his *Doctrine of a Future Life* (1899), pp. 80ff.

25. *APOT* II, pp. 170, 262-65.

26. *Henochs Zehnwochenapokalypse und offene Probleme der Apokalyptik-forschung* (1977).

27. Dexinger does add an introductory verse (92.1), to the Apocalypse. See pp. 110-111, 117-118, for his justification in doing so. In addition, he accepts an Aramaic Vorlage for 91.11 based upon 4QENg.

28. For a critique of Dexinger's hypothesis, see James C. VanderKam, 'Studies in the Apocalypse of Weeks (1 Enoch 93.1-10; 91.11-17)', *CBQ* 46 (1984), pp. 511-23. Dexinger's book is also critically reviewed by G.W.E. Nickelsburg in *JBL* 100 (1981), pp. 669-70.

29. Dexinger wishes to ground the reference to the 'sword' in 91.12 in the concrete, historical confrontation during the time of the author. In this connection we could also note the references to the 'sword' in other books of the Maccabean era (1 Macc. 3.3, 12; Dan. 11.34).

30. Remembering, of course, that the phrase is plural in the Ethiopic and is more accurately translated as 'The Chosen Righteous Ones'.

31. See the fascinating parallels with Qumran materials outlined by Dexinger on pp. 166-69 and 174-78. Compare Shozo Fujita, 'The Metaphor of Plant in Jewish Literature of the Intertestamental Period', *JSJ* 7 (1976), pp. 30-45.

32. Dexinger outlines the parallelism thus (p. 142):

Enoch 91.12	A	Gericht auf der Erde (Bedrücker)
Enoch 91.13	a1	Neuer Tempel
Enoch 91. 14	a2	Universale Ordnung
Enoch 91.15	B	Gericht im Himmel (Engel)
Enoch 91.16	b1	Neuer Himmel
Enoch 91.17	b2	Himmlische Ordnung

33. Follow the discussion in Matthew Black, 'The "Son of Man" in the Old Biblical Literature', *ExpT* 60 (1948-49), p. 13; 'The Eschatology of the Similitudes of Enoch', *JTS* 3 (1952), pp. 1-10; and his *The Book of Enoch or 1 Enoch* (1985), pp. 18, 188-93. Also note the extended footnote in H.H. Rowley, *The Relevance of Apocalyptic* (1963), p. 62 n. 1; James H. Charlesworth, *TOTPNT* (1985), pp. 18, 88-90.

34. Matthew Black, 'Aramaic Barnasha and the "Son of Man"', *ExpT* 95 (1983-84), p. 201, accepts that chs. 70-71 might be a later addition to the *Similitudes*, possibly the invention of late, esoteric cabbalistic Judaism. Also, see the comments of Michael Stone, *JWSTP* (1984), pp. 399-403.

35. Lindars, *Jesus Son of Man* (1983), pp. 13-14.

36. Compare *2 Enoch* 7.2-4. *1 Enoch* 14 plays an important role in descriptions of visionary experiences as they are recorded in many Jewish apocalyptic texts. On this point see: Christopher Rowland, 'The Visions of

God in Apocalyptic Literature', *JSJ* 10 (1979), pp. 39-43; Mary Dean-Otting, *Heavenly Journeys: A Study of the Motif in Hellenistic Jewish Literature* (1984), pp. 39-58; James C. VanderKam, *Enoch and the Growth of an Apocalyptic Tradition* (1984), pp. 130-35.

37. Lindars, commenting on these passages, says (p. 14):

> From these two passages, we can see that Jewish apocalyptic in New Testament times is capable of thinking of celestial assistants in the process of the divine judgment, who may include persons like Enoch who are reserved in heaven. We can also see what the figure of the Messiah is like in an apocalyptic setting. He is not a political deliverer, but the leader of the redeemed in the new and everlasting Kingdom which follows the final judgment.

Lindars, although correct in the general thrust of what he is saying, fails to note that he presupposes *one* particular schematization of the future; namely that of an eternal Messianic Kingdom on earth. We, of course, would want to qualify that presupposition by a more careful analysis of the competing traditions concerning the future Age.

38. Nor, indeed, should our dating of the *Similitudes*!

39. Robert Coughenour, 'The Wisdom Stance of Enoch's Redactor', *JSJ* 13 (1982), pp. 47-55, attempts to come to some understanding of the redactor's thought by his arrangement of material throughout the book.

40. For a comprehensive bibliography on the book of *Jubilees* see Charlesworth, *PMRS* (1981), pp. 143-47 and 293-95; *Semeia* 14: *Apocalypse*, edited by J.J. Collins (1979), pp. 32-33 and 52-53; *AOT* (1984), pp. 7-10.

41. Russell, *Jewish Apocalyptic*, pp. 292-93; Nickelsburg, *Jewish Literature*, pp. 73-80.

42. *The Book of Jubilees* (1902).

43. G.H. Box is critical of this idea. See his Introduction to the popular edition of Charles's *The Book of Jubilees* (1917), pp. viii, xviii-xxii, xxix-xxxiii.

44. The one clear reference to this Messiah is 31.18. See Charles's comments on pp. lxxxvii, 188.

45. Charles pointed to *Ethiopic Enoch* 83-90, the *Testament of Levi* 18, and *1 Macc.* 14.8-15 a advocating such a belief (*op. cit.*, pp. lxxxvii-lxxxviii). Hyrcanus was only to introduce the Messianic Kingdom over which the Judahic Messiah was to rule. Compare, Charles's comments on 1.26 in this regard.

46. In 23.26-28 the length of a man's life is gradually increased as he submits himself to study of an obedience to the Torah. This is a reversal of the process mentioned in 23.9-12 where a shortened life-span is blamed upon the wickedness of man. In the Messianic Age men will live to be 1,000 years old, the age designed by God (23.27). Adam died early, at the age of 930, as a result of his transgression (4.30).

47. The translations are taken from R.H. Charles, *The Book of Jubilees*

(1902). Charles's translations are updated in *AOT* (1984), pp. 1-139.

48. It should be noted that the Day of Judgment is linked to the Genesis flood story in an eschatological context in 4.19, 24 and 5.10.

49. *Op. cit.*, p.150.

50. *The Eschatology of the Book of Jubilees* (1971).

51. For instance, the author does speak of a day of great judgment in 5.1-19 where the story of the Watchers of Genesis 6 is used as a prototype of what lies ahead; but the focus is on the fact of judgment and not its details. The author did evidently feel that his generation was the last before this great judgment since he mentions there were only forty years left in which to study the Torah in preparation (50.4).

52. *Op. cit.*, p. 13. For an up-to-date discussion of the date of *Jubilees*, see James C. VanderKam, *Textual and Historical Studies in the Book of Jubilees* (1977). Vanderkam attempts to include the Qumran fragments of *Jubilees* within his discussion and concludes that a date between 161 and 152 BCE is probable. A crucial basis for his suggested dates is the way in which the author of *Jubilees* has recast the battle stories of 34.2-9 and 37.1-38.14 in light of the Maccabean Revolt (pp. 214ff.) More recently, Ben Zion Wacholder, *The Dawn of Qumran* (1983), pp. 41ff., has argued for a pre-Maccabean date of the book, while G.W.E. Nickelsburg, *JWSTP* (1984), pp. 101-103, has argued for a date 'close to 168 BCE'.

53. Davenport suggests Qumran as a likely place of its writing (*op. cit.*, p. 16). Also note the comments of VanderKam (*op. cit.*, pp. 258-59 n. 94).

54. *Ibid.*, pp. 64-66.

55. Charles feels that 23.29-31 does not teach a resurrection of the body into the Messianic Kingdom but fully harmonizes the passage with *Ethiopian Enoch* 91-104 where a 'blessed immortality' awaits the spirits of the righteous following the great judgment at the end of the Messianic Kingdom. On the whole issue see: H.C.C. Cavallin, *Life After Death* (1974), pp. 36-40; see G.W.E. Nickelsburg, *Resurrection, Immortality and Eternal Life in Intertestamental Judaism* (1972), pp. 31-33 and 46-47; Christopher Rowland, *The Open Heaven* (1982), p. 167.

56. VanderKam argues for the close affinity between *Jubilees* and the Qumran sectarian literature with respect to the teaching contained in them. He feels that *Jubilees* played an important role within the development of the Qumran community and suggests that CD 16.2-4 is an indication of the high respect in which the book was held by the Qumran sectarians. For the importance of 23.14-31 as a key to proper dating of *Jubilees*, see *op. cit.*, pp. 252-54. VanderKam's thesis is critiqued by Philip R. Davies, 'Calendrical Change and Qumran Origins: An Assessment of VanderKam's Theory', *CBQ* 45 (1983), pp. 80-89.

57. *Ibid.*, pp. 267-70.

58. Cavallin suggests that there may be link between 23.31 and the Essene beliefs about the immortality of the soul as recorded in Josephus *BJ* 2 154-

157 and *Ant* 18.8; Hippolytus *Ref.* 9.27; and other Qumran materials (*op. cit.*, pp. 60-72). For a comprehensive study involving Essene concepts, as well as the larger Hellenistic implications, see Martin Hengel, *Judaism and Hellenism* (1974), pp. 196-202.

59. For a listing of the literature on *2 Enoch*, see: James H. Charlesworth, *PMRS* (1981), pp. 103-106, 283; *Semeia* 14: *Apocalypse*, edited by J.J. Collins (1979), pp. 40, 55; *AOT* (1984), pp. 326-28.

60. *The Book of the Secrets of Enoch* (1896). A further translation by N. Forbes is available in *APOT* II (1913), pp. 431-69.

61. See Ulrich Fischer, *Eschatologie und Jenseitserwartung im Hellenistischen Diasporajudentum* (1978), pp. 37-41, for a critical discussion of the relationship between the two versions. Fischer concludes that the shorter (B) version is earlier and more reliable. A. Vaillant, *Le Livre des Secrets d'Hénoch: texte slave et traduction française* (1952), pp. 1ff. and xvff., also discusses the problem of the two versions and opts for the shorter one as earlier. Compare: Arie Rubenstein, 'Observations on the Slavonic Book of Enoch', *JJS* 13 (1962), pp. 1-21; *AOT* (1984), pp. 321-23.

62. Largely based upon the Greek '"Αδαμ' anagram in 30.13 (note the similar anagram in *SO* 3.24), the listing of the planets using their Greek names in 30.3, and the reliance of *2 Enoch* upon the chronology of the LXX. See Fischer, *op. cit.*, p. 37 for details.

63. But see N. Schmidt, 'The Two Recensions of Slavonic Enoch', *JAOS* 41 (1921), pp. 307-12, for a defense of a Palestinian provenance.

64. Russell, *Jewish Apocalyptic* (1964), pp. 61-62 contains a discussion of those who advocate a later date by a Christian author.

65. See Morfil and Charles, *The Book of the Secrets of Enoch* (1896), pp. 85-93, for a discussion and translation. At the time of Charles's edition this section was known in only one minor manuscript. Since that time it has been discovered to exist in several other manuscripts. F.I. Andersen (*TOTP* I [1983], pp. 196-97), lists that five manuscripts contain this concluding section. G.W.E. Nickelsburg, *Jewish Literature* (1981), pp. 185-88 has a running comparison of the parallel structures of *1 Enoch* and *2 Enoch*. He comments that this Melchizedekian Fragment corresponds to *1 Enoch* 106-107. James H. Charlesworth, *TOTPNT* (1985), pp. 23-24. 85, discusses the importance this section might have in helping to explain the virgin birth accounts in the New Testament.

66. See *The Book of the Secrets of Enoch* (1896), pp. xxvii, xxix-xxx, 45-47. Charles's opinions are adopted by Russell, *Jewish Apocalyptic* (1964), p. 293.

67. H.C.C. Cavallin, *Life After Death* (1974), pp. 163-66, feels that the passage in *2 Enoch* supports the teaching of future life after death for the righteous but argues that no explicit statements concerning the resurrection of the body nor the immortality of the soul are contained within the book.

68. See S. Pines, 'Eschatology and the Concept of Time in the Slavonic

Book of Enoch', in *Types of Redemption*, edited by R.J.Z. Werblowsky and C.J. Bleeker (1970), pp. 72-87. Pines explores the possibility of Zoroastrian influence upon the author of Slavonic Enoch in this matter. Just as a matter of interest, this question of influence extends forward into time as well, for Pines goes on to argue that Dostoyevsky was influenced by the Slavonic Book of Enoch in the production of Brothers Karamazov.

69. Of the two manuscripts upon which Charles's edition was based, (A) is from the second half of the seventeenth century while (B) is from the sixteenth century.

70. *TOTP* I (1983), pp. 91-221.

71. Andersen lists 20 manuscripts in *TOTP* I (1983), p. 92. The figure of 23 is mentioned in James H. Charlesworth, 'The SNTS Pseudepigrapha Seminars at Tübingen and Paris on the Books of Enoch', *NTS* 25 (1978-79), pp. 316-18.

72. Andersen notes that this is especially true in chs. 24–33, the section most relevant to our study. As he says (p. 94),

> These chapters contain many wierd notions in the longer recension, some of which could be embellishments. But the shorter account is so incomplete and so disjointed that it seems more like the debris left after drastic revision than an original succinct account. Some, at least, of the creation passages found only in manuscripts of the longer recension are worthy of more serious attention than they have received.

The problem associated with Slavic pseudepigrapha are discussed in James H. Charlesworth, *TOTPNT* (1985), pp. 32-36.

73. I am reliant upon the translation of Kirsopp Lake in the Loeb Classical Library edition (1912-13), for quotations from the *Epistle of Barnabas*.

74. The correspondence between *Urzeit* and *Endzeit* is also found explicitly stated in the *Epistle of Barnabas* 6.19 via an unattributable quotation expounding Gen. 1.26-28.

75. Andersen (*op. cit.*, p. 156), calls attention to Rev. 1.10 in connection with *2 Enoch* 33.2 and contrasts it with the declaration of the first day of creation as being the Lord's day in 28.5. For further discussion of this topic see Wilfred Stott, 'A Note on the Word KYPIAKH in Rev. 1.10', *NTS* 12 (1965-66), pp. 70-75; and Kenneth Strand, 'Another Look at "Lord's" Day in the Early Church and in Rev. 1.10', *NTS* 13 (1966-67), pp. 174-81. For a further fanciful development of this analogical idea within the New Testament, see Thomas Barrosse, 'The Seven Days of the New Creation in St. John's Gospel', *CBG* 21 (1958), pp. 507-16; L. Paul Trudinger, 'The Seven Days of the New Creation in St. John's Gospel: Some Further Reflections', *EQ* 44 (1972), pp. 154-58.

76. See S. Lowy, 'Confutation of Judaism in the Epistle of Barnabas', *JJS* 11 (1960), pp. 1-33.

77. The late date of the *Epistle of Barnabas* (I take it to have been written between 70 and 100 CE) does not remove it from our consideration. It still

embodies Jewish concepts as the foundational ground upon which late Christian reformulations are built. It is this Jewish bedrock which we want to expose in connection with *2 Enoch*.

78. Apparently the opinion of Maxwell Staniforth in *Early Christian Writings: The Apostolic Fathers* (1980), p. 196, when he notes that the preceeding quotation is 'not found in our Book of Enoch'. Kirsopp Lake (*op. cit.*, p. 196) does try to tie in the passage to *1 Enoch* by cross-referencing *Enoch* 89.61-64 and 90.17.

79. Remembering that *2 Enoch* is a midrash on Gen. 5.21-32, and that from the standpoint of Enoch's time this day of judgment is the great Flood.

80. For bibliographical details on the *Ascension of Isaiah*, see James H. Charlesworth, *PMRS* (1981), pp. 125-30. The standard English translation remains R.H. Charles, *The Ascension of Isaiah* (1900), recently revised in *AOT* (1984), pp. 775-812.

81. Although David Flusser, 'The Apocryphal Book of Ascensio Isaiae and the Dead Sea Sect', *IEJ* 3 (1953), pp. 30-47, does attempt to interpret the work apart from the Christian redaction and relate it directly to the Essenes at Qumran. The relevant verse for our consideration (9.9) falls within the Vision of Isaiah itself (6.1-11.4) in which Isaiah's ascent to the seventh heaven is described. Much of the description of this seventh heaven is given over to detailing Christ's descent to earth, his life and death, and his eventual ascent back to heaven. Isaiah views all of this from his vantage point in the seventh heaven. The final granting of crowns and thrones of glory to Enoch and the rest of the transformed righteous is made dependent upon Christ's incarnation and ascension (9.10-18).

82. For a comprehensive bibliography on *3 Enoch*, see James H. Charlesworth, *PMRS* (1981), pp. 106-107, 283.

83. See P. Alexander, *TOTP* I (1983), pp. 223-315. Also note his article, 'The Historical Setting of the Hebrew Book of Enoch', *JJS* 28 (1977), pp. 156-80.

84. This point is further substantiated and clarified in 48D.4.

85. It is intriguing to note that the title does appear in the Gnostic work *Pistis Sophia*. See P. Alexander, *art. cit.*, pp. 161-72, for details. The title is to be contrasted with the set phrase 'the greater YHWH' (48B.44ff.) among the 70 names of God contained in the concluding chapter of 48B. Apparently the highest archangels carried the title 'YHWH' as part of their names: see 6.1; 10.3; 16.5; compare 18.8-24; 19.1; 20.1; 22.1, 16; 25.1; 30.1.

86. P. Alexander, *TOTP* I (1983), pp. 244, 268. Compare p. 264, note i on 10.3.

87. This so-called 'Two Powers in heaven' controversy derives its name from the exclamation of Elisha ben Abuya recorded in *3 Enoch* 16.3. The issue becomes a matter of considerable rabbinic dispute. See P. Alexander, *art. cit.*, pp. 176-78; and Alan F. Segal, *Two Powers in Heaven: Early*

Rabbinic Reports about Christianity and Gnosticism (1977), for details.

88. It may be that the precipitating event for the divine chastisement in this chapter is Metatron's sitting upon the heavenly throne (16.2). This is an action explicitly mentioned as reserved for God alone in 18.24. Indeed, there is some rabbinic discussion of this point, notably *Hagigah* 15a. For details, see Hugo Odeberg, *3 Enoch or the Hebrew Book of Enoch* (1928), pp. 63-64; Alan F. Segal, *op. cit.*, pp. 60-73.

89. In fact, there are several manuscripts of *3 Enoch* which contain this concluding chapter along with two others: 48B and 48D. P. Alexander, *TOTP* I (1983), p. 224, lists them. He also discusses (pp. 310-15) these extra chapters of 48BCD and suggest that they are material taken over from the *Alphabet of Aqiba* and added to the end of certain recensions. Thus they are deemed not original to *3 Enoch*.

90. P. Alexander, *TOTP* (1983), pp. 225-29, for details.

91. For a brief introduction into the importance such Enoch speculations have for New Testament studies, see Barnabas Lindars, 'Enoch and Christology', *ExpT* 92 (1980-81), pp. 295-99.

92. *Christology in the Making* (1980), p. 80, Also note pp. 17ff., 274 n. 36, 299 n. 93. Dunn is here dependent upon the work of Segal.

93. In fact, there is some justification for suggesting a first-century CE context for the initial stages of this debate given the remarkable parallels between the rabbinic materials dealing with the 'Two-Powers' controversy and select passages from Paul's contemporary, Philo. See Segal, *op. cit.*, pp. 159ff. for details. Particularly important here is the way in which Philo speaks of a 'second god' (δεύτερος θεός).

94. In fact, there are two Messiahs mentioned in this verse: one from the tribe of Joseph and one from the tribe of David. Hugo Odeberg (*op. cit.*, pp. 144ff.) discusses this point and suggests that the idea of a Messiah from the tribe of Joseph dates to Tannaitic times.

95. Matthew Black ('The "Two Witnesses" of Rev. II.3F. in Jewish and Christian Apocalyptic Tradition', in *Donum Gentilicium* [David Daube FS], edited by E. Bammel, C.K. Barrett & W.D. Davies [1978], pp. 233ff.), suggestively associates these Enoch speculations with the vindicated 'righteous man' of the Hellenistic book of Wisdom 4.10-5.5. If there is any validity in such an association, an important link with a Wisdom tradition is established.

96. As a point of methodology, any discussion of the importance of the Melchizedek Legends of *2 Enoch* 69-73 must be conducted with the understanding that the Legends form an integral part of some of the extent *2 Enoch* manuscripts. That is to say, we have no independent attestation of the Melchizedek Legends and we should not treat it as if it were an isolated document.

97. F.I. Anderson (*TOTP* I [1983], p. 97), feels that the only point of commonality is that all demonstrate a general tendency to midrashim about Melchizedek.

98. There is much to be said for 53:1-2 as evidence in favour of Jewish authorship of *2 Enoch*. No Christian could have written this.

99. See James H. Charlesworth, 'Christian and Jewish Self-Definition in Light of the Christian Additions to the Apocryphal Writings', in *Jewish and Christian Self-Definition*, II, edited by E.P. Sanders (1981), pp. 46-48.

100. For a discussion as to the original language of the Apocalypse, see Joshua Bloch, 'The Ezra-Apocalypse, was it written in Hebrew, Greek or Aramaic?', *JQR* 48 (1957-58), pp. 279-84.

101. See A.P. Hayman, 'The Problem of Pseudonymity in the Ezra Apocalypse', *JSJ* 6 (1975), pp. 46-57, where the way in which the author uses the pseudonymous prophet to express his own theological concerns and anguishes is explored. Compare Michael Knibb, 'The Exile in Intertestamental Literature', *HJ* 17 (1976), pp. 253-72; Michael Knibb, 'The Exile in the Damascus Document', *JSOT* 25 (1983), pp. 110ff.

102. G.W.E. Nickelsburg, *Jewish Literature between the Bible and the Mishnah* (1981), pp. 277-309, gives a brief introduction to the history of this Revolt and its suppression, as well as a summary of the Jewish literary response which followed. See Jacob Neusner, 'Judaism in a Time of Crisis: Four Responses to the destruction of the Second Temple', *Judaism* 21 (1972), pp. 313-27; Michael Stone, 'Reactions to the Destruction of the Second Temple', *JSJ* 12 (1981), pp. 195-204; Robert Goldenberg, 'Early Rabbinic Explanations of the Destruction of Jerusalem', *JJS* 33 (1982), pp. 517-25; J.J. Collins, *Between Athens and Jerusalem*, (1983), pp. 117-22; Jacob Neusner, *Judaism in the Beginning of Christianity* (1984), pp. 89-99.

103. See Walter Harrison, 'Ezra Among the Wicked in 2 Esdras 3-10', *The Divine Helmsman: Studies of God's Control of Human Events* (Silberman FS; 1980), pp. 21-39; A.L. Thompson, *Responsibility for Evil in the Theodicy of IV Ezra: A Study Illustrating the Significance of Form and Structure for the Meaning of the Book* (SBL Dissertation Series, 29; 1977); D. Boyarin, 'Penitential Liturgy in 4 Ezra', *JSJ* 3 (1972), pp. 30-34; J.C.H. Lebram, 'The Piety of the Jewish Apocalyptists', in *AMWNE* (1983), pp. 199ff. Stephen H. Travis ('The Value of Apocalyptic', *TB* [1979], pp. 57ff.) stresses the connection between theodicy and the positive worth of apocalyptic within Jewish faith.

104. For a helpful introduction to the textual difficulties associated with *4 Ezra*, see Michael Stone, 'Some Remarks on the Textual Criticism of IV Ezra', *HTR* 60 (1967), pp. 107-15.

105. See Joshua Bloch, 'Some Christological Interpolations in the Ezra Apocalypse', *HTR* 51 (2958), pp. 87-94, where it is argued that all six occurrences of 'my Son' in *4 Ezra* are Christian interpolations. Compare Michael Stone, *Features of the Eschatology of IV Ezra* (1965), pp. 71-75, Stephen Gero, '"My Son the Messiah": A Note on 4 Ezra 7:28-29', *ZNW* 66 (1975), pp. 264-67; M. de Jonge's comments in *TDNT* IX (1974), pp. 515-16; James H. Charlesworth, 'Christian and Jewish Self-Definition in Light of the Christian Additions to the Apocryphal Writings', in *Jewish and Christian*

Self-Definition, II, edited by E.P. Sanders (1981), p. 28. There is some evidence for suggesting that the operative word in the Greek vorlage for 'son' is not υἱός but παῖς. See Seyoon Kim, *The Origin of Paul's Gospel* (1982), pp. 210, 215. J. Massyngberde Ford ('"He that Cometh" and the Divine Name', *JSJ* 1 [1970], pp. 144-47), questions whether these are Christian interpolations at all and suggests the possibility that they stem from Jewish sectarian circles. She analyzes the question in connection with the revelation of John, which she takes to derive not from Christian hands but from a Baptist sectarian movement within Judaism.

106. There is a great deal of textual confusion as to the length of the Messianic Kingdom in this verse. Some manuscripts read '30 years', some '400 years', and some '1000 years'. It is generally thought that there was some typological significance to these variations. The '400 years' corresponds to the length of time the Israelites spent in bondage in Egypt, for instance. The reference to '30 years' is thought to reflect a Christian scribal emendation specifically designed to make the length of the Messianic Kingdom correspond to the length of Jesus's life. The reference to '1000 years' is probably dependent upon the widespread notion of a world-week derived from Ps. 90.4. The rabbinic literature abounds with discussions over the length of the Messianic Age. Significant variants from that body of literature include: '40 years'—the length of time the Israelites spent in the wilderness; and '600 years'—the length of a sycamore tree's life. For details, see Strack & Billerbeck, *Kommentar zum Neuen Testament*, III (1926), pp. 823-27; Michael Stone, *Features of the Eschatology of IV Ezra* (1965), pp. 256-57 n. 218; Adela Yarbro Collins, 'Numerical Symbolism in Jewish and Early Christian Apocalyptic Literature', *ANRW* II, 21.2 (1984), pp. 1246-47.

107. Witness the debate over the *Testaments of the Twelve Patriarchs*! See James H. Charlesworth, *PMRS* (1981), pp. 211-20 and 305-307; *TOTPNT* (1985), pp. 38-40; Marius de Jonge, 'Christian Influence in the Testaments of the Twelve Patriarchs', *NovT* 4 (1960-61), pp. 182-235; Howard C. Kee, 'The Ethical Dimensions of the Testaments of the XII as a Clue to Provenance', *NTS* 24 (1977-78), pp. 259-70; *AOT* (1984), pp. 505-600.

108. Whether or not we should label any segment of Palestinian Judaism as 'sectarian' is a controversial issue. Follow the debate, for instance, within *The Journal for the Study of Judaism*: N.J. McEleney, 'Orthodoxy in Judaism of the First Christian Century', *JSJ* 4 (1973), pp. 19-42; D.E. Aune, 'Orthodoxy in First Century Judaism? A Response to N.J. McEleney', *JSJ* 7 (1976), pp. 1-10; Lester Grabbe, 'Orthodoxy in First Century Judaism', *JSJ* 8 (1977), pp. 149-53; N.J. McEleney, 'Orthodoxy in Judaism of the First Christian Century', *JSJ* 9 (1978), pp. 83-88. For an attempt to clarify some of the terms used in this debate, see Robert Murray, 'Jews, Hebrews and Christians: Some Needed Distinctions', *NovT* 24 (1982), pp. 194-208; James H. Charlesworth, *TOTPNT* (1985), pp. 58-62. It is perhaps more accurate,

certainly less controversial, if to say simply that *4 Ezra* represents one 'strand' of first-century Judaism, of which there were many.

109. E.P. Sanders, *Paul and Palestinian Judaism* (1977), pp. 409-18. Also note his 'The Covenant as a Soteriological Category and the Nature of Salvation in Palestinian and Hellenistic Judaism', in *Jews, Greeks and Christians* (Davies FS; 1976), pp. 11-44.

110. *Op. cit.*, p. 418.

111. *Ibid.*, p. 418. Sanders argues that throughout the Palestinian literature under consideration, obedience to the covenant is essential to one's security within the covenant. It is on this basis that the inner connection between the law and the covenant is to be discovered. This connection holds true for *4 Ezra* as well, but with one important qualifier: such obedience to the law must be perfect. In effect, this means that within the dialogues of *4 Ezra* salvation is maintained by a life of perfection; an ideal very difficult to distinguish from belief in the salvific potential of the law itself. Nevertheless, Sanders argues that the formal relationship between law and covenant is maintained in *4 Ezra* (p. 420). In short, according to Sanders analysis, within *4 Ezra* faithfulness to the covenant *is* perfect obedience to the law.

112. The tendency to overcategorize and make unjustified comparisons is the focus of Morna D. Hooker's critique of Sanders's work in 'Paul and "Convenantal Nomism"', in *Paul and Paulinism* (C.K. Barrett FS), edited by M.D. Hooker and S.G. Wilson (1982), pp. 47-56. Also worth examining is R.H. Gundry, 'Grace, Works, and Staying Saved in Paul', *Biblica* 66 (1985), pp. 1-38; James H. Charlesworth, *TOTPNT* (1985), pp. 47-55.

113. It should be noted that there is an abrupt shift in theological tone between the third and fourth sections of the *Ezra Apocalypse* which may be explained in part as a reconciliation to the divine will on the basis of faith in God's abilities. We find the issue of theodicy, so prominent within the first three sections, left strangely unresolved within the rest of the book. It may be that this controversy is deliberately left open as a means of further emphasizing the dependence of Ezra upon God's revelatory acts for an answer to the questions burning so fiercely within his soul. It may even be that such a dialectic is designed to further call attention to the messianic revelations so important throughout the remaining visions of the Apocalypse. Regardless of whether or not faith was understood to have bridged the gap between the third and fourth sections of the book we are still left with a marked difference in emphasis between *4 Ezra* and the New Testament writers as to the nature of such faith. In short, the specifically Christ-centered element is glaringly absent. I am grateful to Dr Knibb for calling my attention to this point. See his brief comments in *The First and Second Book of Esdras* (1979), pp. 218-20.

114. See especially Michael Stone, 'The Concept of the Messiah in IV Ezra', in *Religions in Antiquity* (E.R. Goodenough FS), edited by Jacob Neusner (Studies in the History of Religions 14; 1968), pp. 295-312; James

H. Charlesworth, 'The Concept of the Messiah in the Pseudepigrapha', *ANRW* II, 19.1 (1979), pp. 188-218 and his *TOTPNT* (1985), pp. 111-19; Ulrich Müller, *Messias und Menschensohn in jüdischen Apokalypsen und in der Offenbarung des Johannes* (1972); Maurice Casey, *Son of Man: The Interpretation and Influence of Daniel 7* (1979).

115. Michael Stone, *art. cit.*, p. 295. Also note the discussion in his *Features of the Eschatology of IV Ezra*, (1965), pp. 106-33.

116. For a brief discussion of the teaching of *4 Ezra* pertaining to the resurrection, see Nickelsburg, *Resurrection*, (1981), pp. 138-40; Cavallin, *Life After Death* (1974), pp. 80-86.

117. The critical phrase here is: 'until the end comes, the day of judgment'.

118. *The Ezra Apocalypse* (1912), pp. 108-109. Compare with his contribution in R.H. Charles, *APOT* II (1913), pp. 582-614.

119. Examples of this approach include G.H. Box and W.O.E. Oesterley. Box (*The Ezra Apocalypse* [1912], pp. xxi-xxxiii) argues that the present form of the Apocalypse is due to a redactor (R) who makes use of at least five separate sources. These include: 1. A Salathiel-Apocalypse (S), which incorporates 3.1-31; 4.1-51; 5.13b–6.10; 6.30–7.25; 7.45–8.62; 9.13–10.57; 12.40-48; 14.28-35. This source is dated to about 100 CE. 2. An Ezra-Apocalypse (E), which incorporates 4.52–5.13a; 6.13-29; 7.26-44; 8.63–9.12. This source is dated prior to 70 CE. 3. The Eagle Vision (A), or chs. 11–12, dates to Flavian times. 4. The Son of Man Vision (M), of ch. 13, which is prior to 70 CE. 5. An Ezra Piece (E²), which incorporates 14.1-17a, 19–27, 36-47. This final piece dates between 70 CE and 120 CE with date of 100 CE probable. Box gives a date of about 120 CE to the final redaction of R. Compare this with the work of W.O.E. Oesterley, *II Esdras* (1933), pp. xi-xix and xliv-xlv, where it is similarly argued that the body of 2 Esdras (chs. 3–14) is composed of four independent literary pieces, each of which bears a distinctive messianic teaching and each of which can be more or less dated on the basis of its allusion to historical detail. Oesterley divides and dates the four sources thus: 1. Chapters 3–10: the Apocalypse of Ezra proper; dates to the last decade of the first century CE. 2. Chapters 11–12: The Eagle Vision; dates to 80-96 CE. 3. Chapter 13: The Vision of the Man from the Sea; dates to 66-67 CE. 4. Chapter 14: Ezra and the Holy Scriptures; dates to about 120 CE.

120. Jacob Myers, *I & II Esdras* (1974), pp. 119-21.

121. *Method and Message of Jewish Apocalyptic* (1964), pp. 62-63. See also H.H. Rowley, *The Relevance of Apocalyptic* (1963), pp. 156-59; Michael Stone, *Features of the Eschatology of IV Ezra* (1965), pp. 108ff.; Earl Breech, '"These Fragments I Have Shored Up Against My Ruins": The Form and Function of 4 Ezra', *JBL* 92 (1973), pp. 267-74, where source-critical theories, such as Box's, are criticized and an attempt is made to interpret the whole of *4 Ezra* as a move from despair to consolation under the guidance of

a single author.

122. *Die Verborgenheit Gottes im Weltgeschehen* (1981). Brandenburger focuses on the Vision of the Mourning Woman (9.26–10.59) as a means to solving the interpretation of the book as a unitary composition. His major counterpart in this in-depth literary and theological investigation is Wolfgang Harnisch, who responds to Brandenburger's suggestions in 'Der Prophet als Widerpart und Zeuge der Offenbarung: Erwägungen zur Independenz von Form und Sache im IV Buch Esra', in *AMWNE* (1983), pp. 461-93; and in 'Die Ironie der Offenbarung: Exegetische Erwägungen zur Zionvision im 4 Buch Esra', *ZAW* 95 (1983), pp. 75-95. Harnisch is here following up some of his earlier investigations in *Verhängnis und Verheissung* (1969).

123. *Art. cit.*, p. 298. For a fuller exploration of this theme, see Stone's *Features of the Eschatology of IV Ezra* (1965), pp. 83-97, and his 'Coherence and Inconsistency in the Apocalypses: The Case of "the End" in 4 Ezra', *JBL* 102 (1983), pp. 229-43.

124. See Gregory K. Beale, 'The Problem of the Man from the Sea in IV Ezra 13 and its Relation to the messianic concept in John's Apocalypse', *NovT* 25 (1983), pp. 182-88, for an affirmation of Dan. 7.13f. as influential upon both *4 Ezra* and Revelation. Several of the complexities of the vision in *4 Ezra* 13 are explained as the writer's unusual use of Danielic traditions in a manner similar to that of the author of John's Apocalypse. Of particular note is the use of 'cloud' imagery in *4 Ezra* 13.3 as derived from Dan. 7.13. J.A. Emerton ('The Origin of the Son of Man Imagery', *JST* 9 [1958], pp. 225-42), suggests that such imagery always implied divinity within the Old Testament. Also note the discussion in J.J. Collins, *The Apocalyptic Vision of the Book of Daniel* (1977), pp. 99-101; Jane Schaberg, 'Daniel 7.12 and the New Testament Passion-Resurrection Predictions', *NTS* 31 (1984-85), p. 216.

125. Lindars (*Jesus Son of Man* [1983], p. 192 n. 25) points out that the critical phrase 'something like the figure of a man' is missing from the Latin manuscripts and has to be supplied from the Syriac Version. He is here dependent upon Casey (*Son of Man* [1979], p. 124), who notes that 'there is a lacuna in the Latin and the Syriac reads *'ayk dmutha dbarnasha'*. (Also note the section on 'Son of Man' below in the Appendix.)

126. This controversial topic is thoroughly covered in two articles in *NTS* 25 (1978-79). The first is by Michael Knibb, 'The Date of the Parables of Enoch: A Critical Review', pp. 345-59, where a late-first-century CE date is suggested; the second is by Christopher Mearns, 'Dating the Similitudes of Enoch', pp. 360-69, where an even earlier date (late 40s) is proposed. Both scholars are critical of Milik's unsatisfactory procedures of determining the date of *1 Enoch* 37-71. See also J.C. Hindley, 'Towards a Date for the Similitudes of Enoch'. *NTS* 14 (1967-68), pp. 551-65, where a date during Trajan's reign (115-117 CE) is suggested; Jonas C. Greenfield and Michael

Stone, 'The Enochic Pentateuch and the Date of the Similitudes', *HTR* 70 (1977), pp. 51-65, where a first-century CE date is suggested. Compare C.L. Mearns, 'The Parables of Enoch—Origin and Date', *ExpT* 89 (1977-78), pp. 118-19; G. Bampfylde, 'The Similitudes of Enoch: Historical Allusions', *JSJ* 15 (1984). pp. 9-31, where a date of 50 BCE is suggested for the original parables themselves.

127. Critical for one's assessment of the influence of the *Similitudes* (and *4 Ezra*) upon the New Testament is the question of the oral form of these writings and their dates. It is far too easy to concentrate solely upon the final literary form of these two documents, date them to the second-century CE, and thereby remove them from active consideration. Such a procedure completely ignores the fact that these works embody oral traditions which may prove relevant to New Testament studies in spite of the fact that their completed literary form is indeed second-century. See the comments of Carl R. Holladay, 'New Testament Christology: Some Considerations of Method', *NovT* 25 (1983), pp. 274ff.; James H. Charlesworth, *TOTPNT* (1985), pp. 88-90.

128. And it should be stressed that these associations are not necessarily dependent upon the existence of a title 'Son of Man'.

129. *4 Ezra* 13 is usually given a pre-70 CE date by source scholars. See note 119 above. It is unlikely the *4 Ezra* 13 is directly reliant upon the *Similitudes of Enoch* for its ideas involving the Son of Man figure. It is probable that *4 Ezra* 13 and *1 Enoch* 37-71 are both directly dependent upon Daniel 7 itself, and that they represent independent developments of the Danielic vision. See Johannes Theisohn, *Der auserwählte Richter* (1975), pp. 144-48, for details.

130. As in 12.32!

131. The relevant section in Latin reads: *Demonstra servo tuo per quem visitas creaturam tuam.*

132. The Latin reads: *Finis per me et non per alium.*

133. *I & II Esdras* (1974), p. 201.

134. There is some discrepancy involving the text of v. 26. The Latin text could be taken to have God himself as the intended agent of deliverance. Wellhausen argued that the Latin text misreads the Greek which itself was based on an earlier Hebrew one. The Greek would have read ὅς δι' αὐτοῦ (who through him=Messiah) which the Latin mistakenly reads as δι' αὐτοῦ (through himself—God). See G.H. Box, *The Ezra Apocalypse* (1912), pp. xiv and 293 for details.

135. For a comprehensive bibliography of the literature dealing with the Testament of Moses, see James H. Charlesworth, *PMRS* (1981), pp. 163-66, 297; *AOT* (1984), pp. 604-606. The contribution of J. Priest, 'Testament of Moses (First Century A.D.)', *TOTP* I (1983), pp. 919-34, is also valuable. The Testament is also the subject of investigation in *Studies on the Testament of Moses* (SBL Septuagint and Cognate Studies, 4; edited by George W.E.

Nickelsburg, Jr, 1973). It is generally recognized that the Testament of Moses is part of the Jewish literary response of the Maccabean period, but see Solomon Zeitlin, 'The Assumption of Moses and the Revolt of Bar Kochba', *JQR* 38 (1947-48), pp. 1-45, for an attempt to firmly associate it with the Second Jewish Revolt of 132-135 CE. For a defense of the Maccabean date, see J.J. Collins, *The Apocalyptic Vision of the Book of Daniel* (1977), pp. 198-201.

136. J. Priest (*TOTP* I [1983], p. 932), notes the parallel between this angelic messenger and Melchizedek in 11QM. Both function more as warrior than as priest. Priest thinks the identification between Michael and Melchizedek in later Jewish sources has no bearing for the author of the *Testament of Moses*. We should also note the 'military' imagery surrounding Michael in *2 Enoch* 22.6; 33.10; 71.28; 72.5, where the term *archistratig* is used. This should be compared to the Latin *nuntius* of *Testament of Moses* 10.2. On this, see Adela Yarbro Collins, 'Composition and Redaction of the Testament of Moses 10', *HTR* 69 (1976), pp. 179-86. It is interesting to note that by the middle of the second century Christ becomes identified explicitly with the angel Michael in the *Shepherd of Hermas*. On this, see Jean Daniélou, *The Theology of Jewish Christianity* (1964), pp. 121-27.

137. See R.H. Charles, *The Assumption of Moses* (1897), pp. 40-41.

138. The *Testament of Moses* survives in a single extant Latin manuscript which dates from the sixth century CE. It is generally thought that the original was either in Hebrew or Aramaic. See J. Priest, *TOTP* (1983), pp. 920-21 for details as to textual reconstructions.

139. There have been many attempts to determine the messianic teaching of this mysterious *Testament of Moses*. For an unusual interpretation in this regard, turn to: Cuthbert Lattey, 'The Messianic Expectation in "The Assumption of Moses"', *CBQ* 4 (1942), pp. 9-21, who argues for the sequential placement of chs. 9 and 10 of the *Testament of Moses* in order to support his contention that Taxo (9.1) is to be understood as the Suffering-Servant Messiah of Isaiah 53. This Suffering-Servant is, according to Lattey, to bring the Kingdom of God (10.1ff.) via his vicarious death. While we can agree with Lattey about the relationship between chs. 9 and 10, his messianic interpretation of the *Testament of Moses* is without foundation. A more realistic interpretation of the identity of Taxo is to be found in Sigmund Mowinckel, 'The Hebrew Equivalent of Taxo in *Ass. Mos.* IX', *Supplements to VT*, 1 (1953), pp. 88-96, where a close association between Qumran and the *Testament of Moses* is assumed. H.H. Rowley has an extended discussion in *The Relevance of Apocalyptic* (1963), pp. 149-56. David Carlson, 'Vengeance and Angelic Mediation in Testament of Moses 9 and 10', *JBL* 101 (1982), pp. 85-95, also discusses the unity of these two chapters.

140. Finality is indicated by the reference to 'last days' in vv. 18, 20 and 46.

141. See Bruce Metzger, 'The "Lost" Section of II Esdras (= 4 Ezra)', *JBL*

76 (1957), pp. 153-56. Compare his remarks in *TOTP* I (1983), pp. 519-20.

142. It is perhaps not too unreasonable to suggest that there may be a correlation between the two facts. That is to say, that one of the reasons such a 'monotheistic' passage as 5.56-6.6 might have found its way into *4 Ezra* was because it was an attempt to preserve the transcendent character of the Most High in the face of such a passage as we find preserved in the Armenian text of *4 Ezra* 13.

143. See Myers, *op. cit.* (1974), p. 306.

144. We should not, of course, attempt to argue on the basis of these secondary translations that the original (Hebrew or Greek?) text of *4 Ezra* 13 intended such an outright identification between the son of man-figure and the Most High as we see embodied in the later Armenian text. Such a suggestion would be grossly anachronistic. (Michael Stone [*The Armenian Version of IV Ezra* (1979), pp. 3ff.] has reconstructed the Armenian text based upon all the major available manuscripts and has suggested that the earliest traceable date for the various textual families of the manuscripts is about the 12th century. However, the presence of quotations of *4 Ezra* in other Armenian literature seems to push the date back even further, indicating that a fifth century translation from the Greek is likely.) At the same time we would not wish to ignore completely the fact that these secondary translations do exist. They represent a subsequent develoment of the tradition, but the important question for our concerns is whether this subsequent development is harmonious with the ambiguity we noted between God and messianic agent in ch. 13. I would adjudge the Armenian reading to be a liberal exploitation of the original ambiguity in *4 Ezra* 13. This raises the additional and fascinating question as to what social and theological factors gave rise to the Armenian reading. It would be interesting to know, for instance, if the outright identification of the Most High with the son of man-figure took place in an environment consumed with messianic speculations or not, and at what date? If Kim's suggestions (above pp. 104-105) about the identification of the Danielic son of man-figure with the Ancient of Days in select LXX manuscripts is correct, and his proposed dating for such an identification (second-century CE at the latest) is accurate, one is tempted to insist on the re-evaluation of the different tradition of *4 Ezra* 13 contained within the Armenian text when compared with the Latin text we now possess.

145. For a comprehensive listing of the literature on *2 Baruch* see Charlesworth, *PMRS* (1981), pp. 83-86, 275; *AOT* (1984), pp. 838-41.

146. The classic *The History of the Jewish People in the Age of Jesus Christ (175 B.C.—A.D. 135)*, by Emil Schürer, recently revised by Vermes, Millar and Black, Volume II (1979), pp. 514-47, uses 2 Baruch and 4 Ezra as a framework upon which to provide a systematic presentation of messianism. The fact that the *Similitudes of Enoch* are not included in this systematic presentation is due to the editors assuming *1 Enoch* 37-71 to be a late,

Christian work (possibly under the influence of Milik's investigations?). The work of E.P. Sanders on Paul is open to the same criticism as it also neglects *1 Enoch* 37-71. See James H. Charlesworth, *TOTPNT* (1985), p. 154 n. 33, for details.

147. See A.M. Denis, *Fragmenta Pseudepigraphorum Quae Supersunt Graece* (PVTG III; 1970), pp. 118-20, where a Greek fragment is given corresponding to *2 Baruch* 12.1-13.2, and 13.11-14.3. For an English translation from the Syriac see R.H. Charles, *The Apocalypse of Baruch* (1896), *APOT* II, pp. 481-526; or *AOT* (1984), pp. 841-95.

148. *APOT* II, pp. 472-74.

149. Pierre Bogaert, *L'Apocalypse syriaque de Baruch*, I (1969), pp. 378-80. Compare J. Strugnell's review in *JBL* 89 (1970), pp. 484-85.

150. *The Apocalypse of Baruch* (1896), pp. liii-lxv. The seven sections are: 1. 1.1-5.6; 2. 6.1-9.2; 3. 10.1-12.4; 4. 12.5-20.6; 5. 21.1-35.5; 6. 36.1-46.7; 7. 47.1-77.26. It should be noted that Charles, by adopting this structure, was forced to posulate a fast at the end of ch. 35 since the (anticipated?) reference there is missing.

151. Charles first of all distinguishes between those sources which are optimistic concerning the future Kingdom of Israel on earth and those which are pessimistic concerning it and focus their hopes instead upon the immediate advent of the final judgment and the heavenly world. The former group Charles designates A1, A2, A3 (corresponding to the three Messianic Apocalypses contained in the book: 27.1-30.1; 36-40; 53-74), and B1. The latter group he designates B2 and B3. In addition, B1 is to be differentiated from the three 'A' sources in that it does not associate a Messiah with the Kingdom on earth whereas A1, A2, and A3 all do. Charles assigns 1.1-9.1; 32.2-4; 43.1-44.7; 45.1-46.7; 77.1-82.9; 84.1-11; 86.1-3 to B1 while 10.1-25.4; 30.2-32.1; 32.5-35.5; 41.1-42.8; 44.8-15; 47.1-52.7; 75.1-76.4; 83.1-22 all belong to B2. Chapter 85 is the work of B3.

152. See Louis Ginzberg, 'Apocalypse of Baruch', in *The Jewish Encyclopedia*, Volume II (1904), pp. 554-55; Russell, *Jewish Apocalyptic* (1964), pp. 64-65. The most recent attempt to interpret *2 Baruch* as the work of a solitary author is Gwendolyn B. Sayler, *Have the Promises Failed? A Literary Analysis of 2 Baruch* (SBL Dissertation Series, 72; 1984). Sayler uses the approach employed by Breech with respect to *4 Ezra* and arrives at similar conclusions. See note 121 above.

153. See A.F.J. Klijn, 'The Sources and the Redaction of the Syrian Apocalypse of Baruch', *JSJ* 1 (1971), pp. 65-76.

154. On this see Frederick J. Murphy, '2 Baruch and the Romans', *JBL* 104 (1985), pp. 663-69.

155. Charles thinks the whole passage suffers from an intrusion. See *APOT* II, p. 499.

156. The 'Messiah' is specifically mentioned in 29.3; 30.1; 39.7; 40.1; 70.9; 72.2.

157. For a discussion of *2 Baruch's* teaching on the resurrection see H.C.C. Cavallin, *Life After Death* (1974), pp. 86-94.

158. The contrast between the present corruptible world and the future incorruptible one is a persistent theme throughout *2 Baruch* (see 21.19; 74.2: compare 23.7-24.1).

159. *Art. cit.*, p. 75.

160. *TOTP* I (1983), p. 619.

161. On this issue of the Temple and attitudes concerning its restoration, see R.G. Hamerton-Kelly, 'The Temple and the Origins of Jewish Apocalyptic', *VT* 20 (1970), pp. 1-15.

162. Assuming, of course, that Klijn's analysis of this issue is correct.

163. This heavenly Jerusalem was created along with Paradise and was revealed to Adam, Abraham and Moses (4.1-7). See Michael Stone, 'Lists of Revealed Things in the Apocalyptic Literature', in *Magnalia Dei: The Mighty Acts of God* (G. Ernest Wright FS; edited by F.M. Cross, W.E. Lemke, and P.D. Miller, Jr, 1976), pp. 415-16.

164. For a study of these verses see Jacob Licht, 'An Analysis of Baruch's Prayer (Syr. Bar. 21)', *JJS* 33 (1982), pp. 327-31.

165. Note how throughout the Apocalypse it is emphasized that the destruction of Jerusalem is to last only 'for a time'; that is to say that the earthly Jerusalem is to be replaced by the future heavenly Jerusalem shortly. See 1.4; 4.1; 6.9; 20.3; 32.2-4; 68.5.

166. It should be noted that neither 36-40 nor 53-76 precludes a subsequent judgment by God. We simply have to state that in neither of these Messianic Apocalypses, as we now have them, is such a subsequent confirming judgment of God introduced.

167. One final piece of evidence may be pointed to in connection with the pliability of the judgment theme within *2 Baruch*. This is found in 63.6-8, where the angel Ramiel destroys the army of Sennacherib during the time of Hezekiah. In spite of the fact that the judgment is performed by an angelic representative the result is said to be a work of God. What separates the messianic judgment from being a similar type is the fact of its conclusiveness, its finality.

168. R.H. Charles, *The Revelation of St. John*, Volume II (1920), pp. 142f. also lists *1 Enoch* 91-104 and *Psalms of Solomon* 1-16 as maintaining the distinction. Neither of these works appears to do so, however, and Charles's suggestions have, for the most part, fallen on unsympathetic ears. Brief mention should also be made of the possibility that the Samaritan documents may reflect an eschatology involving a temporary, Messianic Kingdom followed by an eternal Age to Come. John MacDonald (*The Theology of the Samaritans* [1964], pp. 359ff.) speaks of such a distinction within many of the Samaritan texts dealing with their future hope. These expectations center upon a Moses redivivus figure called the Taheb, who was thought to come and usher in the Second Kingdom. This period of

blissfulness was to last approximately 100 years and the Taheb was to die during its course. It was to be followed by a Day of Vengeance and a resurrection of the righteous. Also note John Bowman, 'Early Samaritan Eschatology', *JJS* 6 (1955), pp. 63-72. The great difficulty in using such Samaritan material to help illuminate earlier Jewish belief is, of course, the problem of dating. Most of the Samaritan documents are heavily redacted within the medieval period and thus any comparative work is problematic. They do warrant further consideration by New Testament scholars, however, in spite of these drawbacks.

169. The issue is explored in an introductory manner by Jacob Licht, 'Time and Eschatology in Apocalyptic Literature and in Qumran', *JJS* 16 (1965), pp. 177-82. Also note: Bleddyn J. Roberts, 'Bible Exegesis and Fulfilment in Qumran', in *Word and Meanings* (David Winton Thomas FS; edited by Peter R. Acroyd and Barnabas Lindars, 1968), pp. 195-207; John Pryke, 'Eschatology in the Dead Sea Scrolls', in *The Scrolls and Christianity*, edited by Matthew Black (1969), pp. 45-57; Nils Alstrup Dahl, 'Eschatology and History in the Light of the Dead Sea Scrolls', in *The Future of Our Religious Past* (Rudolf Bultmann FS; edited by James M. Robinson 1971), pp. 9-28; J.J. Collins, 'Patterns of Eschatology at Qumran', in *Traditions in Transformation: Turning Points in Biblical Faith*, edited by Baruch Halpern and Jon D. Levenson (1981), pp. 351-75; Hartmut Stegemann, 'Die Bedeutung der Qumranfunde für die Erforschung der Apokalyptik', in *AMWNE* (1983), pp. 495-530; D. Dimant, *JWSTP* (1984), pp. 538-42; Philip R. Davies, 'Eschatology in Qumran', *JBL* 104 (1985), pp. 39-55.

170. Roger T. Beckwith, The Significance of the Calendar for Interpreting Essene Chronology and Eschatology', *RQ* 10 (1980), pp. 167-202. Also see his 'The Earliest Enoch Literature and its Calendar: Marks of their Origin, Date and Motivation', *RQ* 10 (1981), pp. 365-403. The issue of the Essene sect itself is examined in light of Beckwith's calendrical research in 'The Pre-History and Relationships of the Pharisees, Sadducees and Essenes: A Tentative Reconstruction', *RQ* 11 (1982), pp. 3-46. Also note J. Morgenstern, 'The Calendar of the Book of Jubilees, Its Origin and its Character', *VT* 5 (1955), pp. 34-76; James VanderKam, 'The Origin, Character and Early History of the 364-Day Calendar: A Reassessment of Jaubert's Hypothesis', *CBQ* 41 (1979), pp. 390-402; and his '2 Macc. 6.7a and Calendrical Change in Jerusalem', *JSJ* 12 (1981), pp. 1-23; E.R. Leach, 'A Possible Method of Intercalation for the Calendar of the Book of Jubilees', *VT* 7 (1957), pp. 392-97; *AOT* (1984), pp. 3-5.

171. Beckwith is critical of Milik's restoration of the 4Q 180-181 fragments and suggests an alternative compatible with his own arguments. Milik (*The Books of Enoch* [1976], p. 251) restores the relevant fragment to read 'This is the order of (generations after) the creation [of Adam; and from Noah to] Abraham, when he begat Isaac, there are ten [weeks]'. Beckwith amends the

section to read 'This is the order of the creation to Jared, to Noah, to Eber, and to Abraham, until he begot Isaac: ten [jubilees]'. In light of the phrase '70 weeks' in 4Q 180 1.9 Milik's restoration has the advantage of consistency when in 180 1.5 it reads 'ten weeks' instead of Beckwith's 'ten jubilees'. However, any advantage is lost when we consider that 70 weeks (70 × 7) is equal to 10 jubilees (10 × 49). Such interrelationships among holy numbers and their multiples seems to characterize this literature and makes assured interpretations very difficult.

172.   For a discussion of the contribution of 11QM to this issue of a ten-division eschatology, see M. de Jonge and A.S. van der Woude, '11Q Melchizedech and the New Testament', *NTS* 12 (1965-66), pp. 304f.; A.S. van der Woude, 'Melchisedek als himmlische Erlösergestalt in den neugefundenen eschatologischen Midrashim aus Qumran-Höhle 11', *OTS* 14 (1965), pp. 354-73; Joseph Fitzmyer, 'Further Light on Melchizedech from Qumran Cave 11', *JBL* 86 (1967), p. 35,; Merrill Miller, 'The Function of Isa 61.1-2 in 11Q Melchizedech', *JBL* 88 (1969), pp. 467-469; M. Delcor, 'Melchizedek from Genesis to the Qumran texts and the Epistle to the Hebrews', *JSJ* 2 (1971), pp. 115-35; Daniel Miner, 'A Suggested Reading for 11Q Melchizedek 17', *JSL* 2 (1971), pp. 144-48; F. du Toit Laubscher, 'God's Angel of Truth and Melchizedek', *JSJ* 3 (1972), pp. 46-51; Paul J. Kobelski, *Melchizedek and Melchiresa* (1981), pp. 49-51; D. Dimant, *JWSTP* (1984), pp. 521-22. The larger implications of traditions about the figure Melchizedek and his relationship to the New Testament is the subject of Fred L. Horton, Jr, *The Melchizedek Tradition* (1976). Compare David Flusser, 'Melchizedek and the Son of Man', *Christian News from Israel* 17 (1966), pp. 23-29; Richard Longenecker, 'The Melchizedek Argument of Hebrews: A Study in the Development and Circumstantial Expression of New Testament Thought', in *Unity and Diversity in New Testament Theology* (Ladd FS; 1978), pp. 161-85.

173.   Deduced via the Aramaic *Vorlage* of the *Testaments* found at Qumran!

174.   In particular, I found Beckwith's attempt to explain away the troublesome section of *Jubilees* 47-50 very unsatisfying. He does not seem to give ample weight to the fluctuation among our sources as to the length of a jubilee year (49 or 50 years?) but is content to impose a singular schematization upon a host of diverse literature with little regard to the consequences of rendering the original meaning of those documents irretrievable. Adela Yarbro Collins ('Numerical Symbolism in Jewish and Early Christian Apocalyptic Literature', *ANRW* II, 21.2 [1984], pp. 1234-36), discusses this point of whether the jubilee year was every 49 or 50 years.

175.   See Roger Beckwith, 'Daniel 9 and the Date of Messiah's Coming in Essene, Hellenistic, Pharisaic, Zealot and Early Christian Computation', *RQ* 10 (1981), pp. 521-42; Adela Yarbro Collins, *art. cit.*, pp. 1225-29. The

literal fulfilment of the prophecy with respect to Jesus' death is stressed in R.J.M. Gurney, 'The Seventy Weeks of Daniel 9.24-27, *EQ* 53 (1981), pp. 29-36. As a matter of interest, it should be noted that Daniel 7-12 displays a remarkable diversity with respect to its calculation of the end-time. J.J. Collins, *The Apocalyptic Vision of the Book of Daniel* (1977), p. 154, notes no less than four different calculations. We should take this diversity as supportive evidence for our contention of eschatological variety within a single work.

176. The passage is the Hymn 10 and is found in Column 6 of 1QH. See Geza Vermes, *The Dead Sea Scrolls in English* (1975), pp. 168-72, for the full translation.

177. See Geza Vermes, *The Dead Sea Scrolls: Qumran in Perspective* (1982), p. 197, for bibliographical details about the Qumran belief in the resurrection of the dead.

178. *Art. cit.*, pp. 178-79. Compare Jacob Myers, *I & II Esdras* (1974), p. 127, where *SO* 3.652-660 is described in the same connection. The work of Charles often makes the same claims about earlier sections (3.1-62) of the *Oracles*. See his *Doctrine of a Future Life* (1899), p. 226. Hans-Alwin Wilcke, *Das Problem eines messianischen Zwischenreichs bei Paulus* (1967), pp. 39-41, includes *SO* 3.652-731 in his discussion of theme.

179. Even Bailey himself (p. 178) admits that such a distinction was not the original intention of the relevant passages but arises out of the completed form and character of the *Oracles* as a whole. This is, of course, a very weak foundation upon which to base any interpretation of the *Oracles'* eschatological teaching.

180. The recent work of J.J. Collins on 'The Sibylline Oracles', *TOTP* I (1983), pp. 323, 332, 365 n. u, 380-82 for details. Occasionally a 4-Empire structure is also presented especially in *SO* 2. See David Flusser, 'The Four Empires in the Fourth Sibyl and in the Book of Daniel', *Israel Oriental Studies* 2 (1972), pp. 148-75. Apparently the notion of a 4-Empire structure was quite widespread in the ancient Near East. See J.W. Swain, 'The Theory of the Four Monarchies: Opposition History under the Roman Empire', *CP* 35 (1940), pp. 1-21; M.J. Gruenthaler, 'The Four Empires of Daniel', *CBQ* 8 (1946), pp. 72-82 and 201-12; Edward F. Siegman, 'The Stone Hewn from the Mountain (Daniel 2)', *CBQ* 18 (1956), pp. 366ff.; J.J. Collins, *The Apocalyptic Vision of the Book of Daniel* (1977), pp. 37-43, for further details. On the larger issue of historical reviews within apocalyptic, see J.J. Collins, 'Pseudonymity, Historical Reviews and the Genre of the Revelation of John', *CBQ* 39 (1977), pp. 329-43.

181. See the discussion below in Chapter 3.

182. Despite the strained attempts of J. Massyngberde Ford, *Revelation* (1975), pp. 12ff., to assign chs. 4-21 to a circle of John the Baptist and deny the specifically Christian authorship of the book. James H. Charlesworth (*TOTPNT* [1985] p. 87) discusses fruitless attempts to identify the Jewish

core underlying the Apocalypse. Also worth noting is Ulrich Müller, 'Literarische und formgeschichtliche Bestimmung der Apokalypse des Johannes als einem Zeugnis frühchristlicher Apokalyptik', in *AMWNE* (1983), pp. 599-619.

183. A good example of this tension is the way in which the phrase τὸ Ἀλφα καί το ᾿ Ωμεγα is used within the Apocalypse. In 1.8 it appears to be used of God while in 22.13 it is used of Christ.

184. It should be noted that we disagreed with Russell as to the date of *2 Enoch*. We placed it within the first century CE. However, the comments about its contribution to our subject matter are unaffected by its dating and it is here discussed with *Jubilees*.

Notes to Chapter 2

1. The word παρουσία occurs 14 times within the Pauline corpus. It is used not only with reference to Christ's future advent in glory (as in 1 Cor. 15.23; 1 Thess. 2.19; 3.13; 4.15; 5.23; 2 Thess. 2.1,8), but also with reference to Paul's own 'coming' to the churches (2 Cor. 10.10; Phil. 1.26; 2.2); with reference to the 'coming' of Paul's fellow-workers (1 Cor. 16.17; 2 Cor. 7.6-7); and once with reference to the 'coming' of Satan (2 Thess. 2.9). It is only this first category, speaking of Christ's eschatological arrival, that we are concerned with in this thesis. The second category, that dealing with Paul's own presence within the churches, has been an important factor in form-critical studies within the Pauline epistles. Note, for instance: Robert Funk, 'The Apostolic Parousia: Form and Significance', in *Christian History and Interpretation* (Knox FS; 1967), pp. 249-68; Hendrikus Boers, 'The Form Critical Study of Paul's Letters: 1 Thessalonians as a Case Study', *NTS* 29 (1975-76), pp. 140-58.

2. The best single volume on the subject is still A.L. Moore, *The Parousia in the New Testament* (Supplements to Novum Testamentum, 13; 1966).

3. See Anthony Thiselton, 'The Parousia in Modern Theology: Some Questions and Comments', *TB* 27, (1976), pp. 27-53, who notes the conscpicuous absence of the Parousia belief in many modern philosophical systems concerned with the future. Also note Richard Hiers, 'Eschatology and Methodology', *JBL* 85 (1966), pp. 170-84.

4. Of particular note is Bruce Vawter, '"And He Shall Come Again with Glory"', in *SPCIC 1961* (1963), pp. 143-50; A.L. Moore, *op. cit.*, pp. 35-90; Stephen Travis, *Christian Hope and the Future of Man* (1980).

5. *The Second Advent* (1945). The book was revised in a third edition of 1963. Also note the follow-up article '"The Second Advent"—25 Years Later', *ExpT* 82 (1971), pp. 307-309, where intervening scholarly developments were taken into account but no adjustments to the thesis of the book thought necessary.

6. On Glasson's suggestion that the Caligula episode in 41 CE was the catalyst point for the rise of the doctrine of the Parousia, J. Lowe, in his review of Glasson's *The Second Advent* in *JTS* 47 (1946), p. 85, comments:

> This seems to confuse cause and effect. The excitement over Caligula's proposals and the interpretation of them in terms of the 'abomination of desolation' is itself only intelligible in an atmosphere tense with apocalyptic expectation. That is to say, the Caligula episode presupposes, rather than causes, the note of urgency and imminence.

7. *Jesus and His Coming* (1957). Also note the more popular *In the End, God* (1950).

8. Compare Robinson's 'The Most Primitive Christology of All?', *JTS* n.s. 7 (1956), pp. 177-89, for an investigation into the early Church's kerygma as evidenced in Acts, in which Robinson detects two divergent strands of christological proclamation. Acts 3, he argues, does not originally contain any notion of a Parousia doctrine.

9. See the critical review of Robinson's *Jesus and His Coming* by G.R. Beasley-Murray in *SJT* 10 (1959), pp. 134-40.

10. *Jesus and His Coming*, p. 32.

11. Schweitzer has come under heavy criticism for his un-scholarly handling of many of the pseudepigraphal documents and his fabrication of a 'late-Jewish apocalyptic' viewpoint. There are indications that Schweitzer himself realized the inherent weakness of this 'manufactured' viewpoint, or at least recognized several competing traditions within Jewish eschatological thought of the period. On this point, see the stinging remarks of T.F. Glasson, 'Schweitzer's Influence—Blessing or Bane?', *JTS* 28 (1977), pp. 294ff.; Lou H. Silberman, 'Apocalyptic Revisited: Reflections on the Thought of Albert Schweitzer', *JAAS* 44 (1976), pp. 491ff. Further discussion is found below in note 24.

12. 'The Christian Hope and the Problem of Demythologizing', *ExpT* 65 (1953-54), p. 229.

13. 'New Testament and Mythology', in *Kerygma and Myth*, volume I, edited by Hans Werner Bartsch (1953), pp. 3f.

14. On this issue see, G.H. Parke-Taylor, *Yahweh: The Divine Name in the Bible* (1975), pp. 103ff.

15. The corresponding noun θυμός is also used in Rom. 2.8; 2 Cor. 12.20; Gal. 5.20; Eph. 4.31; Col. 3.8. In all instances but Rom. 2.8 the subject of θυμός is man.

16. Both references in Romans 13 speak of the wrath of the world rulers upon disobedient subjects and thus have God as their subject only by extension. Eph. 4.31 and Col. 3.8 list ὀργή as an undesirable attribute for Christians to possess.

17. See A.T. Hanson, *The Wrath of the Lamb* (1957), pp. 68-111. See G.H.C. Macgregor, 'The Wrath of God in the New Testament', *NTS* 7 (1960-61), pp. 101-109 for a brief survey and a division of the Pauline

passages into time categories. Macgregor follows Dodd in arguing for the tendency of Paul to depersonalize the wrath of God. See C.H. Dodd, *The Epistle of Paul to the Romans* (1932), pp. 45ff. Stephen H. Travis (*The Place of Divine Retribution in the Thought of St. Paul* [1970], pp. 51ff.) argues that ὀργή is both realized and eschatological; that it is a divinely ordained condition of man both present and future. Wrath is essentially a relational concept and hence never directed at Christians. Since it is relational, Travis argues, it is neither retributive nor impersonal (contra Dodd!).

18. See B.N. Kaye, 'Eschatology and Ethics in 1 and 2 Thessalonians', *NovT* (1975), pp. 47-57, and Calvin Roetzel, 'The Judgment Form in Paul's Letters', *JBL* 88 (1969), pp. 305-12, where the ecclesiastical context of Paul's judgment passages is discussed. The wider social function of apocalyptic in Paul's letters is discussed by Wayne Meeks, *The First Urban Christians* (1983), pp. 171-80, and 'Social Functions of Apocalyptic Language in Pauline Christianity', in *AMWNE* (1983), pp. 687-705. Also worth considering on the subject are two additional articles in the *AMWNE* volume: Elizabeth Schüssler Fiorenza, 'The Phenomenon of Early Christian Apocalyptic: Some Reflections on Method', pp. 295-316; and George W.E. Nickelsburg, 'Social Aspects of Palestinian Jewish Apocalypticism', pp. 687-705. Also note the literature cited above in Chapter 1, note 1.

19. Much of the time παραδίδωμι is used either in reference to Christ's redemptive work on the cross (Rom. 4.25, 8.32; 1 Cor. 11.23b; Gal. 2.20; Eph. 5.25) or the handing over of tradition from one witness to the next (Rom. 6.17; 1 Cor. 11.2, 23a, 15.3). See Morna D. Hooker, 'A Further Note on Romans 1' *NTS* 13 (1966-67), pp. 181-83, where it is argued that both Gen. 1.20-26 and Psalm 106 underlie Paul's use of the term παραδίδωμι in Romans 1. Hooker does not discuss 1 Cor. 5.5. A full discussion of the use of παραδίδωμι in Paul's letters is found in Gabriella Berenyi, 'Gal 2, 20: A Pre-Pauline or a Pauline Text?', *Biblica* 65 (1984), pp. 510ff.

20. *The Second Advent* (1963), pp. 157-71. Also note: Ernest Best, *A Commentary on the First and Second Epistles to the Thessalonians* (1972), pp. 205f.; E. Springs Steele, 'The Use of Jewish Scriptures in 1 Thessalonians', *BTB* 14 (1984), pp. 12-17. In addition to the associations made by Glasson we should note:

1.   1 Thess. 5.3—Jer. 6.14, 8.11; Ezek. 13.10
2.   1 Thess. 5.8—Isa. 59.17; Wis. 5.18
3.   2 Thess. 1.7—Zech. 14.5
4.   2 Thess. 1.8—Ps. 79.6; Jer. 10.25
5.   2 Thess. 1.10—Ps. 89.7; Isa. 2.11, 17 49.3
6.   2 Thess. 1.12—Isa 24.15; Mal. 1.11
7.   2 Thess. 2.4—Dan 11.36; Ezek. 28.2
8.   2 Thess. 2.8—Job 4.9; Isa. 11.4

21. The best study of the Old Testament concept remains H.H. Rowley's treatment in *The Faith of Israel* (1956), pp. 177-201. For discussion of the

Amos 5 theophany, which is probably the oldest description contained in the Old Testament, see C. Van Leeuwen, 'The Prophecy of Yom YHWH in Amos V 18-20', *OTS* 19 (1974), pp. 113-34; John D.W. Watts, *Vision and Prophecy in Amos* (1958), pp. 68-84. For an excellent survey of relevant scholarship see Hans M. Barstad, *The Religious Polemics of Amos* (Supplements to Vetus Testamentum, 34; 1984), pp. 89-110.

22. *Op. cit.*, p. 171.

23. Glasson here primarily means that within the *Similitudes* the Messiah always appears simultaneously with God at the final judgment. In contrast, within the New Testament documents, the Parousia of Christ is nowhere spoken of as being accompanied by a theophany of God. While this in itself may be a correct observation on Glasson's part, the important point to note is that he uses this distinction as grounds for rejecting *1 Enoch* (and by implication other Jewish pseudepigrapha as well) as having any contribution to make in our understanding of the New Testament Parousia hope. Note the caustic comments on Glasson's method made by H.H. Rowley in *The Relevance of Apocalyptic* (1963), pp. 164-65. We are here attempting to go beyond the strict Parousia motif and to examine comparatively how God and Messiah are related to each other with respect to the larger judgment theme in both the *Similitudes* of Enoch and the Pauline epistles. In other words, is there a shared perspective within both bodies of literature which united them in spite of this apparently decisive difference suggested by Glasson? I am suggesting that there is indeed such a unity—it focuses on the identification between God and messianic agent in judgment. The shared perspective between *1 Enoch* and the Pauline epistles on this point renders Glasson's estimation of the worth of pseudepigraphal literature questionable. Just because two documents use a common theme in a slightly different manner is no reason for suggesting that any investigation into their respective uses of that theme cannot be aided by a comparative investigation of the theme itself.

24. Contrary to Glasson's general program of eliminating as many of the Jewish pseudepigraphal documents as possible from consideration. Effectively, Glasson rules out of bounds all the relevant texts including: *4 Ezra, 2 Baruch, 2 Enoch, Jubilees, 1 Enoch, Testament of Moses,* and *Psalms of Solomon.* Glasson lays much of the blame for this unjustified attention to such non-biblical literature at the feet of Albert Schweitzer, whom he says has done scholarship a serious disservice in leading it astray by fabricating a 'late-Jewish apocalyptic' viewpoint as dervied from these works. See T.F. Glasson, 'Schweitzer's Influence—Blessing or Bane?', *JTS* 28 (1977), pp. 289-302, and his *Jesus and the End of the World* (1980), pp. 21-35, for details. Glasson's major criticism of Schweitzer on this point is sound, but his application of it to a consideration of the New Testament evidence is self-contradictory. In particular, his dismissing caricature of *4 Ezra* and *2 Baruch* on pp. 22-24 of the book is ludicrous, given the diversity he himself admits is

contained within these works with respect to their eschatological teaching. On p. 24 he criticizes Schweitzer for failing to take seriously these differing eschatological viewpoints current in first-century Judaism, while on p. 22 he summarily dismisses *4 Ezra* (and by implication *2 Baruch* as well) as having any possible influence on Jesus because, 'If Jesus believed anything like this, the end of the world could not be near; it was at least four hundred years away'. Here Glasson is guilty of the same criticism he levels at Schweitzer in that he himself fails to appreciate the diversity of eschatological teaching contained within *4 Ezra* itself. As we attempted to demonstrate above in Chapter 1, it is reductionistic to describe its eschatology as simply teaching 'a temporary, Messianic Kingdom of 400 years duration'. We should not be too quick to dismiss the possibility that Jesus himself might well have been able to be as flexible in his conceptualizations about the future as the author of *4 Ezra* appears to have been. In any event, any definition we might wish to assign to the term 'late Jewish apocalyptic' must of necessity recognize the diversity of eschatological schemes present within Jewish thought of the time.

25. Johannes Theisohn has made an in-depth study of this motif in his monograph *Der auserwählte Richter* (1975). He notes that the phrase Throne of glory (*manbara sebḥat/sebḥatitu*) occurs 14 times in the *Similitudes* in three major forms (pp. 68-98). Of special interest is the third-person singular, masculine, pronominal suffix on the word *sebḥat* (*sebḥatitu*). To whom does this refer? The answer to this question is, of course, critical for our own considerations within this thesis. Theisohn subjects the various passages from the *Similitudes* to a rigorous traditio-historical analysis and concludes that a singular throne is meant throughout—the Throne of God himself. At the same time, it must be emphasized that both God and the Elect One/Son of Man occupy the same throne. One of the important points in the entire issue is the fact that the Lord of the Spirits (God) is said to have placed the Elect One/Son of Man on that Throne of Glory in 51.3; 61.8; 62.2.

26. Matthew Black, 'The Throne-Theophany Prophetic Commission and the "Son of Man"', in *Jews, Greeks and Christians* (Davies FS; 1976), pp. 57-73. Also note the discussion in T.F. Glasson, 'The Son of Man Imagery: Enoch 14 and Daniel 7', *NTS* 23 (1977-78), pp. 82-90; Seyoon Kim, *The Origin of Paul's Gospel* (1982), pp. 92ff.; Matthew Black, *The Book of Enoch or 1 Enoch* (1985), p. 151.

27. Black appeals to the *Testament of Moses* 10 as further evidence of this interpretation of the destiny of Israel (pp. 62f.) Yet, strangely, he does not follow up his point about the 'individualizing' of the nation into a messianic figure by appealing to the angel in *T. Moses* 10.2. This would have been a natural link and would have strengthened Black's thesis, but the connection is left undeveloped.

28. *Art. cit.*, p. 163.

29. He is following up a suggestion made by R.H. Charles in *APOT* II (1913), p. 237.

30. Basically, Kim argues that christological thought developed along two separate paths, both of which find their root in this christophanically based Image christology. The two paths are Wisdom christology and Adam christology; the former affirms Christ's divinity while the latter affirms his humanity. It should be noted that in so arguing Kim reverses the relationship generally thought to exist between Paul's conception of Christ as the Image of God and his Adam christology. Usually, Adam christology is taken to yield an understanding of Christ as the Image of God, instead of the other way around. See Kim, *op. cit.*, pp. 193ff. for details.

31. Indeed, we should not presume that Ezekiel 1 served as the only prophetic-call passage which may have influenced Paul's interpretation of the Damascus christophany, especially with regard to the apostolic commission derived from it. There is strong evidence that the description of Isaiah's call in Isaiah 6 also had an important contribution to make in this regard. See Kim, *op. cit.*, pp. 94ff. for details. Christopher Rowland explores the influence of Ezekiel 1 and Isaiah 6 upon Jewish and Christian documents in 'The Visions of God in Apocalyptic Literature', *JSJ* 10 (1979), pp. 137-54. Particularly important is his discussion of Revelation 4, which Rowland assumes shows no Christian influence. This assumption is challenged by L.W. Hurtado, 'Revelation 4-5 in the Light of Jewish Apocalyptic Analogies', *JSNT* 25 (1985), pp. 105-24.

32. Kim does not, of course, set out to examine this conceptual overlap itself, nor try to apply his conclusions about the origins of Paul's christological thought to the eschatological concept of the Day of the Lord. That is left for our consideration here. Nevertheless, we turn to Kim's important and comprehensive monograph for the valuable provision it makes in allowing us to follow through some of its suggestions, apply them to the Pauline concept of the Day of the Lord, and set them within the larger context of Paul's christological thought.

33. *Ibid.*, pp. 258ff.

34. The quotation comes from pp. 215-16. Kim's work, altogether comprehensive in scope and impressive in its argumentation, is not without its limitations. In particular, the sections dealing with the title 'Son of Man' and its relationship to the title 'Son of God' are of debatable value. Kim suggests (pp. 249-52) that the messianic interpretation of Dan. 7.13 begins with Jesus himself and thus is parallel to yet independent of similar developments in *1 Enoch* 37-71 and *4 Ezra* 13. This, in itself, seems to me to be quite straightforward and well within the realms of possibility. It is, however, the close connection Kim sees between 'Son of Man' and 'Son of God' which stretches the imagination. His association of the two concepts relies very heavily upon what he feels to be a deliberate Pauline exploitation of the ambiguous Greek term ὁ ἄνθρωπος; and his attempt to integrate the

two is motivated by his desire to subsume both christological categories under the heading of the Damascus christophany. Kim's thesis was finished in 1977 (although published in 1981), and was thus too early to interact with either J.D.G. Dunn's *Christology in the Making* (1980), or Barnabas Lindars's *Jesus Son of Man* (1983). One cannot help but wonder how Kim's assessment of the Son of Man/Son of God question is qualified by these, and other, contributions to the field. To be fair to Kim, he does mention in the Preface that the 'Son of Man' section needs strengthening. This he attempts to do in a further book entitled *The 'Son of Man' as the Son of God* (1983), although he does not interact with Dunn as much as one would like. In this second work Kim re-emphasizes Jesus' creative use of Dan. 7.13 and suggests that 'Jesus intended to reveal himself to be the divine figure who was the inclusive representative (or the head) of the eschatological people of God' (p. 36). Kim relies upon 4QpsDanA^a, and the LXX reading of Dan. 7.13f. in Papyrus 967 and Codex 88, as all supporting his contention that the Danielic son of man figure was also designated Son of God in some pre-Christian Jewish literature. In addition, the son of man figure within these same documents was also stressed as being similar to (ὡς) the Ancient of Days himself. (The point was briefly alluded to in J.A. Montgomery, *The Book of Daniel* [1927], p. 324.) This is, of course, to be associated with the merkabah throne visions of Ezek. 1.26 and Kim's contention is that the heavenly Son of Man ideas of Daniel 7 are ultimately derived from throne-theophany and are readily associated with both Son of God and messianic categories. In short, Kim argues that there was indeed a messianic interpretation of the heavenly figure in Daniel 7, contemporaneous with the time of the writing of many of the New Testament documents, which was *not* dependent upon a titular usage of *bar nasha*.

35. Kim is here reliant upon James Barr, 'Theophany and Anthropomorphism in the Old Testament', *Supplement to VT* 7 (1960), pp. 31-38. Christopher Rowland ('The Visions of God in Apocalyptic Literature', *JSJ* 10 [1979], p. 513) notes that there is a tendency in Jewish apocalyptic to 'move away from anthropomorphic conceptions'.

36. Kim comments on Dan. 7.13 in a manner which illustrates his point (p. 208):

> Daniel does not see *the* Son of Man but one like a son of man. It is rather a descriptive, pictorial phrase which expresses that the figure Daniel sees is like a man, has a human form of likeness. The accompaniment of the clouds in his appearance clearly indicates that he is a divine figure. For in the OT clouds regularly accompany theophany. So the figure Daniel sees, 'one like a son of man', is a deity appearing in human form and likeness.

37. An important modification is the *Testament of Abraham*, where a human being (Abel) is described in terms of heavenly appearance. See Kim, *op. cit.*, pp. 205ff. for details.

38. Note for instance his pre-existent interpretation of the sending of

God's Son in Rom. 8.3; Gal. 4.4; Col. 1.13ff. Compare this with the interpretation of J.D.G. Dunn, *Christology in the Making* (1980), pp. 38-44.

39. I do not mean by this that I disagree with Kim's interpretation of Gal. 4.4, or of other similar passages which speak of the sending of God's Son. I happen to concur. But I am suggesting that it is a matter of serious scholarly dispute and these passages cannot be handled in an *a priori* fashion. Instead, I am trying to rescue the essential, relevant point by appealing to an additional line of argument which focuses on the shared eschatological role of Christ and God within a theophanic context. This shared role, in itself, leads to some blurring of the boundaries of God and messianic agent in a manner which is harmonious with Kim's contention that functional and ontological categories interpenetrate within Paul's christological thought under the impact of the Damascus Vision.

40. Morton Smith, 'What is Implied by the Variety of Messianic Figures?', *JBL* 78 (1959), pp. 70f., notes the diversity of expression within *1 Enoch* with regard to the role of the Messiah.

41. Observe the way in which the Lord of the Spirits (another phrase for the Most High) is said to place the Elect One on the throne of Glory in 61.8 and yet is said to sit down upon that throne himself in 62.2. The circle is completed when we note that the Elect One seats himself upon the throne in 69.29. Also note the substitution of Melchizedek for God upon the throne in 11QM (compare 4Q161 and 4Q174 for further instances of this phenomenon of substitution). For an investigation into the different traditio-historical strands within the *Similitudes* which give rise to an Elect One or a Son of Man figure, see Johannes Theisohn, *Der auserwählte Richter* (1975), pp. 47-49.

42. E.P. Sanders ('Testament of Abraham: First to Second Century A.D.', *TOTP* I [1983], pp. 871-80), dates the Testament between 75-125 CE and argues for its essentially Jewish character.

43. G.W.E. Nickelsburg, ('Eschatology in the Testament of Abraham: A Study of the Judgment Scene in the Two Recensions', *Studies on the Testament of Abraham*, edited by G.W.E. Nickelsburg [1976], pp. 23-64) tries to solve the complex puzzle surrounding the three-fold judgment scene. It may well be that the subsequent judgment performed by God in the Testament arises from a desire to interject a theistic element.

44. This same sort of contextual confusion can be traced within *4 Ezra*, beginning with 7.33, where the judgment throne is explicitly said to be occupied by the Most High. This should be examined alongside other sections of the work which speak of the Messiah's role in judgment. We discussed both the *Testament of Moses* 10 and *4 Ezra* more fully within Chapter 1.

45. There is some textual confusion between βήματι τοῦ θεοῦ and βήματι τοῦ Χριστοῦ in Rom. 14.10 with several major manuscripts exhibiting a

222   *Jesus and God in Paul's Eschatology*

corrector's hand and the more difficult θεοῦ being inserted in the place of Χριστοῦ. It is generally thought that the confusion is due to the influence of 2 Cor. 5.10. See Bruce M. Metzger, *A Textual Commentary on the Greek New Testament* (1977), pp. 513, and C.E.B. Cranfield, *Romans*, volume II (1979), p. 709. There is no such textual confusion in the passage from 2 Corinthians 5.

46. The allusion to Isa. 45.23 in Phil. 2.10-11 is discussed on pp. 114-17.

47. It may be that the 'Savior' link within Isaiah 45 is partially responsible for Paul's turning to the passage as he expounds the significance of Christ's accomplishments on behalf of the Church. If so, this seems to demonstrate a certain degree of conceptual overlap as far as the concept of 'Savior' is concerned and thus supports the basic contention of this book. This 'Savior' link has also been extensively examined with respect to the Colossian heresy. Andrew Bandstra ('Did the Colossian Errorists Need a Mediator?', *New Dimensions in New Testament Study*, edited by Richard N. Longenecker and Merrill C. Tenney [1974], pp. 329-43) has sought to solve the complex problem of the nature of the Colossian heresy by examining it in light of Jewish writings which demonstrates a polemic 'against any divine hypostasis being regarded as mediator of creation and/or redemption'. Jewish documents which exhibit this polemic include 1QH 3.19-23 and 6.12ff; *SO* 3.24; 4.41, 181, 183; *2 Baruch* 21.7-10; *4 Ezra* 5.56-6.6 and the *Apocalypse of Abraham* 10 and 16. Simply stated, the Colossian heresy was that members of the church there advocated God's unmediated activity in their salvation and thus failed to give proper authority to Christ's status regarding their salvation. It is notoriously difficult to identify the Colossian heresy. Bandstra's attempt founders on the fact that most of the Jewish works he turns to to construct his 'Jewish polemic' also contain exalted messianic sections which would run counter to his argument. Again we are at the mercy of our presuppositions regarding the ability of monotheistic Jewish authors to juxtapose exalted messianic passages with theistic ones. They simply were not as concerned with the inherent 'contradictions' of such a juxtaposition as we oftentimes are.

48. Note Matthew Black, *Romans* (1973), p. 167, and C.E.B. Cranfield, *Romans*, volume II (1979), p. 710 for details.

49. George Howard, 'The Tetragram and the New Testament', *JBL* 96 (1977), pp. 63-83. Howard is interacting with the work of Siegfried Schulz, 'Maranatha und Kyrios Jesus', *ZNW* 53 (1962), pp. 125-44. Also note the comments of C.F.D. Moule, *The Origin of Christology* (1977), pp. 35-46; D.R. DeLacey, '"One Lord" in Pauline Christology', in *Christ the Lord* (Guthrie FS; edited by Harold H. Rowden; 1982), pp. 191-95.

50. According to Howard the abbreviated form was 'a conscious effort to preserve the sacred nature of the divine name' (p. 77). E.C.B. Maclaurin, 'YHWH: The Origin of the Tetragrammaton', *VT* 12 (1962), p. 462, goes so

far as to suggest that the Christian's rejection of the tetragrammaton in favour of κύριος was largely responsible for its being revered among the Massoretic Jews of later centuries.

51. And within Paul's copy of the LXX from which it is derived!

52. Howard as supportive evidence also points to Rom. 3.6 as speaking of God's judging of the world.

53. At the beginning of his article, Howard rules out the oral factor from his consideration. It is crucial that this factor be taken into account in the issue. Howard's thesis is weakened, possibly undermined entirely, by its omission. For further discussions see: N.A. Dahl and Alan F. Segal, 'Philo and the Rabbis on the Names of God', *JSL* 9 (1978), pp. 1-28; Patrick W. Skehan, 'The Divine Name at Qumran, in the Masada Scroll, and in the Septuagint', *BIOSCS* 13 (1980), pp. 14-44; Albert Pietersma, 'Kurios or Tetragram: A Renewed Quest for the Original LXX' in *De Septuaginta* (Wevers FS; 1984), pp. 85-101. Of special value is W.G. Waddell, 'The Tetragrammaton in the LXX', *JTS* 45 (1944), pp. 158-61, which contains a plate of one of the most important LXX manuscripts (P. Faoud Inv. No. 266) clearly demonstrating the spacing technique used for the name of YHWH.

54. We find this distinction maintained in *QG* 2.16; 2.51; 2.75; 3.39; 4.2; 4.8; 4.53; 4.87; and in *QE* 1.23; 2.62; 2.64; 2.68.

55. Rom. 2.16 is another good example of this co-operative description.

56. Rom. 14.10 avoids this word ἔμπροσθεν altogether and substitutes παραστησόμεθα. Paul uses ἔμπροσθεν five other times (Gal. 2.14; Phil. 3.13; 1 Thess. 1.3; 2.19; 3.9). Only the Galatians reference is void of any eschatological significance. Several of these passages, notably 1 Thess. 2.19, associate God and Christ together in a manner similar to 1 Thess. 3.13, but none quite so clearly.

57. The textual variant ἀποκαταλλάγητε is probably a later attempt to remove the ambiguous subject implied by ἀποκατηλλαξεν and thus shift the focus from who is performing the action of the verb to those receiving it. Also worth noting on this point is Eph. 5.27, where Christ is said to present the Bride (Church) to himself (ἑαυτῷ).

58. Taken from Max Staniforth, *Early Christian Writings: The Apostolic Fathers* (1980), pp. 146-47.

59. Paul speaks of Jesus as Lord (κύριος) 189 times, the majority of references being nominal in character.

60. Paul speaks of its significance in a variety of ways. It is the Day of our glorification or transformation (Rom. 8.17-18, 20; 1 Cor. 15.50-54; 2 Cor. 3.18; 2 Thess. 1.10, 2.14; cp. Rom. 5.2). It is the Day of our adoption as sons (Rom. 8.23). It is the Day in which the Church is presented to Christ as a spotless bride (Col. 1.22, 28; cp. Eph. 5.27). In several places Paul simply calls it the hope of our faith (Col. 1.5, 23).

61. 1 Cor. 1.7; 2 Cor. 1.10; Gal. 5.5; Phil. 3.11-14, 20-21; 1 Thess. 1.10.

62. Consistently Paul speaks of the resurrection of the body of the

believers as dependent upon the already accomplished resurrection of their Lord and mentions the two together (Rom. 8.11, 29; 1 Cor. 6.14, 15.20-28; 2 Cor. 4.14; cp. 2 Cor. 5.1-4; 1 Thess. 5.10; Col. 3.4).

63. Rom. 8.19-22; cp., Eph. 1.10; Phil. 2.9-11.

64. Ernest Best (*A Commentary on the First and Second Epistles to the Thessalonians* [1972], p. 206) explains the difference between the presence and/or absence of the definite article in the phrase 'The Day of the Lord' as a Semitism and as due to the influence of the Hebrew construct state.

65. παρουσία is read in place of ἡμέρα in DFG.

66. John M. Court ('Paul and the Apocalyptic Pattern', *Paul and Paulinism* [Barrett FS; 1982], pp. 57-66) suggests that the plural form may reflect the Jewish 'apocalyptic convention of dividing world history up into a number of epochs' (p. 62). This is probably further evidence of Paul's indebtedness to an inheritance of Jewish apocalyptic forms.

67. There are several other passages which also deserve careful study in this regard, such as 1 Thess. 4.6; Rom. 15.9-12, 21; Eph. 4.8. However, these do not display quite the same eschatological emphasis as the eleven I have selected and therefore must be left for another time.

68. See A.T. Hanson, 'The Midrash in II Corinthians 3: A Reconsideration', *JSNT* 9 (1980), pp. 2-28; Seyoon Kim, *The Origin of Paul's Gospel* (1982), pp. 12-13, note 6, for discussion. An even more remarkable demonstration of Paul's flexibility of referent in Old Testament quotations is to be seen in his use of Exod. 40.13. In 1 Cor. 2.16 this verse is applied to Jesus while in Rom. 11.34 it is applied to God. Also worth noting is the application of Ps. 68.18 to Christ in Eph. 4.8.

69. The eschatological import of this verse is not to be overlooked! It is perhaps worth noting here as well that all three of the pre-Pauline credal formulae within his earliest epistle (1 Thess. 1.10; 4.14; 5.10) also speak of the Lord Jesus' Parousia. See Raymond F. Collins, *Studies on the First Letter to the Thessalonians* (1984), pp. 253-66, for a discussion of the pre-Pauline formulae of these verses.

70. On this, see C.H. Dodd, *According to the Scriptures* (1952), pp. 47-48 and 62-64.

71. The same section of Isaiah is similarly used in Romans 9.33. See p. 124 for a fuller discussion of this reference.

72. The dominant means of interpreting the hymn in recent years has been to focus on it as an expression of Adamic christology. An articulate example of such an approach is J.D.G. Dunn, *Christology in the Making* (1980), pp. 114-21. Dunn argues that 2.6-7c is a piece of Adamic christology and that 7d-8 and 9-11 are properly interpreted in light of that christological theme. In my opinion such an interpretation can be sustained with regard to 7d-8 but does little justice to 9-11 which breaks the mould of any Adamic motif. Dunn himself admits (p. 118) that the strongly monotheistic passage (Isa. 45.23) 'adds a new dimension to the christological claim', but fails to

expound in any way what this new dimension is. Dunn's treatment of the hymn is a classic example of how one particular theological motif (i.e. Adamic christology) is allowed to govern the whole exegesis of the passage even when sections of that hymn do not easily fit within such a motif, or at least are not fully expounded by that motif. I would agree with the Adamic interpretation of vv. 6-8 (in spite of the objections raised by T.F. Glasson, 'Two Notes on the Philippians Hymn (II. 6-11)', *NTS* 21 [1974-75], pp. 137ff.), but would insist that the christological message of 9-11 rests on a different plane.

73. On the subject, see: Joachim Jeremias, 'Zur Gedankenführung in den paulinischen Briefen', in *Studia Paulina*: (De Zwaan FS; 1953), pp. 152ff.; Joachim Jeremias, 'Zu Phil. ii 7: ΕΑΥΤΟΝ ΕΚΕΝΩΣΕΝ', *NovT* 6 (1963), pp. 182-88; Dieter Georgi, 'Der vorpaulinische Hymnus Phil 2, 6-11', *Zeit und Geschichte* (Bultmann FS; 1964), pp. 263-93; Ralph P. Martin, *Carmen Christi* (1964), pp. 24-41; Charles Talbert, 'The Problem of Pre-Existence in Philippians 2.6-11', *JBL* 86 (1967), pp. 142ff.; Ernst Käsemann, 'A Critical Analysis of Philippians 2.5-11', *JTC* 5 (1968), pp. 45-88; J.T. Sanders, *New Testament Christological Hymns* (1971), pp. 9-12; Jerome Murphy-O'Connor, 'Christological Anthropology in Phil., II, 6-11', *RB* 83 (1976), pp. 26ff.; George Howard, 'Phil. 2.6-11 and the Human Christ', *CBQ* 40 (1978), pp. 372ff.

74. On the importance of this phrase within Pauline theology, including its function as a capstone for the Philippians 2 hymn, see Martin Hengel, *Crucifixion* (1977), pp. 62-63.

75. For a discussion of the cosmic implications of these words, see John G. Gibbs, 'The Relation Between Creation and Redemption According to Phil. II 5-11', *NovT* 12 (1970), pp. 270-83.

76. On this point, see Ralph P. Martin, *Carmen Christi* (1964), pp. 42ff.; I. Howard Marshall, 'The Christ-Hymn in Philippians', *TB* 19 (1968), pp. 117ff.; C.F.D. Moule, 'Further Reflections on Philippians 2.5-11', in *Apostolic History and the Gospel*: (Bruce FS; 1970), pp. 265ff.; Graham Stanton, *Jesus of Nazareth in New Testament Preaching* (1974), pp. 99-106; L.W. Hurtado, 'Jesus as Lordly Example in Philippians 2.5-11', in *From Jesus to Paul* (Beare FS; 1984), pp. 113-26.

77. See Martin, *op. cit.*, pp. 247f. for a discussion of J. Jervell's contention that they do not belong together.

78. Note the conjunctions διό (v. 9) and καί (v. 10).

79. Martin, *op. cit.*, pp. 229ff. correctly emphasizes that vv. 9-11 are integrally linked to the rest of the hymn and is critical of any attempt to separate them from it. George Howard, *art. cit.*, pp. 378ff. laments the fact that 9-11 have tended to be overlooked in scholarly investigations in favour of the earliest sections of the hymn. Howard attempts to interpret 9-11 in such a manner as to emphasize the humanity of Christ. While this is commendable in itself, it has led to some fanciful interpretation on Howard's

part. For instance, he takes the verb ὑπερύψωσεν in v. 9 to be a post-resurrection exaltation on earth and not an allusion to Christ's heavenly ascension. In my opinion this is far-fetched and tends to set up a false dilemma between Jesus' bodily, post-resurrection exaltation and his spiritual, heavenly ascension. Why not simply acknowledge that Jesus' ascension was in a spiritual body?

80. Accepting the variant reading of ἐξομολογήσεται in place of ὀμεῖται. Martin, *op. cit.*, p. 256, suggests that the author of the hymn is subconsciously quoting the *Targum of Isaiah* 45.23 in adopting this reading. Jerome Murphy-O'Connor (*art. cit.*, p. 47) points out that in Isa. 45.23 the LXX differs from the MT at one critical point. The LXX drops the specific reference to God in v. 21 and thereby allows easy association with a Wisdom figure (i.e. Jesus) in the general thrust of the verse. Murphy-O'Connor argues that the Wis. 3.8 is responsible for this connection in thought.

81. Contra C.F.D. Moule, *art. cit.*, p. 270. Talbert (*art. cit.*, p. 145) also seems to imply that the name Ἰησοῦς is meant.

82. Not to mention the fact that Ἰησοῦς was a name which was borne by the Lord all of his earthly life and it is hardly likely that it was spoken of as being conferred upon him only at the conclusion of his life of obedient service.

83. As Martin (*op. cit.*, p. 236) comments: 'The important thing is that it is God who gives to the exalted Jesus the all-excelling name. This, then, can be none other than the name of God Himself; and the name of God κατ᾽ ἐχοξήν which, in the Old Testament, distinguishes Him from all rivals and idol powers as 'Lord' (Yahweh).'

84. On the dynamic Hebrew conceptualization of God's Name, see Martin, *op. cit.*, pp. 245f. n. 3, and the literature cited there.

85. See J.B. Lightfoot, *St. Paul's Epistle to the Philippians* (1903), p. 113; Jerome Murphy-O'Connor, *art. cit.*, pp. 48f.; George Howard, *art. cit.*, pp. 381ff., where Howard is also quick to qualify this association of Jesus Christ with the name of Yahweh in functional and not ontic terms. 'The idea is that God gave to Christ the name which is above every name, i.e., the name YHWH, not for him to wear as his own name, but for him to possess and use' (p. 382). Howard criticizes Ralph Martin for what he considers an unjustified ontological association between Jesus and God on the basis of the phrase κύριος Ἰησοῦς Χριστός in v. 11. Howard does go on to try and outline what he imagines to be a three stage process of development of the phrase along an increasingly ontological pathway, but his entire outline suffers from being hypothetical and is without any textual evidence to demonstrate the various stages of the process. Underlying Howard's thesis in this regard is his insistence that the pre-Christian Greek Bible never substituted the tetragrammaton YHWH with the surrogate κύριος. However this idea is not without its difficulties. See above (pp. 108-10) where Howard's proposal is discussed in connection with Rom. 14.10-11.

86. Not to mention the pre-Pauline traditions contained within those letters.

87. Jean-François Collange (*The Epistle of St. Paul to the Philippians* [1979], p. 106) comments: 'early Christian faith was not able to escape the problem which its own confession of Jesus as Lord raised in the face of the strict monotheism of the Old Testament'.

88. Incidentally, Eph. 3.14 speaks of its author bowing his knees before the Father (πατέρα) with an interesting alternate reading being πατέρα τοῦ κυρίος ἡμῶν Ἰησοῦ Χριστοῦ.

89. Note the discussion above in connection with the quotation of Isa. 45.23 in Rom. 14.11 (pp. 107-108).

90. See the details of such a shift outlined in connection with the *Epistle of Barnabas* 12.10ff. in Chapter 3, note 71.

91. Following Lightfoot, *op. cit.*, p. 115, who appeals to Rev. 22.14 for support in future tense verbs. The evidence for the two variants is equally divided. In light of this it seems strange to me that the aorist κάμψη is read in v. 10, especially since the LXX of Isa. 45.23 reads the future κάμψει. Perhaps the answer lies in the fact that the verses offer a capsule-summary of the present/future paradox of Christian hope. In any case, it should be remembered that aorist subjunctives often serve as futures.

92. 'Dissenting Deities and Philippians 2.1-11', *JBL* 88 (1969), p. 290.

93. There is some discussion as to whether Paul understands angelic beings or saints by this use of οἱ ἅγιοι. See A.L. Moore, *I & II Thessalonians* (1969), p. 58, and E. Best, *A Commentary on the First and Second Epistles to the Thessalonians* (1972), pp. 152-53, for details. The question is finally unanswerable; οἱ ἅγιοι could refer to either. See the comments in the text below in connection with 2 Thess. 1.7, 10 (pp. 217-18).

94. On this, see C.H. Dodd, *According to the Scriptures* (1952), pp. 66-67.

95. In connection with the verb ἄξει contained in this verse, Paul Ellingworth ('Which Way Are We Going? A verb of movement, especially in 1 Thess. 4, 14b', *BibTr* 25, [1974], pp. 426-31) has argued that it implies an upward rather than a downward movement on behalf of τοὺς κοιμηθέντας. J.M. Ross ('1 Thessalonians 3.13', *BibTr* 26 [1975], p. 444) goes further, to suggest that part of this confusion of motion in 4.14 is due to the influence of the Jewish theophanic tradition alluded to in 3.13. Ross thus effectively argues that a distinction be made between οἱ ἅγιοι in 3.13 and τοὺς κοιμηθέντας in 4.14 (but see note 93 above). On this whole subject of Paul's use of traditional Jewish apocalyptic, see Raymond F. Collins, *Studies on the First Letter to the Thessalonians* (1984), pp. 9, 247-52. In any case, the christocentric/theocentric ambiguity between 3.13 and 4.14 is a further example of Paul's conceptual overlap on this point.

96. This fact is completely overlooked by Glasson and calls into question his assertion that, as far as the Parousia is concerned, 'in the New Testament,

the Messiah and the Lord are the same person'. (See the quotation above on pp. 101-102 of the text.) Glasson's argument on this point betrays his prejudice against the relevance of pseudepigraphal literature in explaining the origin of the New Testament doctrine of the Parousia of Christ.

97. Jerome Neyrey ('Eschatology in 1 Thessalonians: The Theological Factor in 1.9-10; 2.4-5; 3.11-13; 4.6 and 4.13-18', in *SBL Seminar Papers 1980*, pp. 220ff.) argues strongly for the theocentric element in 1.10 as determinative. He sees the verse as reflective of an older, missionary-preaching tradition which was primarily God-centered and not Christ-centered. For a discussion of the pre-Pauline form of 1.10, see Jerome Havener, 'The Pre-Pauline Christological Credal Formulae of 1 Thessalonians', in *SBL Seminar Papers 1981*, pp. 105ff.

98. Glasson (*The Second Advent*, p. 31) makes a categorical distinction between *1 Enoch* and the New Testament on the basis that the New Testament often speaks of the Messiah as accompanied by angels while 'nowhere is there any hint in Enoch of the Messiah having an angelic retinue'.

99. Zech. 14.5 is quoted in the *Didache* 16 with reference to Christ's Parousia. See Glasson, *ibid.*, p. 169, for details.

100. 'The Relevance of Isaiah 66.7 to Revelation 12 and 2 Thessalonians 1', *ZNW* 67 (1976), pp. 252-68.

101. Additionally, both *Genesis Rabbah* 85 and *Leviticus Rabbah* 14/9 demonstrate this same tendency of messianic reinterpretation.

102. Aus, in another article ('God's Plan and God's Power: Isaiah 66 and the Restraining Factors of 2 Thess. 2.6-7', *JBL* 96 [1977], pp. 537-53), argues that Isaiah 66 contains the interpretative key to the mystery of the meaning of ὁ κατέχον and τὸ κατέχον in 2 Thess. 2.6-7. Basically he solves the question in favor of God as the active subject via an appeal to the verb in Isa. 66.9 where God is spoken of as 'shutting' or 'restraining' the womb. Aus eventually associates this restraining factor with the worldwide proclamation of the Gospel.

103. Aus notes the persecution motif in 2 Thess. 1.4-8; 2.7, 15-17; 3.3, 5.

104. These linguistic associations are: (1) 2 Thess. 1.6 and Isa. 66.6 focusing on the word ἀνταποδοῦναι; (2) 2 Thess. 1.8 and Isa. 66.15 focusing on the phrase ἐν πυρὶ φλογός; (3) 2 Thess. 1.8 and Isa. 66.4, 15 focusing on the words ἐκδίκησιν and ὑπακούουσιν; (4) 2 Thess. 1.12 and Isa. 66.5 focusing on the words ἐνδοξασθῇ and τὸ ὄνομα.

105. The most literal adoption is ἐν φλογὶ πυρός, from Isa. 66.15, which appears in 2 Thess. 1.8 in two major textual forms: ἐν φλογὶ πυρός and ἐν πυρὶ φλογός. The textual evidence is fairly evenly divided for both readings. See Peter Katz, 'ἐν πυρὶ φλογός', *ZNW* 46 (1955), pp. 133-38, for details.

106. The *Targum of Isaiah* 66.7 speaks of the revelation of a king (יהגלי מלכה) while the MT speaks of a son being delivered (זכר המלימה).

107. Exactly the same phrase occurs in vv. 19 and 21.

108. Probably because of its acting as a depersonalizing and unnecessary noun which detracts from the theocentric use of κύριος.

109. It is exactly the same in 11c and 17c.

110. It is likely that the allusion to Psalm 88 was prompted by the judgment motif in the larger context of v. 8.

111. See Barnabas Lindars, *New Testament Apologetics*, (1961), p. 202. the minor variant Ἰησους following κύριος should be excluded. Bruce Metzger (*A Textual Commentary on the Greek New Testament* [1975], p. 636) suggests that its omission might be due to a later attempt to make the allusion more closely allign with Isaiah 11.

112. Charles Giblin (*The Threat to Faith* [1967], p. 95) associates the use of this verb with Holy War imagery.

113. See Ernest Best, *A Commentary on the First and Second Epistles to the Thessalonians* (1972), pp. 302-303.

114. Ronald Clements (*Isaiah 1-39* [1980], pp. 121-22) comments that vv. 1-5 are a post-exilic redactional addition designed to engender assurance about the Davidic monarchy. At the same time, it is attached to another strand of prophecy in vv. 6-9 which involves the wider, universal hope of the future.

115. Paul shows himself familiar with the Davidic prophecy via the quotation of 11.10 (cp. 11.1) contained in Rom. 15.12. There the reference to Isaiah forms part of a string of Old Testament quotations revolving around the theme of the hope of the Gentiles. Thus the specifically messianic element is secondary, which probably explains the deletion of ἐν τῇ ἡμέρα ἐκείνῃ from the middle of the quotation.

116. As Joachim Jeremias (*The Unknown Sayings of Jesus* [1964], pp. 80-83) argues. Jeremias's argument involves the understanding that originally the saying would have spoken of ὁ υἱός τοῦ ἀνθρώπου instead of αὔτος ὁ κύριος. See Raymond Collins, *op. cit.*, pp. 39ff., and Gebhard Löhr, '1 Thess. 4.15-17: Das Herrenwort', *ZNW* 71 (1980), pp. 269-73, for further details.

117. Joseph Plevnik, 'The Parousia as Implication of Christ's Resurrection (An Exegesis of 1 Thess. 4, 13-18)', in *Word and Spirit* (Stanley FS; 1975), pp. 199-277.

118. Plevnik (*art. cit.*, p. 236) notes that the word is found 28 times in the Old Testament, 16 instances of which involve theophanies.

119. Its use is also readily associated with 'Holy war' traditions in Israel's history, especially within the book of Judges.

120. Mt. 24.30; 26.64; Mk 13.26; 14.62; Lk. 21.27. Also note Rev. 1.7 and 14.14-16. In Rev. 10.1 an angel is clothed in the cloud. The motif also is used with reference to ascension, as Acts 1.9 and Rev. 11.12 indicate.

121. Follow this argument in Glasson's, *The Second Advent*, pp. 31ff.

122. 'Behold, He Cometh with Clouds', *NTS* 5 (1959-60), pp. 127-32. Scott argues that this accounts for the fact that within the *Similitudes* of Enoch (46.1-2; 43.3; 69.27, 29) the reference to the 'clouds of heaven' is

missing from the description of the coming of the Son of Man.

123. Remembering that Scott's article is 25 years old and the 'Son of Man' question has been somewhat refined during the interval.

124. We have already noted in connection with 1 Thess. 3.13 and 4.14 that there exists a christocentric/theocentric overlap with respect to the Coming of the Lord.

125. The passage from Isaiah was apparently a favourite one among early Christians exegetes. We find a similar use of it in 1 Pet. 2.6. See Barnabas Lindars, *New Testament Apologetic* (1961), pp. 169-86, for details.

126. A fact emphasized by his use of the future καταισχυνθήσεται in both Rom. 9.33 and 10.11. the quotation contained in 1 Pet. 2.6 retains the aorist verb καταισχύνθη as derived from the LXX.

127. The addition also occurs in the reference in 1 Peter.

128. It does occur in A Q Sy¹ ᵐᵍ 88. For a discussion of the variant, see J. De Waard, *A Comparative Study of the Old Testament Text in the Dead Sea Scrolls and in the New Testament* (1966), pp. 54-60. De Waard thinks it should be seriously considered whether the phrase comes into the LXX via the Targum on Isa. 28.16.

129. The LXX reads: καὶ οὐχ ὡς λίθου προσκόμματι συναντήσεσθε.

130. The verse begins in the LXX: κύριον αὐτὸν ἁγιάσατε.

131. The major divergence from the LXX is Paul's substitution of ἐκ Σίων for ἕνεκεν Σιών. On this point, see Berndt Schaller, 'ΗΞΕΙ ΕΚ ΣΙΩΝ Ο ΡΥΟΜΕΝΟΣ', in *De Septuaginta* (Wevers FS; edited by Albert Pietersma and Claude Cox; 1984), pp. 201-206.

132. See the extended discussion in Markus Barth, *Ephesians* 2 (1974), pp. 758-808.

133. The imagery of Isa. 59.17 might also lie behind the military phrases in Rom. 13.12 (ἐνδυσώμεθα τὰ ὅπλα τοῦ φωτός) and 2 Cor. 6.7 (τῶν ὅπλων τῆς δικαιοσύνης).

134. For details of how such war-imagery is applied to an eschatological figure, including the Messiah, see below, Chapter 3, note 80. Robert A. Wild ('The Warrior and the Prisoner: Some Reflections on Ephesians 6.10-20', *CBQ* 46 [1984], p. 287) emphasizes that the armor which the Christian is exhorted to put on 'is that worn by God himself'.

Notes to Chapter 3

1. In Gal. 1.4 this present age is specifically called 'evil' (πονηρός) Compare Rom. 8.18; 1 Cor. 7.26; Eph. 5.16.

2. In 1 Cor. 13.8-12 and 2 Cor. 4.16-18 Paul speaks metaphorically of the present age as opposed to the future in a manner recognizing the overlap of the two. Compare 2 Cor. 3.18; Col. 2.16-17.

3. For a good discussion of the relationship between justification and this

final judgment, see K.P. Donfried, 'Justification and Last Judgment in Paul', *ZNW* 67 (1976), pp. 90-110, where it is argued that justification is the starting point for understanding Paul's ideas about the final judgment. Ultimate obedience to the gospel message is essential to secure a favourable verdict on the Judgment Day. Thus it is only proper for the Christian to proclaim 'I am in the process of being saved' and never 'I have been saved'. The same article appears, slightly condensed, in *Interpretation* 30 (1976), pp. 140-52. Stephen Travis (*Divine Retribution in the Thought of St. Paul* [1970], pp. 102-15) discuss the relationship between justification and judgment and arrives at similar conclusions. For a discussion of the parallel clauses 'the revelation of righteousness of God' and 'the revelation of the wrath of God' in Rom. 1.17-18, see Gunter Bornkamm, 'The Revelation of God's Wrath: Romans 1-3' in his *Early Christian Experience* (1969), pp. 47-50.

4. For a discussion of the relationship between the Synoptic apocalyptic material and Paul, see: G.H. Waterman, 'The Sources of Paul's Teaching on the Second Coming of Christ in 1 and 2 Thessalonians', *JETS* 18 (1975), pp. 105-13; David Wenham, 'Paul and the Synoptic Apocalypse', *Gospel Perspectives: Studies of History and Tradition in the Four Gospels*. Volume II, edited by R.T. France and David Wenham (1981), pp. 345-375. The larger question of the basic continuity between Jesus and Paul is explored by W.G. Kümmel, 'Jesus und Paulus', *NTS* 10 (1963-64), pp. 163-81. The fluctuating attitude with respect to the eschatological traditions inherited by Paul as evidenced by comparing 1 Cor. 15.3-5 and Gal. 1.11f. is discussed in W. Grundmann, 'Überlieferung und Eigenaussage im eschatologischen Denken des Apostels Paulus', *NTS* 8 (1961-62), pp. 12-26.

5. The noun βασιλεύς occurs in 2 Cor. 11.32 in reference to Aretus but is beyond our consideration.

6. The literature on the subject is vast. A good overview and bibliography is to be found in George Eldon Ladd's *The Presence of the Future* (1974). W.G. Kümmel's *Promise and Fulfilment* (1957) is worth noting. Also worth noting is Kümmel's 'Eschatological Expectation in the Proclamation of Jesus', in *The Future of Our Religious Past* (Bultmann FS; 1971), pp. 29-48.

7. On this, see George Johnson, '"Kingdom of God" Sayings in Paul's Epistles', in *From Jesus to Paul* (Beare FS; 1984)), pp. 143-56. Unfortunately, Johnson does not distinguish within his discussion between the Kingdom of Christ and the Kingdom of God.

8. The present/future dichotomy is discussed in W.G. Kummel, 'Futuristic and Realized Eschatology in the Earliest Stages of Christianity', *JourRel* 43 (1963), pp. 303-14. This is a translation of the German article which appears in *NTS* 5 (1958-59), pp. 113-26.

9. Paul uses κυριεύω in Romans with much the same force in 6.9, 14; 7.1; 14.9.

10. Eduard Schweizer discusses Paul's teaching on the Kingdom of God and its present/future dimensions in connection with baptism in 'Dying and Rising with Christ', *NTS* 14 (1967-68), pp. 1-14.

11. See Joachim Jeremias, 'Flesh and Blood Cannot Inherit the Kingdom of God', *NTS* 2 (1955-56), pp. 151-59, where it is persuasively argued that the phrase is in reference to the transformation of the believers alive at the time of the Parousia. A distinction is thus made between the metamorphosis of the live believer (15.50b) and the deceased one (15.50c). Refer also to Ronald J. Sider, 'The Pauline Conception of the Resurrection Body in I Corinthians XV. 35-54', *NTS* 21 (1974-75), pp. 428-39.

12. See Bruce M. Metzger, *A Textual Commentary on the Greek New Testament* (1975), p. 607, for a discussion of the variant readings of this phrase.

13. This is not the place to discuss the thorny issue of the authenticity of either Colossians or Ephesians. The problems are complex and would take us too far afield without having much direct bearing on our topic. Although I personally tend to accept Pauline authorship of Colossians (albeit with heavy editing?) and take Ephesians to be the work of a later disciple, we can safely assume that any teaching on the Kingdom of Christ in either of the disputed epistles has the apostle as its ultimate source. For a discussion of the problem, see John Coutts, 'The Relationship of Ephesians and Colossians', *NTS* 4 (1957-58), pp. 201-207; J.B. Polhill, 'The Relationship between Ephesians and Colossians', *RevExp* 70 (1975), pp. 439-50. A good survey of the whole Deutero-Pauline issue is to be found in Arthur G. Patzia, 'The Deutero-Pauline Hypothesis: An Attempt at Clarification', *EQ* 52 (1980), pp. 27-42. For debate about the Pauline authorship of Eph. 5.5, see P.L. Hanmer, 'A Comparison of KLERONOMIA in Paul and Ephesians', *JBL* 79 (1960), pp. 267-72; D.R. Denton, 'Inheritance in Paul and Ephesians', *EQ* 54 (1982), pp. 157-62. A short article on the subject of eschatology within the Ephesian letter is Stephen S. Smalley's, 'The Eschatology of Ephesians', *EQ* 28 (1956), pp. 152-57.

14. B. Klappert in his article on 'King' in *NIDNTT* II (1976), p. 387, remarks: 'The phrase "basileia of Christ" and the equation of "Kingdom of God" with Jesus Christ are thus seen to be the result of the change-over from an implicit to an explicit christology'. For a discussion of the special christocentric emphasis within New Testament eschatology (especially with regards to Mk. 14.62), see George R. Beasley-Murray, 'New Testament Apocalyptic: A Christological Eschatology', *RevExp* 72 (1975), pp. 317-30.

15. Eduard Schweizer argues for the essential harmony between Jesus and Paul with respect to the eschatological message of the Kingdom in '1 Korinther 15, 20-28 als Zeugnis paulinischer Eschatologie und ihrer Verwandtschaft mit der Verkündigung Jesu', *Jesus und Paul* (Kümmel FS; 1975), pp. 301-14. He includes a brief discussion of the present/future dimension of this shared proclamation.

16. For a standard exposition of the chiliastic position, see Hans Bietenhard, *Das tausendjährige Reich* (1955). The post-Apostolic Church's belief in the millennium is traced in his 'The Millennial Hope in the Early Church', *SJT* 6 (1953), pp. 12-30. The classic post-millennial interpretation is simplistically advocated in Allen Ford, 'The Second Advent in Relation to the Reign of Christ', *EQ* 23 (1951), pp. 30-39. This article imposes a rigid structure upon the relevant New Testament passages while containing not a single reference to Jewish apocalyptic within pseudepigraphal literature. Clark Pinnock, 'The Structure of Pauline Eschatology', *EQ* 37 (1965), pp. 9-20, also objects to a chiliastic interpretation of 1 Cor. 15.23-28 on the grounds that it does 'exegetical violence' (p. 19) to the text. Once again no attention is given to the flexibility of apocalyptic in this regard and Paul is forced into a straight-jacket of interpretation. There is no discussion of pseudepigraphal material in the article either.

An even more incredible feat is Anthony Hoekema's recent *The Bible and the Future* (1979), pp. 180-87, which argues vehemently for an a-millennialist interpretation of the whole of the New Testament. This book purports to be a scholarly work; yet, remarkably, within its 343 pages there is not a single reference to any pseudepigraphal book. No doubt this approach is theologically inspired and there is a certain virtue thought to be attached to such strict adherence to 'Biblical' evidence; but efforts such as this make a mockery of scholarly attempts to interpret the meaning of the New Testament using all the critical tools available (including the use of pseudepigraphal material as a background source). Sadly, I feel books such as Hoekema's are in the end counterproductive. They convince only those who are pre-disposed to their particular viewpoint and merely serve to further entrench poisoned attitudes about historical/critical studies by blinding readers as to the vitality of eschatological teaching within the New Testament as well as the rich apocalyptic milieu of the pseudepigraphal literature.

17. Scholarship has been far from unanimous in its assessment of the meaning of the millennium in Rev. 20.4ff. For a useful attempt to clarify the various interpretations of this critical passage through an extended dialectical discussion, see R.G. Clouse (ed.), *The Meaning of the Millennium: Four Views* (1977). Here there are several interpretative suggestions given: G.E. Ladd on historic premillennialism; H.A. Hoyt on dispensational premillennialism; L. Boettner on postmillennialism; and A.A. Hoekema on amillennialism. Each scholar responds to the viewpoints of the other within this book. See also Michel Gourges, 'The Thousand-Year Reign (Rev. 20.1-6): Terrestrial or Celestial?', *CBQ* 47 (1985), pp. 676-81.

18. Recent commentators on the book of Revelation are divided as to whether 1 Cor. 15.20-28 should be taken as a parallel to 20.1-11. Those opposed to such a connection include: G.B. Caird, *A Commentary on the Revelation of St. John the Divine* (1966), pp. 249-51; Robert Mounce, *The Book of Revelation* (1977), p. 357; Eduard Lohse, *Die Offenbarung des*

Johannes (1979), p. 104. (It is worth noting that most commentators who reject the Pauline connection are critical of a pre-millennial interpretation of Revelation 20 as well. More often than not their a-millennial presuppositions are determining their exegesis in this regard.) Commentators sympathetic to such an idea include: Martin Rist, *The Revelation of St. John the Divine* (1957), p. 519; Matthias Rissi, *Time and History: A Study on the Revelation* (1966), pp. 119ff.; George Eldon Ladd, *A Commentary on the Revelation of John* (1972), pp. 161, 267ff.; G.R. Beasley-Murray, *The Book of Revelation* (1974), pp. 290ff. Both Martin Kiddle (*The Revelation of St. John* [1940], p. 395) and Ronald H. Preston and Anthony T. Hanson (*The Revelation of St. John the Divine* [1962], p. 125) think such an association is 'doubtful'.

Commentators on the Pauline Epistles are also divided on the issue. Advocates include: H.A.W. Meyer, *Critical and Exegetical Handbook to the Epistles to the Corinthians* (1881), pp. 59-63; Johannes Weiss, *Der erste Korintherbrief* (1910), pp. 358-59; Phillip Bachmann, *Der erste Brief des Paulus an die Korinther* (1910), pp.438-40; Hans Lietzmann, *An die Korinther I & II*, (1949), pp. 80-82; James Moffatt, *The First Epistle of Paul to the Corinthians* (1938), p. 249. Opponents include: H.L.Goudge, *The First Epistle to the Corinthians*, 4th edn (1915), pp. 148-50 and 165-66; R. St. John Parry, *The First Epistle of Paul the Apostle to the Corinthians* (1957), pp. 225-26; Jean Héring, *The First Epistle of Saint Paul to the Corinthians* (1962), pp. 167-68; C.K. Barrett, *A Commentary on the First Epistle to the Corinthians* (1968), pp. 356-61; I. Howard Marshall, *1 and 2 Thessalonians* (1983), p. 121. Robertson and Plummer (*A Critical and Exegetical Commentary on the First Epistle of St. Paul to the Corinthians* [1914], p. 314) argue that it is 'impossible to say' one way or the other.

For additional discussion of the issue, see: Otto Pfleiderer, *Paulinism: A Contribution to the History of Primitive Christian Theology I* (1877), pp. 267-76; George Eldon Ladd, *Crucial Questions about the Kingdom of God* (1952), pp. 177ff.; Maurice Goguel, *The Birth of Christianity* (1953), pp. 248-49; L. Cerfaux, *Christ in the Theology of St. Paul* (1959), pp. 51-52; C.K. Barrett, *From First Adam to Last* (1962), pp. 101ff.; Robert H. Mounce, 'Pauline Eschatology and the Apocalypse', *EQ* 46 (1974), pp. 164-66; Ralph P. Martin, *New Testament Foundations*, Volume II (1978), pp. 408-17, and *The Spirit and the Congregation: Studies in 1 Corinthians 12-15* (1984), pp. 107-18; Murray J. Harris, *Raised Immortal* (1983), pp. 178-80. Of special note is C.F.D. Moule, *The Birth of the New Testament*, 3rd edn (1981), p. 145, where it is argued that vestiges of the distinction between the concept of a temporary Messianic Kingdom and the Eternal Age to Come are thought to be embodied in 1 Cor. 15.20-28. This is similar to the thought of Hans Conzelmann, *1 Corinthians* (1975), pp. 269-75, where it is argued that the Kingdom does not primarily lie in the future for Paul but it seems clear that Paul is indebted to the traditional Jewish eschatological schema we see outlined in *4 Ezra*. Christophe Senft, *La Première Épitre de Saint Paul aux*

Corinthiens (1979), p. 199, arrives at a similar judgment.

19. For a helpful introduction into Schweitzer's work on Paul and its impact upon New Testament scholarship, see Anthony C. Thiselton, 'Schweitzer's Interpretation of Paul', *ExpT* 90 (1978-79), pp. 132-37.

20. *The Mysticism of Paul the Apostle* (1931), p. 90

21. Schweitzer suggests that Paul was the originator of such an idea (*op. cit.*, p. 94). He assumes throughout that Paul, along with the authors of *4 Ezra* and *2 Baruch*, expects the resurrection of the dead at the end of the Messianic Kingdom.

22. Apparently apocalyptic literature as a whole struggled with the problem of the status of the living and of the dead at the time of the consummation (note especially the exchanges between Ezra and God in the first three sections of the Ezra Apocalypse!). Such a dilemma within apocalyptic may help to explain in part the climate of opinion within the churches at Corinth and Thessaloniki which necessitates Paul's letters to them, but we should not press the point too far. See A.F.J. Klijn, '1 Thessalonians 4.13-18 and its Background in Apocalyptic Literature', in *Paul and Paulinism* (Barrett FS; 1982), pp. 67-73, for an attempt to use this problematic feature of apocalyptic in illuminating the first epistle to the Thessalonians. For a related discussion of how 1 Cor. 15.20-28 fits within the larger issue of the resurrection of both Christ and the believers in the rest of the chapter, see William Dykstra, '1 Corinthians 15.20-28: An Essential Part of Paul's Argument Against Those Who Deny the Resurrection', *CTR* 4 (1969), pp. 195-211. Dykstra emphasizes vv. 20-28 as an important part of Paul's teaching in countering the Corinthian heresy alluded to in 15.12.

23. See Schweitzer's *Paul and his Interpreters* (1912), pp. 50ff. Also note the concluding remarks on page 240, which draw their inspiration in a large part from a healthy consideration of 1 Cor. 15.20-28. Schweitzer laments the way in which first-century Jewish parallels were overlooked in the history of Pauline scholarship and credits Richard Kabisch, *Die Eschatologie des Paulus in ihren Zusammenhängen mit dem Gesamtbegriff des Paulinismus* (1893), with the first breakthrough in this area.

24. 3rd edn (1970), pp. 285ff. The first edition appeared in 1948.

25. *Ibid.*, p. 291. He cites Héring as a source for this interpretation and quotes him as support with regards to the Corinthian situation: 'We do not err in affirming that Paul himself at an early period had expressly denied the future resurrection and that the anti-resurrectionists at Thessaloniki and Corinth were after all the representatives of the unchanged Pauline belief' ('Saint-Paul a-t-il enseigné deux resurrections?', *RHPR* 12 [1932], p. 318). The quote in Davies is found on p. 292. A further discussion of Héring's ideas on the subject can be found in his *The First Epistle of St. Paul to the Corinthians* (1962), pp. 164-68.

26. The 'two-stage appearance' is, of course, another way of expressing the delay of the Parousia!

27. *Ibid.*, p. 297.

28. These six passages are: 1 Thess. 2.12; 2 Thess. 1.4-5; Gal. 5.21; 1 Cor. 15.50; Col. 4.11.

29. It is perhaps not unreasonable to suggest that τὸ τέλος of 1 Cor. 15.24 and the frequently used *finis* of *4 Ezra* share a common root. No doubt if the Greek version of *4 Ezra* had survived it would have read τὸ τέλος where the Latin now has *finis*.

30. 'The Problem of an Intermediate Kingdom in 1 Corinthians 15.20-28', *JETS* 18 (1975), pp. 229-42. Also see his 'The Use of Psalms 8 and 110 in 1 Corinthians 15.25-27 and in Hebrews 1 and 2', *JETS* 15 (1972), pp. 25-29.

31. Hans-Alwin Wilcke, *Das Problem eines messianischen Zwischenreichs bei Paulus* (1967).

32. Remembering, of course, that what is implied by a doctrine of two resurrections is an intervening Messianic Kingdom of temporary duration!

33. A good illustration of this is found on pp. 69-72 of Wilcke's book, where the interpretative history of 1 Cor. 15.22b is given. The meaning of the two occurrences of πάντες has been vigorously debated among the Church Fathers!

34. *Ibid.*, pp. 65-75.

35. As F.C. Burkitt ('On 1 Corinthians xv 26', *JST* 17 [1916], pp. 384-85) interprets the phrase. Burkitt appeals to 1 Pet. 3.8 for support in this adverbial interpretation.

36. Colin Brown concurs in his article on 'Number' in *NIDNTT* II (1976), pp. 702-703.

37. See William Crockett, 'The Ultimate Restoration of all Mankind: 1 Corinthians 15.22', *Studia Biblica 1978, III. Papers on Paul and Other New Testament Authors* (1980), pp. 83-87.

38. *Art. cit.*, p. 234.

39. Must the comprehensiveness of Christ's saving efficacy be restricted to an anthropological sphere? What are we to make of passages which introduce a cosmic dimension (such as Rom. 8.19-22)? Markus Barth ('Christ and All Things', in *Paul and Paulinism* [Barrett FS; 1982], pp. 160-72) critiques the bias modern scholarship has against such a dimension and suggests that only a christology 'from above' is sufficient to explain some of the claims of the New Testament. According to Barth, this cosmic comprehensiveness of Christ leads to confession of the deity of Christ.

40. Wallis appeals to Acts 24.15 for support of his assertion that Paul's believes in a dual resurrection but notes that Wilcke does not accept Acts as an historically reliable source of Paul's teaching. See *art. cit.*, pp. 236-37. For a critique of the skeptical attitude towards Luke's historical reliability, which seems to prevade German scholarship, see Martin Hengel, *Acts and the History of Earliest Christianity* (1979).

41. *Art. cit.*, p. 230. On this point, see also Friedrich Wilhelm Maier, 'Ps. 110, 1 (LXX 109, 1) im Zusammenhang von 1 Kor. 15, 24-26', *BibZ* 20 (1932),

pp. 139-56.

42. *Ibid.*, p. 232.

43. 'The Kingship of Christ and the Church in the New Testament', in *The Early Church*, edited by A.J.B. Higgins, (1956), pp. 111ff.

44. See *Christ and Time* (1951) and *Salvation in History* (1967).

45. See W.R.G. Loader, 'Christ at the Right Hand—Ps. CX.1 in the New Testament', *NTS* 24 (1977-78), pp. 199-217.

46. *The Christology of the New Testament* (1959). It should be noted here that Heb. 10.13 is also thought by Cullmann to be a future reference of Ps. 110.1.

47. *Art. cit.*, pp. 112f.

48. H.A.A. Kennedy, *St. Paul's Conception of the Last Things* (1904), pp. 319ff. lists several instances where does not denote a time sequence. However, none of the Johannine parallels he gives have both the ἔπειτα and εἶτα clauses. In addition, the only other Pauline occurrence of the dual ἔπειτα/εἶτα clause structure is contained earlier within 1 Corinthians 15 itself. In vv. 5-7 we have a chronological sequence of resurrection appearances of the risen Christ to various disciples in which full force of the temporal dimension should be accorded.

49. Wilcke does make mention of this important point in his monograph (pp. 94-100), but fails to take it into serious consideration as he develops his arguments. He does describe the construction as 'clumsy' ('schwerfällig', p. 97). It is Wallis who turns this clumsiness to his advantage and reinterprets the whole passage with the awkward tense considerations in mind. G.G. Findlay, *St. Paul's First Epistle to the Corinthians* (1900), p. 927, notes that the two phrases denote 'distinct, but connected and complementary acts'.

50. See C.H. Dodd, *According to the Scriptures* (1952), pp. 34-35; J.D.G. Dunn, *Christology in the Making* (1980), pp. 108ff.; Barnabas Lindars, *New Testament Apologetics* (1961), pp. 45-51 and 222-50. Martin Hengel ('Hymns and Christology', in *Between Jesus and Paul* [1982], pp. 78-96) analyses the Church's adoption of this Psalm, among others, within her worship hymns in his effort to trace the earliest christological development of thought. On the development issue, see I. Howard Marshall, 'The Development of Christology in the Early Church', *TB* 18 (1967), pp. 77-93; Ralph Martin, 'New Testament Hymns: Background and Development', *ExptT* 94 (1982-83), pp. 132-36; Martin Hengel, 'Christology and New Testament Chronology', in *Between Jesus and Paul* (1983), pp. 30-47; Seyoon Kim, *The Origin of Paul's Gospel* (1982), pp. 105ff., where pupil criticizes professor with regards to development in his (Hengel's) own thought on the matter. Of special note is P.M. Casey's discussion of the Jewish antecedents to Paul's christological development in 'Chronology and the Development of Pauline Christology', in *Paul and Paul in Paulinism* (Barrett FS; 1982), pp. 124-34. His distinction between 'static' and 'dynamic' categories is particularly useful, even if it is

somewhat artificial.

51. D.M. Hay, *Glory at the Right Hand: Psalm 110 in Early Christianity* (1973), lists 33 occurrences within the New Testament alone. See pp. 163-66 in this book for a list.

52. W.R.G. Loader *art. cit.*, pp. 200ff.

53. *Ibid.*, pp. 202ff. where Loader tries to make a distinction between the interim heavenly activity of the exalted Jesus and the present rule of the enthroned Christ. I find such a distinction strained at best and ultimately derived from the unsatisfactory practice of driving a wedge between Jesus' Lordship and his Messiahship. Surely the very passage Loader begins his discussion with (Acts 2.32-36) renders such an interpretation invalid by its dual proclamation 'God has made him both Lord and Christ'. We are very much nearer the truth if we see Jesus' Lordship as inseparably linked with and stemming from his Messiahship. The 'Archilles-heel' of an interpretation such as Loader's is its dependence upon a theory of the essential incompatibility between the task of intercession and the messianic rule. Loader himself admits the problem (p. 207), yet persists with the false distinction. For a sound discussion of the delay of the Parousia, note: Stephen Smalley, 'The Delay of the Parousia', *JBL* 83 (1964), pp. 41-54; David E. Aune, 'The Significance of the Delay of the Parousia for Early Christianity', in *Current Issues in Biblical and Patristic Interpretation* (Tenney FS; 1975), pp. 87-109; and Richard Bauckham, 'The Delay of the Parousia', *TB* 31 (1980), pp. 3-36. Bauckham treats the subject from the standpoint of its being an issue within Jewish literature and argues that this awareness of the Jewish problem provides an excellent backdrop against which the New Testament concern must be viewed. Christopher Rowland (*Christian Origins* [1985], pp. 285-94) also has some excellent material.

54. Generally the exaltation of Christ and the Church's worship of him was understood to be grounded in the destruction by means of the resurrection of Christ of the powers of evil enslaving mankind. Mankind is thus released from bondage and granted the freedom in which the Christian life is able to develop. Passages such as Col. 2.15, Phil. 2.10, and the various uses of Ps. 110.1 in the New Testament were thought to support such an interpretation. See G.H.C. Macgregor, 'Principalities and Powers: The Cosmic Background of Paul's Thought', *NTS* 1 (1954-55), pp. 17-28; Heinrich Schlier, *Principalities and Powers in the New Testament* (1961); Jung Young Lee, 'Interpreting the Demonic Powers in Pauline Thought', *NovT* 12 (1970), pp. 54-69; Roy Yates, 'Christ and the Powers of Evil in Colossians', in *Studia Biblica 1978, III. Papers on Paul and Other New Testament Authors* (1980), pp. 461-68. (For a recent investigation into the verb θριαμβεύω in Col. 2.15, see Rory B. Egan, 'Lexical Evidence on Two Pauline Passages', *NovT* 19 [1977], pp. 34-62). This type of interpretation has been recently challenged by Wesley Carr in his *Angels and Principalities* (1981); compare 'The Rulers of this Age—1 Corinthians II, 6-8', *NTS* 23

(1976-77), pp. 20-35, and 'Two Notes on Colossians', *JTS* 24 (1973), pp. 492-500, where it is argued that neither Paul nor his contemporaries believed the world to be dominated by hostile spiritual powers which had to be conquered through the cross. Instead, the references to enemies, powers and authorities are thought to speak of the human need before God and are thus anthropologically and soteriologically based. As Carr concludes (pp. 122-23): 'The phrase αἱ ἀρχαὶ καὶ αἱ ἐξουσίαι that occurs in Colossians and Ephesians contributes to the Christology, not by pointing to any achievement of Christ in battle against hostile powers, but by associating him with God as the one who receives the recognition and worship of the heavenly host'. This christologically crucial issue of worship of Jesus within a monotheistic faith is the subject of Richard Bauckham's, 'Worship of Jesus in Apocalyptic Christianity', *NTS* 27 (1980-81), pp. 322-41. Bauckham specifically discusses the Apocalypse of John and the *Ascension of Isaiah*. Also worth noting on the subject is C.F.D. Moule, 'The Influence of Circumstances on the Use of Christological Terms', *JTS* n.s. 10 (1959), pp. 248ff.; R.T. France, 'The Worship of Jesus: A Neglected Factor in Christological Debate?', in *Christ the Lord* (Guthrie FS; edited by Harold H. Rowden; 1982), pp. 17-37. In any case, it should be noted that Col. 3.1-4 still retains the present/future tension of the Christian life as based upon the exaltation of Christ to the right hand of God.

55. As Hay (*op. cit.*, pp. 60-62 and 123-25) argues. He similarly points to Rom. 8.34 as primarily concerned with Christ's intercession on behalf of the saints at the last judgment (pp. 59-60). Contra Loader, *art. cit.*, pp. 204-205 (Romans 8) and 208 (1 Corinthians 15).

56. *Op. cit.*, pp. 61-62. Hay does also list the *Apocalypse of Peter* 6 and *SO* 2.243 as Christian parallels to this notion of a future Messianic Age as related to Ps. 110.1.

57. Terence Callan ('Psalm 110.1 and the Origin of the Expectation that Jesus Will Come Again', *CBQ* 44 [1982], pp. 622-36) argues that Psalm 110.1 plays a critical role in the development of the doctrine of the Parousia. According to Callan, the Psalm becomes associated with Dan. 7.13-14 and Jesus' enthronement as the Son of Man. Under the impact of the delay of the end of the world the κύριος link in the Psalm was exploited and Old Testament theophanies readily transposed into expressions of christophany. Thus we can readily see the influence of Glasson upon Callan's work. Unfortunately, his results fall under the same criticism as Glasson's ideas do. That is to say, that it deprecates the value of parallels in Jewish pseudepigraphal literature and ignores the critical identity between God and Messiah with respect to Final Judgment which occurs within those documents. It is this identity which we are suggesting helps to give rise to a doctrine of the Parousia of Christ.

58. A recent example is H.N. Ridderbos, *Paul: An Outline of his Theology* (1975), pp. 556-62. It should be noted that these types of objections are often

raised by those who attempt to systematize Paul's theology at the expense of its flexibility and vitality. More often than not this drive to systematize is motivated by the dogmatic theological presuppositions of the interpreter. See also D.E.H. Whiteley, *The Theology of St. Paul* (1964), pp. 270-71. Compare note 18 above.

59. The relationship between imminence and transcendence within apocalyptic literature is the subject of A.T. Lincoln's *Paradise Now and Not Yet* (1981). Lincoln deals specifically with the Pauline corpus and seeks to explore what role the heavenly dimension plays within Paul's thought. He points out that the imminence/transcendence tension within apocalyptic has a spatial axis (earthly/heavenly), as well as the more recognized temporal one (now/not yet). These dual axial emphases, Lincoln feels, were derived from the apocalyptic spirit existent in Paul's time. Paul's unique contribution to the issue is the christological context and orientation given to the matter. Of particular note for our study is the discussion on pp. 174ff. Lincoln is quite right in using the idea of a realized eschatology involving a heavenly dimension as a means to uncovering the close ties Paul's thought has with other apocalyptic writing. What is not sufficiently taken into account within the monograph is the fact that apocalyptic also provided a ready-made conceptual link between Messiah and God which also is easily adapted to Paul's christological categories. The 'spatial' dimension of apocalyptic is also discussed in J.J. Collins, 'Apocalyptic Eschatology as the Transcendence of Death', *CBQ* 36 (1974), pp. 21-43. Collins restricts his discussion to Jewish apocalypses of the first century CE and argues cogently that a future expectation and present experience of the heavenly realm were mutually interdependent in apocalyptic.

60. See Amos Wilder, 'Eschatological Imagery and Earthly Circumstance', *NTS* 5 (1958-59), pp. 229-45, for a penetrating study of the comprehensiveness of eschatological thought as an expression of the human mythological and sociological interests. G.B. Caird, *The Language and Imagery of the Bible* (1980), pp. 243-71, devotes a chapter to demonstrating the ability of eschatological language to be used metaphorically in expounding the present. His thesis is conveniently synthesized on p. 256:

> 1. The Biblical writers believed literally that the world has had a beginning in the past and would have an end in the future. 2. They regularly used end-of-the-world language metaphorically to refer to that which they knew was not the end of the world. 3. As with some other uses of metaphor, we have to allow for the likelihood of some literalist misinterpretation on the part of the hearer, and for the possibility of some blurring of the edges between vehicle and tenor on the part of the speaker.

Unfortunately, Caird does not tackle the larger question of the historical and objective reality of these eschatological beliefs in light of this blurring he describes between vehicle and tenor. Essentially this question must be answered in two parts: (1) the implications for the Biblical writers (such as

Paul) who make use of this eschatological material; (2) the implications for use today as we attempt to interpret its relevant meaning. This demythologization question and its relationship to history remain the crucial issues.

61. We have not even touched on the possibility of deliberate divergence by Paul as a means for accounting for the inconsistency!

62. Note Kümmel's cautious remark on the subject in his 'Anhang' to H. Lietzmann, *An die Korinther I & II* (1949), 4th edn p. 193:

> Da durch nicht angedeutet ist, dass ein grosser zeitlicher Abstand zwischen παρουσία und τέλος angenommen ist, in dem man das συμβασιλεύειν usw. ansetzen dürfte, und da es keineswegs klar ist, ob der Kampf gegen die Geistermächte erst mit der Parusie beginnt, ist es durchaus unbegründet, durch die Annahme eines 'Zwischenreiches' eine systematische Reihenfolge der beim Paulus da und dort begegnenden eschatologischen Erwartungen zu konstruieren. Paul will hier nur betonen, dass beim Eintritt des τέλος Christus alle Geistermächte besiegt hat und Gott allein Herr ist.

63. *Paul the Apostle* (1980).

64. Beker comments that the shift in emphasis within the second century CE from resurrection as the focus of Christian faith to incarnation as the focus, involves a shift from the theocentric to the christocentric dimension of the gospel. Indeed, Beker argues, the development of hermeneutic along Trinitarian lines compels an interpretation of Paul's Christology in ontological rather than functional terms. This may all be true, but the crucial point at issue here is whether or not the apocalyptic texts themselves promote such a shift of interpretation. Beker seems to imply that such a shift is a very denial of the nature of apocalyptic itself. With this I cannot agree. Victor Branick ('Apocalyptic Paul?', *CBQ* 47 [1985], pp. 664-75) is certainly correct in his criticism of Beker for overstating his case on Paul's use of eschatological language, especially in connection with the passage 1 Cor. 15.24-28. For a discussion of the role 1 Cor. 15.24-28 plays in the christological debates of the post-apostolic era, see: Aloys Grillmeier, *Christ in Christian Tradition* (1965), pp. 311ff.; and John F. Jansen, '1 Corinthians 15.24-28 and the Future of Jesus Christ', in *Texts and Testaments* (edited by W.E. March, 1980), pp. 173-97, who specifically discusses the interpretation of Marcellus of Ancyra in this regard.

65. It is interesting to note that the prime Pauline text called upon by Beker to support such a theocentric interpretation of Paul's apocalyptic teaching is 1 Cor. 15.28. This verse, as we shall see directly below, is the concluding phrase of a very complicated section (vv. 20-28), which fluctuates between theocentric and christocentric poles of emphasis. Beker may be placing too much weight upon this verse as evidence for an essentially theocentric outlook within the whole of Paul's apocalyptic thought.

66. Richard Longenecker, 'The Nature of Paul's Early Eschatology', *NTS* 31 (1985-86), pp. 85-95, argues that Paul's eschatological hope was founded on a functional christology: 'Paul's basic Christian conviction and the

starting point for all his Christian theology was not apocalypticism but functional christology—that is, that his commitment was not first of all to a programme or some timetable of events but to a person: Jesus the Messiah' (p. 93). My contention that a close relationship existed between eschatology and christology is sustained by such a remark; but I would go a step beyond Longenecker and suggest that the division between functional christology and ontology in many eschatological texts is not as clear-cut as we often presume.

67. 'Paul's Christological Use of Scripture in 1 Cor. 15.20-28', *NTS* 28 (1981-82), pp. 502-27. Also worth noting are: Gerhard Barth, 'Erwägungen zu 1 Korinther 15, 20-28', *EvT* 30 (1970), pp. 515-27; and T.G. Bücher's investigations into the larger context of the passage in 'Nochmals zur Beweisführung in 1 Korinther 15.12-20', *TZ* 36 (1980), pp 129-52 and 'Die logische Argumentation in 1 Korinther 15.12-20', *Biblica* 55 (1974), pp. 465-86.

68. *Art. cit.*, pp. 508ff.

69. For the larger issue of how Paul quotes from the MT and the LXX, see E. Earle Ellis, 'A Note on Pauline Hermeneutics', *NTS* 2 (1955-56), pp. 127-33; and his *Prophecy and Hermeneutic in Early Christianity* (1978), pp. 147ff. Of related interest is Joseph Fitzmyer's investigation into the Qumran community's practices in 'The Use of Explicit Old Testament Quotations in Qumran Literature and in the New Testament', *NTS* 7 (1960-61), pp. 297-333; Matthew Black, 'The Christological Use of the Old Testament in the New Testament', *NTS* 18 (1971-72), pp. 1-14; Richard Longenecker, *Biblical Exegesis in the Apostolic Period* (1975), pp. 104-32; Max Wilcox, 'On Investigating the Use of the Old Testament in the New Testament', in *Text and Interpretation* (Black FS; 1979), pp. 231-43; C.F.D. Moule, *The Birth of the New Testament*, 3rd edn (1981), pp. 68-106; A.T. Hanson, *The Living Utterances of God* (1983), pp. 34-35, 39-40, and 44-62.

70. A parallel phenomenon has been noted within Essene practice by J.V. Chamberlain, 'The Functions of God as Messianic Titles in the Complete Qumran Isaiah Scroll', *VT* 5 (1955), pp. 366-72. Chamberlain points out that certain Isaianic passages (notably 51.4-8 and 56.10) were understood messianically by the Essene community at Qumran with attributes and emanations of God personified as descriptive names for the Messiah. This process is detected by the consistent substitution of third-person pronouns for first-person ones thus effecting the transfer in thought from God to these personifications.

71. The *Epistle of Barnabas* quotation in 12.10 is particularly interesting in that it is immediately followed by a supporting quotation taken from Isa. 45.1. The Isaiah quote, of course, is based upon a corrupted reading of the LXX and substitutes κύριος for κύρος. The same corrupted reading also occurs in Tertullian *Against Praxis* 11 and Novatian *Concerning the Trinity*. See T.F. Glasson, '"Plurality of Divine Persons" and Quotations in

Hebrews 1.6ff.', *NTS* 12 (1965-66), pp. 270-72.

72. Lambrecht, *art. cit.*, pp. 508ff.

73. On the Old Testament context of this passage, see Leslie C. Allen, *Psalms 101-150* (1983), pp. 78-87.

74. E.B. Allo, *Première Épître aux Corinthiens* (1934), pp. 408ff.; Lambrecht, *art. cit.*, p. 520 note 31.

75. For a discussion of God as the subject of ὑποτάξαντα and ὑπετάγη in Rom. 8.20, see C.E.B. Cranfield, 'Some Observations on Romans 8.19-21', in *Reconciliation and Hope* (Morris FS; 1974), pp. 227f.; G.B. Caird, 'The Development of the Doctrine of Christ in the New Testament', in *Christ For Us Today* (1968), pp.73-74.

76. Lambrecht, *ibid.*, pp. 510f. argues that the literal quotation of Ps. 8.6 is not as certain as is often claimed and that we should not underestimate the differences between it and 27a.

77. Matthew Black, 'πᾶσαι ἐξουσίαι αὐτῷ ὑποταγήσονται', in *Paul and Paulinism* (C.K. Barrett FS; edited by M.D. Hooker and S.G. Wilson; 1982), pp. 74-82. What is exciting about this possibility is the fact that it also allows for a connection of thought between the Saints of the Most High in 27a and their messianic representative. Compare G.R. Beasley-Murray, 'The Interpretation of Daniel 7', *CBQ* 45 (1983), pp. 44-58, where a messianic interpretation of the son-like figure representing the saints and exercising the rule of God over the world is suggested with special attention given to the theophany of the coming of the Ancient of Days in v. 22 as an interpretative comment by the author of Daniel to elucidate v. 13.

The identity of the 'Son of Man' figure within the Danielic vision is a matter of considerable debate. Basically, the issue revolves around whether he represents an angelic being or the people of God. For details and discussion, see J.J. Collins, 'The Son of Man and the Saints of the Most High in the Book of Daniel', *JBL* 93 (1974), pp. 50-66; and his *The Apocalyptic Vision of the Book of Daniel* (1977), pp. 123-52, where Collins proposes the 'angelic' interpretation. In fact, Collins specifies the 'son of man' figure as the archangel Michael. He is opposed in this interpretation by Gerhard F. Hasel, 'The Identity of the Saints of the Most High', *Biblica* (1975), pp. 173-92; V.S. Poythress, 'The Holy Ones of the Most High in Daniel VII', *VT* 26 (1976), pp. 208-13. Both Hasel and Poythress reject Collins's conclusions and propose identification of the 'Son of Man' directly with the people of God. Also worth noting is Alexander A. Di Lella, 'The One in Human Likeness and the Holy Ones of the Most High in Daniel 7', *CBQ* 39 (1977), pp. 1-19.

78. On this, see C.H. Dodd, *According to the Scriptures* (1952), pp. 32-34. John M. Court, 'Risen, Ascended, Glorified', *KTR* 6 (1983), pp. 39-42, makes a valiant attempt to uncover the early Christian use of traditional material as demonstrated via these two Psalms. He rightly calls attention to the temporal difference between the two proof-texts (Ps. 110.1 is essentially

future in orientation; Psalm 8 essentially looks into the past), and suggests
that these temporal distinctions are related to two separate conceptualizations
of ascension and enthronement. These differing conceptualizations reflect a
much more dynamic atmosphere for the development of christology than is
often realized.

79. On this subject, note Robert D. Rowe, 'Is Daniel's "Son of Man"
Messianic?', in *Christ the Lord* (Guthrie FS; edited by Harold H. Rowden;
1982), pp. 71-96.

80. It may well be that the idea of a Divine Warrior is partially responsible
for this emphasis on the subjection of enemies. If so, it easily helps to
demonstrate how a theocentric idea is re-invested with christocentric
meaning. On this, see Bruce A. Stevens, 'Jesus as the Divine Warrior', *ExpT*
94 (1982-83), pp. 326-29. The eschatological Warrior-figure of Melchizedek
may prove to be especially relevant in this regard. It should not be
overlooked that there is some evidence for the pre-Christian, Jewish use of
Ps. 110.1 in connection with such an eschatological figure. There is some
justification for asserting that the Psalm was associated with Melchizedek in
11QM. This mysterious figure of Melchizedek very probably bears some
relationship with 'Son of Man' speculations such as that found in the
Similitudes of Enoch. See Paul J. Kobelski, *Melchizedek and Melchiresa*
(1981), pp. 49-54 and 130-137; compare Marius de Jonge, 'The Role of
Intermediaries in God's Final Intervention in the Future According to the
Qumran Scrolls', in *Studies on the Jewish Background of the New Testament*
(9169), pp. 44-63; J.J. Collins, 'The Heavenly Representative: The "Son of
Man" in the Similitudes of Enoch', in *Ideal Figures in Ancient Judaism*,
edited by J.J. Collins and G.W.E. Nickelsburg (1980), pp. 111-33; Joseph M.
Baumgarten, 'The Heavenly Tribunal and the Personification of Sedeq in
Jewish Apocalyptic', *ANRW* II, 19.1 (1979), pp. 219-39; Martin Hengel, *Son
of God* (1976), pp. 80-83, where the larger issue of transcendent, representative
figures in pre-Christian Judaism is discussed.

81. Indeed, in both the other references to Ps. 8.6 contained within the
New Testament God is consistently the subject of ὑπέταξεν (see Eph. 1.16-
22 and Heb. 2.6-8). Daniel Cohn-Sherbok, 'Paul and Rabbinic Exegesis',
SJT 35 (1982), p. 120, discusses Paul's use of Ps. 8.4 in 1 Cor. 15.25-27 and
points to the rabbinic parallels in which confusion over the precise meaning
of a Scriptural quotation are clarified in some manner by the author
concerned. On the whole, Paul's use of Old Testament texts is seen by this
Jewish scholar, himself a Rabbi, as following in the tradition of Pharisaic
Judaism in this regard.

82. *Christology in the Making* (1980), pp. 108-11.

83. Follow the debate about this issue through S.I. Edgar, 'Respect for
Context in Quotations from the Old Testament', *NTS* 9 (1962-63), pp. 55-62
and Richard T. Mead, 'A Dissenting Opinion About Respect for Context in
Old Testament Quotations', *NTS* 10 (1963-64), pp. 279-89.

84. There is some justification for asserting that Ps. 8.6 was interpreted eschatologically in the Hellenistic world as the future granting of responsibility for rule over God's Kingdom to the faithful community. See Howard C. Kee, *Community of the New Age* (1977), p. 72 and p. 194 note 61, where CD 3.12b-21; 1QS 3.16-18; Sir. 17.1-11; and Wis. 9.1-13 are all appealed to. Whether or not Ps. 8.6 was used in such a manner (and it appears to me quite likely that it was), is not directly relevant to our discussion as to the nature of the conceptual relationship between God and his messianic agent. It does, however, echo harmoniously with veiled hints as to the saints' co-rule with Jesus in the Messianic Age (note 1 Cor. 6.2-3). Recently Francis Moloney, 'The Reinterpretation of Psalm VIII and the Son of Man Debate', *NTS* 27 (1980-81), pp. 656-72, has called attention to the Aramaic Targum of Psalm 8 in an effort to help illuminate the murky atmosphere of the Son of Man debate. Moloney asserts that the Targum does exhibit a messianic redaction and a tendency towards individualization which makes it an invaluable piece of evidence in the search for a Jewish, non-Christian origin of a transcendent, messianic, Son of Man figure. For a brief introduction into the problems of using the Targums in illuminating New Testament research, see Merrill Miller, 'Targum, Midrash and the Use of the Old Testament in the New Testament', *JSJ* 2 (1971), pp. 29-82; Anthony D. York, 'The Dating of Targumic Literature', *JSJ* 5 (1974), pp. 49-62. Of special interest in the Targum on Psalm 8 is the expansive reference to Leviathan in v. 9 which should be compared to *4 Ezra* 6.49-53 and *2 Baruch* 29.3-8. See J.J. Collins, *The Apocalyptic Vision of the Book of Daniel* (1977), pp. 96-99, for a discussion of the mythological imagery surrounding this creature of the deep.

We should not think that messianic interpretation of the Psalms is restricted to Psalm 8. Recently Gunter Reim ('Jesus as God in the Fourth Gospel: The Old Testament Background', *NTS* 30 [1983-84], pp. 158-60) has sought to show that the messianic understanding given to Psalm 45 in the Gospel of John is reliant upon a pre-Christian interpretation of that unusual passage. The crucial phrase in v. 8 reads in the LXX: ἔχρισεν σε ὁ θεός, ὁ θεός σου.

85. For a discussion as to whether Phil. 3.20-21 might be pre-Pauline, see Seyoon Kim, *The Origin of Paul's Gospel* (1982), pp. 150ff. Neal Flanagan, 'A Note on Philippians 3.20-21', *CBQ* 18 (1956), pp. 8-9, calls attention to the structural parallel to Phil 2.6-11 within these verses. Of special note is John Reumann, 'Philippians 3.20-21—A Hymnic Fragment?', *NTS* 30 (1983-84), pp. 593-609, where the specifically christocentric force of 3.21b is acknowledged as a step beyond the theocentric force of 1 Cor. 15.27. Reumann also takes the αὐτῷ of 3.21b to be reflexive.

86. As J.D.G. Dunn, *Christology in the Making* (1980), pp. 109f. interprets. Also note the discussion in Seyoon Kim, *The Origin of Paul's Gospel* (1982), pp. 183ff. Kim's concluding remark on this suggestion is: 'To make it certain

we need more solid evidence that Paul indeed rendered Jesus' self-designation 'The Son of Man' by ὁ ἄνθρωπος, took it as his claim to be the Man representing the new humanity, and used Ps. 8 to show Christ as much' (p. 186).

87. Ralph P. Martin (*Colossians* [1972], p. 126) notes:

> the person of Christ is seen in relation to His work and the christology as functional, not speculative. But inasmuch as He accomplished what God alone could do—the pacification of the hostile powers of the universe, in particular, and has taken His place on His Father's throne (Phil. 2.9-11; 1 Tim. 3.16; Heb. 1.3-4; Rev. 3.21, 5.1-4) as the divinely appointed world-ruler and judge of all history, it was a short step for the early Christians to take to set Him 'in the place of God' in their cultic worship.

88. Marcus Barth, *Ephesians*, Volume II (1974), pp. 564-65.

89. Conzelmann (*1 Corinthians* [1975], p. 275) gives some parallels within classical literature for this enigmatic phrase.

90. As Robertson and Plummer (*A Critical and Exegetical Commentary on the First Epistle of St. Paul to the Corinthians* [1914], p. 358) correctly note.

91. *An Idiom Book of New Testament Greek* (1953), p. 160.

92. The textual evidence for the inclusion of τά is divided. If we accept it as original, it strengthens the case for πάντα as a neuter plural noun referring to the created order.

93. See J.D.G. Dunn, *Christology in the Making* (1980), pp. 36-45, for a discussion of this theme within the Pauline letters.

94. *The Christology of the New Testament* (1959), p. 293.

95. *Op. cit.*, p. 235. J. Christiaan Beker, *Paul the Apostle* (1980), echoes Cullmann's ideas. See the discussion above on pp. 146-49.

96. Various possible meanings of the verb, including the literal Latin translation 'recapitulation', are presented by Marcus Barth, *Ephesians* 1, (1974), pp. 89-92. The verb occurs only one other time in the New Testament, in Rom. 13.9. It has no christological significance there.

97. On this see Marcus Barth, *Ephesians* 1 (1974), pp. 183ff.

98. For a discussion of the meaning of Col. 1.18 within the Colossians hymn, especially with reference to the theme of cosmic reconciliation contained therein, see Ralph P. Martin, *Reconciliation* (1981), pp. 111-26.

99. See Chapter 2, pp. 112-13 for details.

100. *Carmen Christi* (1964), p. 273.

101. Thus the question as to whether this is a Pauline insertion to a pre-Pauline hymn *may* offer some insight into the Apostle's monotheistic presuppositions. Although I tend to accept 11c as a Pauline interpolation, I feel it has little to contribute in uncovering those presuppositions. It seems to me that Paul's ability to identify conceptually Christ with God is such that it renders such speculations about his 'rigid' Jewish monotheism secondary, or at least in need of qualification by those passages which do indeed genuinely

identify Christ with God.

102. 'A Critical Analysis of Philippians 2.5-11', *JTC* (1968), p. 82.

103. See Joachim Jeremias, 'Zur Gedankenführung in den Paulinischen Briefen', in *Studia Paulina* (Zwaan FS; 1953), p. 154; Ralph P. Martin, *Carmen Christi* (1964), p. 34.

104. Indeed Jewish literature gives many examples of such functional identification between God and messianic agent. The ontological relationship is much more difficult to pin down, partly because of linguistic limitations and partly because of our own theological presuppositions. This ontological relationship has been the crucial point of criticism of J.D.G. Dunn's *Christology in the Making* (1980), especially by more conservative scholars who feel Dunn's approach has undermined the christological truth of scripture (notably, I. Howard Marshall's 'Incarnational Christology in the New Testament' and John F. Balchin's 'Paul, Wisdom and Christ' both in *Christ the Lord: Studies in Christology Presented to Donald Guthrie* [edited by Harold H. Rowden; 1982], pp. 1-16 and 204-19 respectively). In particular, Dunn's interpretation of Phil. 2.6-11 has been called into question. Yet Dunn is quite right to insist that any interpretation of such an exalted passage as Philippians 2 must be governed by the 'historical context of meaning' ('In Defense of a Methodology', *ExpT* 95 [1983-84], p. 296). We must not presume that since it is clear to us in 1987 that Paul believed in Christ's divinity because he (Christ) exercised divine functions, it must also have been equally clear to the Christians of Philippi around 50 CE. Perhaps Dunn is right to subject this treasure of a passage to as rigorous and searching a scrutiny as he does. On the other hand, he is at times too dismissive in his assessment of evidence and tends to judge consistently on the side of caution.

Let us start from another vantage point and suppose, for just a moment, that in Phil. 2.6-11 Paul *did* mean to affirm the divinity of Jesus Christ. How could he have made such a teaching understandable to his audience and yet remain true to his monotheism? What words or phrases would he employ? In what ways would such an affirmation differ in presentation from what we presently have in Philippians 2? When put in this way, it becomes all the more apparent just how difficult it is for us to divorce ourselves from our presuppositions when it comes to exegeting such a passage as the Christ hymn of Philippians 2.

105. The comments of G.B. Caird on Philippians 2 in *Paul's Letters From Prison* (1976),p. 124, drive this point home while at the same time they betray a certain understanding of how Caird conceives Jewish monotheism to have operated: 'It is not surprising therefore that at an early date it (κύριος) became the most popular designation for Jesus, or that its ambiguity provided a setting in which Christian devotion to Jesus could expand. But Paul at least never took the step of calling Jesus God. He retained his Jewish monotheism to the end. Even if Jesus could be described as equal with God,

even if 'the highest place that heaven affords' belonged to him by right, yet at the last he must surrender his sovereignty to God, so that God may be all in all (1 Cor. 15.28)'. The critical question is whether Paul ever did indeed take the step of calling Jesus God. Caird seems clearly to answer in the negative. I am not as sure and would suggest that at times Paul does indeed identify Jesus with God, while at the same time he interjects clarifying notes of christological subordination in certain key passages. In any case, we make progress in solving this thorny question if we suggest that Paul's monotheism was able, to a certain extent, to absorb the theocentric/christocentric paradox and offered at the same time 'corrective' concluding remarks such as Phil. 2.11c and 1 Cor. 15.28c.

106. Ἰησοῦ is read in 4.16 in B.

Notes to Appendix

1. 'Parallelomania', *JBL* 81 (1962), pp. 1-13.
2. The call for purification of method is continued by Philip S. Alexander, 'Rabbinic Judaism and the New Testament', *ZNW* 74 (1983), pp. 237-46.
3. See Chapter 1 note 126, for a brief comment on this.
4. See Chapter 1 note 118, for details.
5. Published as 'Appendix E' to Matthew Black's *An Aramaic Approach to the Gospels and Acts*, 3rd edn (1967), pp. 310-28.
6. The details may be followed in Geza Vermes, 'The Present State of the "Son of Man" Debate', *JJS* 29 (1978), pp. 123-34.
7. 'The Son of Man Problem', *ZNW* 67 (1976), pp. 147-54. With respect to the often appealed-to 'Son of Man' passage from *4 Ezra* 13, Casey also undermines any use of it as evidence of a title. He argues that it is highly contentious that the phrase 'Son of Man' in *4 Ezra* 13 is direct evidence for the existence of a pre-Christian, Jewish understanding of a transcendent, messianic figure. In his book *Son of Man* (1979), pp. 124-26, Casey notes that in *4 Ezra's* use of the Danielic vision in ch. 13 a distinction is maintained between the word for 'man' in the vision (13.3, 5, 12) and in the interpretation (13.25, 32, 51). Casey conjectures that this distinction holds for several languages, any one of which may have been the original language of *4 Ezra*. These languages, along with the respective word distinctions, include: Hebrew (אדם and איש), Aramaic (אניש and גברא), Latin (*homo* and *vir*), Syriac (*bar nasha* and *gabra*), and Greek (ἄνθρωπος and ἀνήρ. Nevertheless, *4 Ezra* may still hold a position of conceptual relevance to the New Testament documents with respect to the 'Son of Man' issue even if the literary certainty is lost.
8. 'The Contribution of Qumran Aramaic to the Study of the New Testament', *NTS* 20 (1973-74), pp. 382-407; and his "The New Testament

Title "Son of Man" Philologically Considered', in *A Wandering Aramean: Collected Aramaic Essays* (SBL Monograph Series 25, 1979), pp. 143-60.

9. 'The Son of Man', *JST* 28 (1977), pp. 19-48.

10. 'Die älteste Schicht der Menschensohn-Logien', *ZNW* 58 (1967), pp. 159-72.

11. See Maurice Casey, *Son of Man* (1979).

12. Follow the discussion in Matthew Black, 'The Eschatology of the Similitudes of Enoch', *JTS* 3 (1952), pp. 1-10; Maurice Casey, 'The Use of the Term "Son of Man" in the Similitudes of Enoch', *JSJ* 7 (1976), pp. 11-29; Matthew Black, 'The "Parables" of Enoch (1 Enoch 37-71) and the "Son of Man"', *ExpT* 88 (1976-77), pp. 5-8.

13. 'Exit the Apocalyptic Son of Man', *NTS* 18 (1972-73), pp. 243-67.

14. 'Re-enter the Apocalyptic Son of Man', *NTS* 22 (1975-76), pp. 52-72. Also note his 'Jesus as Advocate: a Contribution to the Christology Debate', *BJRL* 62 (1979-80), pp. 476-97.

15. Also note the foundational article 'The New Look on the Son of Man' *BJRL* 63 (1981), pp. 437-62, of which this book is an expansion; cf. the subsequent discussion generated by the book between Lindars and Richard Bauckham in *JSNT* 23 (1985): Richard Bauckham, 'The Son of Man: "A Man in my Position" or "Someone"?', pp. 23-33; Barnabas Lindars, 'Response to Richard Bauckham: The Idiomatic Use of Bar Enasha', pp. 35-41. P.M. Casey, 'General Generic and Indefinite: The Use of the Term "Son of Man" in Aramaic Sources and in the Teaching of Jesus', *JSNT* 29 (1987) pp. 21-56, also enters the debate.

16. In particular, we should not fail to consider the abiding influence of Dan. 7.13f. upon such a developing messianism. Its contribution to a pre-Christian messianism is virtually certain and demands more scholarly attention regardless of how the titular '*bar nasha*' question is ultimately resolved.

17. 'Aramaic Barnasha and the "Son of Man"', *ExpT* 95 (1983-84), pp. 200-206. Compare this with the slightly different approach of Seyoon Kim, *The 'Son of Man' as the Son of God* (1983), pp. 15-37. Kim avoids the titular issue itself but does make a valuable contribution to the question by suggesting a messianic interpretation of the Dan. 7.13 figure which is not dependent upon the emphatic state of the Aramaic phrase *bar-nasha*.

18. Black emphasizes that both 'The Elect One' and 'The Anointed One' are clearly titles within the Ethiopic text.

19. Black here is criticizing Vermes and Lindars, who base their contentions upon the fact that the East Aramaic, Syriac, and Targumic Aramaic all display a weak, emphatic state. This, Black counters, is *not* the case for the old West Aramaic dialect. It is this ability of the old West Aramaic to display an emphatic state which Black exploits to posit a titular force of the expression *barnasha* which he feels underlies the Greek ὁ υἱός τοῦ ἀνθρώπου (p. 202).

20. This is the underlying point of C.F.D. Moule in his *The Origin of Christology* (1977). For Moule's more direct discussion of 'Son of Man' along related lines, see 'Neglected Features in the Problem of "The Son of Man"', in *Neues Testament and Kirche* (Schnackenburg FS; edited by J. Gnilka, 1974), pp. 413-28.

21. *Op. cit.*, p. 12. We should of course note that it is just such a theophanic passage from *1 Enoch* that becomes applied christologically in Jude; see C.D. Osburn, 'The Christological Use of 1 Enoch 1.9 in Jude 14, 15', *NTS* 23 (1976-77), pp. 334-41; James H. Charlesworth, *TOTPNT* (1985), p. 374.

22. One cannot overestimate the seminal work by C.H. Dodd in this area. His two articles on the subject appeared as: 'The Mind of St. Paul: A Psychological Approach', *BJRL* 17 (1933). pp. 91-105, and 'The Mind of Paul: Change and Development', *BJRL* 18 (1934), pp. 69-110. They have been reprinted in Dodd's *New Testament Studies* (1953), pp. 67-128.

23. For an excellent summary of this evaluation of Colossians and Ephesians with respect to the question of eschatological development, see the recent article by Paul Achtemeier, 'An Apocalyptic Shift in Early Christian Tradition: Reflections on Some Canonical Evidence', *CBQ* 45 (1983), pp. 234-37. On the subject, also note the important article by William Baird, 'Pauline Eschatology in Hermeneutical Perspective', *NTS* 17 (1970-71), pp. 314-27, where a word of caution is interjected.

24. On the relationship between 1 Corinthians 15 and 2 Cor. 5.1-10, see Baird, *art. cit.*, pp. 315ff.; R.F. Hettlinger, '2 Corinthians 5.1-10', *SJT* 10 (1957), pp. 174-94; E. Earle Ellis, 'II Corinthians V. 1-10 in Pauline Eschatology', *NTS* 6 (1959-60), pp. 211-24; C.F.D. Moule, 'The Influence of Circumstances on the Use of Eschatological Terms', *JTS* n.s. 15 (1964), pp. 1-15; Karel Hanhart, 'Paul's Hope in the Face of Death', *JBL* 88 (1969), pp. 445-57; Murray J. Harris, '2 Corinthians 5.1-10: Watershed in Paul's Eschatology?', *TB* 22 (1971), pp. 32-57; William Lillie, 'An Approach to II Corinthians 5.1-10', *SJT* 30 (1977), pp. 59-70.

25. 'Early Eschatological Development in Paul: The Evidence of I and II Thessalonians', *NTS* 27 (1980-81), pp. 137-57. Mearns accepts 2 Thessalonians as genuinely Pauline, without comment.

26. Implicit in this thoroughly realized eschatology are: (1) belief that the Kingdom of God had come immediately after the Cross and Passion of Christ; (2) belief that the exaltation of Jesus was in fact the awaited Parousia event; (3) belief that the Christian already possessed the resurrection body.

27. In this regard, Mearns argues that the congregation at Thessaloniki bears a remarkable resemblance to that at Corinth. Both are thought to share the same over-realized perspective which manifests itself in tensions within the churches. Incidentally, Mearns supports his interpretation of the Thessalonian correspondence with a similar study involving the Corinthians

correspondence ('Early Eschatological Development in Paul: The Evidence of 1 Corinthians', *JSNT* 22 [1984], pp. 19-35).

28. Mearns is here consciously following the pattern of 'backwards extrapolation' set by J.C. Hurd, in *The Origin of 1 Corinthians* (1965), with respect to the Corinthian letters. His article in *JSNT* sets forth the modifications he feels are needed within Hurd's work.

29. This point was made a generation ago by John Lowe, 'An Examination of Attempts to Detect Developments in St. Paul's Theology', *JTS* 42 (1941), who queries (p. 133): 'It may fairly be asked whether one is entitled to look for a marked transformation or even modification of ideas during that (late) stage of a man's life, a man who had already been preaching and teaching for years'. John Drane, 'Theological Diversity in the Letters of St. Paul', *TB* 27 (1976), pp. 3-26, in critiquing the work of Charles Buck and Greer Taylor (*Saint Paul: A Study of the Development of his Thought* [1969]), which is very similar to that of Mearns, characterizes it as argument which 'is based on inference' and adds that 'the central evidence on which the whole hypothesis is constructed is of an indirect nature' (p. 14). The same criticisms may be justifiably levelled at Mearns's effort.

30. Difficult passages which speak of the death of Christians as ordinary, such as 1 Thess. 5.10, are explained in terms of being 'odd' or 'abnormal' and associated with unusual texts like Acts 5.1-11 or 1 Cor. 11.30.

31. Mearns unreservedly adopts the position of T.F. Glasson on this point about the origin of the doctrine of the Parousia.

32. Note how Mearns ('Early Eschatological Development in Paul: The Evidence of 1 Corinthians', [*JSNT* 22] 1984, pp. 19-35), associates the rise of the doctrine of the Parousia directly with the doctrine of the future final resurrection: 'once belief in a future final resurrection was accepted by Christians, the Lord of that resurrection was conceived as coming dramatically to earth, in order to superintend this aspect of the eschatological drama' (p. 21).

33. Walther Schmithals (*Paul and the Gnostics* [1972], pp. 160-69) focuses on 4.13-18 in his attempt to relate the eschatological question in Paul's debate with the Gnostics at Thessaloniki.

34. 'The Taking Up of the Faithful and the Resurrection of the Dead in 1 Thessalonians 4.13-18', *CBQ* 46 (1984), pp. 274-83. John Gillman ('Signals of Transformation in 1 Thessalonians 4.13-18', *CBQ* 47 [1985], pp. 263-81) also argues that there is much more continuity between Paul's teaching in 1 Thessalonians and 1 Corinthians than is allowed by Mearns's program of eschatological development. Gillman argues that the idea of transformation is central to Paul's belief and if we feel compelled to outline development in Paul's ideas on the subject of eschatology, it is a move from the implicit (1 Thess. 4.13-18) to the explicit (1 Cor. 15.51-52 and Phil. 3.20-21). Incidentally, Gillman consistently misspells 'Mearns' as 'Mears' although the *NTS* article is correctly cited. Apparently, Gillman was unaware of

Mearns's subsequent work on 1 Corinthians.

35. See the discussion of Mearns's article above.

36. Plevnik is here reliant upon the work of G. Lohfink, *Die Himmelfahrt Jesu: Untersuchungen zu den Himmelsfahrts- und Erhöhungstexten bei Lukas* (1971).

37. *Art. cit.*, p. 282.

38. *Ibid.*, p. 282.

39. See the discussion in Chapter 2 pp. 123-24.

40. *Untersuchungen zum zweiten Thessalonicherbrief* (Erfurter Theologische Studien, 27; 1972), pp. 46-66. Also note the comments on this point by Béda Rigaux, *Les Épîtres aux Thessaloniciens* (Études Bibliques; 1956), pp. 76-111.

41. '"The Jesus Whom Paul Preaches" (Acts 19.13)', in *From Jesus to Paul* (Beare FS; edited by Peter Richardson and John C. Hurd, 1984), pp. 79ff.

42. 'Who Wrote II Thessalonians?', *NTS* 25 (1978-79), pp. 131-45.

43. *Ibid.*, p. 136.

44. '1 Thessalonicher 5, 1-11, der apologetische Einschub eines Späteren', *ZTK* 70, (1973), pp. 288-315. Also note the relevant section in his commentary, *Der erste Brief an die Thessalonicher* (1976). A similar source-critical analysis of 1 Thess. 4.13-18 is occasionally put forward as well. See Wolfgang Harnisch, *Eschatologische Existenz* (1973), pp. 26ff., for details.

45. For a sensitive and thoughtful critique of interpolation and redactional theories of 1 Thessalonians as a whole, see Raymond F. Collins, *Studies on the First Letter to the Thessalonians* (1984), pp. 96-135 and 154-72. The authenticity of 1 Thessalonians 5.1-11 is also maintained by Joseph Plevnik, '1 Thessalonians 5.1-11: Its Authenticity, Intention and Message', *Biblica* 60 (1979), pp. 71-90.

BIBLIOGRAPHY

1. TEXTS AND TRANSLATIONS

A. *Old and New Testaments*

Biblia Hebraica, 2 volumes, edited by R. Kittel (Stuttgart: Bibelanstalt, 1945).

The Old Testament in Greek, 3 volumes, by Henry Barclay Swete (Cambridge University Press, 1905).

Novum Testamentum Graece (Nestle-Aland, 26th edn; Stuttgart: Deutsche Bibelstiftung, 1979).

B. *The Apocryphal and Pseudepigraphal Documents*

Unless otherwise noted all English translations of the pseudepigraphal documents are taken from the various contributions contained within *The Old Testament Pseudepigrapha*, 2 Volumes, edited by James H. Charlesworth (London: Darton, Longman & Todd 1983-85). In addition, the following specialized textual works, studies and translations were used:

The Apocrypha and Pseudepigrapha of the Old Testament, 2 volumes, edited by R.H. Charles (Oxford: Clarendon Press, 1913; reprinted 1963).

The Apocryphal Old Testament, edited by H.F.D. Sparks (Oxford: Clarendon Press, 1980).

1. *1 Enoch*

Black, Matthew, *The Book of Enoch or 1 Enoch: A New English Edition* (Leiden: E.J. Brill, 1985)

Charles, R.H., *The Book of Enoch or 1 Enoch* (2nd edn; Oxford: Clarendon Press, 1912).

Isaac. E., '1 (Ethiopic Apocalypse of) Enoch Second Century B.C.–First Century A.D.)', *TOTP* I (1983), pp. 5-89.

Knibb, Michael, *The Ethiopic Book of Enoch: A New Edition in the Light of the Aramaic Dead Sea Fragments*, 2 volumes (Oxford: Clarendon Press, 1978).

—'1 Enoch' in *AOT*. (1984), pp. 169-319.

Milik, J.T., *The Books of Enoch: Aramaic Fragments of Qumran Cave 4* (Oxford: Clarendon Press, 1976).

2. *Jubilees*

Charles, R.H., *The Book of Jubilees, or the Little Genesis*, (London: A. & C. Black, 1902).

—*The Book of Jubilees, or the Little Genesis*, Introduction by G.H. Box (Translations of Early Document; London: SPCK, 1917).

Rabin, C., 'Jubilees', in *AOT* (1984), pp. 1-139.

3. *2 (Slavonic) Enoch*

Andersen, F.I., '2 (Slavonic Apocalypse of) Enoch (Late First Century A.D.) with Appendix: 2 Enoch in Merilo Pravednoe', *TOTP* I (1983), pp. 91-221.

Charles, R.H. and Morfill, W.R., *The Book of the Secrets of Enoch* (Oxford: Clarendon Press, 1896).
Pennington, A., '2 Enoch', in *AOT* (1984), pp. 321-62.

4. *3 (Hebrew) Enoch*
Alexander, P.S., '3 (Hebrew Apocalypse of) Enoch (Fifth to Sixth Century A.D.)', *TOTP* I (1983), pp. 223-315.
Odeberg, Hugo, *3 Enoch or The Hebrew Book of Enoch* (Cambridge: University Press, 1928).

5. *4 Ezra (2 Esdras)*
Klijn, A.F.J. (ed.), *Der lateinische Text der Apokalypse des Esra* (Berlin: Akademie Verlag, 1983).
Metzger, Bruce, 'The Fourth Book of Ezra (Late First Century A.D.)', *TOTP* I (1983), pp. 517-59.
Stone, Michael (ed. and tr.), *The Armenian Version of IV Ezra* (Missoula, Montana: Scholars Press, 1979).

6. *2 (Syriac) Baruch*
Bogaert, P., *L'Apocalypse Syriaque de Baruch* (Paris: Cerf, 1969).
Brockington, L.H., 'The Syriac Apocalypse of Baruch', in *AOT* (1984), pp. 835-95.
Charles, R.H., *Apocalypse of Baruch* (London: A. & C. Black, 1896).
Klijn, A.F.J., '2 (Syriac Apocalypse of) Baruch (Early Second Century A.D.)', *TOTP* I (1983), pp. 615-52.

8. *The Testament of Moses*
Charles, R.H., *The Assumption of Moses* (London: A. & C. Black, 1897).
Nickelsburg, G.W.E. Jr (ed.), *Studies in the Testament of Moses*, (SBL Septuagint and Cognate Studies, 4, Cambridge, Massachusetts: Society of Biblical Literature, 1973).
Priest, J., 'Testament of Moses (First Century A.D.)', *TOTP* I (1983), pp. 919-34.
Sweet, J.P.M., 'The Assumption of Moses' in *AOT* (1984), pp. 601-16.

9. *The Apostolic Fathers*
Lake, Kirsopp, *The Apostolic Fathers*, 2 Volumes (The Loeb Classical Library; London: Heinemann, 1914-17).
Staniforth, Maxwell, *Early Christian Writings: The Apostolic Fathers* (New York: Penguin Books, 1980).

10. *Philo of Alexandria*
Coulson, F.H. & G.H. Whittaker, *Philo*, 12 Volumes (The Loeb Classical Library; London: Heinemann, 1949-53).

11. *Josephus*
Thackeray, H. St. J., *Josephus*, 9 Volumes, (The Loeb Classical Library; London: Heinemann, 1926-65).

12. *The Ascension of Isaiah*
Barton, J.M.T., 'The Ascension of Isaiah', in *AOT* (1984), pp. 775-812.
Charles, R.H., *The Ascension of Isaiah* (London: A. & C. Black; 1900).

13. *The Testament of Abraham*
Nickelsburg, G.W.E. Jr (ed.), *Studies on the Testament of Abraham* (SBL Septuagint

and Cognate Studies 6; Missoula, Montana: Scholars Press, 1976).

Sanders, E.P., 'Testament of Abraham (First to Second Century A.D.)', *TOTP* I (1983), pp. 871-902.

2. DICTIONARIES AND ENCYCLOPEDIAS

The Encyclopedia of Theology edited by Karl Rahner (London: Burns & Oates, 1975).

The Interpreter's Dictionary of the Bible, edited by George A. Buttrick, 4 volumes (Nashville, Tennessee: Abingdon, 1962).

The Interpreter's Dictionary of the Bible Supplementary Volume, edited by Keith Crim, (Nashville, Tennessee: Abingdon, 1976).

The Jewish Encyclopedia, edited by Isisdore Singer, 12 volumes, (New York: Funk & Wagnalls, 1901-1906).

Jewish Writings of the Second Temple Period: Apocrypha, Pseudepigrapha, Qumran Sectarian Writings, Philo, Josephus (Compendia Rerum Iudaicarum ad Novum Testamentum, Section Two: The Literature of the Jewish People in the Period of the Second Temple and the Talmud), edited by Michael Stone (Philadelphia: Fortress Press, 1984).

The New International Dictionary of New Testament Theology, edited by Colin Brown, 3 volumes (Exeter: Paternoster, 1975-78).

The Theological Dictionary of the New Testament, edited by Gerhard Kittel and Gerhard Friedrich, 10 volumes (Grand Rapids, Michigan: Eerdmans, 1964-76).

3. PERIODICAL ARTICLES, COLLECTED ESSAYS
AND CONTRIBUTIONS TO FESTSCHRIFTEN

Achtemeier, Paul J., 'An Apocalyptic Shift in Early Christian Tradition: Reflections on Some Canonical Evidence', *CBQ* 45 (1983), pp. 231-48.

Alexander, P.S., 'The Historical Setting of the Hebrew Book of Enoch', *JJS* 28 (1977), pp. 156-80.

—'Rabbinic Judaism and the New Testament', *ZNW* 74 (1983), pp. 237-46.

Aune, David E., 'The Significance of the Delay of the Parousia for Early Christianity', in *Current Issues in Biblical and Patristic Interpretation: Studies in Honor of Merrill C. Tenney*, edited by Gerald F. Hawthorne (Grand Rapids, Michigan: Eerdmans, 1975), pp. 87-109.

—'Orthodoxy in First Century Judaism? A Response to N.J. McEleney', *JSJ* 7 (1976), pp. 1-10.

Aus, Roger D., 'The Relevance of Isaiah 66.7 to Revelation 12 and 2 Thessalonians 1', *ZNW* 67 (1977), pp. 252-68.

—'God's Plan and God's Power: Isaiah 66 and the Restraining Factors of 2 Thess. 2.6-7', *JBL* 96 (1977), pp. 537-53.

Balchin, John F., 'Paul, Wisdom and Christ', in *Christ the Lord: Studies in Christology Presented to Donald Guthrie*, edited by Harold H. Rowden (Leicester: IVP, 1982), pp. 204-19.

Bailey, John A., 'Who Wrote II Thessalonians?', *NTS* 25 (1978-79), pp. 131-45.

Bailey, J.W., 'The Temporary Messianic Reign in the Literature of Early Judaism', *JBL* 53 (1934), pp. 170-87.

Bampfylde, G., 'The Similitudes of Enoch: Historical Allusions', *JSJ* 15 (1984), pp. 9-31.

Bandstra, Andrew J., 'Did the Colossian Errorists Need a Mediator?', *New Dimensions in New Testament Study*, edited by Richard N. Longenecker and Merrill C. Tenney (Grand Rapids, Michigan: Zondervan, 1974), pp. 329-43.

Barker, Margaret, 'Slippery Words: Apocalyptic', *ExpT* 89 (1977-78), pp. 324-29.

Barrosse, Thomas, 'The Seven Days of the New Creation in St. John's Gospel', *CBQ* 21 (1958), pp. 507-16.

Barth, Gerhard, 'Erwägungen zu 1 Korinther 15.20-28', *EvT* 30 (1970), pp. 515-27.

Barth, Markus, 'Christ and All Things', *Paul and Paulinism: Essays in Honour of C.K. Barrett*, edited by M.D. Hooker and S.G. Wilson (London: SPCK, 1982), pp. 160-72.

Bauckham, Richard, 'The Delay of the Parousia', *TB* 31 (1980), pp. 3-36.

—'Worship of Jesus in Apocalyptic Christianity', *NTS* 27 (1980-81), pp. 322-41.

—'The Son of Man: "A Man in my Position" or "Someone"?', *JSNT* 23 (1985), pp. 23-33.

Baumgarten, Joseph M., 'The Heavenly Tribunal and the Personification of Sedeq in Jewish Apocalyptic', *ANRW*, Volume II 19.1 (1979), pp. 219-39.

Beale, Gregory K., 'The Problem of the Man from the Sea in IV Ezra 13 and its Relation to the Messianic Concept in John's Apocalypse', *NovT* 25 (1983), pp. 182-88.

Beasley-Murray, George R., Review of J.A.T. Robinson's *Jesus and His Coming*, *SJT* 10 (1959), pp. 134-40.

—'New Testament Apocalyptic: A Christological Eschatology', *RevExp* 72 (1975), pp. 317-30.

—'The Interpretation of Daniel 7', *CBQ* 45 (1983), pp. 44-58.

Beckwith, Roger T., 'The Significance of the Calendar for Interpreting Essene Chronology and Eschatology', *RQ* 10 (1980), pp. 167-202.

—'Daniel 9 and the Date of Messiah's Coming in Essene, Hellenistic, Pharisaic, Zealot and Early Christian Computation', *RQ* 10 (1981), pp. 521-42.

—'The Earliest Enoch Literature and its Calendar: Marks of their Origin, Date and Motivation', *RQ* 10 (1981), pp. 365-403.

—'The Pre-History and Relationships of the Pharisees, Sadducees and Essenes: A Tentative Reconstruction', *RQ* 11 (1982), pp. 3-46.

Berenyi, Gabriella, 'Gal 2.20: A Pre-Pauline or a Pauline Text?', *Biblica* 65 (1984), pp. 490-537.

Bietenhard, Hans, 'The Millennial Hope in the Early Church', *SJT* 6 (1953), pp. 12-30.

Black, Matthew, 'The "Son of Man" in the Old Biblical Literature', *ExpT* 60 (1948-49), pp. 11-15.

—'The Eschatology of the Similitudes of Enoch', *JST* 3 (1952), pp. 1-10.

—'The Christological Use of the Old Testament in the New Testament', *NTS* 18 (1971-72), pp. 1-14.

—'The Throne-Theophany Prophetic Commission and the "Son of Man"', in *Jews, Greeks and Christians: Religious Cultures in Late Antiquity, Essays in Honor of William David Davies*, edited by Robert Hamerton-Kelly and Robin Scroggs (Studies in Judaism in Late Antiquity 21; Leiden: E.J. Brill, 1976), pp. 57-73.

—'The "Parables" of Enoch (1 Enoch 37-71) and the "Son of Man"', *ExpT* 88 (1976-77), pp. 5-8.

—'The Apocalypse of Weeks in the Light of 4QENg', *VT* 28 (1978), pp. 464-69.

—'The "Two Witnesses" of Rev. II.3f. in Jewish and Christian Apocalyptic Tradition', *Donum Gentilicium: New Testament Studies in Honour of David Daube*, edited by E. Bammel, C.K. Barrett & W.D. Davies (Oxford: Clarendon Press, 1978), pp. 227-37.

—'Πᾶσαι ἐξουσίαι αὐτῷ ὑποταγήσονται', *Paul and Paulinism: Essays in Honour of C.K. Barrett*, edited by M.D. Hooker and S.G.Wilson (London: SPCK, 1982), pp. 74-82.

—'Aramaic Barnasha and the "Son of Man"', *ExpT* 95 (1983-84), pp. 200-206.

Bloch, Joshua, 'The Ezra-Apocalypse, Was it Written in Hebrew, Greek or Aramaic?', *JQR* 48 (1957-58), pp. 279-84.

—'Some Christological Interpolations in the Ezra Apocalypse', *HTR* 51 (1958), pp. 87-94.

Boers, Hendrikus, 'The Form Critical Study of Paul's Letters: 1 Thessalonians as a Case Study', *NTS* 22 (1975-76), pp. 140-58.

Boobyer, G.H., 'Jesus as "Theos" in the New Testament', *BJRL* 50 (1967-68), pp. 247-61.

Bowman, John, 'Early Samaritan Eschatology', *JJS* 6 (1955), pp. 63-72.

Bowker, John '"Merkabah" Visions and the Visions of Paul', *JSS*, 16 (1971), pp. 157-73.

—'The Son of Man', *JTS* 28 (1977), pp. 19-48.

Boyarin, D., 'Penitential Liturgy in 4 Ezra', *JSJ* 3 (1972), pp. 30-34.

Braaten, Carl E., 'The Significance of Apocalypticism for Systematic Theology'; *Interpretation* 25 (1971), pp. 480-99.

Branick, Vincent, 'Apocalyptic Paul?', *CBQ* 47 (1985), pp. 664-75.

Breech, Earl, 'These Fragments I Have Shored Up Against My Ruins: The Form and Function of 4 Ezra', *JBL* 92 (1973), pp. 267-74.

Brown, Colin, article on 'Number' in *NIDNITT* II (1976), pp. 702-703.

Brown, Raymond E., 'Does the New Testament Call Jesus God?', *TS* 26 (1965), pp. 545-73.

Bücher, T.G., 'Die logische Argumentation in 1 Korinther 15.12-20', *Biblica* 55 (1974), 465-86.

—'Nochmals zur Beweisführung in 1 Korinther 15.12-20', *TZ* 36 (1980), pp. 129-52.

Bultmann, Rudolf, 'The New Testament and Mythology', in *Kerygma and Myth*, volume I, edited by Hans Werner Bartsch (London: SPCK, 1953), pp. 1-44.

—'The Christian Hope and the Problem of Demythologizing', *ExpT* 65 (1953-54), pp. 228-30 and 276-78.

Burkitt, F.C., 'On 1 Corinthians xv 26', *JTS* 17 (1916), pp. 384-85.

Caird, G.B., 'The Development of the Doctrine of Christ in the New Testament', in *Christ For Us Today: Papers from the Conference of Modern Churchman, Somerville College, Oxford, July 1967*, edited by Norman Pittenger (London: SCM, 1968), pp. 66-80.

Callan, Terrance, 'Psalm 110.1 and the Origin of the Expectation that Jesus Will Come Again', *CBQ* 44 (1982), pp. 622-36.

Carlson, David, 'Vengeance and Angelic Mediation in Testament of Moses 9 and 10', *JBL* 101 (1982), pp. 85-95.

Carr, Wesley, 'Two Notes on Colossians', *JTS* 24 (1973), pp. 492-500.

—'The Rulers of this Age—1 Corinthians II. 6-8', *NTS* 23 (1976-77), pp. 20-35.

Casey, P.M., 'The Son of Man Problem', *ZNW* 67 (1976), pp. 147-54.

—'The Use of the Term "son of man" in the Similitudes of Enoch', *JSJ* 7 (1976), pp. 11-29.

—'Chronology and the Development of Pauline Christology', in *Paul and Paulinism: Essays in Honour of C.K. Barrett*, edited by M.D. Hooker and S.G. Wilson (London: SPCK, 1982), pp. 124-34.

—'General, Generic and Indefinite: The Use of the Term 'Son of Man' in Aramaic Sources and in the Teaching of Jesus', *JSNT* 29 (1987), pp. 21-56.

Chamberlain, J.V., 'The Functions of God as Messianic Titles in the Complete Isaiah Scroll', *VT* 5 (1955), pp. 366-72.

Charlesworth, James H., 'The Renaissance of Pseudepigraphal Studies: The SBL

Pseudepigrapha Project', *JSJ* 2 (1971), pp. 107-14.

—'The SNTS Pseudepigraphal Seminars at Tübingen and Paris on the Books of Enoch', *NTS* 25 (1978-79), pp. 315-23.

—'The Concept of Messiah in the Pseudepigrapha', in *ANRW*, Volume II 19.1 (1979), pp. 168-218.

—'A History of Pseudepigraphal Research: The Re-emerging Importance of the Pseudepigrapha', in *ANRW*, II 19.1, (1979), pp. 54-88.

—'Christian and Jewish Self-Definition in Light of the Christian Additions to the Apocryphal Writings', in *Jewish and Christian Self-Definition*, Volume II, edited by E.P. Sanders (London: SCM, 1981), pp. 27-55.

—'A Prolegomenon to a New Study of the Jewish Background of the Hymns and Prayers in the New Testament', *JJS* 33 (1982), pp. 265-85.

Chernus, Ira, 'Visions of God in Merkabah Mysticism', *JSJ* 13 (1982), pp. 123-46.

Cohn-Sherbok, Daniel, 'Paul and Rabbinic Exegesis', *SJT* 35 (1982), pp. 117-32.

Collins, Adela Yarbro, 'Composition and Redaction of the Testament of Moses 10', *HTR* 69 (1976), pp. 179-86.

—'Numerical Symbolism in Jewish and Early Christian Apocalyptic Literature', in *ANRW*, II 21.2 (1984), pp. 1221-87.

Collins, J.J., 'Apocalyptic Eschatology as the Transcendence of Death', *CBQ* 36 (1974), pp. 21-43.

—'The Son of Man and the Saints of the Most High in the Book of Daniel', *JBL* 93 (1974), pp. 50-66.

—'Jewish Apocalyptic against its Hellenistic Near Eastern Environment', *BASOR* 220 (1975) pp. 27-36.

—'Pseudonymity, Historical Reviews and the Genre of the Revelation of John', *CBQ* 39 (1977), pp. 329-43.

—'The Heavenly Representative: The "Son of Man" in the Similitudes of Enoch', *Ideal Figures in Ancient Judaism*; edited by J.J. Collins and G.W.E. Nickelsburg, (SBL Septuagint and Cognate Studies, 12; Chico, California: Scholars Press, 1980), pp. 111-33.

—'Patterns of Eschatology at Qumran', *Traditions in Transformation: Turning Points in Biblical Faith*, edited by Baruch Halpern and Jon D. Levenson (Winona Lake, Indiana: Eisenbrauns, 1981), pp. 351-75.

—'The Genre Apocalypse in Hellenistic Judaism', in *AMWNE* (1983), pp. 531-48.

Collins, Raymond F., *Studies on the First Letter to the Thessalonians* (Bibliotheca Ephemeridum Theologicarum Lovaniensium 66; Leuven University Press, 1984).

Coughenour, Robert, 'The Wisdom Stance of Enoch's Redactor', *JSJ* 13 (1982), pp. 47-55.

Court, John M., 'Paul and the Apocalyptic Pattern', *Paul and Paulinism: Essays in Honour of C.K. Barrett*, edited by M.D. Hooker and S.G. Wilson (London: SPCK, 1982), pp. 57-66.

—'Risen, Ascended, Glorified', *KTR* 6 (1983), pp. 39-42.

Coutts, John, 'The Relationship of Ephesians and Colssians', *NTS* 4 (1957-58), pp. 201-207.

Cranfield, C.E.B., 'Some Observations on Romans 8.19-21', in *Reconciliation and Hope: New Testament Essays on Atonement and Eschatology Presented to L.L. Morris on his 60th Birthday*, edited by Robert Banks (Exeter: Paternoster Press, 1974), pp. 224-30.

Crockett, William, 'The Ultimate Restoration of all Mankind: 1 Corinthians 15.22', *Studia Biblica 1978, III. Papers on Paul and Other New Testament Authors*

(JSNT Supplement Series 3; Sheffield: JSOT, 1980), pp. 83-87.

Cullmann, Oscar, 'The Kingship of Christ and the Church in the New Testament', in *The Early Church*, edited by A.J.B. Higgins (London: SCM, 1956), pp. 105-37.

Dahl, Nils Alstrup, 'Eschatology and History in the Light of the Dead Sea Scrolls', *The Future of our Religious Past: Essays in Honour of Rudolf Bultmann*, edited by James M. Robinson (London: SCM, 1971), pp. 9-28.

Dahl, N.A. (with Alan F. Segal), 'Philo and the Rabbis on the Names of God', *JSJ* 9 (1978), pp. 1-28.

Davies, G.I., 'Apocalyptic and Historiography', *JSOT* 5 (1978), pp. 15-28.

Davies, Philip R., 'Calendrical Change and Qumran Origins: An Assessment of Vanderkam's Theory', *CBQ* 45 (1983), pp. 80-89.

—'Eschatology at Qumran', *JBL* 104 (1985), pp. 39-55.

De Lacey, D.R., '"One Lord" in Pauline Christology', in *Christ the Lord: Studies in Christology presented to Donald Guthrie*, edited by Harold H. Rowden (Leicester: IVP, 1982), pp. 191-203.

Denton, D.R., 'Inheritance in Paul and Ephesians', *EQ* 54 (1982), pp. 157-62.

Delcor, M., 'Melchizedek from Genesis to the Qumran Texts and the Epistle to the Hebrews', *JSJ* 2 (1971), pp. 115-35.

Di Lella, Alexander A., 'The One in Human Likeness and the Holy Ones of the Most High in Daniel 7', *CBQ* 39 (1977), pp. 1-19.

Dimant, D., 'Qumran Sectarian Literature', in *JWSTP* (1984), pp. 483-550.

Dodd, C.H., 'The Mind of St. Paul: A Psychological Approach', *BJRL* 17 (1933), pp. 91-105.

—'The Mind of Paul: Change and Development', *BJRL* 18 (1934), pp. 69-110.

Donfried, K.P., 'Justification and Last Judgment in Paul', *ZNW* 67 (1976), pp. 90-110.

Drane, John, 'Theological Diversity in the Letters of St. Paul', *TB* 27 (1976), pp. 3-26.

Dunn, J.D.G., 'In Defence of a Methodology', *ExpT* 95 (1983-4), pp. 295-99.

Dykstra, William, '1 Corinthians 15.20-28: An Essential Part of Paul's Argument Against Those Who Deny the Resurrection', *CTR* 4 (1969), pp. 195-211.

Edgar, S.I., 'Respect for Context in Quotations from the Old Testament', *NTS* 9 (1962-63), pp. 55-62.

Egan, Rory B., 'Lexical Evidence on Two Pauline Passages', *NovT* 19 (1977), pp. 34-62.

Ellingworth, Paul, 'Which Way Are We Going? A Verb of Movement, Especially in 1 Thess. 4.14b', *BibTr* 25 (1974), pp. 426-31.

Ellis, E. Earle, 'A Note on Pauline Hermeneutics', *NTS* 2 (1955-56), pp. 127-33.

—'II Corinthians V. 1-10 in Pauline Eschatology', *NTS* 6 (1959-60), pp. 211-24.

Elwell, Walter, 'The Deity of Christ in the Writings of Paul', *Current Issues in Biblical and Patristic Interpretation: Studies in Honor of Merrill C. Tenney*, edited by Gerald F. Hawthorne (Grand Rapids, Michigan: Eerdmans, 1975), pp. 297-308.

Emerton, J.A., 'The Origin of the Son of Man Imagery', *JTS* 9 (1958), pp. 225-42.

Fiorenza, Elizabeth Schüssler, 'The Phenomenon of Early Christian Apocalyptic: Some Reflections on Method', in *AMWNE* (1983), pp. 295-316.

Fitzmyer, Joseph A., 'The Use of Explicit Old Testament Quotations in Qumran Literature and in the New Testament', *NTS* 7 (1960-61), pp. 297-333.

—'Further Light on Melchizedek from Qumran Cave 11', *JBL* 86 (1967), pp. 25-41.

—'The Contribution of Qumran Aramaic to the Study of the New Testament', *NTS*

20 (1973-74), pp. 382-407

—'The New Testament Title "Son of Man" Philologically Considered', in *A Wandering Aramean: Collected Aramaic Essays* (SBL Monograph Series 25; Missoula, Montana: Scholars Press, 1979), pp. 143-60.

Flanagan, Neil, 'A Note on Philippians 3.20-21', *CBQ* 18 (1956), pp. 8-9.

Flusser, David, 'The Apocryphal Book of Ascensio Isaiae and the Dead Sea Sect', *IEJ* 3 (1953), pp. 30-47.

—'Melchizedek and the Son of Man', *Christian News from Israel* 17 (1966), pp. 23-29.

—'The Four Empires in the Fourth Sibyl and in the Book of Daniel', *Israel Oriental Studies* 2 (1974), pp. 148-75.

Ford, Allan, 'The Second Advent in Relation to the Reign of Christ', *EQ* 23 (1951), pp. 30-39.

Ford, J. Massingberde, '"He that Cometh" and the Divine Name', *JSJ* 1 (1970), pp. 144-47.

France, R.T., 'The Worship of Jesus: A Neglected Factor in Christological Debate?', in *Christ the Lord: Studies in Christology Presented to Donald Guthrie*, edited by Harold H. Rowden (Leicester: IVP, 1982), pp. 17-37.

Friedrich, Gerhard, '1 Thessalonicher 5.1-11, der apologetische Einschub eines Späteren', *ZTK* 70 (1973), pp. 288-315.

Fujita, Shozo, 'The Metaphor of Plant in Jewish Literature of the Intertestamental Period', *JSJ* 7 (1976), pp. 30-45.

Funk, Robert, 'The Apostolic Parousia: Form and Significance', in *Christian History and Interpretation: Studies Presented to John Knox*, edited by W.R. Farmer, C.F.D. Moule and R.R. Niebuhr (Cambridge: Cambridge University Press, 1967), pp. 249-68.

Gager, John G., 'Functional Diversity in Paul's Use of End-Time Language', *JBL* 89 (1970), pp. 325-37.

Georgi, Dieter, 'Der vorpaulinische Hymnus Phil 2.6-11', in *Zeit und Geschichte: Dankesgabe an Rudolf Bultmann zum 80. Geburtstag*, edited by Erich Dinkler (Tübingen: J.C.B. Mohr, 1964), pp. 263-93.

Gero, Stephen, '"My Son the Messiah": A Note on 4 Ezra 7.28-29', *ZNW* 66 (1975), pp. 264-67.

Gibbs, John G., 'The Relation between Creation and Redemption according to Phil. II 5-11', *NovT* 12 (1970), pp. 270-83.

Gillman, 'Signals of Transformation in 1 Thessalonians 4.13-18', *CBQ* 47 (1985), pp. 263-81.

Ginzberg, Louis, article on 'The Apocalypse of Baruch', in *The Jewish Encyclopedia*, Volume II (1902), pp. 554-55.

Glasson, T.F., '"Plurality of Divine Persons" and the Quotations in Hebrews 1.6ff.', *NTS* 12 (1965-66), pp. 270-72.

—'"The Second Advent"—25 Years Later', *ExpT* 82 (1971-72), pp. 307-309.

—'Two Notes on the Philippians Hymn (II. 6-11)', *NTS* 21 (1974-75), pp. 133-39.

—'Schweitzer's Influence—Blessing or Bane?', *JTS* 28 (1977), pp. 289-302.

—'What is Apocalyptic?', *NTS* 27 (1980-81), pp. 98-105.

—'The Son of Man Imagery: 1 Enoch and Daniel 7', *NTS* 23 (1976-77), pp. 82-90.

Goldenberg, Robert, 'Early Rabbinic Explanations of the Destruction of Jerusalem', *JJS* 33 (1982), pp. 517-25.

Gourges, Michael, 'The Thousand-Year Reign (Rev. 20.1-6): Terrestrial or Celestial?', *CBQ* 47 (1985), pp. 676-81.

Grabbe, Lester, 'Orthodoxy in First Century Judaism', *JSJ* 8 (1977), pp. 149-53.

—'Chronology in Hellenistic Jewish Historiography', in *SBL 1979 Seminar Papers*, Volume II (1979), pp. 43-68.

Greenfield, Jonas, C. (with Michael Stone), 'The Enochic Pentateuch and the Date of the Similitudes', *HTR* 70 (1977), pp. 51-65.

Gruenthaler, M.J., 'The Four Empires of Daniel', *CBQ* 8 (1946), pp. 72-82, 201-12.

Grundmann, W., 'Überlieferung und Eigenaussage im eschatologischen Denken des Apostels Paulus', *NTS* 8 (1961-61), pp. 12-26.

Gundry, R.H., 'Grace, Works, and Staying Saved in Paul', *Biblica* 66 (1985), pp. 1-38.

Gurney, R.J.M., 'The Seventy Weeks of Daniel 9.24-27', *EQ* 53 (1981), pp. 29-36.

Halperin, David J., 'Merkabah Mysticism in the Septuagint', *JBL* 101 (1982), pp. 351-63.

Hamerton-Kelly, R.G., 'The Temple and the Origins of Jewish Apocalyptic', *VT* 20 (1970), pp. 1-15.

Hanhart, Karel, 'Paul's Hope in the Face of Death', *JBL* 88 (1969), pp. 445-57.

Hanmer, P.L., 'A Comparison of KLERONOMIA in Paul and Ephesians', *JBL* 79 (1960), pp. 267-72.

Hanson, Paul D., 'Jewish Apocalyptic Against its Near Eastern Environment', *RB* 78 (1971), pp. 31-58.

—'Prolegomena to the Study of Jewish Apocalyptic', in *Magnalia Dei: The Mighty Acts of God*, edited by F.M. Cross, W.E. Lemke & P.D. Miller, Jr (Garden City, New York: Doubleday, 1976), pp. 389-413.

—Article on 'Apocalypticism', in *IDB Supplementary Volume* (1976), pp. 28-34.

Harnisch, Wolfgang, 'Die Ironie der Offenbarung: Exegetische Erwägungen zur Zionvision im 4. Buch Esra', *ZAW* 95 (1983), pp. 75-95.

—'Der Prophet als Widerpart und Zeuge der Offenbarung: Erwägungen zur Independenz von Form und Sache im IV Buch Esra', in *AMWNE* (1983), pp. 461-93.

Harrington, Daniel J., 'Research on the Jewish Pseudepigrapha During the 1970s', *CBQ* 42 (1980), pp. 147-59.

Harris, Murray J., '2 Corinthians 5.1-10: Watershed in Paul's Eschatology?', *TB* 22 (1971), pp. 32-57.

Harrison, Walter, 'Ezra Among the Wicked in 2 Esdras 3-10', in *The Divine Helmsman: Studies of God's Control of Human Events, Presented to Lou H. Silberman*, edited by J.L. Crenshaw and Samuel Sandmel (New York: Ktav, 1980), pp.21-39.

Hartman, Lars, 'The Functions of Some So-Called Apocalyptic Timetables', *NTS* 22 (1975-76), pp. 1-14.

—'Survey of the Problem of Apocalyptic Genre', in *AMWNE* (1983), pp. 329-43.

Hasel, Gerhard F., 'The Identity of the Saints of the Most High', *Biblica* 56 (1975), pp. 173-92.

Hauer, Chris, Jr, 'When History Stops: Apocalypticism and Mysticism in Judaism and Christianity', in *The Divine Helmsman: Studies of God's Control of Human Events, Presented to Lou H. Silberman*, edited by J.L. Crenshaw and Samuel Sandmel (New York: Ktav, 1980), pp. 21-39.

Havener, Ivan, 'The Pre-Pauline Christological Credal Formulae of 1 Thessalonians', in *SBL Seminar Papers 1981*, pp. 105-28.

Hayman, A.P., 'The Problem of Pseudonymity in the Ezra Apocalypse', *JSJ* 6 (1975), pp. 47-56.

Hengel, Martin, 'Christology and New Testament Chronology', in *Between Jesus and Paul* (London: SCM, 1983), pp. 30-47.

—'Hymns and Christology', in *Between Jesus and Paul* (London: SCM, 1983), pp. 78-96.

Héring, J., 'Saint-Paul a-t-il enseigné deux résurrections?', *RHPR* 12 (1932), pp. 300-20.

Hettlinger, R.F., '2 Corinthians 5.1-10', *SJT* 10 (1957), pp. 174-94.

Hickling, C.J.A., 'Centre and Periphery in the Thought of Paul', *Studia Biblica 1978, III. Papers on Paul and Other New Testament Authors* (JSNT Supplement Series, 3; Sheffield: JSOT, 1980), pp. 199-214.

Hiers, Richard H., 'Eschatology and Methodology', *JBL* 85 (1966), pp. 170-84.

Hindley, J.C., 'Towards a Date for the Similitudes of Enoch', *NTS* 14 (1967-68), pp. 551-65.

Holladay, Carl R., 'New Testament Christology: Some Considerations of Method', *NovT* 25 (1983), pp. 257-78.

Hooker, Morna D., 'A Further Note on Romans 1', *NTS* 13 (1966-67), pp. 181-83.

—'Paul and "Convenantal Nomism"', in *Paul and Paulinism: Essays in Honour of C.K. Barrett*, edited by M.D. Hooker and S.G. Wilson (London: SPCK, 1982), pp. 47-56.

Howard, George, 'The Tetragram and the New Testament', *JBL* 96 (1977), pp. 63-83.

—'Phil. 2.6-11 and the Human Christ', *CBQ* 40 (1978), pp. 368-87.

Hurd, John C., '"The Jesus Whom Paul Preaches" (Acts 19.13)', in *From Jesus to Paul: Studies in Honour of Francis Wright Beare*, edited by Peter Richardson and John C. Hurd (Ontario: Wilfrid Laurier University Press, 1984), pp. 73-89.

Hurtado, L.W., 'Jesus as Lordly Example in Philippians 2.5-11', in *From Jesus to Paul: Studies in Honour of Francis Wright Beare*, edited by Peter Richardson and John C. Hurd, (Ontario: Wilfrid Laurier University Press, 1984), pp. 113-26.

—'Revelation 4-5 in the Light of Jewish Apocalyptic Analogies', *JSNT* 25 (1985), pp. 105-24.

Isenberg, S.R., 'Millenarism in Greco-Roman Palestine', *Religion* 4 (1974), pp. 26-46.

Jansen, John F., '1 Corinthians 15.24-28 and the Future of Jesus Christ', in *Texts and Testaments*, edited by W.E. March (San Antonio, Texas: Trinity University Press, 1980), pp. 173-97.

Jeremias, Joachim, 'Zur Gedankenführung in den Paulinischen Briefen', in *Studia Paulina: In Honour of Johannis De Zwaan* (Haarlem: Bohn, 1953), pp. 146-54.

—'Flesh and Blood Cannot Inherit the Kingdom of God', *NTS* 2 (1955-56), pp. 151-59.

—'Zu Phil. ii 7: ΈΑΥΤΟΝ ΕΚΕΝΩΣΕΝ', *NovT* 6 (1963), pp. 182-88.

—'Die älteste Schicht der Menschensohn-Logien', *ZNW* 58 (1967), pp. 159-72.

Johnson, George, '"Kingdom of God" Sayings in Paul's Letters', in *From Jesus to Paul: Studies in Honour of Francis Wright Beare*, edited by Peter Richardson and John C. Hurd (Ontario: Wilfrid Laurier University Press, 1984), pp. 143-56.

Jonge, Marius de, 'Christian Influence in the Testaments of the Twelve Patriarchs', *NovT* 4 (1960-61), pp. 182-235.

—(with A.S. van der Woude), '11Q Melchizedech and the New Testament', *NTS* 12 (1965-66), pp. 301-26.

—'The Role of Intermediaries in God's Final Intervention in the Future According to the Qumran Scrolls', *Studies on the Jewish Background of the New Testament* (Assen, Netherlands: Van Gorcum, 1969), pp. 44-63).

—Contribution to the article on 'Messiah' in *TDNT*, IX (1974), pp. 511-17.

Käsemann, Ernst, 'The Beginnings of Christian Theology', *JTS* 6 (1969), pp. 17-46.

—'A Critical Analysis of Philippians 2.5-11', *JTC* 5 (1968), pp. 45-88.

Katz, Peter, "Εν πυρὶ φλογός', *ZNW* 46 (1955), pp. 133-38.

Kaye, B.N. 'Eschatology and Ethics in 1 and 2 Thessalonians', *NovT* 17 (1975), pp. 47-57.

Kee, Howard, C., 'The Ethical Dimensions of the Testaments of the XII as a Clue to Provenance', *NTS* 24 (1977-78), pp. 259-70.

Klappert, B., article on 'King' in *NIDNTT* II (1976), pp. 377-90.

Klijn, A.F.J., 'The Sources and the Redaction of the Syrian Apocalypse of Baruch', *JSJ* 1 (1971), pp. 65-76.

—'1 Thessalonians 4.13-18 and its Background in Apocalyptic Literature', in *Paul and Paulinism: Essays in Honour of C.K. Barrett*, edited by M.D. Hooker and S.G. Wilson (London: SPCK, 1982), pp. 67-73.

Knibb, Michael, 'The Exile in Intertestamental Literature', *HJ* 17 (1976), pp. 253-72.

—'The Date of the Parables of Enoch: A Critical Review', *NTS* 25 (1978-79), pp. 345-59.

—'The Exile in the Damascus Document', *JSOT* 25 (1983), pp. 99-117.

Kümmel, W.G., 'Futuristic and Realized Eschatology in the Earliest Stages of Christianity', *JourRel* 43 (1963), pp. 303-14.

—'Jesus und Paulus', *NTS* 10 (1963-64), pp. 163-81.

—'Eschatological Expectation in the Proclamation of Jesus', in *The Future of our Religious Past: Essays in Honour of Rudolf Bultmann*, edited by James M. Robinson (London: SCM, 1971), pp. 29-48.

Lambrecht, J., 'Paul's Christological Use of Scripture in 1 Cor. 15.20-28', *NTS* 28 (1981-82), pp. 502-27.

Laubscher, F. Du Toit, 'God's Angel of Truth and Melchizedek', *JSJ* 3 (1972), pp. 46-51.

Lattey, Cuthbert, 'The Messianic Expectation in "The Assumption of Moses"', *CBQ* 4 (1942), pp. 9-21.

Laws, Sophie, 'Can Apocalyptic Be Relevant?', in *What About the New Testament? Essays in Honour of Christopher Evans*, edited by Morna Hooker and Colin Hickling (London: SCM, 1975), pp. 89-102.

Leach, E.R., 'A Possible Method of Intercalation for the Calendar of the Book of Jubilees', *VT* 7 (1957), pp. 392-97.

Lebram, J.C.H., 'The Piety of the Jewish Apocalyptists', in *AMWNE* (1983), pp. 171-210.

Lee, Jung Young, 'Interpreting Demonic Powers in Pauline Thought', *NovT* 12 (1970), pp. 54-69.

Leivestad, Ragnar, 'Exit the Apocalyptic Son of Man', *NTS* 18 (1972-73), pp. 243-67.

Licht, Jacob, 'Time and Eschatology in Apocalyptic Literature and in Qumran', *JJS* 16 (1965), pp. 177-82.

—'An Analysis of Baruch's Prayer (Syr. Bar. 21)', *JJS* 33 (1982), pp. 327-31.

Lillie, William,'An Approach to II Corinthians 5.1-10', *SJT* 30 (1977), pp. 59-70.

Lindars, Barnabas, 'Re-enter the Apocalyptic Son of Man', *NTS* 22 (1975-76), pp. 52-72.

—'Jesus as Advocate: A Contribution to the Christology Debate', *BJRL* 62 (1979-80), pp. 476-97.

—'Enoch and Christology', *ExpT* 92 (1980-81), pp. 295-99.

—'The New Look on the Son of Man', *BJRL* 63 (1981), pp. 437-62.

—'Response to Richard Bauckham: The Idiomatic Use of Bar Enasha', *JSNT* 23 (1985), pp. 35-41.

Loader, W.R.G., 'Christ at the Right Hand—Ps. CX.1 in the New Testament', *NTS* 24 (1977-78), pp. 199-217.

Löhr, Gebhard, '1 Thess. 4.15-17: Das Herrenwort', *ZNW* 71 (1980), pp. 269-73.

Longenecker, Richard, 'The Melchizedek Argument of Hebrews: A Study in the Development and Circumstantial Expression of New Testament Thought', in *Unity and Diversity in New Testament Theology: Essays in Honor of George E. Ladd*, edited by Robert E. Guelich (Grand Rapids: Eerdmans, 1978), pp. 161-85.

—'The Nature of Paul's Early Eschatology', *NTS* 31 (1985-86), pp. 85-95.

Lorimer, W.L., 'Romans IX. 3-5', *NTS* 13 (1966-67), pp. 385-86.

Lowe, John, 'An Examination of Attempts to Detect Developments in St. Paul's Theology', *JTS* 42 (1941), pp. 129-42.

—Review of T.F. Glasson's *The Second Advent* in *JTS* 47 (1946), pp. 80-85.

Lowy, S., 'Confutation of Judaism in the Epistle of Barnabas', *JJS* 11 (1960), pp. 1-33.

Macgregor, G.H.C., 'Principalities and Powers: The Cosmic Background of Paul's Thought', *NTS* 1 (1954-55), pp. 17-28.

—'The Wrath of God in the New Testament', *NTS* 7 (1960-61), pp. 101-109.

Maclaurin, E.C.B., 'YHWH: The Origin of the Tetragrammaton', *VT* 12 (1962), pp. 439-63.

Maier, Friedrich Wilhelm, 'Ps. 110.1 (LXX 109.1) im Zusammenhang von 1 Kor. 15.24-26', *BibZeit* 20 (1932), pp. 139-56.

Marshall, I. Howard, 'The Development of Christology in the Early Church', *TB* (1967), pp. 77-93.

—'The Christ-Hymn in Philippians', *TB* 19 (1968), pp. 104-27.

—'Slippery Words: Eschatology', *ExpT* 89 (1977-78), 264-69.

—'Pauline Theology in the Thessalonian Correspondence', in *Paul and Paulinism: Essays in Honour of C.K. Barrett*, edited by M.D. Hooker and S.G. Wilson (London: SPCK, 1982), pp. 173-83.

—'Incarnational Christology in the New Testament', in *Christ the Lord: Studies in Christology Presented to Donald Guthrie*, edited by Harold H. Rowden (Leicester: IVP, 1982), pp. 1-16.

Martin, Ralph P. 'New Testament Hymns: Background and Development', *ExpT* 94 (1982-83), pp. 132-36.

McEleney, N.J., 'Orthodoxy in Judaism of the First Christian Century', *JSJ* 4 (1973), pp. 19-42.

—'Orthodoxy in Judaism of the First Christian Century', *JSJ* 9 (1978), pp. 83-88.

Mead, Richard T., 'A Dissenting Opinion about Respect for Context in Old Testament Quotations', *NTS* 10 (1963-64), pp. 279-89.

Mearns, C.L., 'The Parables of Enoch—Origin and Date', *ExpT* 89 (1977-78), pp. 118-19.

—'Dating the Similitudes of Enoch', *NTS* 25 (1978-79), pp. 360-69.

—'Early Eschatological Development in Paul: The Evidence of I and II Thessalonians', *NTS* 27 (1980-81), pp. 137-57.

—'Early Eschatological Development in Paul: The Evidence of 1 Corinthians', *NTS* 22 (1984), pp. 19-35.

Meeks, Wayne, 'Social Functions of Apocalyptic Language in Pauline Christianity', in *AMWNE* (1983), pp. 687-705.

Metzger, Bruce, 'The "Lost" Section of II Esdras (= IV Ezra)', *JBL* 76 (1957), pp. 153-56.

—'The Punctuation of Rom. 9.5', in *Christ and Spirit in the New Testament: Essays in Honour of C.F.D. Moule*, edited by Barnabas Lindars and Stephen S. Smalley

(Cambridge: Cambridge University Press), (1973), pp. 95-112.

Miller, Merrill, 'The Function of Isa 61.1-2 in 11Q Mechizedech', *JBL* 88 (1969), pp. 467-69.

—'Targum, Midrash and the Use of the Old Testament in the New Testament', *JSJ* 2 (1971), pp. 29-82.

Miner, Daniel F., 'A Suggested Reading for 11Q Melchizedek 17', *JSJ* 2 (1971), pp. 144-48.

Moloney, Francis, 'The Reinterpretation of Psalm VIII and the Son of Man Debate', *NTS* 27 (1980-81), pp. 656-72.

Morgenstern, J., 'The Calendar of the Book of Jubilees, its Origin and its Character', *VT*, (1955), pp. 34-76.

Moule, C.F.D., 'The Influence of Circumstances on the Use of Christological Terms', *JTS* n.s. 10 (1959), pp. 247-63.

—'The Influence of Circumstances on the Use of Eschatological Terms', *JTS* n.s. 15 (1964), pp. 1-15.

—'Further Reflections on Philippians 2.5-11', in *Apostolic History and the Gospel: Biblical and Historical Essays Presented to F.F. Bruce on his 60th Birthday*, edited by W. Ward Gasque and Ralph P. Martin (Exeter: Paternoster Press, 1970), pp. 264-76.

—'Neglected Features in the Problem of "The Son of Man"', in *Neues Testament und Kirche (Festschrift für Rudolf Schnackenburg)*, edited by J. Gnilka (Freiburg in Breislau: Harder, 1974), pp. 413-28.

—'The New Testament and the Doctrine of the Trinity', *ExpT* 88 (1976-77), pp. 16-20.

—'The Borderlands of Ontology in the New Testament', in *The Philosophical Frontiers of Christian Theology: Essays in Honour of Donald MacKinnon*, edited by Brian Hebblethwaite and Stewart Sutherland (Cambridge: Cambridge University Press, 1982), pp. 1-11.

Mounce, Robert H., 'Pauline Eschatology and the Apocalypse', *EQ* 46, (1974), pp. 164-66.

Mowinckel, Sigmund, 'The Hebrew Equivalent of Taxo in Ass. Mos. IX', *Supplements to VT, 1* (Leiden: E.J. Brill, 1953), pp. 88-96.

Müller, Ulrich B., 'Literarische und formgeschichtliche Bestimmung der Apokalypse des Johannes als einem Zeugnis frühchristlicher Apokalyptik', in *AMWNE* (1983), pp. 599-619.

Murphy, Frederick J., '2 Baruch and the Romans', *JBL* 104 (1985), pp. 663-69.

Murphy-O'Connor, Jerome, 'Christological Anthropology in Phil., II, 6-11', *RB* 83 (1976), pp. 25-50.

Murray, Robert, 'Jews, Hebrews and Christians: Some Needed Distinctions', *NovT* 24 (1982), pp. 194-208.

Neusner, Jacob, 'The Development of the Merkavah Tradition', *JSJ* 2 (1971), pp. 149-60.

—'Judaism in a Time of Crisis: Four Responses to the Destruction of the Second Temple', *Judaism* 21 (1972), pp. 313-27.

—'"Judaism" After Moore: A Programmatic Statement', *JSJ* 31, (1980), pp. 141-56.

Neyrey, Jerome, 'Eschatology in 1 Thessalonians: The Theological Factor in 1.9-10; 2.4-5; 3.11-13; 4.6 and 4.13-18', in *SBL Seminar Papers 1980*, pp. 219-31.

Nickelsburg, G.W.E. Jr, 'Eschatology in the Testament of Abraham: A Study of the Judgment Scene in the Two Recensions', in *Studies on the Testament of Abraham*, edited by G.W.E. Nickelsburg (SBL Septuagint and Cognate Studies, 6; Missoula, Montana: Scholars Press, 1976), pp. 23-64.

—Review of Dexinger's *Zehnwochenapokalypse und offene Probleme der Apokalyptik-forschung*, in *JBL* 100 (1981), pp. 669-70.

—'The Epistle of Enoch and the Qumran Literature', *JJS* 33, (1982), pp. 333-48.

—'Social Aspects of Palestinian Jewish Apocalypticism' in *AMWNE* (1983), pp. 641-54.

—'The Bible Rewritten and Expanded', in *JWSTP* (1984), pp. 89-156.

Osburn, C.D. 'The Christological Use of 1 Enoch 1.9 in Jude 14.15', *NTS* 23 (1976-77), pp. 334-41.

Patzia, Arthur G., 'The Deutero-Pauline Hypothesis: An Attempt at Clarification', *EQ* 52 (1980), pp. 27-42.

Perrin, Norman, 'Eschatology and Hermeneutics: Reflections on Method in the Interpretation of the New Testament', *JBL* 93 (1974), pp. 3-14.

Perry, Victor, 'Does the New Testament Call Jesus God?', *ExpT* 87 (1975-76), pp. 214-15.

Pietersma, Albert, 'Kurios or Tetragram: A Renewed Quest for the Original LXX' in *De Septuaginta: Studies in Honour of John William Wevers on his 65th Birthday*, edited by Albert Pietersma and Claude Cox (Ontario: Benben, 1984), pp. 85-101.

Pines, S., 'Eschatology and the Concept of Time in the Slavonic Book of Enoch', in *Types of Redemption: Contributions to the Theme of the Study-Conference Held at Jerusalem, 14th to 19th July 1968*, edited by R.J.Z. Werblowsky and C.J. Bleeker (Supplement to Numen, 18; Leiden: E.J. Brill, 1970), pp. 72-87.

Pinnock, Clark, 'The Structure of Pauline Eschatology', *EQ* 37 (1965), pp. 9-20.

Plevnik, Joseph, 'The Parousia as Implication of Christ's Resurrection', in *Word and Spirit: Essays in Honor of David Michael Stanley*, edited by Joseph Plevnik, (Willowdale, Ontario: Regis College Press, 1975), pp. 199-277.

—'1 Thessalonians 5.1-11: Its Authenticity, Intention and Message', *Biblica* 60 (1979), pp. 71-90.

—'The Taking Up of the Faithful and the Resurrection of the Dead in 1 Thessalonians 4.13-18', *CBQ* 46 (1984), pp. 274-83.

Polhill, J.B., 'The Relationship Between Ephesians and Colossians' *RevExp* 70 (1973), pp. 439-50.

Poythress, V.S., 'The Holy Ones of the Most High in Daniel VII', *VT* 26 (1976), pp. 208-13.

Pryke, John, 'Eschatology in the Dead Sea Scrolls', in *The Scrolls and Christianity*, edited by Matthew Black (Theological Collections, 11; London: SPCK, 1969), pp. 45-57.

Rahner, Karl, article on 'Trinity, Divine', in *The Encyclopedia of Theology*, edited by Karl Rahner (1975), pp. 1755-64.

Reim, Gunter, 'Jesus as God in the Fourth Gospel: The Old Testament Background', *NTS* 30 (1983-84), pp. 158-60.

Reumann, John, 'Philippians 3.20-21—A Hymnic Fragment?', *NTS* 30 (1983-84), pp. 593-609.

Roberts, Bleddyn J., 'Bible Exegesis and Fulfilment in Qumran', in *Word and Meanings: Essays Presented to David Winton Thomas*, edited by Peter R. Ackroyd and Barnabas Lindars (Cambridge: Cambridge University Press, 1968), pp. 195-207.

Robinson, J.A.T., 'The Most Primitive Christology of All?', *JTS* NS 7 (1956), pp. 177-89.

Roetzel, Calvin, 'The Judgment Form in Paul's Letters', *JBL* 88 (1969), pp. 305-12.

Ross, J.M. '1 Thessalonians 3.13', *BibTr* 26 (1975), p. 444.

Rowe, Robert D., 'Is Daniel's "Son of Man" Messianic?', in *Christ the Lord: Studies in Christology Presented to Donald Guthrie*, edited by Harold H. Rowden (Leicester: IVP, 1982), pp. 71-96.

Rowland, Christopher, 'The Visions of God in Apocalyptic Literature', *JSJ* 10 (1979), pp, 137-54.

—'Apocalyptic Visions and the Exaltation of Christ in the Letter to the Colossians', *JSNT* 19 (1983), pp. 73-83.

Rubenstein, Arie, 'Observations on the Slavonic Book of Enoch', *JJS* 13, (1962), pp. 1-21.

Sanders, E.P. 'The Covenant as a Soteriological Category and the Nature of Salvation in Palestinian and Hellenistic Judaism', in *Jews, Greeks and Christians: Religious Cultures in Late Antiquity, Essays in Honor of William David Davies*, edited by Robert Hamerton-Kelly and Robin Scroggs (Studies in Judaism in Late Antiquity, 21; Leiden: E.J. Brill, 1976), pp. 11-44.

—'The Genre of Palestinian Jewish Apocalypses', in *AMWNE* (1983), pp. 447-59.

Sanders, J.A., 'Dissenting Deities and Philippians 2.1-11', *JBL* 88 (1969), pp. 279-90.

Sandmel, Samuel, 'Parallelomania', *JBL* 81 (1962), pp. 1-13.

Schaberg, Jane, 'Daniel 7.12 and the New Testament Passion-Resurrection Predictions', *NTS* 31 (1984-85), pp. 208-22.

Schaller, Berndt, 'ΗΞΕΙ ΕΚ ΣΙΩΝ Ο ΡΥΟΜΕΝΟΣ', in *De Septuaginta: Studies in Honour of John William Wevers on his 65th Birthday*, edited by Albert Pietersma and Claude Cox (Ontario: Benben, 1984), pp. 201-206.

Schmidt, N. 'The Two Recensions of Slavonic Enoch', *JAOS* 41 (1921), pp. 307-12.

Schulz, Siegfried, 'Maranatha und Kyrios Jesus', *ZNW* 53 (1962), pp. 125-44.

Schweizer, Eduard, 'Dying and Rising with Christ', *NTS* 14 (1967-68), pp. 1-14.

—'1 Korinther 15.20-28 als Zeugnis paulinischer Eschatologie und ihrer Verwandt-schaft mit der Verkündigung Jesu', in *Jesus und Paulus: Festschrift für Werner George Kümmel zum 70. Geburtstag*, edited by E. Earle Ellis and Erich Grässer (Göttingen: Vandenhoeck & Ruprecht, 1975), pp. 301-14.

Scott, R.B.Y., '"Behold, He Cometh with"', *NTS* 5 (1959-60), pp. 127-32.

Segal, Alan F. (with N.A. Dahl), 'Philo and the Rabbis on the Names of God', *JSJ* 9 (1978), pp. 1-28.

—'Heavenly Ascent in Hellenistic Judaism, Early Christianity and their Environment', in *ANRW*, II 23.2 (1980), pp. 1333-94.

Sider, Ronald J., 'The Pauline Conception of the Resurrection Body in 1 Corinthians XV. 35-54', *NTS* 21 (1974-75), pp. 428-39.

Siegman, Edward F., 'The Stone Hewn from the Mountain (Daniel 2)', *CBQ* 18 (1956), pp. 364-79.

Silberman, Lou H., 'Apocalyptic Revisited: Reflections on the Thought of Albert Schweitzer', *JAAR* 44 (1976), pp. 489-501.

Skehan, Patrick W., 'The Divine Name at Qumran, in the Masada Scroll, and in the Septuagint', *BIOSCS* 13 (1980), pp. 14-44.

Smalley, Stephen S., 'The Eschatology of Ephesians', *EQ* 28 (1956), pp. 152-57.

—'The Delay of the Parousia', *JBL* 83 (1964), pp. 41-54.

Smith, Morton, 'What is Implied by the Variety of Messianic Figures?', *JBL* 78 (1959), pp. 66-72.

Stegemann, Hartmut, 'Die Bedeuting der Qumranfunde für die Erforschung der Apokalyptik', in *AMWNE* (1983), pp. 495-530.

Steele, E. Springs, 'The Use of Jewish Scriptures in 1 Thessalonians', *BTB* 14 (1984), pp. 12-17.

Stevens, Bruce A., 'Jesus as the Divine Warrior', *ExpT* 94 (1982-83), pp. 326-29.

Stone, Michael, 'Some Remarks on the Textual Criticism of IV Ezra', *HTR* 60 (1967), pp. 107-15.

—'The Concept of the Messiah in IV Ezra', *Religions in Antiquity: Essays in Memory of E.R. Goodenough*, edited by J. Neusner (Studies in the History of Religions, 14; Leiden: Brill, 1968), pp. 295-312.

—'Lists of Revealed Things in Apocalyptic Literature', in *Magnalia Dei: The Mighty Acts of God: Essays on the Bible and Archeology in Memory of G. Ernest Wright*, edited by F.M. Cross, W.E. Lemke, and P.D. Miller, Jr (Garden City, New York: Doubleday, 1976), pp. 414-52.

Stone, Michael (with Jonas C. Greenfield), 'The Enochic Pentateuch and the Date of the Similitudes', *HTR* 70 (1977), pp. 51-65.

—'The Book of Enoch and Judaism in the Third Century B.C.E.', *CBQ* 40 (1978), pp. 479-92.

—'Coherence and Inconsistency in the Apocalypses: The Case of "the End" in 4 Ezra', *JBL* 102 (1983), pp. 229-43.

—'Apocalyptic Literature', in *JWSTP* (1984), pp. 383-441.

Stott, Wilfrid, 'A Note on the Word ΚΥΡΙΑΚΗ in Rev. 1.10', *NTS* 12 (1965-66), pp. 70-75.

Strand, Kenneth 'Another Look at "Lord's Day" in the Early Church and in Rev. 1.10', *NTS* 13 (1966-67), pp. 174-81.

Strugnell, J., Review of Bogaert's *L'Apocalypse de Baruch*, in *JBL* 89 (1970), pp. 484-85.

Sturch, Richard L., 'Can One Say "Jesus is God"?', in *Christ the Lord: Studies in Christology Presented to Donald Guthrie*, edited by Harold H. Rowden (Leicester: IVP, 1982), pp. 326-40.

Swain, J.W., 'The Theory of the Four Monarchies: Opposition History under the Roman Empire', *CP* 35 (1940), pp. 1-21.

Talbert, Charles, 'The Problem of Pre-Existence in Philippians 2.6-11', *JBL* 86 (1967), pp. 141-53.

Taylor, Vincent, 'Does the New Testament Call Jesus God?', *ExpT* 72 (1961-62), pp. 116-18.

Thiselton, Anthony C., 'The Parousia in Modern Theology: Some Questions and Comments', *TB* 27 (1976), pp. 27-53.

—'Schweitzer's Interpretation of Paul', *ExpT* 90 (1978-79), pp. 132-37.

Thoma, Clemens, 'Jüdische Apokalyptik am Ende des ersten nachchristlichen Jahrhunderts: Religionsgeschichtliche Bemerkungen zur syrischen Baruchapokalypse und zum vierten Esrabuch', *Kairos* 11 (1969), pp. 134-44.

Thomas, J. Douglas, 'Jewish Apocalyptic and the Comparative Method', in *Scripture in Context: Essays and the Comparative Method*, edited by Carl D. Evans, William W. Hallo and John B. White (Pittsburgh, Pennsylvania: Pickwick Press, 1980), pp. 245-62.

Thompson, A.L., *Responsibility for Evil in the Theodicy of IV Ezra: A Study Illustrating the Significance of Form and Structure for the Meaning of the Book* (SBL Dissertation Series 29; Missoula, Montana Scholars Press, 1977).

Thorndike, J.P. 'The Apocalypse of Weeks and the Qumran Sect', *RQ* 3 (1961), pp. 163-84.

Travis, Stephen H., 'The Value of Apocalyptic', *TB* 30 (1979), pp. 53-76.

Trudinger, L. Paul, 'The Seven Days of the New Creation in St. John's Gospel: Some Further Reflections', *EQ* 44 (1972), pp. 154-58.

Tupper, E. Frank, 'Revival of Apocalyptic in Biblical and Theological Studies',

RevExp 72 (1975), pp. 279-303.

VanderKam, J.C., 'The Origin, Character and Early History of the 364-Day Calendar: A Reassessment of Jaubert's Hypothesis', *CBQ* 41 (1979), pp. 390-401.

—'2 Macc. 6.7a and Calendrical Change in Jerusalem', *JSJ* 12 (1981), pp. 1-23.

—'Studies on the Apocalypse of Weeks (1 Enoch 93.1-10; 91.11-17)', *CBQ* 46 (1984), pp. 511-23.

Van der Woude, A.S., 'Melchisedek als himmlische Erlösergestalt in den neugefundenen eschatologischen Midrashim aus Qumran-Höhle 11 (With Plate)', *OTS* 14 (1965), pp. 354-73.

—(with Marius de Jonge), '11Q Melchizedech and the New Testament', *NTS* 12 (1965-66), pp. 301-326.

Van Leeuwen, C., 'The Prophecy of the Yom YHWH in Amos V 18-20', *OTS* 19 (1974), pp. 113-34.

Vawter, Bruce, 'And He Shall Come Again with Glory', in *SPCIC 1961* (1963), pp. 143-50.

Vermes, Geza, 'The Use of barnash/bar nasha in Jewish Aramaic', printed as 'Appendix E' in Matthew Black's *An Aramaic Approach to the Gospels and Acts* (3rd edn; Oxford: Clarendon Press, 1967), pp. 310-28.

—'The Present State of the "Son of Man" Debate', *JJS* 29 (1978), pp. 123-34.

Waddell, W.G., 'The Tetragrammaton in the LXX', *JTS* 45 (1944), pp. 158-61.

Wallis, Wilber, 'The Use of Psalms 8 and 110 in 1 Corinthians 15.25-27 and in Henrews 1 and 2', *JETS* 15 (1972), pp. 25-29.

—'The Problem of an Intermediate Kingdom in 1 Corinthians 15.20-28, *JETS* 18 (1975), pp. 229-42.

Watermann, G.H., 'The Sources of Paul's Teaching on the Second Coming of Christ in 1 and 2 Thessalonians', *JETS* 18 (1975), pp. 105-13.

Wenham, David, 'Paul and the Synoptic Apocalypse', in *Gospel Perspectives: Studies of History and Tradition in the Four Gospels*, Volume II, edited by R.T. France and David Wenham (Sheffield: JSOT, 1981), pp. 345-75.

Widengren, Geo, 'Iran and Israel in Parthian Times with Special Regard to the Ethiopian Book of Enoch', in *Religious Syncretism in Antiquity: Essays in Conversation with Geo. Widengren*, edited by Birger A. Pearson (Missoula, Montana: Scholars Press, 1975), pp. 85-129.

Wilcox, Max, 'On Investigating the Use of the Old Testament in the New Testament', in *Text and Interpretation: Studies in the New Testament Presented to Matthew Black*, edited by Ernest Best and R. McL. Wilson (Cambridge: Cambridge University Press, 1979), pp. 231-43.

Wild, Robert A., 'The Warrior and the Prisoner: Some Reflections on Ephesians 6.10-20', *CBQ* 46 (1984), pp. 284-98.

Wilder, Amos, 'Eschatological Imagery and Earthly Circumstance', *NTS* 5 (1958-59), pp. 229-45.

Yates, Roy, 'Christ and the Powers of Evil in Colossians', in *Studia Biblica 1978, III. Papers on Paul and Other New Testament Authors* (JSNT Supplement Series, 3; Sheffield: JSOT, 1980), pp. 461-68.

York, Anthony D., 'The Dating of Targumic Literature', *JSJ* 5 (1974), pp. 49-62.

Zeitlin, Solomon, 'The Assumption of Moses and the Revolt of Bar Kochba', *JQR* 38 (1947-48), pp. 1-45.

4. BOOKS, COMMENTARIES AND MONOGRAPHS

Allen, Leslie C., *Psalms 101-150* (Word Biblical Commentary, 21; Waco, Texas: Word Books, 1983).

Allo, E.B., *Première Épitre aux Corinthiens* (Études Bibliques; Paris: Gabalda, 1934).

Barr, James, 'Theophany and Anthropomorphism in the Old Testament', *Supplements to Vetus Testamentum*, 7; Leiden: E.J. Brill, 1960), pp. 31-38.

Barrett, C.K., *From First Adam to Last* (London: A. & C. Black 1962).

—*A Commentary on the First Epistle to the Corinthians* (Black's New Testament Commentaries; London: A. & C. Black 1968).

—*Essays on John* (London: SCM, 1982).

Barstad, Hans M., *The Religious Polemics of Amos* (Supplements to Vetus Testamentum, 34; Leiden: E.J. Brill, 1984).

Barth, Marcus, *Ephesians* (2 Volumes; Anchor Bible; New York: Doubleday, 1974).

Beasley-Murray, George R., *The Book of Revelation* (The New Century Bible; London: Marshall, Morgan, & Scott, 1974).

Beker, J. Christiaan, *Paul the Apostle: The Triumph of God in Life and Thought* (Edinburgh: T. & T. Clark, 1980).

—*Paul's Apocalyptic Gospel* (Philadelphia, Pennsylvania: Fortress, 1983).

Bietenhard, Hans, *Das tausendjährige Reich* (Zürich: Theologischer Verlag, 1955).

Billerbeck, Paul (with Hermann L. Strack), *Kommentar zum Neuen Testament aus Talmud und Midrasch* (4 volumes; München: Beck, 1926).

Box, G.H., *The Ezra Apocalypse* (London: Pitman, 1912).

Brandenburger, Egon, *Die Verborgenheit Gottes im Weltgeschehen* (Abhandlungen zur Theologie des Alten und Neuen Testaments, 68; Zürich: Theologischer Verlag, 1981).

Buck, Charles (with Greer Taylor), *Saint Paul: A Study of the Development of his Thought* (New York: Scribners, 1969).

Caird, G.B., *A Commentary on the Revelation of St. John the Divine* (Black's New Testament Commentaries; London: A. & C. Black, 1966).

—*Paul's Letters from Prison* (New Claredon Bible; Oxford: Oxford University Press, 1976).

—*The Language and Imagery of the Bible* (London: Duckworth, 1980).

Carr, Wesley, *Angels and Principalities* (Society of New Testament Studies Monograph Series, 42; Cambridge: Cambridge University Press, 1981).

Casey, P.M., *Son of Man: The Interpretation and Influence of Daniel 7* (London: SCM, 1979).

Cavallin, H.C.C., *Life After Death: Paul's Argument for the Resurrection of the Dead in 1 Cor. 15; Part I: An Enquiry into the Jewish Background* (Coniectanea biblica, New Testament 7.1; Lund: Gleerup, 1974).

Cerfaux, l., *Christ in the Theology of St. Paul* (New York: Herder & Herder, 1959).

Charles, R.H., *A Critical History of the Doctrine of a Future Life in Israel, in Judaism, and in Christianity* (London: A. & C. Black, 1899).

—*The Revelation of St. John* (2 volumes; The International Critical Commentary; Edinburgh: T. & T. Clark, 1920).

Charlesworth, James, H., *The Pseudepigrapha and Modern Research with a Supplement* (Septuagint and Cognate Studies, 7; Chico, California: Scholars Press, 1981).

—*The Old Testament Pseudepigrapha and the New Testament* (Society for New Testament Studies Monograph Series, 54; Cambridge: Cambridge University Press, 1985).

Clements, Ronald, *Isaiah 1-39* (The New Century Bible; London: Marshall, Morgan & Scott, 1980).

Clouse, R.G., (ed.), *The Meaning of the Millennium: Four Views* (Downers Grove Grove, Illinois: IVP, 1977).

Collange, Jean-François, *The Epistle of St. Paul to the Philippians* (London: Epworth Press, 1979).

Collins, J.J. *The Apocalyptic Vision of the Book of Daniel* (Harvard Semitic Monographs, 16; Missoula, Montana: Scholars Press, 1977).

—*Between Athens and Jerusalem* (New York: Crossroad Press, 1983).

Conzelmann, Hans, *1 Corinthians* (Hermeneia; Philadelphia: Fortress, 1975).

Cranfield, C.E.B., *A Critical and Exegetical Commentary on the Epistle to the Romans* (2 volumes; International Critical Commentary; Edinburgh: T. & T. Clark, 1979).

Cullmann, Oscar, *Christ and Time* (London: SCM, 1951).

—*The Christology of the New Testament* (London: SCM, 1959).

—*Salvation in History* (London: SCM, 1967).

Daniélou, Jean, *The Theology of Jewish Christianity* (London: Darton, Longman & Todd, 1964).

Davies, W.D., *Paul and Rabbinic Judaisn* (3rd edn; London: SPCK, 1970).

Davenport, G.L. *The Eschatology of the Book of Jubilees* (Studia postbilica, 20; Leiden: Brill, 1971).

Dean-Otting, Mary, *Heavenly Journeys: A Study of the Motif in Hellenistic Jewish Literature* (Judentum und Umwelt, 8; Frankfurt: Peter Lang, 1984).

Deichgräber, Reinhard, *Gotteshymnus und Christushymnus in der frühen Christenheit* (Studien zur Umwelt des Neuen Testaments, 5; Göttingen: Vandenhoeck & Ruprecht, 1967).

Delling, Gerhard, *Bibliographie zur jüdisch-hellenistischen und intertestamentarischen Literatur 1900-1970* (Berlin: Akademie Verlag, 1975).

Denis, A.-M., *Fragmenta pseudepigraphorum quae supersunt graeca* (Pseudepigrapha Veteris Testamenti Graece, 3; Leiden: Brill, 1970), pp. 118-20.

De Waard, J., *A Comparative Study of the Old Testament Text in the Dead Sea Scrolls and in the New Testament* (Studies on the Texts of the Desert of Judah, 4; Leiden: Brill, 1966).

Dexinger, F., *Henochs Zehnwochenapokalypse und offene Probleme der Apokalyptik-forschung* (Studia postbilica, 29; Leiden: Brill, 1977).

Dodd, C.H., *The Epistle of Paul to the Romans* (The Moffatt New Testament Commentaries; London: Hodder and Stoughton, 1932).

—*According to the Scriptures* (London: Nisbet, 1952).

—*New Testament Studies* (Manchester: Manchester University Press, 1953).

Drane, John, *Paul: Libertine or Legalist?* (London: SPCK, 1975).

Dunn, J.D.G., *Christology in the Making* (Philadelphia: Westminster, 1980).

Ellis, E. Earle, *Prophecy and Hermeneutic in Early Christianity* (Grand Rapids, Michigan: Eerdmans, 1978).

—*Paul's Use of the Old Testament* (Grand Rapids, Michigan: Baker Book House, 1981; reprint of 1957 edn).

Findlay, G.G., *St. Paul's First Epistle to the Corinthians* (The Expositor's Greek Testament, Volume II; London: Hodder & Stoughton, 1900).

Fischer, Ulrich, *Eschatologie und Jenseitserwartung im hellenistischen Diasporajudentum* (BZNW, 44; New York: de Gruyter, 1978).

Fitzmyer, Joseph A., *The Dead Sea Scrolls: Major Publications and Tools for Study* (Sources for Biblical Study, 8; Missoula, Montana: Scholars Press, 1977).

Ford, J. Massyngberde, *Revelation* (The Anchor Bible; Garden City, New York: Doubleday, 1975).

Friedrich, Gerhard, *Der erste Brief an die Thessalonicher* (Das Neue Testament Deutsch, 8; 14th edn; Göttingen: Vandenhoeck & Ruprecht, 1978).

Giblin, Charles, *The Threat to Faith*: An Exegetical and Theological Re-examination of 2 Thessalonians 2 (Analecta Biblica, 31; Rome: Pontifical Biblical Institute, 1967).

Glasson, T.F., *The Second Advent: The Origin of the New Testament Doctrine* (3rd edn; London: Epworth Press, 1963).

—*Jesus and the End of the World* (Edinburgh: St. Andrew Press, 1980).

Goguel, Maurice, *The Birth of Christianity* (London: George Allen & Unwin, 1953).

Goudge, H.L., *The First Epistle to the Corinthians* (4th edn; Westminster Commentaries; London: Methuen, 1915).

Gruenwald, Ithamar, *Apocalyptic and Merkabah Mysticism* (Cologne: E.J. Brill, 1980).

Hanson, A.T., *The Wrath of the Lamb* (London: SPCK, 1957).

— (with Ronald H. Preston), *The Revelation of St. John the Divine* (The Torch Bible Commentaries; London: SCM, 1962).

— *The Living Utterances of God* (London: Darton, Longman & Todd, 1983).

Hanson, Paul D., *The Dawn of Apocalyptic* Philadelphia: Fortress, 1979).

Harnisch, Wolfgang, *Verhängnis und Verheissung der Geschichte: Untersuchungen zum Zeit- und Geschichtsverständnis im 4. Buch Esra und in der syr. Baruchapokalypse* (Göttingen: Vandenhoeck & Ruprecht, 1969).

— *Eschatologische Existenz: Ein exegetischer Beitrag zum Sachanliegen von 1 Thessalonicher 4.13-5.11* (Göttingen: Vandenhoeck & Ruprecht, 1973).

Harris, Murray J., *Raised Immortal: The Relation between Resurrection and Immortality in New Testament Teaching* (Marshall's Theological Library; London: Marshall, Morgan & Scott, 1983).

Hay, D.M., *Glory at the Right Hand: Psalm 110 in Early Christianity* (SBL Monograph Series, 18; Nashville, Tennessee: Abingdon, 1973).

Hengel, Martin, *Judaism and Hellenism* (2 volumes; London: SCM, 1974).

— *The Son of God* (Philadelphia: Fortress, 1976).

— *Crucifixion* (London: SCM, 1977).

— *Acts and the History of Earliest Christianity* (London: SCM, 1979).

— *The Atonement* (London: SCM, 1981).

Héring, Jean, *The First Epistle of Saint Paul to the Corinthians* (London: Epworth Press, 1962).

Hoekema, Anthony A., *The Bible and the Future* (Exeter: Paternoster Press, 1979).

Horton, Fred L. Jr, *The Melchizedek Tradition* (Society for New Testament Studies Monograph Series, 30; Cambridge: Cambridge University Press, 1976).

Hurd, J.C., *The Origin of 1 Corinthians* (London: SPCK, 1965).

Kabisch, Richard, *Die Eschatologie des Paulus in ihren Zusammenhängen mit dem Gesamtbegriff des Paulinismus* (details of publication unknown, 1893).

Käsemann, Ernst, *New Testament Questions of Today* (London: SCM, 1969).

Kee, Howard C., *Community of the New Age* (London: SCM. 1977).

— *Miracle in the Early Christian World* (London: Yale University Press, 1983).

Kennedy, H.A.A., *St. Paul's Conceptions of the Last Things* (London: Hodder and Stoughton, 1904).

Kiddle, Martin, *The Revelation of St. John* (Moffat New Testament Commentary; London: Hodder & Stoughton, 1940).

Kim, Seyoon, *The Origin of Paul's Gospel* (Grand Rapids, Michigan: Eerdmans, 1982).

— *The 'Son of Man' as the Son of God* (Tübingen: J.C.B. Mohr, 1983).

Knibb, Michael (with R.J. Coggins), *The First and Second Books of Esdras* (Cambridge Bible Commentary; Cambridge: Cambridge University Press, 1979).

Kobelski, Paul J., *Melchizedek and Melchiresa* (The CBQ Monograph Series, 10; Washington, D.C.: The Catholic Biblical Association of America, 1981).

Koch, Kurt, *The Rediscovery of Apocalyptic* (London: SCM, 1972).

Kreitzer, L.J., 'Christ as Second Adam in Paul' (Unpublished MTh Thesis: University of London, 1982).

Kümmel, W.G., *Promise and Fulfilment* (London: SCM, 1957).

Ladd, George Eldon, *Crucial Questions about the Kingdom of God* (Grand Rapids, Michigan: Eerdmans, 1952).

— *A Commentary on the Revelation of John* (Grand Rapids, Michigan: Eerdmans, 1972).

— *The Presence of the Future: The Eschatology of Biblical Realism* (London: SPCK, 1980).

Lietzmann, H., *An die Korinther I & II* (Handbuch zum Neuen Testament, 9; 4th edn; Tübingen: Mohr, 1949).

Lightfoot, J.B., *St. Paul's Epistle to the Philippians* (London: Macmillan, 1903).

Lincoln, A.T., *Paradise Now and Not Yet* (Society for New Testament Studies Monograph Series, 43; Cambridge: Cambridge University Press, 1981).

Lindars, Barnabas, *New Testament Apologetic* (London: SCM, 1961).

— *Jesus Son of Man* (London: SPCK, 1983).

Lohfink, G., *Die Himmelfahrt Jesu: Untersuchungen zu den Himmelfahrts- und Erhöhungstexten bei Lukas* (Studien zum Alten und Neuen Testament, 26; Munich: Kosel, 1971).

Lohse, Eduard, *Colossians and Philemon* (Hermeneia; Philadelphia, Pennsylvania: Fortress, 1971).

— *Die Offenbarung des Johannes* (Das Neue Testament Deutsch, 11; Göttingen: Vandenhoeck & Ruprecht, 1979).

Longenecker, Richard, *Biblical Exegesis in the Apostolic Period* (Grand Rapids, Michigan, Eerdmans, 1975).

MacDonald, John, *The Theology of the Samaritans* (London: SCM, 1964).

Marshall, I Howard, *1 and 2 Thessalonians* (New Century Bible; Grand Rapids, Michigan: Eerdmans, 19183).

Martin, Ralph P., *Carmen Christi: Philippians II. 5-11 in Recent Interpretation and in the Setting of Early Christian Worship* (Society for New Testament Studies Monograph Series, 4; Cambridge: Cambridge University Press, 1967).

— *Colossians: The Church's Lord and the Christian's Liberty* (Exeter: Paternoster, 1972).

— *Colossians and Philemon* (The New Century Bible; London: Marshall, Morgan & Scott, 1974).

— *New Testament Foundations*, Volume II (Grand Rapids, Michigan: Eerdmans, 1978).

— *Reconciliation: A Study of Paul's Theology* (Marshall's Theological Library; London: Marshall, Morgan & Scott, 1981).

— *The Spirit and the Congregation: Studies in 1 Corinthians 12-15* (Grand Rapids, Michigan: Eerdmans, 1984).

Meeks, Wayne, *The First Urban Christians* (New Haven, Connecticut: Yale University Press, 1983).

Metzger, Bruce, *An Introduction to the Apocrypha* (New York: Oxford University Press, 1957).

— *A Textual Commentary on the Greek New Testament* (London: United Bible Societies, 1975).

Miller, William R., *Isaiah 24-27 and the Origin of Apocalyptic* (Harvard Semitic Monograph Series, 11; Missoula, Montana: Scholars Press, 1976).

Moffatt, James, *The First Epistle of Paul to the Corinthians* (The Moffatt New Testament Commentaries; London: Hodder and Stoughton, 1938).

Montgomery, J.A., *The Book of Daniel* (The International Critical Commentary; (Edinburgh: T. & T. Clark, 1927).

Moore, A.L., *The Parousia in the New Testament* (Supplements to Novum Testamentum, 13; Leiden: E.J. Brill, 1966).

— *I & II Thessalonians* (The New Century Bible; London: Thomas Nelson, 1969).

Moore, G.F., *Judaism in the First Centuries of the Christian Era: The Age of Tannaim* (3 volumes; Cambridge, Massachusetts: Harvard University Press, 1927).

Morris, Leon, *The Cross in the New Testament* (Exeter: Paternoster Press, 1965).

Moule, C.F.D., *An Idiom Book of New Testament Greek* (Cambridge: Cambridge University Press, 1953).

— *The Origin of Christology* (Cambridge: Cambridge University Press, 1977).

— *The Birth of the New Testament* (3rd edn; London: A. & C. Black, 1981).

Mounce, Robert H., *The Book of Revelation* (The New International Commentaries on the New Testament; Grand Rapids, Michigan: Eerdmans, 1977).

Mowinckel, Sigmund, *He That Cometh*, translated by G.W. Anderson (Oxford: Blackwell, 1956).

Müller, Ulrich, *Messias und Menschensohn in jüdischen Apokalypsen und in der Offenbarung des Johannes* (Gütersloh: Mohn, 1972).

Myers, Jacob M., *I and II Esdras* (The Anchor Bible; Garden City, New York, Doubleday, 1974).

Neusner, Jacob, *Judaism in the Beginning of Christianity* (London: SPCK, 1984).

Nickelsburg, G.W.E. Jr, *Resurrection, Immortality and Eternal Life in Intertestamental Judaism* (Harvard Theological Studies, 26; Cambridge, Massachusetts: Harvard University Press, 1972).

— *Jewish Literature between the Bible and the Mishnah* (London: SCM, 1981).

Oesterley, W.O.E., *II Esdras* (Westminster Commentaries; London: Methuen, 1933).

Parke-Taylor, G., *Yahweh: The Divine Name in the Bible* (Waterloo, Ontario: Wilfred Laurier University Press, 1975).

Parry, R. St. John, *The First Epistle of Paul to the Corinthians* (Cambridge Greek Testament; Cambridge: Cambridge University Press, 1957).

Pfleiderer, Otto, *Paulinism: A Contribution to the History of Primitive Christian Theology* (2 volumes; London: Williams & Norgate, 1877).

Plummer, Alfred (with Archibald Robertson), *A Critical and Exegetical Commentary on the First Epistle of St. Paul to the Corinthians* (2nd edn; Edinburgh: T. & T. Clark, 1914).

Preston, Ronald H. (with Anthony T. Hanson), *The Revelation of St. John the Divine* (The Torch Bible Commentaries; London: SCM, 1962).

Reumann, John, *Righteousness in the New Testament* (Philadelphia, Pennsylvania: Fortress, 19182).

Ridderbos, *Paul: An Outline of His Theology* (London: SPCK, 1975).

Rigaux, Béda, *Les Épitres aux Thessaloniciens* (Études Bibliques; Paris: Gabalda, 1956).

Rissi, Matthias, *Time and History: A Study on the Revelation* (Richmond, Virginia: John Knox Press, 1966).

Rist, Martin, *The Revelation of St. John the Divine* (The Interpreters Bible, Volume XII; Nashville, Tennessee: Abingdon Press, 1957).

Robinson, J.A.T., *In the End, God* (London: SCM, 1950).

— *Jesus and His Coming* (London: SCM, 1957).

— *Truth is Two-Eyed* (London: SCM, 1979).

Rowland, Christopher, *The Open Heaven* (London: SPCK, 1982).

— *Christian Origins* (London: SPCK, 1985).

Rowley, H.H., *The Faith of Israel* (London: SCM, 1956).

— *The Relevance of Apocalyptic* (3rd edn; London: Lutterworth, 1963).

Russell, David S., *The Method and Message of Jewish Apocalyptic* (Old Testament Library; Philadelphia: Westminster, 1964).

Sanders, E.P., *Paul and Palestinian Judaism* (London: SCM, 1977).

Sanders, J.T., *The New Testament Christological Hymns* (The Society for New Testament Studies Monograph Series, 15; Cambridge: Cambridge University Press, 1971).

Sayler, Gwendolyn B., *Have the Promises Failed? A Literary Analysis of 2 Baruch* (SBL Dissertation Series, 72; Chico, California: Scholars, 1984).

Schlier, Heinrich, *Principalities and Powers in the New Testament* (London: Nelson, 1961).

Schmithals, Walther, *Paul and the Gnostics* (Nashville: Abingdon, 1972).

Schürer, Emil, *A History of the Jewish People in the Time of Jesus Christ (175 BC—AD 135)* (3 Volumes; Edinburgh: t. & T. Clark, 1896).

— *A History of the Jewish People in the Time of Jesus Christ (175 BC—AD 135)*, revised and edited by Geza Vermes, Fergus Millar, and Matthew Black (Edinburgh: T. & T. Clark), Volume I (1973), Volume II (1979), Volume III (1986).

Schweitzer, Albert, *Paul and His Interpreters*, Translated by William Montgomery (London: A. & C. Black, 1912).

— *The Mysticism of Paul the Apostle*, translated by William Montgomery (New York: Holt, 1931).

Schweizer, Eduard, *The Letter to the Colossians* (London: SPCK, 1982).

Segal, Alan F., *Two Powers in Heaven: Early Rabbinic Reports about Christianity and Gnosticism* (Studies in Judaism in Late Antiquity, 25; Leiden: E.J. Brill, 1977).

Semeia 14: 'Apocalypse: The Morphology of a Genre', edited by J.J. Collins (Missoula, Montana: Scholars Press, 1979).

Senft, Christophe, *La Première Épitre de Saint Paul aux Corinthiens* (Commentaire du Nouveau Testament, 7; Lausanne: Delachaux & Niestlé, 1979).

Stanton, Graham, *Jesus of Nazareth in New Testament Preaching* (Society for New Testament Studies Monograph Series, 27; Cambridge: Cambridge University Press, 1974).

Stone, Michael, 'Features of the Eschatology of IV Ezra' (Unpublished PhD Thesis: Harvard University, 1964).

— *Scriptures, Sects, and Visions: A Profile of Judaism from Ezra to the Jewish Revolts* (Philadelphia: Fortress, 1980).

Strack, Hermann L. (with Paul Billerbeck), *Kommentar zum Neuen Testament aus Talmud und Midrasch* (4 volumes; München: Beck, 1926).

David Winston Suter, *Tradition and Composition in the Parables of Enoch* (SBL Dissertation Series, 47; Missoula, Montana: Scholars Press, 1979).

Taylor, Greer (with Charles Buck), *Saint Paul: A Study of the Development of His Thought* (New York: Scribners, 1969).

Taylor, Vincent, *The Atonement in New Testament Teaching* (2nd edn; London:

Epworth, 1945).

Theisohn, Johannes, *Der auserwählte Richter: Untersuchungen zum traditionsgeschichtlichen Ort der Menschensohngestalt der Bilderreden des Äthiopischen Henoch* (Göttingen: Vandenhoeck & Ruprecht, 1975).

Tillich, Paul, *Systematic Theology* (3 volumes; London: SCM, 1978).

Travis, Stephen H., 'The Place of Divine Retribution in the Thought of St. Paul' (Unpublished PhD Thesis: University of Cambridge, 1970).

— *Christian Hope and the Future of Man* (Leicester: IVP, 1980).

— *I Believe in the Second Coming of Jesus* (London: Hodder & Stoughton, 1983).

Trilling, Wolfgang, *Untersuchungen zum zweiten Thessalonicherbrief* (Erfurter Theologische Studien, 27; Leipzig: St. Benno, 1972).

Vaillant, A., *Le Livre des secrets d'Hénoch: Texte slave et traduction française* (Textes publiés par l'institut d'études slaves, 4; Paris: Institut d'études slaves, reprint, 1976).

VanderKam, J.C., *Textual and Historical Studies in the Book of Jubilees* (Harvard Semitic Monographs, 14; Missoula, Montana: Scholars Press, 1977).

— *Enoch and the Growth of an Apocalyptic Tradition* (CBQ Monograph Series, 16; Washington, D.C. Catholic Biblical Association of America, 1984).

Vermes, Geza, *The Dead Sea Scrolls in English* (2nd edn; New York: Penguin, 1975).

— *The Dead Sea Scrolls: Qumran in Perspective* (2nd edn; London: SCM, 1982).

Wacholder, Ben Zion, *The Dawn of Qumran* (Cincinnati: Hebrew Union College Press, 1983).

Watts, John D.W., *Vision and Prophecy in Amos* (Leiden: E.J. Brill, 1958).

Wengst, Klaus, *Christologische Formeln und Lieder des Urchristentums* (Studien zum Neuen Testament, 7; Gütersloh: Mohn, 1973).

Whiteley, D.E.H., *The Theology of St. Paul* (Oxford: Blackwell, 1964).

Wilcke, Hans-Alwin, *Das Problem eines messianischen Zwischenreichs bei Paulus* (Abhandlungen zur Theologie des Alten und Neuen Testaments, 51; Zürich: Zwingli, 1967).

Williams, Sam K., *Jesus' Death as Saving Event: The Background and Origin of a Concept* (Harvard Dissertations in Religion, 2; edited by Caroline Bynum and George Rupp (Missoula, Montana: Scholars Press, 1975).

INDEX

INDEX OF TEXTUAL REFERENCES

Old Testament

Genesis

1.20-26	216n19
1.26-28	198n74
2.2	45
5.21-32	199n79
6	196n51

Exodus

15	50
15.3	49
19.20	100
24	50
34.5	100
34.34	113
40.13	224n68

Numbers

11.25	101

Deuteronomy

30.12-14	114

Job

4.9	122, 216n20

Psalms

8	153, 244n78, 246n86
8.1-3	152
8.4-6	151
8.4	244n81
8.6	141, 142, 149-53, 156, 168, 243n76, 244n81, 245n84
8.6b	152
32.6	122
45.8	245n84
68.18	224n68
68.35	100
79.6	216n20

88	229n110
88.8	121, 229n110
89.7	216n20
90.4	45, 202n106
106	216n19
110.1	143, 145, 146, 150-53, 156, 237n46, 238n54, 239n56, 239n57, 243n78, 244n80
110.1b	150
110.1c	147, 149, 150, 168

Proverbs

8.22ff.	17

Ecclesiastes

12.14	107

Isaiah

1.13	45
2	120, 121
2.10-11	114
2.10	100, 120
2.11	121, 216n20
2.11c	229n109
2.17	121, 216n20
2.17c	229n109
2.19	100
2.21	100
6	219n31
8.14	124
9.1	123
11	122, 229n111
11.1-5	229n114
11.1	229n115
11.3-5	121, 122
11.4	216n20

11.4c-d	121
11.5	121
11.6-9	229n114
11.10	229n115
13.6	101
24.15	216n20
24.23	100
26.19	101
26.21	101
27.9	125
27.12	101
27.13	101
28.16	114, 124, 230n125
31.4	101
40.13	19
42.13	96
45	116, 117, 222n47
45.1	108, 242n71
45.13	108
45.15	108
45.18-25	117
45.21	108, 226n80
45.23	107, 108, 114-17, 222n46, 226n80, 227n89, 227n91
49	107
49.3	216n20
49.18	107, 114
51.4-8	242n70
53	207n139
55.11	50
56.10	242n70
59	125, 127
59.17	126-28, 216n20, 230n133
59.20	125, 127

Isaiah (cont.)		28.2	216n20	7.27a	243n77
66	119, 120,			7.27b	151
	228n102	Daniel	192n10	9.24-27	83
66.4-6	119	2.21	50	11.36	216n20
66.4	228n104	7-12	213n177	11.34	194n29
66.5	100, 120,	7	49, 50, 62,		
	228n104		71, 103, 104,	Joel	
66.6	228n104		106, 167,	2.28-32	114
66.7	119, 120		174,	2.32	114
66.9	228n102		206n129,		
66.15	119,		220n34	Amos	
	228nn104,	7.9-14	106	5	217n21
	105	7.9ff.	49, 50		
66.15-18	100	7.13f.	49, 62,	Micah	
			205n124,	1.3	100, 123
Jeremiah			220n34,		
6.14	216n20		239n57,	Zechariah	
8.11	216n20		249n16	9.14	123
10.25	216n20	7.13	49, 96, 105,	12-14	118, 119
31.33	125		123, 151,	14	118
			205n124,	14.3-5	96
Ezekiel			219n34,	14.5	100, 117,
1	104, 167,		220nn34,36,		118, 119,
	219n31		243n77,		216n20,
1.26-28	103		249n17		228n99
1.26	220n34	7.13a	123	Malachi	
13.10	216n20	7.22	243n77	1.11	216n20

Apocrypha and Pseudepigrapha

Apocalypse of Abraham		4.1	210n165
10	222n47	6.1-9.2	209n150
16	222n47	6.1-8.5	71
		6.9	210n165
2 (Syriac) Baruch	29, 31, 52, 69-80, 87-	10.1-25.4	209n151
	90, 137, 139, 145,	10.1-20.6	69
	147, 154, 156, 157,	10.1-12.4	209n150
	163, 164, 166, 168,	11.3	78
	169, 172, 182,	12.1-13.2	209n147
	208nn145,146,	12.5-20.6	209n150
	209nn152,157,158,	13.3-12	79
	210n167, 217n24,	13.11-14.3	209n147
	218n24, 235n21	14.17	79
1-77	69	19.3	79
1.1-9.2	69, 70	20.3	210n165
1.1-9.1	209n151	21.1-35.5	209n150
1.1-5.6	209n150	21.1-30.5	69
1.4	78, 210n165	21.4-5	79
4.1-7	210n163	21.7-10	78, 90, 164, 222n47

2 (Syriac) Baruch (cont.)

21.19	210n158
23.4-7	71
23.7-24.1	210n158
26.1	72
27-30	72, 77, 79
27.1-30.1	209n151
29.3-30.1	72
29.3-8	245n84
29.4	73
30.1	72, 75, 76, 209n156
30.2-32.1	209n151
31.1-34.1	69
32.2-4	71, 209n151, 210n165
32.2-3	76
32.5-35.5	209n151
35.1-40.4	69
35	209n150
36-40	71, 77, 79, 209n151, 210n166
36.1-46.7	209n150
39.7	209n156
40.1-4	73
40.1-3	75, 76
40.1	209n156
40.3	75
41.1-43.33	69
41.1-42.8	209n151
43.1-44.7	209n151
44.1-47.2	69
44.8-15	209n151
45.1-46.7	209n151
47.1-77.26	209n150
47.1-52.7	209n151
48.1-52.7	69
48.32-41	79
49.1-51.6	71
53-76	73, 77, 78, 80, 210n166
53.1-76.5	69, 77
53-74	209n151
54.13	79
63.6-8	210n167
68.5-6	76
68.5	210n165
70.9	209n156
72.2-74.3	73-74
72.2	209n156
73.1	80
73.2-74.4	80
74.2-3	75, 76

74.2	77, 210n158
75.1-76.4	209n151
77.1-82.9	209n151
77.1-26	69
78-87	69, 79
78.1-87.1	69, 70
78.3	79
82.2	79
83.1-22	209n151
83.1-2	79
83.6-7	79
84.1-11	209n151
85	209n151
86.1-3	209n151

1 (Ethiopic) Enoch	32, 35, 36, 86-88, 90, 94, 101-105, 123, 154, 166, 167, 175, 192nn12,13, 193n23, 197n65, 199n78, 217n23, 221n40, 228n98, 250n21
6-36	34, 192n10, 192n13, 192n14
12-14	35
14	194n36
37-71 (The Similitudes of Enoch)	25, 35, 36, 62, 89, 101-106, 111, 128, 167, 174, 176, 188n30, 192n10, 195n38, 205n126, 206nn127,129, 208n146, 209n146, 217nn23, 218n25, 219n34, 221n41, 229n122, 244n80
37-70	35
43.3	229n122
45-57	106
45.3-6	106
46	105
46.1-2	229n122
46.1	106
46.1b	103
47.3	106
51.3	106, 218n25
55.4	106
60.1-3	106
61.8	106, 218n25, 221n41
62.2-5	106
62.2	218n25, 221n41

1 (Ethiopic) Enoch (cont.)

69.27	229n122
69.29	106, 221n41, 229n122
70–71	194n34
71	35, 103
71.10	103
71.14	35
83–90	34, 101, 192n10, 193n23, 195n45
85–90	36
89.61-64	199n78
90.17	199n78
91–104	32, 34, 35, 193n21, 196n55, 210n168
91.1-10	192n16, 193n19
91.5-10	193n19
91.11-17	33, 193n19
91.11	192n19, 193nn19,22, 194n27
91.12-17	31-34, 76, 81, 83, 86-
(The Apocalypse	88, 145, 192nn12,
of Weeks)	14, 193nn21,22, 193n23
91.12-14	35
91.12	194n29, 194n32
91.13	194n32
91.14	194n32
91.15-17	82
91.15	194n32
91.17	193n29, 194n32
92.1	194n27
92.3	193n19
92.5	193n19
93.1-10	31, 33, 76, 81, 83,
(The Apocalypse	86-88, 145,
of Weeks)	192nn12,14, 193nn21,22,23
93.1-2	34
93.3-8	192n14
93.8-10	193n22
93.9-10	33, 34
93.10	35
106–107	197n65
2 (Slavonic) Enoch	31, 41-52, 76, 86, 166, 197nn59,62, 197nn59,62, 197nn65,67, 199nn77,79, 200n96, 201n98, 214n184, 217n24

3–21	42
7.2-4	194n36
18.6	46
19.4	46
20.3	46
21.2	46
21.4	46
22–58	42
22–24	51
22.1	46
22.2	46
22.6-10	46
22.6	207n136
24–33	198n72
24.2-5	46
24.3-5	47
25.4-5	46
28.5	198n75
30.3	197n62
30.13	197n62
31–33	44, 46
32.1–33.2	42-44, 46, 86
32.2	45
33.1-2	45
33.2	46, 198n75
33.4	46
33.10	207n136
44.3-5	46
47.3-6	46
50.4	46
53.1-2	47, 210n98
59–66	42
65.1-2	46
65.6-11	46
65.6-10	42, 43, 86
66.3-5	46
69–73	42, 200n96
71.28	207n136
72.5	207n136
3 (Hebrew) Enoch	47-52, 89, 157, 199n82, 200n89
3–16	48
3–15	47, 48
3.2	47
4.1	47
4.2	47
4.7	47
4.8-9	47
6.1	199n85
6.2	47

3 (Hebrew) Enoch (cont.)

6.3	47
10.3	199n85, 199n86
12.5	47
16	47, 48
16.2	200n88
16.3	199n87
16.5	199n85
18.8-24	199n85
18.24	200n88
19.1	199n85
20.1	199n85
22.1	199n85
22.16	199n85
25.1	199n85
30.1	199n85
44.7-10	50
44.7-8	50
45.5	50
48A.10	50
48B	199n85, 200n89
48B.44ff.	199n85
48C	48, 50, 200n89
48C.9	50
48C.10-11	51
48C.90	48
48D	200n89
48D.4	199n84
48D.90	47

4 Ezra (2 Esdras) — 29, 31, 52-69, 74, 77, 78, 80, 87-90, 136, 137, 139, 144, 145, 147, 154, 156, 157, 163, 164, 166, 168, 169, 172, 176, 182, 201nn104,105, 203nn108,111,113, 204nn116,121, 205n124, 206n127, 208nn142,144,145, 209n152, 217n24, 218n24, 221n44, 234n18, 235nn21,22, 236n29, 248n7

1-2	52
3-14	52, 204n119
3-10	204n119
3.1-9.25	54, 55, 64
3.1-5.19	52
3.1-31	204n119
3.1	52
3.4-5	65
3.35-36	55
4.1-51	204n119
4.21b	63
4.52-5.13a	204n119
5.13b-6.10	204n119
5.20-6.34	52
5.23-29	64
5.38	64
5.41	60
5.56-6.6	67, 68, 78, 90, 164, 208n142, 222n47
5.56	65
6.1f-g	68
6.6	65, 68
6.7-10	60
6.13-29	204n119
6.25	60
6.30-7.25	204n119
6.35-9.25	52, 57
6.49-53	245n84
6.49-52	73
7.20	54
7.26-44	204n119
7.26-30	53, 55, 57-59, 61, 68
7.26-27	59
7.28ff.	56
7.28-30	61
7.28	53, 56
7.29-30	55, 73
7.31-44	57
7.33-34	61
7.33	221n44
7.45-8.62	204n119
7.61	54
7.113	60
7.118	54
8.7	65
8.52-54	59
8.63-9.12	204n119
9.13-10.57	204n119
9.26-10.59	52, 54, 205n122
9.29-37	54
9.30-31	54
10.38-58	59
10.60-12.51	52, 57
11-12	204n119
11.36-39	60
11.37-12.1	56
11.39-46	60

4 Ezra (cont.)

12	71
12.10-11	73
12.21-49	61
12.31-34	56-58, 61, 68
12.32	206n130
12.34	59, 60, 61
12.40-48	204n119
13–14	54
13	55, 62-65, 67, 69, 105, 156, 164, 172, 204n119, 205n124, 206n129, 208nn142, 144, 219n34, 248n7
13.1-58	52, 62, 68
13.3-52	56
13.3	62, 205n124, 248n7
13.5	248n7
13.12	248n7
13.18	207n140
13.20	207n140
13.25-26	65, 68
13.25	248n7
13.26	67, 206n134
13.29	67
13.32-36	58, 59
13.32	68, 248n7
13.37-38	67
13.44	67
13.46	207n140
13.47	67
13.49-50	67
13.49	67, 69
13.51-52	63, 64
13.51	248n7
13.53-56	63
14	204n119
14.1-48	52
14.1-17a	204n119
14.9	56, 60
14.19-27	204n119
14.28-35	204n119
14.36-47	204n119
15–16	52

Jubilees

	31, 37-41, 81, 82, 83, 86, 166, 195n40, 196nn52,56, 214n184, 217n24
1.4b-26	39
1.10b	39

1.17-18	38
1.17a	39
1.26	195n45
1.27-29	37-38
1.27-28	39
1.29	38, 39
1.29c	39
2.1	39
4.19	196n48
4.24	196n48
4.26	39
4.30	195n46
5.1-19	196n51
5.10	196n48
23.9-12	195n46
23.11	38, 39
23.14-31	196n56
23.14-20	39
23.21-31	39
23.21	39
23.23-27	38
23.26-31	37-38
23.26-28	195n46
23.27	195n46
23.29-31	196n55
23.30	39, 40
23.30b	40
23.31	40, 41, 86, 196n58
23.31a-b	40
31.14	39
31.18	39, 195n44
34.2-9	196n52
37.1-38.14	196n52
47-50	82, 212n174
50.4	39, 196n51
50.5	39
50.6-13	39

1 Maccabees

3.3	194n29
3.12	194n29
14.8-15	195n45

4 Maccabees   187n24

Psalms of Solomon   29, 217n24

1–16	210n168
17	192n10
18	192n10

Sibylline Oracles   81, 84, 166, 188n29,

Sibylline Oracles (cont.)
	213nn178-80
2	213n180
2.243	239n56
3	192n10
3.1-62	213n178
3.24	197n62, 222n47
3.40-62	84
3.652-731	145, 213n178
3.652-660	213n178
3.741-761	84
3.767-784	84
3.796-808	84
4.41	222n47
4.181	222n47
4.183	222n47
8.424-427	46

Sirach
17.1-11	245n84

Testament of	128, 220n37, 221nn42,
Abraham	43
13.1-2	106

Testament of Levi
16–18	82
18	195n45

Testament of Moses	66, 67, 89, 128,
(Assumption of	192n10, 206n135,
Moses)	207nn134,138,139,
	217n24
9	207n139
9.1	207n139
10	207n139, 218n27,
	221n44
10.1-10	66
10.1ff.	207n139
10.1-2	66, 207n136
10.2	218n27
10.3-10	66
10.3-7	106
10.7	66

Testament of	189n33, 192n10,
Twelve Patriarchs	202n107, 212n173

Wisdom
	128
3.8	226n80
4.10–5.5	200n95
5	128
5.17-20	128
5.18	216n20
9.1-13	245n84

Qumran Materials

CD
1	193n22
3.12b-21	245n84
16.2-4	196n56

1QH
	81, 84
3.19-23	222n47
6.12ff.	222n47
10	213n176

1QM
	81
1	81

1QS
3.16-18	245n84
8	193n22

4Q161
	221n41

4Q174	221n41

4Q180-181	82, 211n171, 212n171
1.9	212n171

4QENg	33, 81, 194n27
I iii 23-25	33
I iv 11-26	33

4QpsDanA	220n34

11QMelchizedek	82, 207n136,
	212n172, 221n41,
	244n80

Pseudo-Ezekiel	82
Document	

Testament of Levi	
16–18	82

Other Jewish Writings

Alphabet of Aqiba	200n89	Philo of Alexandria	109, 110, 172, 200n93
		Questions on	222n54
Genesis Rabbah		Genesis	
85	228n101		
		Questions on	222n54
Hagigah 15a	200n88	Exodus	
Josephus		Targum of Isaiah	119
Antiquities		28.16	230n128
18.8	197n58	45.23	226n80
		66.7	119, 228n106
The Jewish War			
2.154-157	196n58	Targum of Psalm 8	245n84
		8.9	245n84
Leviticus Rabbah			
14.9	228n101		

New Testament

Matthew		1.7	187n.18	5.14	132
22.44	150, 151	1.17-18	231n3	5.16	100
24.30	229n120	1.18	99	5.17	132
26.64	229n120	1.24	100	5.18	100
		1.26	100	5.21	132
Mark		1.28	100	6.1-14	136
12.36	150, 151	2.1	99	6.9	231n9
13.26	229n120	2.2	100	6.12	132, 133
14.62	146, 151,	2.3	99, 100	6.14	231n9
	229n120,	2.5	100	6.17	216n19
	232n14	2.5a	99	7.1	231n9
		2.5b	99	8	239n55
Luke		2.8	99, 215n15	8.1	100
20.43	150	2.12	99	8.3	99, 221n38
21.27	229n120	2.16	99, 223n55	8.11	224n62
		2.27	99	8.17-18	223n60
John	16, 245n84	3.4	99	8.18	230n1
		3.5	99	8.19-22	224n63,
Acts	236n40	3.6	99, 223n52		236n39
1.9	229n120	3.7	99, 160	8.20	243n75
2.16-21	114	3.8	100	8.22-23	132
2.32-36	238n53	4.15	99	8.23	223n60
2.35	150	4.25	216n19	8.29	224n62
5.1-11	251n30	5.2	223n60	8.32	216n19
24.15	236n40	5.6	99	8.34	99, 239n55
		5.9	99	9.5	15
Romans		5.12-21	18, 54	9.22a	99
1	216n19	5.14-21	133	9.22b	99

Romans (cont.)

9.33	124, 224n71
10.5-13	114
10.9	114
10.11	114, 124
10.13	114, 124
11	125
11.26-27	125
11.26	125, 127
11.27a	125
11.27b	125
11.33	100
11.34	224n68
12.19	99
13	215n16
13.2	100
13.4	99
13.5	99
13.9	246n96
13.12	230n133
13.14–14.8	110
14	107, 108
14.3	99
14.4	99
14.5	99
14.9-11	108
14.9	108, 231n9
14.10-11	109, 226n85
14.10	99, 107, 108, 109, 111, 114, 156, 157, 221n45, 223n56
14.11	107, 108, 109, 227n89
14.12	110
14.13	99
14.17	110, 132, 133
14.22	99
14.23	99
15.7	160
15.9-12	224n67
15.12	229n115
15.21	224n67

1 Corinthians 251n34, 252n34

1.3	187n18
1.7	113, 163, 223n61
1.8	111, 112, 113, 162
1.17	162
2.2	99
2.6-16	19
2.6	132
2.13	99
2.14	99
2.15	99
2.16	224n68
3.23	159, 162
4.1	162
4.3	99
4.4	99, 162
4.5	99, 112, 162
4.8	132, 133
4.20	132, 133
5.3	99
5.5	100, 112, 162, 163, 216n19
5.12	99
5.13	99
6.1	99
6.2-3	245n84
6.2	99
6.3	99
6.6	99
6.7	100
6.9-10	133
6.9	132
6.10	132
6.14	224n62
7.29-31	132
7.26	230n1
7.37	99
8.6-7	18
9.3	99
10.11	113, 132, 155
10.15	99
10.25	99
10.27	99
10.29	99
10.31	160
11.2	216n19
11.3	159
11.13	99
11.23	162
11.23a	216n19
11.26	112, 162
11.29-32	100
11.29	100
11.30	215n30
11.31	99
11.32	99
11.32b	216n19
11.34	100
13.8-12	230n2
14.24	99
15	140, 143, 145, 147, 177, 180, 237n48, 239n55, 250n24
15.3ff.	180
15.3-5	231n4
15.3	216n19
15.5-7	237n48
15.12	235n22
15.20-28	26, 97, 134, 41, 144-49, 153-56, 158, 159, 163, 164, 168, 181, 182, 224n62, 233n18, 234n18, 235nn22,23, 241n65
15.20ff.	98, 145, 146
15.20-22	18, 127
15.20	140
15.22ff.	137
15.22	139, 141, 142, 144, 145
15.22a	141
15.22b	140-42, 236n33
15.23-28	142, 151, 153, 163, 233n16
15.23-26	151, 152, 163, 168
15.23ff.	96
15.23	112, 145, 146, 151, 214n1
15.23a	142
15.23b	142

1 Corinthians (cont.)

15.24ff.	151
15.24-28	241n64
15.24-25	134
15.24	113, 132,
	137, 139,
	141, 142,
	145, 236n29
15.24a	143
15.24b	143
15.24c	150
15.25-27	143, 244n81
15.25	132, 143,
	147, 149,
	150, 153,
	168
15.25a	150
15.25b	150
15.26	142, 151
15.27-28	151-53, 163,
	168
15.27	141, 142,
	149-51,
	245n85
15.27a	150, 152,
	153, 168,
	243nn76,77
15.27b	150
15.27c	150
15.28	142, 150,
	151, 159,
	241n65,
	248n105
15.28a	143, 150
15.28b	143, 150,
	158, 159
15.28c	143, 158-60,
	169, 248n105
15.44-49	18
15.50-57	182
15.50-54	223n60
15.50ff.	147
15.50	132, 236n28
15.50b	134, 232n11
15.50c	232n11
15.51-52	251n34
16.17	214n1
16.22	114

2 Corinthians

1.9	125
1.10	125, 223n61
1.13	113
1.14	112, 162
1.22	132
2.1	99
2.2	187n18
3.9	100
3.16	113
3.18	132, 223n60,
	230n2
4.14	224n62
4.15	160
4.16-18	230n2
5	107
5.1-10	155, 177,
	182, 250n24
5.1-4	224n62
5.5	132
5.10	107, 109,
	111, 156,
	222n45
5.14	99
6.7	230n133
7.3	100
7.6-7	214n1
10.10	214n1
10.12	99
11.32	231n5
12.20	215n15

Galatians

1.3	187n18
1.4	126, 230n1
1.11f.	231n4
2.14	223n56
2.20	216n19
4.4-5	126
4.4	221nn38,39
5.5	223n61
5.10	100
5.20	215n15
5.21	132, 133,
	236n28

Ephesians

1.2	187n18
1.3-6	160
1.10	224n63
1.10b	159, 160
1.14	132
1.16-22	244n81
1.20-22	151
1.22	159
1.23	158
2.3	99
3.14	227n88
4.8	224nn67,68
4.15	159
4.30	113
4.31	99,
	215nn15,16
5.5	132, 134,
	153, 154, 157
5.6	99
5.16	230n1
5.23	159
5.27	223nn57,60
6.10-17	127, 128
6.11	127
6.13	127
6.23	187n18

Philippians

1.2	187n18
1.6	111, 112, 163
1.10	111, 112, 163
1.11	160
1.26	214n1
1.27-2.18	115
2	225n74,
	247n104,
	247n105
2.1	117
2.2	214n1
2.5	115
2.6-11	15, 18, 114,
	160, 225n74,
	247n104
2.6-8	225n72
2.6-7c	224n72
2.6-7a	115
2.7b-8	115
2.7d-8	224n72
2.8	115
2.9-11	115, 116,
	224nn63,72,
	225n79,
	246n87
2.9	116, 117,
	225n78,

Philippians (cont.)
226n79
2.10-11   114, 115, 222n46
2.10   115, 116, 225n78, 227n91, 238n54
2.11   115-17, 226n85
2.11c   160, 161, 169, 246n101, 248n105
2.15   111
2.16   112, 163
3.10-14   140
3.11-14   223n61
3.13   223n56
3.20-21   156, 223n61, 245n85, 251n34
3.20   126
3.21   152, 153
3.21b   245n85

Colossians   185n2, 232n13, 250n23
1.2   187n18
1.5   223n60
1.13ff.   221n38
1.13f.   153
1.13   126, 132, 134, 138, 154
1.15-20   15, 18, 154
1.16-17   17
1.18   159, 246n98
1.18c   160
1.22   111, 223n60
1.23   223n60
1.28   223n60
2.10   159
2.15   238n54
2.16-17   230n2
2.16   99
2.19   159
3.1-4   239n54
3.4   113, 163, 224n62
3.6   99

3.8   99, 215nn15,16
3.11   158
4.11   132, 133, 236n28

1 Thessalonians   155, 177, 178, 181, 182, 252n45
1.1   187n18
1.3   223n56
1.9   126
1.10   99, 126, 223n61, 224n69, 228n97
2.2   132
2.12   133, 160, 236n28
2.16   99
2.19   112, 162, 214n1, 223n56
3.9   223n56
3.11-13   110, 111
3.11   110
3.12-13   110
3.12   111
3.13   100, 110-12, 117, 118, 162, 214n1, 227n95, 230n124
4   101, 180
4.6   224n67
4.13ff.   147
4.13-5.11   155, 162
4.13-18   136, 140, 179, 180, 183, 251n34, 252n44
4.14   118, 224n69, 227n95, 230n124
4.15-18   122
4.15ff.   98, 122
4.15   112, 162, 214n1
4.15a   122
4.16ff.   98
4.16   100, 101, 122, 162, 248n106
4.17   101, 122, 123
5   127
5.1-11   126, 182, 183, 252n45
5.2-3   101
5.2   112, 162
5.3   216n20
5.8   126, 127, 128, 216n20
5.9   99
5.10   224nn62,69, 251n30
5.23   112, 214n1
6.23   111

2 Thessalonians   119-22, 155, 177, 178, 181-83, 185n2, 250n25
1   101, 119
1.2   187n18
1.4-8   228n103
1.4-5   235n29
1.5-12   140
1.5   100, 132, 133
1.6-12   119, 120
1.6   228n104
1.7-10   118
1.7   113, 118, 119, 162, 216n20, 227n93
1.8   100, 216n20, 228n104, 228n105
1.9   100, 101, 120
1.10   100, 112, 118, 119, 162, 216n20, 227n93
1.10a   121
1.10c   120, 121
1.12   100, 120, 216n20, 228n104
2   96
2.1-10   181
2.1   162, 214n1

2 Thessalonians (cont.)
2.2   112, 162
2.4   216n20
2.6-7   228n102
2.7   228n103
2.8   101, 121,
           122, 214n1,
           216n20
2.9   214n1
2.12   99
2.15-17   228n103
3.3   228n103
3.5   228n103

1 Timothy
3.16   246n87

Philemon
3   187n18

Hebrews
1.3-4   246n87

1.13-2.8   151
1.13   150
2.6-8   244n81
10.13   150, 237n46

1 Peter
2.6   230nn125,
           127
3.8   236n35
3.2   151

Jude   250n21

Revelation 81, 84-85,
           135, 137,
           143, 144,
           205n124,
           239n54
1   105
1.7   229n120
1.8   214n183
3.21   246n87

1.10   45, 198n75
4-21   213n182
4   219n182
5.1-4   246n87
10.1   229n120
11.12   229n120
14.14-16   229n120
20   234n18
20.1-11   233n18
20.1-6   135
20.4ff.   233n17
20.4-6   84, 85
20.4-5   146
20.11-16   135
22.13   214n183
20.14-15   147
22.14   227n91

Other Early Christian Literature

Apocalypse of Peter
6   239n56

Ascension of Isaiah 199n81, 239n54
6.1-11.4   199n81
9.9   47, 199n81
9.10-18   199n81

Epistle of Barnabas 44, 45, 46, 52, 198n73,
           198n77
4   46
6.19   198n74
12.10ff.   227n90
12.10   150, 242n71
15.2-4   45
15.8   45

1 Clement
36.5   150

The Didache
16   228n99

Hippolytus
Refutations   197n58

Novatian
Concerning the   242n71
Trinity

Pistis Sophia   199n85

Polycarp
Letter to the
Philippians
6.2   111

Shepherd of   207n136
Hermas

Tertullian
Against Praxis
11   242n71

INDEX OF MODERN AUTHORS

Achtemeier, P. 250n23
Alexander, P.S. 47, 48, 199nn83,85,86,87, 200nn89,90, 248n2
Allen, L.C. 243n73
Allo, E.B. 243n74
Andersen, F.I. 44, 197n65, 198n71, 198n72, 198n75, 200n97
Aune, D.E. 202n108, 238n53
Aus, R. 119, 120, 228n102, 228n103

Bachmann, P. 234n18
Bailey, J.A. 181, 182, 213n179
Bailey, J.W. 30, 84
Baird, W. 250n23, 250n24
Balchin, J.F. 247n104
Bampfyde, G. 206n126
Bandstra, A. 222n47
Barker, M. 188n29
Barr, J. 220n35
Barrett, C.K. 16, 234n18
Barrosse, T. 198n75
Barstad, H.M. 217n21
Barth, M. 230n132, 236n39, 246n88, 246n96, 246n97
Barth, G. 242n67
Bauckham, R. 238n53, 239n54, 249n15
Baumgarten, J.M. 244n80
Beale G.K. 205n124
Beasley-Murray, G.R. 215n9, 232n14, 234n18, 243n77
Beckwith, R. 81, 82, 83, 211nn170,171, 212nn171,174,175
Beker, J.C. 23, 148, 149, 188n31, 189n32, 241nn64, 65, 246n95
Bengel, J.A. 154
Berenyi, G. 216n19
Best, E. 216n20, 224n64, 227n93, 229n113
Bietenhard, H. 233n16
Billerbeck, P. 202n106
Black, M. 103, 104, 175, 176, 177, 191n3, 192nn12,13,19, 193n21, 194nn33,34, 200n95, 208n146, 218nn26,27, 222n48, 242n69, 243n77, 248n5, 249nn12,18,19
Bloch, J. 201nn100,105
Boers, H. 214n1

Boettner, L. 233n17
Bogaert, P. 69, 209n149
Boobyer, G.H. 185n1
Bornkamm, G. 231n3
Bowker, J. 174, 188n30
Bowman, J. 211n168
Box, G.H. 59, 195n43, 204nn119,121, 206n134
Boyarin, D. 201n103
Braaten, C.E. 187n28
Brandenburger, E. 59, 205n122
Branick, V. 241n64
Breech, E. 204n121, 209n152
Brown, C. 236n36
Brown, R.E. 185n1
Bücher, T.G. 242n67
Buck, C. 251n29
Bultmann, R. 95, 97, 98
Burkitt, F.C. 236n35

Caird, G.B. 17, 233n18, 240n60, 243n75, 247n105, 248n105
Callan, T. 239n57
Carlson, D. 207n139
Carr, W. 238n54, 239n54
Casey, P.M. 174, 204n114, 205n125, 237n50, 248n7, 249nn11,12,15
Cavallin, H.C.C. 40, 196nn55,58, 197n67, 204n116, 210n157
Cerfaux, L. 234n18
Chamberlain, J.V. 242n70
Chardin, T. de 95
Charles, R.H. 23, 30, 34, 35, 37, 38, 41-45, 66, 69, 70, 191n4, 192n16, 193n24, 195nn43,44,45,47, 196n55, 197nn65,66, 198n68, 199n80, 204n118, 207n137, 209nn147,150, 151,155, 210n168, 213n178, 219n29
Charlesworth, J.H. 23, 187n19, 189nn33,34, 36, 192n13, 194n33, 195n40, 197nn59,65, 198n71,72, 199nn80,82, 201nn99, 105, 202nn107,108, 203n112, 204n114, 206n127,134, 208n145, 209n146, 213n182, 250n21
Chernus, I. 188n30
Clements, R.E. 229n114

Clouse, R.G. 233n17
Cohn-Sherbok, D. 244n81
Colani, T. 95
Collange, J. 185n5, 227n87
Collins, A.Y. 193n21, 202n106,
    207n136, 212nn174,175
Collins, J.J. 188n29, 191n1, 192n13,
    201n102, 205n124, 207n134,
    211n169, 213nn175,180, 240n59,
    243n77, 244n80, 245n84
Collins, R.F. 224n69, 227n95, 229n116,
    252n45
Conzelmann, H. 191n6, 234n18, 246n89
Coughenour, R. 195n39
Court, J.M. 224n66, 243n78
Coutts, J. 232n13
Cranfield, C.E.B. 222nn45,48, 243n75
Crockett, W. 236n37
Cullmann, O. 143, 146, 147, 159,
    237n46, 246n95

Dahl, N.A. 211n169, 223n53
Daniélou, J. 207n136
Davenport, G. 38-41, 196n53
Davies, G.I. 193n21
Davies, P.R. 196n56, 211n169
Davies, W.D. 135-139, 235n25
Dean-Otting, M. 188n30, 195n36
Deichgräber, R. 187n19
De Lacey, D.R. 222n49
Delcor, M. 212n172
Delling, G. 189n33
Denis, A.M. 209n147
Denton, D.R. 232n13
Dexinger, F. 34, 194nn27,28,29,31,32
Di Lella, A.A. 243n77
Dimant, D. 211n169, 212n172
Dodd, C.H. 216n17, 224n70, 227n94,
    237n50, 243n78,250n22
Donfried, K.P. 231n3
Drane, J. 189n31, 251n29
Dunn, J.D.G. 49, 151, 186n14, 200n92,
    220n34, 221n38, 224n72, 225n72,
    237n50, 245n86, 246n93, 247n104
Dykstra, W. 235n22

Edgar, S.I. 244n83
Egan, R.B. 238n54
Ellingworth, P. 227n95
Ellis, E.E. 18, 242n69, 250n24
Elwell, W. 185n3

Emerton, J.A. 205n124

Findlay, G.G. 237n49
Fiorenza, E.S. 216n18
Fischer, U. 197n61, 197n62
Fitzmyer, J. 174, 212n172, 242n69
Flanagan, N. 245n85
Flusser, D. 199n81, 212n172, 213n180
Forbes, N. 197n60
Ford, A. 233n16
Ford, J.M. 202n105, 213n182
France, R.T. 239n54
Friedrich, G. 182
Fujita, S. 194n31
Funk, R. 214n1

Gager, J.G. 189n31
Georgi, D. 225n73
Gero, S. 201n105
Gibbs, J.G. 225n75
Giblin, C. 229n112
Gillman, J. 251n34
Ginzberg, L. 209n152
Glasson, T.F. 95, 96, 100-102, 123,
    188n29, 215nn6,11, 216n20,
    217nn23,24, 218nn24,26, 225n72,
    227n96, 228nn96,98,99, 229n121,
    239n57, 242n71, 251n31
Goguel, M. 234n18
Goldenberg, R. 201n102
Goudge, H.L. 234n18
Gourges, M. 233n17
Grabbe, L.L. 193n21, 202n108
Greenfield, J.C. 205n126
Grillmeier, A. 241n64
Gruenthaler, M.J. 213n180
Gruenwald, I. 188n30
Grundmann, W. 231n4
Gundry, R.H. 203n112
Gurney, R.J.M. 213n175

Hanhart, K. 250n23
Halperin, D.J. 188n30
Hamerton-Kelly, R.G. 210n161
Hanmer, P.L. 232n13
Hanson, A.T. 215n17, 224n68, 234n18,
    242n69
Hanson, P.D. 190n1
Harnisch, W. 205n122, 252n44
Harrington, D.J. 189n33
Harris, M.J. 234n18, 250n24

Harrison, W. 201n103
Hartman, L. 188n29, 193n21
Hasel, G.F. 243n77
Hauer, C. 188n30
Havener, J. 228n97
Hay, D. 146, 238n51, 239n55, 239n56
Hayman, A.P. 201n101
Hengel, M. 21, 193n21, 197n58, 225n74, 236n40, 237n50, 244n80
Héring, J. 234n18, 235n25
Hettlinger, R.F. 250n24
Hickling, C.J.A. 189n32
Hiers, R. 214n3
Hindley, J.C. 205n126
Hoekema, A.A. 233n16, 233n17
Holladay, C.R. 206n127
Hooker, M.D. 203n112, 216n19
Horton, F.L. 212n172
Howard, G. 108, 109, 110, 222nn49,50, 223nn52,53, 225nn73,79, 226n85
Hoyt, H.A. 233n17
Hurd, J.C. 181, 251n28
Hurtado, L.W. 219n31, 225n76

Isenberg, S.R. 190n1

Jansen, J.F. 241n64
Jeremias, J. 115, 174, 225n73, 229n116, 232n11, 247n103
Jervell, J. 225n77
Johnson, G. 231n7
Jonge, M. de 201n105, 202n107, 212n172, 244n80

Kabisch, R. 235n23
Käsemann, E. 22, 160, 187nn25,26, 225n73
Katz, P. 228n105
Kaye, B.N. 216n18
Kee, H.C. 191n1, 202n107, 245n84
Kennedy, H.A.A. 237n48
Kiddle, M. 234n18
Kim, S. 103-105, 185n7, 202n105, 208n144, 218n26, 219nn30,31,32,34, 220nn35,36,37, 221n39, 224n68, 237n50, 245n86, 249n17
Klappert, B. 232n14
Klijn, A.F.J. 70, 71, 75, 76, 209n153, 210n162, 235n22
Knibb, M. 32, 192nn16,17,18,19, 201n101, 203n113, 205n126

Kobelski, P. 212n172, 244n80
Koch, K. 187n28
Kreitzer, L.J. 186n15
Kümmel, W.G. 231nn4,6,8, 241n62

Ladd, G.E. 231n6, 233n17, 234n18
Lake, K. 198n73, 199n78
Lambrecht, J. 149, 150, 243nn72,74,76
Lattey, C. 207n139
Laubscher, F. 212n172
Laws, S. 187n26
Leach, E.R. 211n170
Lebram, J.C.H. 201n103
Lee, J.Y. 238n54
Leeuwen, C. Van 217n21
Leivestad, R. 174
Licht, J. 210n164, 211n169
Lietzmann, H. 234n18, 241n62
Lightfoot, J.B. 226n85, 227n91
Lillie, W. 250n24
Lincoln, A.T. 240n59
Lindars, B. 174-176, 194n35, 195n37, 200n91, 205n125, 220n34, 229n111, 230n125, 237n50, 249nn15,19
Loader, W.R.G. 237n45, 238nn52,53, 239n55
Lohfink, G. 252n36
Löhr, G. 229n116
Lohse, E. 185n6, 233n18
Longenecker, R. 18, 212n172, 241n66, 242nn66,69
Lorimer, W.L. 185n4
Lowe, J. 215n6, 251n29
Lowy, S. 198n76

Marshall, I.H. 188n29, 225n76, 234n18, 237n50, 247n104
Martin, R.P. 20, 185nn5,6, 225nn73, 76,77,79, 226nn80,83,84,85, 234n18, 237n50, 246nn87,98, 247n103
MacDonald, J. 210n168
Macgregor, G.H.C. 215n17, 216n17, 238n54
Maclaurin, E.C.B. 222n50
Maier, F.W. 236n41
McEleney, N.J. 202n108
Mead, R.T. 244n83
Mearns, C.L. 177-79, 190n37, 205n126, 206n126, 250nn25,27, 251nn28,29,31,32, 252n34

Meeks, W. 216n18
Metzger, B.M. 185n4, 207n141, 222n45, 229n111, 232n12
Meyer, H.A.W. 234n18
Milik, J.T. 33, 192nn14,18, 193nn20,21, 205n126, 209n146, 211n171, 212n171
Millar, F. 191n3, 208n146
Miller, M. 212n172, 245n84
Miller, W.R. 191n1
Miner, D. 212n172
Moffatt, J. 234n18
Moloney, F. 245.184
Montgomery, J.A. 220n34
Moore, A.L. 214nn2,4, 227n93
Moore, G.F. 31, 191n8
Morfil, W.R. 42, 197n65
Morgenstern, J. 211n170
Morris, L. 20
Moule, C.F.D. 27, 158, 185n1, 187nn18,24, 190n38, 222n49, 225n76, 226n81, 234n18, 239n54, 242n69, 250nn20,24
Mounce, R. 233n18, 234n18
Mowinckel, S. 30, 207n139
Müller, U. 204n114, 214n182
Murphy, F.J. 209n154
Murphy-O'Connor, J. 225n73, 226nn80,85
Murray, R. 202n108
Myers, J. 59, 65, 204n120, 208n143, 213n178

Neusner, J. 188n30, 191n8, 201n102
Neyrey, J. 228n97
Nickelsburg, G.W.E. 192n11, 193n22, 194n28, 195n41, 196nn52,55, 197n65, 201n102, 204n116, 216n18, 221n43

Odeberg, H. 200n88, 200n94
Oesterley, W.O.E. 204n119
Osburn, C.D. 250n21

Parke-Taylor, G.H. 215n14
Parry, R. 234n18
Patzia, A.G. 232n13
Perrin, N. 190n37
Perry, V. 185n1
Pfleiderer, O. 234n18
Pietersma, A. 223n53

Pines, S. 197n68
Pinnock, C. 233n16
Plevnik, J. 179, 180, 229nn117,118, 252nn36,45
Plummer, A. 234n18, 246n90
Polhill, J.B. 232n13
Poythress, V.S. 243n77
Preston, R.H. 234n18
Priest, J. 66, 206n134, 207nn136,138
Pryke, J. 211n169

Rahner, K. 15
Reim, G. 245n84
Reumann, J. 189n32, 245n85
Ridderbos, H.N. 239n58
Rigaux, B. 252n40
Rissi, M. 234n18
Rist, M. 234n18
Roberts, B.J. 211n169
Robertson, A. 234n18, 246n90
Robinson, J.A.T. 95, 96, 190n37, 215nn8,9
Roetzel, C. 216n18
Ross, J.M. 227n95
Rowe, R.D. 244n79
Rowland, C. 186n10, 188nn29,30, 193n23, 194n36, 196n55,219n31, 220n35, 238n53
Rowley, H.H. 194n33, 204n121, 207n139, 216n21, 217n23
Rubenstein, A. 197n61
Russell, D.S. 30, 31, 59, 86, 191nn2,10, 192n11, 195n41, 197nn64,66, 209n152, 214n184

Sanders, E.P. 53-55, 188n29, 203nn109, 111, 112, 209n146, 221n42
Sanders, J.A. 117
Sanders, J.T. 19, 225n73
Sandmel, S. 171, 172
Sayler, G.B. 209n152
Schaberg, J. 205n124
Schaller, B. 230n131
Schier, H. 238n54
Schmidt, N. 197n63
Schmithals, W. 251n33
Schürer, E. 30, 191n3, 208n146
Schulz, S. 222n49
Schweitzer, A. 30, 95, 97, 135, 136, 137, 139, 142, 180, 186n10, 191n6, 215n11, 217n24, 218n24, 235nn19, 21,25

Schweizer, E. 185n6, 232nn10,15
Scott, R.B.Y. 123, 229n122, 230n123
Segal, A.F. 49, 188n30, 199n87,
    200nn88,92,93, 223n53
Senft, C. 234n18
Sider, R.J. 232n11
Siegman, E.F. 213n180
Skehan, P.W. 223n53
Smalley, S.S. 232n13, 238n53
Smith, M. 221n40
Sparks, H.F.D. 23
Staniforth, M. 199n78, 223n58
Stanton, G. 225n76
Steele, E.S. 216n20
Stegemann, H. 211n169
Stevens, B.A. 244n80
Stone, M. 60, 191n1, 192nn12,16,
    194n34, 201nn102,104,105,
    202n106, 203n114, 204nn115,121,
    205n123, 206n126, 208n144,
    210n163
Stott, W. 198n75
Strack, H.L. 202n106
Strand, K. 198n75
Strugnell, J. 209n149
Sturch, R.L. 185n1
Suter, D.W. 188n30
Swain, J.W. 213n180

Talbert, C. 225n73
Taylor, G. 251n29
Taylor, V. 20, 185n1
Theisohn, J. 206n129, 218n25, 221n41
Thiselton, A. 214n3, 235n19
Thomas, J.D. 191n1
Thompson, A.L. 201n103
Thorndike, J.P. 193n22
Tillich, P. 95, 189n37

Travis, S.H. 102n103, 214n4, 216n17,
    231n3
Trilling, W. 181
Trudinger, P. 198n75
Tupper, E.F. 187n28

Vaillant, A. 197n61
VanderKam, J.C. 40, 192n12, 194n28,
    195n36, 196nn52,53,56, 211n170
Vawter, B. 214n4
Vermes, G. 174, 191n3, 208n146,
    213nn176,177, 248n6, 249n19

Waard, J. De 230n128
Wacholder, B.Z. 196n52
Waddell, W.G. 223n53
Wallis, W. 139, 141-45, 237n49
Waterman, G.H. 231n4
Watts, J.D.W. 217n21
Weiss, J. 186n10, 234n18
Wellhausen, J. 206n134
Wengst, K. 187n19
Wenham, D. 231n4
Whiteley, D.E.H. 240n58
Widengren, G. 193n20
Wilcke, H.-A. 139-42, 144, 145,
    213n178, 236nn31,33,40, 237n49
Wilcox, M. 242n69
Wild, R.A. 230n134
Wilder, A. 240n60
Williams, S. 187n24
Woude, A.S. Van der 212n172

Yates, R. 238n54
York, A.D. 245n85

Zeitlin, S. 207n135
Zimmerli, W. 103

JOURNAL FOR THE STUDY OF THE NEW TESTAMENT
Supplement Series

1 THE BARREN TEMPLE AND THE WITHERED TREE
William R. Telford

2 STUDIA BIBLICA 1978
II. Papers on the Gospels
E.A. Livingstone (ed.)

3 STUDIA BIBLICA 1978
III. Papers on Paul and Other New Testament Authors
E.A. Livingstone (ed.)

4 FOLLOWING JESUS
Discipleship in Mark's Gospel
Ernest Best

5 THE PEOPLE OF GOD
Markus Barth

6 PERSECUTION AND MARTYRDOM IN THE
THEOLOGY OF PAUL
John S. Pobee

7 SYNOPTIC STUDIES
The Ampleforth Conferences 1982 and 1983
C.M. Tuckett (ed.)

8 JESUS ON THE MOUNTAIN
A Study in Matthean Theology
Terence L. Donaldson

9 THE HYMNS OF LUKE'S INFANCY NARRATIVES
Their Origin, Meaning and Significance
Stephen Farris

10 CHRIST THE END OF THE LAW
Romans 10.4 in Pauline Perspective
Robert Badenas

11 THE LETTERS TO THE SEVEN CHURCHES OF ASIA
IN THEIR LOCAL SETTING
Colin J. Hemer

12 PROCLAMATION FROM PROPHECY AND PATTERN
Lucan Old Testament Christology
Darrell L. Bock

13 JESUS AND THE LAWS OF PURITY
Tradition History and Legal History in Mark 7
Roger P. Booth

14 THE PASSION ACCORDING TO LUKE
The Special Material of Luke 22
Marion L. Soards

15 HOSTILITY TO WEALTH IN THE SYNOPTIC GOSPELS
T.E. Schmidt

16 MATTHEW'S COMMUNITY
The Evidence of his Special Sayings Material
S.H. Brooks

17 THE PARADOX OF THE CROSS IN
THE THOUGHT OF ST PAUL
A.T. Hanson

18 HIDDEN WISDOM AND THE EASY YOKE
Wisdom, Torah and Discipleship in Matthew 11.25-30
C. Deutsch

19 JESUS AND GOD IN PAUL'S ESCHATOLOGY
L.J. Kreitzer

20 LUKE: A NEW PARADIGM
M.D. Goulder

21 THE DEPARTURE OF JESUS IN LUKE-ACTS
The Ascension Narratives in Context
M.C. Parsons

22 THE DEFEAT OF DEATH
Apocalyptic Eschatology in 1 Corinthians 15 and Romans 5
M.C. De Boer